HOUSING
Symbol, Structure, Site

Lisa Taylor

Editor

Cooper-Hewitt Museum
The Smithsonian Institution's National Museum of Design

Table of Contents

Editor's Notes

By Lisa Taylor

Considering the pervasive importance of design in our lives, it is astonishing that there was so little general interest in the subject as recently as a dozen years ago when the Cooper-Hewitt became the Smithsonian Institution's National Museum of Design. In order to show the relevance of the Museum's collection and programs to contemporary concerns, I initiated a series of outdoor exhibitions of "immovable objects" that had a significant impact on the public and/or on the environment. Among the designs featured were oversized ones such as subway systems and downtown areas that could not be shown adequately in a museum setting through drawings and models that were out of context or scale. Some of the newspaper tabloids that served as catalogues for these exhibitions later became books. *Housing: Symbol, Structure, Site* is a part of that series. The designation of 1987 as the International Year of the Homeless provided the impetus to examine the subject of housing and the meaning of home. A distinguished group of specialists in various disciplines has joined us in exploring that theme.

Humanity has been concerned about shelter since the fall from Eden, and an immense body of scholarly and general writings on the subject exists. This selection favors housing in America and concerns itself largely with design-related issues. One of its main concerns is the influences that cultural values, technological innovations, the media, and political and economic forces have had on housing. Some topics that one might have thought would be included here or would be presented in greater depth, such as population growth, changing family structures, waste disposal, ghettos, regional architectural styles, and street life, are extensively covered in companion volumes. Readers are referred particularly to three of them, *Cities: The Forces That Shape Them*, *Urban Open Spaces*, and *The Phenomenon of Change*.

The global housing situation is deeply alarming. According to the United Nations, a staggering quarter of the world's population lacks adequate housing, and over 100 million people have no housing at all. As overwhelming as the problem seems, we cannot allow its magnitude to freeze us into inaction. Through international cooperation, willpower, and imagination, we have been able to alleviate the consequences of some major world disasters. It will take a similar united global effort to make progress in improving human shelter. What constitutes decent housing varies from place to place and will require many different approaches and solutions.

We Americans are privileged to have some of the best housing in the world—housing that is considered luxurious by most standards—the majority with electricity, full plumbing, and adequate space. With so many people lacking roofs over their heads, it is almost embarrassing to talk about how housing can be improved. Often, however, our very affluence has been the cause of problems. The comforts and conveniences that have made our lives easier and more pleasurable have produced many unintended health hazards and ecological side effects.

Not long ago we were rooted to the land. Home was the center of life, a place where we were born, lived, worked, played, and ultimately died. It was there where our values were formed and where we learned how to cope with life. We knew the landscape, the neighborhood, the people, and the places in it. The warmth of the fireside and light of the lamp bonded us together. Home provided continuity, stability, and tradition. But technological progress has taken us outside the rhythm of Nature. There is no longer the same feeling toward home. How could there be? Almost 42 percent of our population moved between 1980 and 1985. More than half of all women work. The divorce rate is phenomenally high, and an enormous number of young people are growing up in broken homes. Increased mobility has taken us away

The Expulsion from Paradise. Kubler Collection, Cooper-Hewitt Museum.

from the home; simultaneously, television has made us less dependent on each other for companionship. Surely all this has contributed to the isolation and alienation that many feel.

Unlike most countries, the populations of which are homogeneous, the United States enjoys a mix of every conceivable nationality, religion, race, and economic and educational background. Geographically, our country represents an enormous range of climates, natural resources, and terrains. Our choices of accommodations are endless—providing options to live in old cities, new towns, historic districts, cluster developments, in suburbs or country, as renters or owners of single or multiple dwellings, condominiums or cooperatives, in apartment buildings or brownstones, embodying every conceivable style from neoclassical to ultramodern. The life-styles we embrace and their resulting household configurations are probably more varied than anywhere on earth. We have the knowledge and technical ability to build in the most advanced and least environmentally destructive way. This rich diversity should be reflected in an architecture that is more varied, caring, and satisfying. Yet there is a great deal of sameness in contemporary housing, both stylistically and in its component parts. While a certain amount of standardization can be attributed to cost-cutting measures and regulations that dictate the size and positioning of a building, poor and unimaginative design cannot be overlooked. Modern architecture so freqently is wasteful of land and natural resources and fails to meet the physical, psychological, and cultural needs of the people for whom it is designed.

The American dream of owning one's own home has been realized by almost two-thirds of our population. A good hedge against inflation, home ownership represents the largest single investment for most middle-class families. Our government has promoted such ownership by offering tax benefits to home owners, guaranteeing and providing low-interest loans, constructing efficient roads and mass transit, and making inexpensive land available. Similar tax incentives and government grants have been used to encourage the saving of historic buildings and the construction and rehabilitation of low-income housing, as well as to benefit other target areas and groups. In spite of these and many other well-intentioned programs, not all Americans have adequate shelter.

Anything that affects our lives as seriously as housing cannot be tackled on a happen-as-happen, hit-or-miss basis, as often has been the case. It is vital that we concern ourselves with the future development of our cities and towns, and that we plan intelligently for our future housing needs. There must be better coordination among federal, regional, state, municipal and community agencies, and private organizations in the effort to improve housing, and dare one say, to ensure more flexibility and less corruption. Legislation has a powerful influence on housing. We must review policies concerning land use and our building codes and zoning ordinances. Strong efforts should be made to cut red tape and remove other barriers that prevent us from giving greater help to the disadvantaged. We should continue to use whatever tax or other incentives are required to encourage the building of decent, affordable housing.

Although we have learned a great deal, we are still paying the price for the insensitive urban renewal policies of the past, which razed whole neighborhoods and dislocated their inhabitants. The poor and disadvantaged have less mobility and fewer options; neighborhood ties, therefore, are critically important and should be reinforced. Steps must be taken to upgrade borderline neighborhoods that are in danger of becoming slums. Low-density housing, and housing in which tenants can control common areas and access, have been shown to reduce crime and vandalism. We should reclaim and rehabilitate as many old buildings as we can and make certain that new public housing becomes an integral part of the community. Pride in one's surroundings boosts self-image; good public housing should do this. Increased aid should be given to prevent poor families from being evicted and thus requiring relocation. Expanded rent supplements that are transferable to other locations would give greater freedom to choose one's living space and are often more economical and desirable than public housing. Our welfare system has not fostered personal advancement, but one hopes that the recently established program to sell housing units to non-profit organizations, tenant management groups, and individual residents will meet with great success.

Newspapers and television remind us daily of the plight of the homeless in America. Although homelessness is not a recent phenomenon, it is tragic that it exists at all in a country as prosperous as ours. The number of visible homeless is steadily increasing and includes not only vagrants and derelicts, but the sick, abused, and poor as well. All of us are keenly aware of the problem and some of its causes, yet too many of us feel that the homeless are someone else's responsibility rather than our own. We need to take preventive steps and provide appropriate long-range solutions.

For those already on the streets, temporary shelters and soup kitchens are clearly not enough. Medical care, rehabilitation, job counseling, and training must be provided along with whatever additional assistance is needed to enable homeless individuals to function in society again. Private citizens, businesses, religious and philanthropic organizations have responded with generosity, but there is a limit to what they can do. What is required is a massive coordinated effort, on a national to local level, with government taking the lead.

There is another kind of homelessness—painful, too, to talk about—that of having lost, or worse still, never having found what in one's heart is home. The social upheaval that has been experienced in this century is extraordinary. Millions of people in far-flung parts of the globe have been forced to leave their homes for political, economic, or other catastrophic reasons. Some have settled into better lives; many remain displaced. This is one of the great tragedies of our time and not easily solvable because to most of us home means more than shelter. It is more than where we come from or where we live—it is how we feel about ourselves and our place in the world.

Caring and commitment can make a critical difference. When the Museum first began observing the built environment, the future for American cities looked bleak. Depending on whom one listened to, urban areas in the Northeast were doomed either to decay and to be abandoned or to sprawl into a megalopolis spanning much of the Atlantic coast. Neither has happened; and in fact, quite a few of the cities that were thought to be in jeopardy are undergoing a renaissance. Regrettably, the infrastructure of some cities is still fragile, and problems like air pollution, contaminated water, waste disposal, crime, congestion, discrimination, and homelessness persist. Yet, urban life has continued to survive, and in some ways to improve.

Fortunately, the problems related to our country's housing are not nearly so overwhelming as elsewhere. We have the resources to solve them. What we need to do is to make the commitment. Philosophers, politicians, and poets have long recognized the home as the strength of the nation. The promise of America represented a decent place to live for the millions and millions of "tired, poor and homeless" who emigrated here from all over the world. We should make it a shared national goal to fulfill that promise for all Americans by the end of this millennium.

As with so many Cooper-Hewitt publications, this one would not have been possible without the financial support of the J. M. Kaplan Fund and the encouragement of its president, Joan Davidson. The Joyce Mertz-Gilmore Foundation also contributed generously toward its production. Income from the sale of previous publications provided the remaining costs. *Housing: Symbol, Structure, Site* is gratefully dedicated to the patrons, writers, illustrators, photographers, and others who participated in this endeavor.

It gives me pleasure to acknowledge C. Ray Smith's valuable help in editing the text and that of Lucy Fellowes in carefully overseeing the photographic research and writing picture captions. Marian Page, Christopher Flacke, Janet Marks, and Nancy Aakre provided important editorial assistance; the latter supervised production as well. Larry Deemer served as coordinator of the project in its early stages; he and Bernd Dams thoughtfully assisted in the initial search for illustrations and were later joined by Lorraine Bloomstrom, Ysabella Hincapie-Gara, Dorothy Twining Globus, Madeline Greenberg, Mary Humphreys, Jacqueline Rea, Betty Ann Schoenfeld, Milton Sonday and Elaine Vogel. Ann Dorfsman, Randall Cherry, Camille Landau, Edward Rock-Herrera, and Piera Watkins provided extra eyes in proofreading. Caren Grogan, Greta Wharton, George Nichols, Harold Pfister, Denny Ryus, Peter Scherer, and especially Cynthia Plaut helped in other critical ways. For the physical appearance of this publication, we are indebted to its designer, Heidi Humphrey of H + , and Trufont Typographers and Eastern Press who were responsible for typesetting and printing. Once again, we are fortunate to work with Rizzoli International Publications on a joint venture.

Lisa Taylor is Director Emeritus of the Cooper-Hewitt Museum, The Smithsonian Institution's National Museum of Design.

Published by the Cooper-Hewitt Museum, the Smithsonian Institution's National Museum of Design. All articles were specifically commissioned for *Housing*. The opinions expressed are those of the authors and do not necessarily reflect the position of the Museum.

Distributed by Rizzoli International Publications, Inc. 300 Park Avenue South, New York, N.Y. 10010

LC 88-71867   ISBN 0-8478-1016-X
Printed in the United States of America in 1990
© 1990 by The Smithsonian Institution

Library of Congress Cataloging-in-Publication Data

Housing: symbol, structure, site.

  Edited by Lisa Taylor.
  Bibliography: p.
  1. Housing—United States.   2. Housing.   3. Dwellings—United States.   4. Dwellings.   5. Architecture, Domestic—United States.   6. Architecture, Domestic.   I. Taylor, Lisa.   II. Cooper-Hewitt Museum.
HD7293.H7824   1990   363.5   88-71867
ISBN 0-8478-1016-X

Abide/Abode

Some philosophical assumptions can be made.

By Arthur C. Danto

In the summer of 1974, the American artist Jennifer Bartlett set out to create a work of extreme ambition, as much in scale as in subject. *Rhapsody* is composed of nearly a thousand panels, each a foot square, and was intended, as she put it, to "have everything in it." In fact it has but four things in it, repeated in different combinations and executed in various styles: water, mountain, tree, and house. These, she tells us, were the first four things to have occurred to her, and it is hardly matter for surprise that "everything" resolves, analytically, into certain basic components out of which whatever else there is must be composed, nor that the house should at once have been on the short list of basic entities and have come immediately to the consciousness of an artist poised to reenact the fabrication of the whole world.

Nothing, on the other hand, more exactly divides a human sensibility from a divine one than this charged symbol, for in framing the universe, God of course put water, mountains, and trees together to make a world, but there would have been no houses in the pre-lapsarian condition of human existence: the house is *Menschenwerk*—our contribution to the overall scheme—and testifies to that condition of vulnerability defined as ours since the Expulsion.

It was, on the Biblical account, shame that moved Eve and Adam to cover themselves when they became conscious of their fallen condition, so clothing was, initially, less a matter of protection from sun and chill than the expression of a moral intuition in the language of garmentry. By the same criterion, one would suppose the house, as a form of covering—as essentially a roof—must have been the spontaneous symbol of our difference from the angels, the second mark of our deep humanity. It is this, perhaps, that justifies the stirring claim of the German philosopher Martin Heidegger that *dwelling* is the primary attribute of our being—our essence in effect: "We do not dwell because we have built," he wrote, "but we build because we dwell, because we are *dwellers*." Dwelling, if indeed the human condition, entails that the house is as much a meaning as a means.

In drawing a house as the first, or nearly the first, thing it draws, the child expresses an innate understanding of its condition as human (and it is suitable that one of the styles Bartlett appropriates for the house is that of a child's drawing). A work of art that has a house in it has *us* in it, in our basic condition as dwellers. It is the basic symbol, if Heidegger is right, and all other symbols for ourselves derive from it. Defined as "structures intended for dwelling," houses of different styles imply different forms of life. And different interpretations of the house as symbol define different philosophies of life.

As with the other objects that, as we say today, encode the metaphors through which we represent our nature to ourselves, the house connects, in a single uneasy whole, both aspects of our difficult metaphysical nature as spirit and body. Consider, for example, the chair. As the *seat*, it is where we sit in judgment and from whence we rule—so it is the emblem of superiority and domination. The throne, the bench, the seat, the chair, the *cathedra* specify different foci of authority when occupied by the monarch, the magistrate, the representative, the professor (or the chairman), the bishop—and often the design reflects the symbolic weight of the figure whose role requires ritual sitting as a perquisite. But we also sit just to take the weight off our feet—to repose, relax, recuperate—acknowledging through the act the limits of our powers as physically embodied beings, flesh and blood, heir to shocks, weary and weak.

The house, too, is a ruling-place, as in the Houses of Parliament and the House of Representatives. And it is the ruling families that are synecdochically designated a "house," as in the House of Hanover or the House of Orange. This, I think, is not the primary connotation of "house" in English, which as a word carries an

Jennifer Bartlett, *Rhapsody*, 1975, detail. Courtesy Paula Cooper Gallery. © Geoffrey Clements. Collection of Sid Singer, New York.

opposite meaning, connected with the dimension of frailty in our image of ourselves. But there is a family of English terms that refer back to the Latin *domus*: domicile, domesticate, dominate, dominion, domain, (con)dominium, dominus, domineer; and through these the house speaks to us precisely as the symbol of rulership, ownership, mastery, power.

Dwelling, in this interpretation, is having in effect conquered, having made the world one's own (*owning* it), and so having the rights and privileges that such honorifics as those that refer to *domus* carry like badges: Don, Dona, Dame, Madame (or madam, whose house is not a home.) That which is in*domi*table is literally that which we cannot bring within our house: untamable, wild, undisciplined, undomesticable. Just to have a house is to possess symbolic authority (under an older system of government, to have a voice or vote), and the house is the embodiment of our dominance. The philosophical picture projected by the house-as-*domus* is one where we impose ourselves on the world through possession, transforming the heretofore untamed into the means of habitation. The house is the form that our will-to-power takes as characteristically human.

A house, as an architectural entity, exemplifies the philosophy conveyed by the concept of the *domus*. A house has to stand (a house divided against itself must fall), and the straight line, the level surface, the right angle imply the ruler, in both senses of the term: the house communicates the proposition: I stand, I am upright, I am straight, I am rational, I *am order*. These propositions are conveyed through the vocabulary of columns and beams, which must be respectively plumb and level to "house" the thought we ascribe to them. But these same propositions, which belong instead to the language of enclosure and connect us to the other range of meanings that belongs to the concept of the house—meanings that have little to do with domination, but instead with our essential weakness, as needing shelter from the wild world without.

As a word, *house* carries us back to the

dark forests of Germania, in contrast with *domus*, through which order and civilization are defined in the sunlit peninsulas of the Mediterranean. In Old English, *hus* means exactly shelter. It is cognate with *huden*—to hide, conceal, cover; and it expands into such modern terms as hut, huddle, hoard, and, through its first syllable, into *hus*-band (house-bound, tied to a dwelling as a condition of survival). This is the fragile, threatened, exposed side of our self-image as dwellers: beings that need protection, a place to crawl into, if only a hole or cave—and our walls announce our vulnerability.

The idea of the *home*, as a place where goods are stored and husbanded, is already inscribed in the house as *hus*, where rationality has less the implication of rule and order than of reasonableness, thrift, frugality, moderation. For who

knows what the future may bring or what needs will have to be met? The house as home is the place of comfort, safety, where we can let down our defenses. It contrasts with the jungle world of savages and predators "out there." It implicitly characterizes the world as precariousness.

Hegel sees the house as the primary artistic product of the human intellect, since its form has no direct model in nature. It differs, thus, from sculpture, which initially takes its form from that of natural objects, and especially the human body. So, as spiritual product, the house inevitably gives an outward embodiment of our inner reality, hence to our nature as rational. And this translates into the political metaphors of domination, as with *domus*. But as shelter, I think, the house draws initially upon what nature itself pro-

vides: the cliff, which protects me from behind as I sit between it and my fire, or the cavern, which surrounds me. It is thus that frame and wall speak in different voices, and together express our nature as reason and as flesh, as order and disorder, as beings of thought and need. It is our most eloquent philosophical symbol, and it is not difficult to understand how it would have forced itself immediately into Jennifer Bartlett's consciousness.

It is instructive, in the light of this symbol, to consider the temple as the dwelling of the god. Clearly, as *dominus*, God does not need shelter. But God must be present among us in the condition of the *domus*, and it is as *domus* that the architecture of the Lord's house impresses itself upon the community: it will be the highest structure, and the *dome* transmits absolute authority. This means, in effect, that the walls must themselves aspire to an absolute nonfunctional role, which is to say: non-load-bearing, to express the fact that God is not, like us, in need of housing. The Gothic cathedral, of course, in reducing wall to window, executes this imperative to perfection. The Gothic genius lies in discovering how to make walls possess purely symbolic value, and for this purpose, glass is the ideal material. It says, accordingly, a great deal about our increasing security in the world that glass itself grows larger and takes up greater and greater portions of our total domestic enclosures. The glass house is the final emblem of a world well-ordered. What immense optimism is expressed by the glass towers of the modern city!

Glass today is a social partition that divides many dwellers from the homeless, those whose powerlessness is double. Deprived of the house as *domus*, their impotence is multiplied by their lack of the house as shelter. As dwellers without where to dwell, the homeless are at the farthest edges of humanity. They are mirror images of us whose meaning resides in our means.

Arthur C. Danto is Johnsonian Professor of Philosophy at Columbia University and art critic for *The Nation*.

The History of Housing

Cultural values have shaped it.

By Eugenie Ladner Birch

Tracing the evolution of living units reiterates the cultural values and economic life of entire civilizations, for shelter is a basic human need, and the architectural history of dwellings is long and cyclical. Archaeologists have found evidence of purposeful sheltering as far back as 360,000 years, and the housing types of the earliest periods have been repeated in later eras.

In its earliest expression, domestic architecture met the simplest survival needs of prehistoric society. Hunters and food gatherers needed only temporary or semipermanent shelter. On the move, following animal migratory patterns or harvesting seasonal grains and berries, they sought refuge from the elements and from predators in caves or trees. Later, they erected mobile units—skin- or bark-covered frames quickly assembled—to provide a base of operations and protection for the young or the vulnerable. Humans have used this technique repeatedly: twenty thousand years ago mammoth-hunters on the Russian tundra dug pits and roofed them with hide huts; in the nineteenth century nomadic American Indians employed similar elements in their portable tepees.

Advances in technology that permitted the development of agriculture and the domestication of animals allowed foragers to become villagers who erected permanent dwellings. In early Middle Eastern settlements, residential styles developed that are still in use today. At first, windowless one-room mud-brick dwellings were built, arranged on terraces linked by wood ladders. Later, more complex houses were erected with many rooms that served for storage, sleeping, and a combination of work and living spaces. In addition, courtyards were placed at the center of each unit and houses were clustered on wandering streets that ultimately created dense urban precincts. The resulting street fa-

cades were pierced with doors and a few small openings for ventilation, creating unpretentious, inward-looking houses that focused architecturally on the interior courtyard rather than on the street. Other early village societies built freestanding houses, but overall, one tradition remained the same: villagers combined work and living spaces in one unit.

The Greeks adopted this modest introverted housing and modified it slightly. They surrounded the internal courtyard with a colonnade and placed an altar at its center. More significantly, they created separate public rooms for men and women. (Women were second-class citizens in democratic Greece and led sheltered, restricted lives. They did not mix with male guests even in their own living rooms.)

The Romans, too, used the courtyard house with its windowless facade, but made it more elaborate. To enhance the entrance they added a decorative door and vestibule that led to the courtyard (now called an atrium), which they surrounded with guest and reception rooms. They also constructed a second interior open space (the peristyle), which they enclosed with domestic areas—bedrooms, dining rooms, family gathering places, and kitchens.

In addition, the Romans introduced high-rise living. To accommodate the burgeoning population in important cities, they built six- or seven-story apartment buildings. This form, which came to dominate the housing stock in Rome, was much like the nineteenth-century New York City tenement. It had stores on the street floor and walk-up apartments on the upper levels. It did not, however, have water or sanitary facilities, covered windows, or a central heating system.

With the fall of Rome and the subsequent decline of urban life in Western Europe, an agricultural economy rose. Domestic architecture reflected this change

as the population built simple functional shelter. Crude cottages and the occasional reuse of former Roman public buildings—the colosseum at Arles became a circular apartment village—were the pattern.

In subsequent centuries, as trading based on the exchange of surplus agricultural goods and raw materials grew, a merchant economy emerged. This new form of organization stimulated the growth of small fortified cities, which became the characteristic medieval urban form. Inside city walls the burghers con-

structed multistory homes that were two rooms deep and designed to accommodate both work and domestic functions. They reserved the ground floor for offices or shops and storage, placing living rooms on the second level and bedrooms above. Depending on need and geographic location, they sometimes employed an open courtyard or multistoried hall on the ground floor. Despite this feature, the medieval house had little in common with that of the Greeks and Romans. Its focus was on the street, not on the interior. Bays or several large openings on the street

"Jerusalem," from *The Nuremberg Chronicle*, Nuremberg, 1493. Cooper-Hewitt Museum Library.

floor and a liberal number of shuttered windows on the upper levels accentuated its outward orientation.

As cities grew more densely populated, their inhabitants increasingly clamored for more street frontage for commercial use. To accommodate this need they arranged buildings in attached masses on long narrow lots, a custom that is common today in many places. One result of this practice was the loss of side-wall windows. Residential units became totally dependent for light and air on shuttered openings at the front and rear. By the end of the medieval period, city dwellers had created a prototypical house that would dominate the urban single-family form throughout the nineteenth century—the row or terrace house.

During the Renaissance, aristocratic home owners began to make the one major functional adjustment that would come to characterize modern housing—the separation of work and home. In addition, this period contributed several stylistic changes: the addition of larger, glazed windows, and the use of uniform facades aligning cornice lines, windows, and doors.

In the industrial age, as national economies based on manufacturing and the delivery of services flourished, the separation of home and work became common for all classes. The growth of central business districts in large, densely populated cities pushed residential sectors outward. In the evolving neighborhoods, residents lived in a variety of dwellings. At one extreme, the wealthy found comfort in spacious Victorian houses with numerous rooms designed for any number of special purposes; at the other, the poor found some protection in crowded slums, such as multifamily tenements or poorly serviced wood row houses.

Advances in technology, particularly in construction techniques and transportation, further stimulated a revolution in the form and location of housing. The invention of the elevator and the use of steel in construction resulted in apartment buildings of unprecedented heights. The proliferation of mass transit and automobiles and the invention of the balloon frame (a quickly assembled

Thomas Girten, *View of the Gate of St. Denis*, 1802. Cooper-Hewitt Museum, Gift of Museum of Graphic Arts.

wood-stud skeleton) allowed for the extension of residential suburbs containing masses of speculatively built single-family dwellings. These areas became affordable to increasing numbers of middle-class residents. This group, in fact, with its heavy dependence on the automobile, inspired a significant architectural change in house design: the garage was brought to the front and made a central feature of the residential unit.

Modern housing is the product of many generations. It comes in various forms—the single-family detached unit, the high-rise apartment, the row house, the tenement. It has various orientations—to the street or into itself. It has various contents—one room or several that combine

work and living spaces or are used for domestic functions only. It has various locations—in metropolitan areas or in farmlands.

In today's world, examples of every housing type are evident, and new ones are appearing. In the United States, major demographic changes including the rise of dual-income families, the proliferation of single-person or single-parent households, and the increased numbers of elderly have generated new demands for different types of shelter. Congregate housing with shared dining and living facilities and accessory apartments and the subdivision of a single-family house into two smaller units are among the current responses. Others include flexible

houses designed to accommodate work and living spaces and minimum dwelling units stripped of all but basic amenities but affordable to the low-income single-person household. Clearly, the long architectural history of housing will continue to unfold and reveal new types of dwellings. It will also include the repetition of earlier forms adapted for contemporary purposes.

Eugenie Ladner Birch teaches planning history and demography in the Department of Urban Affairs and Planning at Hunter College in New York City. She is editor of *The Unsheltered Woman: Women and Housing in the Eighties.*

An Enduring Theme

Clockwise from upper left:

Edmund Charles Tarbell, *My Family*, 1914, Private Collection.

Miyagawa Chosun, *Festivals of the Twelve Months* (detail), Edo period, Ukiyoe School, 59.12. Courtesy of the Freer Gallery of Art, Smithsonian Institution, Washington, D.C.

"Nahkte and his wife leave their house to greet the rising sun and also the god Osiris," from the *Book of the Dead of Nahkte*, early Nineteenth Dynasty (c. 1320–1290 B.C.), British Museum EA 10471. By permission of the Trustees of the British Museum.

Banquet Scene, Persian miniature, probably 18th century. Cooper-Hewitt Museum, Gift of Ely Jacques Kahn.

Fernand Léger, *Three Women* (*Le grand déjeuner*), 1921, oil on canvas. Collection, The Museum of Modern Art, New York. Mrs. Simon Guggenheim Fund .

Pieter de Hooch, *The Bedroom*, about 1660. National Gallery of Art, Washington, D.C.; Widener Collection .

Henri Matisse, *Interior at Nice*, 1921, oil on canvas, Charles H. and Mary F.S. Worcester Collection, 1956.339. © 1988, The Art Institute of Chicago. All rights reserved.

Housing and Culture

By Amos Rapoport

It is generally assumed, usually implicitly, that housing is housing, that its nature is unproblematic; that it began as shelter and that shelter and other instrumental functions dominate; that what is "good housing" is also unproblematic and standards are universal: what suits one group suits all. All these assumptions about housing are mistaken, because of the relation of housing (indeed all human artifacts) to culture. Looking at that relation is, therefore, essential for a better understanding of housing, because it changes one's ideas about what housing is, what it does, and what "better housing" might mean in different contexts. This, in turn, should change policy and design.

Why these mistaken views? One reason is the ubiquity of housing and the ethnocentrism of most people. That is, most people feel their own culture is superior. One grows up in a particular kind of housing that leads to "self-evident" values and standards whereby other housing is judged. Also, housing is rarely considered comparatively, for example, cross culturally. When it is, mistaken assumptions change because evidence to the contrary is abundant and inescapable. This also follows from the ubiquity of housing: all known human groups build. Since many animals do too, there is evolutionary continuity, as in other aspects of human behavior, including culture. Moreover, humans began building remarkably early: hominids built in Olduvai Gorge in Africa almost two million years ago. This followed stone tools but preceded the use of fire. Yet climate made shelter relatively unimportant. These early origins of housing therefore need other explanations; one possibility is marking special places where food was brought back and shared.

This not only changes assumptions about the origins of housing. It also means that housing has an extraordinary spread through time, as well as across space: it is found wherever and whenever humans have lived. Yet this vast body of evidence has been neglected and its essential lessons ignored—hence the mistaken views about housing.

Comparative work, however, requires comparable units. Trying to identify these, quickly reveals that what housing is taken to be is neither self-evident nor unproblematic. This is because, like all built environments, housing is more than buildings; people and their behavior must be considered. Housing is that part of the built environment in which particular activities take place—and in different cultures these activities occur in many different settings, with different linkages and separations, with different enclosure or openness, that is, privacy. Asking who does what, where, when, including or excluding whom and why shows that housing is best conceptualized as *that system of settings in which particular systems of activities occur*. It is these systems of settings that constitute housing and need to be compared.

It follows that what housing is needs to be *discovered* not *assumed*. What is included varies greatly; sometimes it may include unexpected parts of the settlement if any, or even areas beyond; sometimes the dwelling may be sufficient. In some cases, such as communal dwellings found in various traditional societies, the dwelling and settlement are one, although outside settings are typically also used. Always, how the included settings are combined, linked, separated, or used varies greatly.

Thus one basic assumption is changed just while preparing to do comparative work; doing such work changes the others.

A most striking aspect of housing when considered comparatively is its extraordinary diversity. There must be many hundreds, perhaps thousands, of distinct kinds of dwellings, varying in form, shape, materials, size, spatial organization, and in what meanings, if any, they communicate, and how dwelling and larger milieu are linked and used.

Why should that be? Why should the relatively few things people do result in so many different forms of housing? This diversity and the reasons for it are key issues, because they challenge the remaining assumptions and have implications for policy and design.

Even a dwelling is not just a structure; it is an institution, a social and cultural unit of space created to support the way of life of people. This makes it a complex phenomenon for which no single explanation will suffice. All possible explanations, however, are variations on a single theme: people with very different attitudes and ideals respond to various imperatives—physical, economic, social, cultural, ritual. Housing was always more than shelter; "function" was always much more than a physical, utilitarian, or instrumental concept. Not only is meaning not separate from function; frequently it *is* the most important function.

Functions and activities have four components: the activity itself (its most manifest aspect); how it is carried out; how it is associated with other activities to form activity systems; its meaning (its most latent aspect). Cultural variability goes up as one moves from manifest to latent aspects. Since housing is so diverse, these latent aspects, for example meaning, must be more important than the manifest or instrumental ones.

Consider cooking. It is a cultural universal—all human groups transform raw food. How that is done, however, varies as do the activities associated with it, with very different requirements. The meaning of the activity varies most; among many possible meanings it may be a core ritual or central in establishing status hierarchies; it may then need large settings so that efficiency kitchens are inappropriate. Cooking may involve notions of purity and pollution or need to be hidden; open settings will be inappropriate. The consequence is that the location, size, organization, equipment, and many other aspects of cooking settings are extremely variable. Since that also applies to all other settings and how they are related, the overall diversity becomes even greater.

Put differently: in housing, *wants* are more important than *needs*; wants are also much more variable. Wants play an important role because of what I call the *low criticality* of housing—there are always many ways of satisfying needs. This also means that there is *choice*, which is central to the understanding of housing. There are also constraints, and the relative roles of choice and constraints are an important aspect of the study of housing.

Wants and the different choices made among available alternatives vary with culture, which distinguishes among human groups. Culture, however, is a complex concept difficult to use in analyzing or designing housing because it is both too broad and too abstract. The conclusion of a rather complex analysis is that the concept needs to be "dismantled." This can be done in two ways. One leads via world views and values, to life-style with its associated activity systems; the other—to social variables, such as family and kinship, roles, social networks, and the like. Both can be shown to help understand the variability of housing with culture and to respond to it.

Given all this, the assumption that standards are universal or unproblematic is incorrect. In fact, what makes for good housing (or other environments) varies greatly with culture. Housing quality can be described by a set of attributes, which I call an *environmental quality profile*. These are evaluated as desirable or undesirable and thus chosen or rejected.

Four things can vary: the attributes themselves, their ranking, their importance vis-à-vis other things, and whether they are positive or negative. As in the case of what housing is, environmental quality needs to be *discovered*, not assumed because it is *culture-specific*; what is seen as good in one context may be bad in another. All attributes of housing can be evaluated differently: climate, settlement size, location, size, internal and external space and their organization, vegetation, destiny, privacy, what is communicated and how, and so on.

The choice among alternatives that results in a particular environmental quality profile is made to achieve congruence with life-style and be supportive of it. Life-style can also be seen as the choices made about how to allocate resources—time, money, effort, and so on; it also can be expressed as a profile. The two profiles can be related, which is why it is useful to "dismantle" culture to life-style.

This applies generally, but becomes particularly useful in countries like the United States, where ethnicity, race, and class seem less useful and where income is an *enabling* rather than determining variable: people with identical incomes make very different housing choices. Recall that culture also leads to social variables such as family structure, roles, and life cycle stages. These remain useful, but they also typically have life-style implications (as ethnicity, race, and class often do also.) *Overall, life-style is the most useful concept in considering the relation of housing to culture*—although not the only one.

This is also the case with culture change, whether in developed or developing countries. That also changes life-styles and hence housing. Consider a small example. One typical change in traditional societies is a great increase in possessions; people begin to accumulate *things*. This apparently trivial change can be shown to have a whole set of consequences for housing, including increased need to communicate resulting status variations, increased amount of space needed, and the number and specialization of settings, and increased physical enclosure to protect possessions. These, in turn, greatly change privacy. And so on.

In the past, diversity occurred mainly cross-culturally and over time. Any one traditional society tended to be remarkably homogeneous; so were its dwellings and settlements, which frequently symbolized the group. Today, in countries like the United States, extraordinary cultural diversity is found *within* the society—in life-styles and hence allocation of resources, privacy, space use, communication of status or identity, family arrangements, trajectories of life-cycle stages, and so on. Yet while life-style diversity increases greatly (some marketing analyses use over fifty life-style groups), *housing* diversity seems to decrease. There is thus a potential, and possibly a real, misfit.

Rates of change in all these variables, as well as forms of sharing of dwellings, institutions, technology, work patterns, time use, and so on also increase. The need is thus not only for greater diversity of housing but also for *open-endedness* to accommodate rapid change, to allow users to participate, complete, add, and modify. Also, meanings are increasingly communicated through objects, furnishings, landscaping, and the like (semi-fixed elements) — through *personalization*. Open-endedness thus becomes an important latent function of housing, particularly since the need to communicate identity also goes up with rapid change and proliferation of groups.

Since housing is a system of settings, the larger milieu (neighborhoods, for example) may also play a role in responding to specific life-styles in their specialized institutions and settings, spatial organization, forms of social homogeneity and behavior, and ways of communicating identity. Whereas the need seems to be for culture-specific housing, the opposite is the case; standards tend to become more uniform both in countries like the United States, Australia, or Canada and in developing countries like Indonesia, the Philippines, or India. There was even talk in the United Nations (mercifully dropped) about a uniform world housing code! Thus not only is there insufficient diversity in housing—there are pressures for even less. Even those concerned with changes in family structure, roles, and the like, tend not to advocate *additional* housing forms but argue for the *replacement* by new forms.

Whereas all built environments need to be culture-specific, this applies particularly to housing. As the primary setting for life it needs to be highly supportive of culture; sometimes the very survival of certain cultures may depend on this. It is thus imperative that, first, the mistaken assumptions about housing be revised and, second, the implications for policy and design be faced. In both these endeavors the study of the relation of housing and culture is central.

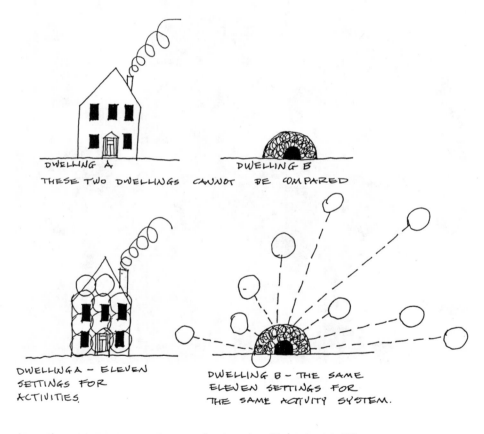

DWELLING A

DWELLING B

THESE TWO DWELLINGS CANNOT BE COMPARED

DWELLING A — ELEVEN SETTINGS FOR ACTIVITIES.

DWELLING B — THE SAME ELEVEN SETTINGS FOR THE SAME ACTIVITY SYSTEM.

THE TWO SYSTEMS OF ELEVEN SETTINGS EACH CONSTITUTE THE UNITS OF COMPARISON, I.E. THEY CONSTITUTE "HOUSING" IN THE TWO CASES

Courtesy of Amos Rapoport.

Amos Rapoport, one of the founders of the field of environment-behavior studies, has published extensively. He is currently Distinguished Professor of Architecture at the University of Wisconsin-Milwaukee.

Amenities and Comforts

By Anthony Ridley

The need for a home lies deep in human nature. Three million years ago in Africa our hominid ancestors focused their lives around base sites—no more than a pile of stones for a windbreak and soft vegetation as furnishing, but still home.

Fire, the earliest real home comfort, came later when a recognizably human species, Homo erectus, broke free of Africa and settled in the colder lands of Asia and Europe. Here warmth in winter became a necessity for survival. When fire was first captured and tamed will never be known, but ancient hearths have been found in the Chinese cavern of Choukoutien, occupied by Homo erectus six-hundred thousand years ago.

Gradually other home comforts were added. Discoveries on the French Riviera show that two-hundred thousand years later Homo erectus had learned to build primitive huts and provide himself with furnishings. Preserved in the long-buried floors are impressions of animal hides used for couches and beds. With the advent of modern man some fifty thousand years ago came a quickening advance. Improvements in stone chisels enabled bone, horn, and ivory to be worked as never before. Bone needles made it easier to stitch pelts together for clothing and coverings. Indoor and outdoor life became a little more comfortable.

Early on in the use of fire, brands must have been plucked from the flames to act as torches. Longer-lasting lights would have been needed to explore the recesses of caves. When the great age of European cave painting flowered twenty thousand years ago, the lamp was already well established. A hundred were discovered in the Lascaux caves alone, some so well shaped as to suggest a long tradition of manufacture. The Stone Age lamp was simply a moss wick, supplied with grease from a depression gouged into a piece of soft rock, yet the technology of lighting was to show little improvement until the Industrial Revolution of the eighteenth century.

Between ten and twelve thousand years ago, as the world grew warmer in the wake of the last Ice Age, a new way of life became possible. In certain well-watered areas of the Middle East, people who had long gathered the local edible grasses took the giant step of planting and harvesting their own crops. Settled farming communities appeared. Temporary huts gave way to permanent houses, and the chances for home comforts began to improve.

Eventually the food surpluses provided by agriculture allowed complex societies to develop. By the fourth millennium B.C. cities and civilizations were beginning to emerge in Egypt and Mesopotamia. In many ways these early cities were premature. Drinking water still came mainly from the increasingly polluted rivers; farmyard sanitation was the general rule. Egypt, with its scanty rainfall, had little need for drains and never developed sewers. Even Pharaoh made do with an earth closet. Mesopotamia was more progressive and some of its palaces had sewers by the end of the third millennium. Over the next few centuries the use of sewers spread down as far as the wealthy merchant class, but never reached the mass of the population.

In terms of the niceties of home life, a younger civilization, further east, was superior to both older cultures. The cities that flourished along the Indus Valley from about 2300 B.C. to 1750 B.C. enjoyed adequate water supply and simple but effective sanitation. Each housing block had at least one well of its own, and even quite humble homes often had a room, with a sunken floor, set aside for bathing. Many of the houses had a privy that could be cleansed with a flush of water from a pitcher kept close by. Wastes were discharged into a network of street drains that, though open, were

Robert Campin (active by 1406–d.1444), *Triptych of the Annunciation* (detail), 15th century, oil on wood. Metropolitan Museum of Art, The Cloisters Collection, 1956 (56.70).

well constructed and easily scoured out by a flow of water. Domestic lighting was simple but ingenious. Bricks, which had been left projecting from the walls at various convenient points around the house, were hollowed out to take the oil and wicks needed for unspillable lamps.

Eventually the Indus heritage was lost, as its cities succumbed to barbarian attack. But another civilization was stirring, whose influence is felt to this day. China was emerging from the twilight of legend. From the Shang dynasty of about 1600 B.C. down to the present, China has maintained a thread of continuity despite all the vicissitudes of plague, famine, foreign invasion, and civil war.

By the middle of the second millennium B.C. Chinese agriculture could support numerous sizable towns. The city of Ch'eng-tzu-yai, for instance, occupied a rectangular area of fifteen-hundred feet by thirteen-hundred feet, completely enclosed by a defensive wall. Though houses were built of mud, timber, and thatch, and water supply and sanitation were basic, the Chinese were already great potters and, certainly before 1300 B.C., had mastered the use of bronze. Elegant pottery would have graced the homes of the rich, and their kitchens would have featured huge bronze tripods and cauldrons. Even the humble would have possessed a cooking pot.

While China continued on its own individual way, powers rose and fell in the West. By the fifth century B.C. Greece had reached the peak of its influence, with its thinkers and artists making lasting contributions to Western civilization. But the genius of Greece was directed toward civic life rather than domestic comfort. Though the best of its public buildings command admiration to this day, its private houses were utterly unpretentious. Exterior simplicity was matched by austerity within. There were no cupboards, and clothes and personal possessions hung from hooks in the walls. Stools and chairs were few. Dining couches doubled as beds. But with the sunny courtyard as an extension to the house, life would have been pleasant enough. Some houses had kitchens with flues extending up to roof level, but much of the cooking must have been done in the open air, using portable ranges. When guests came, lamplight extended entertainment and talk far into the night. Perhaps the use of artificial light is a measure of civilization. Certainly the Greeks were great users and makers of lamps. Thousands have been found in Athens alone.

However, Greek home life did lack two great amenities—running water and sanitation. The first deficiency could be partially remedied. Each city maintained public fountain-houses, supplied with pure water from local springs. Women went to fill their jugs every day and often stayed to gossip, making the fountain-house a focus of social life. Although water was precious, the Greeks liked to keep clean, and many houses set aside a special room for bathing.

The Romans, with an even greater passion for baths, became the premier water engineers of antiquity. At its peak Rome was supplied by thirteen aqueducts, delivering forty gallons a day for each inhabitant. But very little of this water reached private dwellings directly. The bulk went to public fountain-houses, as in the Greek cities, or to the great public baths. Only the wealthy could afford the tariff for direct connection to the mains. Besides, most ordinary citizens lived in tall tenement blocks, and piping water to the upper floors would have been beyond even Roman technical ability.

At first sight the Roman tenement looked surprisingly modern—elegantly proportioned with balconies, large windows, and tiled roofs—but there were many hidden deficiencies. Buildings were thrown together with little thought of safety, so that collapse and fire were commonplace. With no fireplaces or chimneys, heating was limited to feeble charcoal braziers—all the more serious since the windows were unglazed. Newfangled glass was much too expensive for poor tenants. Sanitation, at best, was access to a communal privy built over a cesspit on the ground floor. Rome had reason to be thankful for its numerous splendid public lavatories served by water-flushed sewers.

By contrast the homes of the wealthy Romans were comfortable and spacious, with water on tap and sewers to carry off the wastes. Occasionally privies were even flushed from above in a thoroughly modern manner, with a stopcock controlling the flow of water from a raised cistern. Heating was not neglected. Hot air was circulated through underfloor and wall cavities, distributing a pleasant warmth from a central furnace. Window glass, used for the very first time, added a unique touch of luxury. Artificial lighting was the only real deficiency. Smoky, flamed lamps remained the mainstay, though candles were also manufactured.

Domestic comfort was swept away by the tide of barbarian invasion that destroyed the Western Empire in the fifth century. Rome itself was sacked by Germanic tribesmen in 410 A.D. Everywhere the invaders destroyed or shunned what they could not understand, and kept to their own traditions of house building. Not until the nineteenth century were Roman standards once again matched and exceeded.

Israhel van Meckenem (about 1440–1503?), *The Children's Bath*, before 1500, engraving. Cooper-Hewitt Museum, Gift of Mrs. Leo Wallerstein.

The Anglo-Saxons who occupied the province of Britain had no time for Roman niceties. Even the most powerful noble was content with a barn-like hall of wood construction and a scattering of outhouses. Communal life centered around the hall, where the chief's entourage ate, drank, and slept. Furniture was crude. Planks laid over trestles served as tables; backless benches as seating. In the center of the earth floor stood a clay hob for the fire. Smoke found its way out through a hole in the thatch. Windows were mere openings, with no trace of glass. Artificial light came from the great central fire and torches of pitch pine or fat-soaked wood spluttering in holders ranged along the walls. At night tables were stacked and benches pushed together to make beds for the retainers. Only the master and mistress, and perhaps a few honored guests, withdrew to the outer buildings.

Without the civilizing influence of Christianity the losses might have been even more profound. Candles still burned before the altar; glass, too precious for domestic windows, continued to grace the house of God. As monasteries grew, the old Roman idea of waterborne sanitation was revived. From at least the tenth century onward a stream would sometimes be diverted to pass under the sanitary block adjacent to the brothers' dormitory. It was also the church that took the lead in restoring water supplies. The Abbaye of St. Laurent, near Paris, began to pipe in spring water as early as the sixth century and by the ninth had enough to provide a public fountain for its lay neighbors.

As the medieval era advanced, secular standards began to improve, with royalty leading the way. Once the old rough manners were put aside, no king would deny himself amenities enjoyed by mere monks. Also, Crusading contacts with the East, where many of the old Roman comforts still lingered, had awakened a new desire for luxury. Within a year of his return from the last Crusade in 1274, England's Edward I had extended the water service at his Palace of Westminster to include a cold supply piped directly into his bathroom. Three-quarters of a century later his grandson, Edward III, added piped hot water to the glories of the royal tub. But this was most unusual. The wood, barrel-like baths of the medieval period were normally filled by hand.

Among the aristocracy the bath was not the only means of personal hygiene. Custom demanded that on rising in the morning hands and face should be washed and teeth rinsed. To cater to this need stone handbasins, complete with drains, were often built into wall alcoves in the living quarters of great houses and castles. Water, however, was not on tap, but came from a hand-filled container suspended above the sink.

For many townspeople any sort of water was a luxury. Cities were expanding and fast outgrowing the capacity of local springs and wells. But the monasteries had shown the way. Gradually major towns began to establish conduits of their own to supply their public fountains with fresh, clean waters. London's first conduit was completed in 1237; others were added regularly but never quite kept up with demand.

All medieval households suffered to some extent from poor sanitation. Not that there was any lack of privies—numerous stone "garderobes" can still be found in any self-respecting castle ruin. The fault lay in final disposal. An isolated monastery could divert a stream and turn it into a private sewer, but this was never a viable solution for a crowded town. Some castles with a river frontage built privies jutting out from the wall to take advantage of the passing tide. Those less fortunately sited allowed their privies to void into seldom-emptied cesspits or the waters of a stagnant moat.

Progress was more obvious in the matter of domestic glass which, from the middle of the thirteenth century, staged a slow comeback. Henry III, who reigned from 1216 to 1272, was the first great English glazier. Many of the king's wealthier subjects followed his example, though often, to save on expense, only the top of a window was glazed, leaving the bottom to old-fashioned wood shutters. Until the sixteenth century the cost of glass remained so high that casements were sometimes taken down and stored away during any protracted absence from home.

The art of domestic heating also began to advance, in unlikely partnership with military architecture. Though the central hearth and roof louvre were long retained in the traditional great hall, they were useless to heat the lower floors of the massive stone castles that became fashionable in the eleventh century. To solve the problem of what to do with the smoke, the castle builders moved the fireplace to a recess in an external wall from which a flue angled its way through the masonry to emerge in a simple vent. By the middle of the twelfth century the more efficient vertical flue had come into use, sometimes topped by a cylindrical chimney to further improve the draft. At the end of the medieval age, as the single-story hall gave way to more complex buildings, wall-fireplaces and chimneys came into their own. But the process took a long time to work down the social scale, and as late as 1577 William Harrison could imply in his *Description of England* that cottage chimneys were a recent innovation.

So the people of the Middle Ages had won back some of the old Roman comforts; it remained for modern technology to complete the process and set new standards of its own.

One of the greatest amenities of modern home life is a copious supply of safe, unpolluted water. The spring-fed conduits of the medieval city gave reasonable purity but were sadly lacking in quantity. Then technology found a partial answer. By setting waterwheels in the arches of a bridge a river's own power could be used to pump its waters into city fountains. A much greater supply became available and for the first time water was connected to modest private homes. Town after town established such waterworks—Breslau in 1479, Toledo in 1526, Augsburg in 1548, London in 1582. But quantity had been bought at the expense of quality; even in those days major rivers were heavily contaminated.

The invention of the steam engine opened the way for still greater supplies. Steam-driven pumps were tried out tentatively in London from 1712, but it was not until 1742 that the Chelsea Water Works established a viable system. Other companies, both in Britain and abroad, began to install pumping engines. The Watering Committee of Philadelphia introduced the steam-driven pump to America in 1797.

Another benefit of technology was the development of cast-iron water mains capable of withstanding high internal pressures. The hollowed-out tree trunks used previously had been so notoriously leaky that pressures had seldom allowed water to be raised further than a ground-floor cistern. Water for the higher stories had to be carried up or pumped by hand. London began a large-scale replacement of its wooden mains in 1811 and by 1817 pioneering Philadelphia was importing British cast-iron piping and once again showing America the way. With the combination of powerful pumps and high-pressure mains, it at last became possible to supply piped water to upper floors and loft cisterns.

Water could be delivered efficiently, but unpolluted sources were becoming difficult to find. Some cities, like New York in 1842, built lengthy aqueducts to tap distant sources of pure water. London came up with the sand filter-bed, introduced in 1829, which removed all gross impurities and greatly reduced bacterial contamination. At last a way had been found to clean up suspect waters. After 1852 all river-derived water supplied to London had first to be passed through filter-beds. The age of pure water had almost arrived. With the introduction of the chlorination process in 1908, which killed any residual bacteria, the story was complete.

The ability of high-pressure mains to deliver water to every floor of the house was not fully exploited for many years. The single tap over the kitchen sink remained the norm for many working-class city families well into the twentieth century. But the idea of the bathroom as a necessity was taking root. New products began to appear in response to demand, quickening still further the pace of development. After about 1880 freestanding cast-iron baths and simple earthenware washbasins began to make their way onto the market. The bathroom was becoming cheaper and more functional. In the present century, stripped of unnecessary ostentation, it has become accepted as one of the essential amenities of home life.

It was probably the increasing availability of water that rekindled interest in waterborne sanitation. During the 1590s the Elizabethan courtier Sir John Harington had devised an effective water closet, but with piped water in its infancy he was greatly ahead of his time. After a further hundred years water closets reappeared in England, though at first only as great rarities. In these early appliances the water-seal was maintained by a simple plug on the end of a long handle, which was raised for emptying and flushing. The first British patent for a water closet, granted to Alexander Cumming in 1775, featured a sliding valve actuated by a lever that simultaneously opened a water-cock to admit a cleansing flush. More significant, however, than this piece of mechanical ingenuity was the S-bend water trap inserted in the drain below the toilet to prevent the entry of sewer gases.

Although valve closets of one sort or another remained in use for a further hundred years, it was realized, in the earlier part of the nineteenth century, that an S-trap could maintain an efficient water-seal on its own. By the late 1840s British trade journals were carrying increasing numbers of advertisements for cheap, valveless closets consisting of a glazed-pottery bowl, which tapered sharply into an S-trap and was provided at the top with a side-pipe for flushing water. Here was the true prototype of the present-day toilet. With the addition of the flushing rim in 1849, progressive improvements in shape, and the advent in the 1880s of freestanding pedestal models without unhygienic surrounds, the modern sanitary age had arrived.

Window glass roundels were already established at the close of the medieval period and plate glass was developed in France around 1680; by the end of the eighteenth century its use was widespread throughout Western Europe. Improvements in glass technology provided ever-larger window panes, encouraging changes in fashion. From the late seventeenth century, wooden glazing bars, more suited to the larger panes, began to take over from the old-fashioned leaded lights. A less explicable innovation was the advent of the sliding sash, which in Georgian architecture temporarily eclipsed the hinged casement. By Victoria's reign such large sheets of glass could be manufactured that single panes were sometimes used to fill an entire frame. From then on windows could be made virtually as large or small as the architect wished. With the development of sealed double-glazed units in the mid-twentieth century, window design has moved another step forward. Light can now be admitted without serious loss of heat.

Domestic lighting emerged from the Middle Ages much as it had entered it, with flame the only source of illumination. It was not until 1782 that the first real breakthrough in millennia was achieved, when the Swiss scientist Ami Argand made a lamp that outshone twenty candles. The secret lay in the extra draft created by a glass chimney and a tubular wick. Within two years the new lamp was under manufacture in England.

Other changes were in the offing. In 1792 the mining engineer William Murdoch succeeded in lighting his office with a gas distilled from coal. Thanks largely to the enthusiasm of German-born Frederick Winser, the London-based Gas Light and Coke Company was founded in 1812. After struggling for some years the company paid a dividend in 1817, but prejudice against gas persisted and its use was long confined to lighting streets, factories, and public buildings. Not until the 1840s was it taken up on a large scale for domestic lighting.

The possibility of electric light had been recognized as far back as 1802, but the problem of thin filaments burning through proved intractable. It was not until 1878 that the British inventor Joseph Swan produced the first practicable electric light bulb, with a carbon filament enclosed in a highly evacuated glass globe. Within a few months Thomas Edison, working independently in the United States, hit on the same idea. Both Swan and Edison were producing commercially by 1881 and in 1883 the two inventors joined forces to form the Edison and Swan United Electric Light Company. For the first time light could be produced without the need for flame.

With the advent of cool-running fluorescent tubes in the 1930s new design possibilities were opened up. Although strip lighting was more rapidly accepted in the work setting, its advantages for domestic applications have won increasing recognition. Its efficiency allows kitchens and workrooms to be brilliantly lit without glare or sharp shadows, while living rooms can benefit from the soft light provided by concealed fittings.

The chimney and open fire of the Middle Ages were wasteful of fuel and poorly suited to the requirements of a multi-roomed house. Gas and electric fires have been introduced as replacements but more significant is the development of methods of central heating that allow the temperature of the whole house to be controlled. Heating by steam and hot water were suggested by the Elizabethan Sir Hugh Platt but neither idea was taken

Mary Cassatt (1844–1926), *Woman Bathing*, about 1891, drypoint and aquatint in color. The Brooklyn Museum, Dick S. Ramsay Fund (39.107).

up practically until the eighteenth century. Appropriately the earliest known example of heating by steam is attributed to James Watt, the famous engineer who, during the winter of 1784–85, heated his office with a simple box-like radiator fed with steam from a boiler on the lower floor.

As more factories went over to steam power, steam heating became an increasingly attractive proposition, and by the first decade of the nineteenth century was well established. Because of the high temperature of the pipework, steam proved less suited to domestic needs,

though it has enjoyed some success in American cities since the 1880s, when district heating companies came into prominence.

Gentler hot-water heating was first put to practical use in 1789, when the French inventor Bonnemain designed an incubator to hatch chicks for the Paris market. The Marquis de Chabanne adapted Bonnemain's idea to domestic heating and in 1816 introduced the system into Britain. Robert Briggs began to install hot-water heating appliances in the United States in the 1840s. The system gradually won support, but real success had to wait until the second half of the twentieth century, when the application of electrical pumping allowed the use of easily hidden narrow-bore tubing and thin, elegant radiators.

Warm-air heating can also be traced back to the eighteenth century, when, to reduce the risk of fire, factory owners took to moving the heating stove into a side room from where hot air was circulated back into the main building. In about 1792 William Strutt improved on this system by enclosing the furnace within an arched, brick-built jacket, leaving a gap of about ten inches all round. Cool air was drawn into the gap, strongly heated by the furnace, and piped away for distribution. Early domestic warm-air systems relied, in the same way, on natural convection and required the furnace to be situated in a basement, below the living rooms. The use of an electric circulating fan has freed warm air from this restraint and led to increased popularity. A further attraction is that with fan operation, air-conditioning can easily be incorporated.

Modern humanity—cushioned from the environment by central heating and air-conditioning, able to turn night into day at the flick of a switch, provided with pure water no further away than the kitchen, and served by an unobtrusive sewage disposal system—has come a long way since the first home comfort of fire was won six-hundred thousand years ago.

Anthony Ridley lectures on science subjects at London's Middlesex Polytechnic and is the author of *Living in Cities* and *At Home: An Illustrated History of Houses and Homes.*

Houses are for Living In

Comfort has become a major requirement.

By Paul Oliver

Francis Bacon wrote in *Of Building* in 1625, "Houses are built to live in and not to look on; therefore let use be preferred before uniformity, except where both may be had."

Bacon was writing at a time when the houses of the wealthy were getting grander in scale and more symmetrical in design under the new Renaissance influence in Britain, at a time too, when the houses of ordinary people were frequently unsanitary hovels. He was making a plea for efficient houses rather than beautiful ones. Today we may prefer that "both may be had," but we still place greater importance on their efficiency.

We ask a lot of our houses: we expect them to keep out rain and snow; we require protection from the wind, and shade from the sun. But we also want our houses to be well ventilated, and the interiors to be light. If we need our houses to be warm in winter, we also like them to be cool in summer—and comfortable between times. We may like a fire, but we do not want smoke; we want hot and cold running water, but we do not expect leaks. We assume that the building will stand up, that the floors are going to be level and will take the weight of furniture, that the walls will not crack, the timbers rot, or the foundations sink. All this and much more we take for granted, and we are hardly aware of our presumption—until some part or other fails.

Comfort has become a major requirement of our houses in modern Western societies. So much so that we are prepared to overheat them with the heavy consumption of fuels in the winter, and to refrigerate them with air-conditioning in the summer. High levels of servicing have enabled us to enjoy open-plan living in an ambient temperature; electricity has facilitated every kind of domestic chore from cleaning carpets to washing dishes. It provides levels of luxury and freedom from drudgery that are unthinkable for millions of families in Latin America, Africa, or Asia.

Almost without exception the peoples of the world live in houses of some kind or another: from tree shelters in the Philippines to cave dwellings in Cappadocia, from scattered cylindrical houses in the South African veldt to apartment houses in Sweden, and from black tents in Saudi Arabia to mobile homes in Southern California. Diverse in form, construction, materials, and size though they may be, houses in every part of the globe have many similar functions for living, even if the spaces in and around them are employed differently. They all are used for the preparation of food and the eating of meals, even if some societies have their stoves outdoors and take their meals in the yard. Houses generally provide shelter for sleeping, though in many parts of the Middle East beds are placed on the roofs in the hot season. Houses afford safety and the protection of property, where possessions or stores are important; they can provide a haven of privacy, even though, in places as far apart as Brazil and Burma, numbers of families may share the same community building. We can generalize about the uses of houses, but in the details, every dwelling type is culturally specific.

Sometimes the differences between house types have an environmental basis: in northern Greenland or Siberia year-round insulation is necessary, not only from extremes of cold but from biting winds and low ground temperatures due to building on permafrost. In the hot and humid regions of Southeast Asia houses must deflect heavy tropical rains, yet the walls must be sufficiently open to permit the cross-ventilation that is necessary if occupants are to gain any measure of comfort. Comfort conditions are, like all aspects of living in houses, relative to the specific circumstances, and they are compounded when, in this case, Malay houses are required to accommodate many people, are extended and partitioned, and must ensure the privacy of the occupants while maintaining through ventilation.

Privacy is essentially cultural, and the degree of separation from public or semi-public space that it implies differs widely from one society to another. Sometimes privacy is principally related to the sleeping quarters of parents; sometimes it may extend to the apartments of unmarried daughters; and sometimes it is codified and virtually embodied in common law. This is the case in some strict Muslim societies, and most Islamic communities require the separation of women from men. This fact has had profound effects upon house form from Iraq to Northern Nigeria.

At the base of all societies lies the family, but the nature of the family is perceived differently in various cultures. The nuclear family of parents and children, common in Western Europe, is considerably enlarged to accommodate the grandparents' generation in "stem families," and laterally to include, for instance, brothers of the parents, their wives, and children in an "extended family," as may be found in many parts of Africa and Asia. Such family structures require large houses capable of supporting many people—built vertically in the Yemen, horizontally in eastern Turkey. Marriage customs determine whether a son remains in his parents' house, whether a bride receives a dowry. And rules of inheritance define who, and how many, benefit from the property when a house owner dies. Many societies place great importance on ancestral homes and lands, identifying with the places where their forefathers lived.

We all identify with our houses: there is "no place like home," and we are intimately bound up with it. Home is often a symbol of ourselves, and when it is entered without our knowledge we feel violated. Home is for many, a model of our own universe, where we act out all the dramas of life—and often, of death—and where our possessions, some utilitarian, some for decoration, are signs of the things that matter to us. "House and home" are one and the same, but "home" implies the emotional ties that we have with the house.

In Western society, where the majority of householders had not been involved in the building of their homes, where many have bought a house that has already had many previous occupants, the term *homemaking* is applied to a process of personalizing the dwelling with furniture and objects. In societies throughout much of the world homemaking is more literally the process of actually building the house. For families who have been physically involved in the preparation of the materials, the dedication of the site, often with religious rites that also accompany stages in its construction, and who have themselves assembled the structural elements to their requirements within the norms of their tradition, identification is with the house from its inception.

Among the peoples of Mali and Burkino Faso the house is anthropomorphic, every part being associated with the parts and organs of the human body. For other societies, including Native American nations such as the Navajo, the dwelling unit symbolizes the cosmos: the roof may be associated with the heavens, the floor with the earth, the corner posts dedicated to deities. For them, the house *is* temple. And in many other societies the house is part shrine where offerings are made to the protective deities, as they are in Hindu dwellings.

Such associations with the dwelling are customary among rural peoples and, in spite of modernization, frequently persist in modified form in urban areas. The need

A Gurunsi compound, including altar shrine and headman's house, in Northern Ghana. © Paul Oliver, 1964.

for trade and the marketing of produce, the desire for social intercourse and increased choice, and the natural gregariousness of human beings have always led to the clustering of houses. The location of communities, which may range in scale from hamlet to village to town and, ultimately, to city, depends on many factors, such as access to water and communication routes. Climatic and environmental constraints also condition their location as well as the numbers of people that can be supported by them. But in the past forty years changes in technology, the "green revolution" in some regions and famine in others, and many other fac-

tors both economic and political have accelerated the process of movement to the cities.

In the West the expansion of the cities has been met by the growth of the suburbs and the housing developments of speculative builders. An important distinction can be made here between "houses" and "housing"—between individual dwellings and the process of accommodating people. "Housing" as a product of that process may also refer to large-scale solutions of the accommodation problem. Some housing is produced for sale or rent—the eighteenth-century London squares were of this kind—and

such speculative housing continued in the nineteenth and twentieth centuries in Europe and the United States. The provision of low-cost or rental units by charitable organizations and, later, by local and federal governments expanded to meet the demands of the newly urbanized but economically disadvantaged migrants to the cities.

Mass housing is to be seen all over the world; Hong Kong, for example, has extraordinarily high densities on limited space. The most extensive housing programs were those undertaken in the wake of World War II, when the devastated cities of Warsaw and Coventry, London and Berlin, Dresden and Stalingrad, and literally hundreds of others throughout Europe had to be swiftly rebuilt. Vast housing complexes in the obliterated Russian cities were designed to house millions of homeless people. Modernist high-rise "slab" blocks following the theories, if not the example, of Le Corbusier rose in the thousands from Scandinavia to Italy and eventually throughout the world. But many proved to be structurally and socially disastrous. Apart from the failure of poorly tested prefabrication systems, there were signs of social breakdown when families were isolated in their apartments, because walkways were dangerous and elevators virtually unusable. For countless families high-rise living enforced separation from land and community, and destroyed the bond of identification with the home.

Today the world faces massive housing problems as millions of people continue to migrate to cities, where the attractions of urban living and opportunities for marginal "spin-off" employment draw the poor in droves to the urban conurbations. There they settle in makeshift shelters and illegal settlements. From Casablanca to Calcutta, from Manila to Mexico City the growth of these slums has been phenomenal. In the 1950s Mexico City's slums represented less than 15 percent of its total housing stock; now three-quarters of the population live in them and the city is likely to be the largest in the world before the end of the century.

Exacerbated by growth through natural increase, the problems of the expanding cities are immense. Low-rise development creates difficulties in maintaining communications and transport, and the infrastructure of such services as sewers and water supply is costly; yet the slum populace is too poor to contribute to the expense. In many countries—Peru and Kenya, for instance—migrants to the cities are offered low-rental serviced sites on which to build their own houses. In Indonesia and elsewhere methods of upgrading and improving the conditions of existing squatter settlements are being introduced, though not without considerable expense. Such measures can generate new difficulties: in Calcutta improved and legalized bustees, as they call such settlements, tended to attract still more migrants from the impoverished rural areas. If high-rise fails and low-rise is too extravagant, what kinds of housing can meet these unprecedented demands? It may be that the answer to the problems of expanding cities may lie not in the urban areas themselves but in rural development and the planned growth of decentralized secondary and tertiary towns.

The era of mass-housing solutions dedicated, in Francis Bacon's terms, to "uniformity" may be near an end, but too few architects, planners, and social scientists are yet addressing the scale of the problems that reside in any alternative approaches. Those who are confronting the issues now prefer "use before uniformity," realizing that the immediate need is more for houses "to live in" than ones that are good "to look on." But if future urban environments are to have any quality, it is the task of designers to ensure that ultimately "both may be had." Implicit in Francis Bacon's wise words of more than three-and-a-half centuries ago is the warning that if houses, and housing, are to succeed, they must satisfy the physical, cultural, and qualitative needs of the societies concerned.

Paul Oliver, formerly Head of the Architectural Association Graduate School and more recently, Associate Head of the School of Architecture at Oxford Polytechnic, specializes in the study of vernacular architecture. He is the author of *Dwellings: The House Across the World*.

The Contradictions of Housing

The driving force is economics.

By Peter Marcuse

Housing in the United States is contradiction. Private enterprise has created a tremendously productive, tremendously unequal housing system. Some live in a post-shelter society; others can no longer find even minimal shelter. Ingrained racism and sexism shape housing opportunities; housing shapes racist and sexist patterns. Our best architects build some of the finest and most luxurious housing in the world. Other architects (some also prizewinning) build massive minimal-standard housing projects that are dynamited to destroy their evils twenty years after they are built.

Housing is pride and joy, status and sanctuary for some; it is shame and fear, stigma and prison for others. Home ownership is the cherished goal of all "true" Americans; but less and less it differs from tenancy in cost, in security, in restrictions on use, in location, in amenities. Efficiency in production and cost savings in management are hallmarks of our compulsively energetic private market; yet we are more wasteful of land and the natural environment than any other advanced private-market economy.

The key to these contradictions is twofold: polarization and privatization. The two are related. The polarization of society, the increasing gap between the well-off and the badly-off, leads to and is reinforced by the transfer of many normal public functions to the realm of private concern—for those that can afford them—and public neglect—for those that cannot. Both polarization and privatization are directly reflected in the housing we see (or do not see) about us.

The rich have always been with us. The United States need bow to no other country's feudal tradition in the splendor of its housing for the upper classes. The quality of Fifth Avenue's mansions, Newport's estates, California's ranches, Texas's ostentation, or the design of second and third homes in Colorado or apartments in Chicago yield to none.

The poor also have always been with us, although their number and the permanence of their marginality is on a historic increase. Here the competition is with the Third World rather than with aristocratic patterns: the homeless that fill bus and train stations, that sleep on the sidewalks and park benches (when the good citizens of communities like Santa Barbara do not make sleeping outdoors a criminal offense) have hit a post-depression high. Estimates, according to the Coalition for the Homeless, are sixty thousand in New York, twenty-five thousand in Houston, fifty thousand in Los Angeles. Children number almost a third of the homeless in New York. Despite the stereotype, less than a quarter of those living on the streets were previously mentally ill.

Some imaginative design skills and creative financing goes into a few shelters for the homeless, but nowhere near enough. Nor are shelters the answer to those without homes: homes are what they need, not armories or church basements or public flophouses. The abdication of the public sector compounds the failure of the private sector to provide housing where housing is most needed.

The division among those neither very rich nor very poor is the most striking feature of the 1980s housing scene. No longer is there an amorphous "middle class," spreading out in socially differentiated but similarly bland suburbs on the edges of every metropolitan area. The division between managerial and professional on the one hand, white- and blue-collar working class on the other, is growing and is directly reflected in the changing of neighborhoods and the restructuring of cities.

The yuppies, for the moment in high demand, are gentrifying neighborhoods, "reclaiming" older housing, displacing poorer residents, reversing the filtering process that for so long was looked to for the improvement of working-people's housing. Working-class people, in the same process, are forced to move; their commute to work becomes longer, the space they can afford dwindles, the hassles they have to endure in less tended-to neighborhoods increase.

Household patterns both contribute to and reflect the division: single young professionals move to the center city, couples with children and limited incomes find only older fringe areas or remote suburbs affordable, and even then only with two incomes. Single parents, predominantly women, find themselves left out in the cold (often literally) more and more. Increasing renovation activity, neighborhood revitalization, unfortunately even some historic preservation, are all parts of this process. The driving force is straight economics: when the private sector allocates housing, effective demand determines who gets what where—and who has to leave to make it all possible.

The abdication of the public sector contributes mightily to these developments. Both city planning and housing policies fail their ideals, in what they do not do as much as in what they do do. But the big

Demolition of Pruitt-Igoe housing project, St. Louis, Missouri, 1972–77. St. Louis Housing Authority.

issues are not in the control of the professionals and the civic volunteers who attempt to guide these policies directly; housing is more influenced by developments outside the housing sector than by those within it.

Take taxes, for instance. The biggest of all public subsidies for housing is that going to home owners via the deductibility of mortgage interest and taxes, and the failure to tax the imputed income derived from owner-occupancy. Current estimates are that this runs to $48 billion, and is growing; the current subsidy to lower-income housing is only $8.9 billion, and is shrinking.

The framers of the Income Tax Amendment hardly had a shift from rental to owner-occupancy in mind in 1916, yet that is what has been produced. It plays directly into the hands of a long-standing ideological bias toward home ownership as a symbol of social status and personal freedom, the "foundation of American life," as Herbert Hoover called it. Despite the fact that home ownership for many is more of a burden than a blessing, that mortgage foreclosures are at a postwar high, that leases can give every bit as much protection to a tenant as a deed to an owner, the bias continues. Real tax advantages give it substance. Not even repeal of the favored deductions for second homes survived in the tax reform negotiations of 1986.

Fiscal and monetary policy affecting interest rates is thus the single most decisive public action affecting housing in the United States, yet its primary concerns have little to do with shelter. Interest rates—not need, not planning, not social priorities—have, year in and year out, been the prime determinant of how much new housing is supplied in the United States. Thus the huge fluctuations in the volume of production; in 1982, when interests rates were 15 percent, only 1,072,000 units were started; in 1972, when they were 5 percent, 2,378,000 units were built.

By comparison, public policy designed to produce housing according to social need is a sad orphan. We may well have less publicly assisted housing stock for the benefit of poor people than any other

industrialized nation on the face of the earth: 4 percent this year, and likely to decline as limited-duration subsidies and restrictions expire. What was publicly built has always been shabbily treated. We now ridicule the architectural fashions that produced a high-rise, high-density Pruitt-Igoe in St. Louis, but those architects worked in the financial straitjacket imposed by conservative political leaders and a tax-shy voting public. The dynamiting of these projects is less a failure of public housing than of the commitment to such housing on the part of government—under pressure, of course, from those private sector interests that have never accepted government intruding on their real estate turf.

Professionals, be they planners, architects, designers, civil servants, or community leaders, have only been able to influence these events at their edges. They have been most successful in the area of environmental protection, because this is where the threat has been most visible and has most cut across class and race lines. The courts, somewhat more insulated from the pressures of the private housing industry than legislatures, have tended to provide broad interpretations of environmental mandates; some of the worst abuses in city planning have been halted in the name of seemingly minor concerns under environmental legislation, as the striped bass of the Hudson River halted Westway in New York, for instance. But the larger, more pervasive, but "accepted" forms of environmental degradation have remained outside the purview of environmental legislation: the waste of land in suburban single-family, large-lot developments; locational choices that force reliance on automobiles rather than mass transit; densities that consume open space, light and air; assaults on air and water quality; excessive noise levels; ugliness, monotony, and dirt: these are still largely immune to public control in fact if not in theory.

Racism has proved an enduring aspect of the American housing scene. Segregation indexes—on a scale where zero means that each census tract in a city reflects the distribution of races in the city as a whole and 100 means absolute sepa-

ration by race—have remained in the vicinity of 75 in most cities. Where suburbs are opened up, often after major confrontations, to members of minority groups, new smaller ghettos are likely to be formed; in the heart of older cities, black and hispanic areas are likely to have the highest rates of abandonment, of public neglect and private disinvestment.

For women, escape from the constricting patterns of patriarchal household relationships that are built into most housing is as remote as ever. Locations that are not accessible by public transportation, cooking and maintenance arrangements that assume a full-time household worker, lack of day care or supportive services for single mothers, prejudice in the public as well as private market against "non-traditional" (even if long-standing) household patterns, affect white as well as minority women, middle class as well as poor women, but minority and poor women most of all. Despite a strong body of research and advocacy on the issue and some examples of striking success (in New York City's city-owned tax-foreclosed housing stock, for instance) progress is hardly visible; for poor single women, housing is one of the most difficult and mounting problems.

Privatization in housing has different results for these various groups. Private security guards instead of adequate public policing, private health spas instead of public recreational facilities, private automobiles or commuter buses instead of public mass transit, private garbage pickup instead of public sanitation, even whole private residential complexes instead of public communities; private streets, private gates, private schools, private dining rooms, private and exclusive lives—in each case public contraction and private expansion go hand in hand. The results are uneven: privatization accentuates polarization. As the well-to-do become better off in ever narrower circles, the less well-off become less well off in ever larger numbers.

But the picture is not all bleak; on the average, in fact, much is improving, and remarkably so. The proportion of substandard housing in the nation was 46 percent in 1940; today, by the same measure, it is

less than 4 percent (a majority of all renters complain about their neighborhoods, though). Overcrowding has gone down; average household size, and average number of persons per room, are at a historic low (but may have turned a corner in the early 1980s, and three million households are even more overcrowded). Two-thirds of our households own their own homes, more than ever before (even if others who would like to own them cannot and even if it takes twice the median income to afford a new home). Real estate values are at an all-time high, and most of those who have used their own housing as an investment have made out well. The real estate industry is prospering; twenty-six of the four-hundred richest individuals in the United States made their money in New York real estate alone (but some also go bankrupt). Americans have been in the forefront of housing architecture and design internationally, although in mass production and in social housing design we have much to learn. Visitors come from all over the world to see what we have accomplished in the planning of unbelievably elaborate and huge complexes (the pros and cons of many of which are hotly debated at home).

Does this contradictory picture reflect healthy diversity, or social failure? In some cases, surely a desirable diversity: the range of choices open to many Americans is without peer in the world; the skylines of our great cities are striking in the boldness of their statements; the richness of architectural expression is without peer; the mobility that an advanced financial and marketing system allows is greater than in any other nation on earth. But, just as surely, diversity can be a euphemism for injustice and inequality, ugliness and waste, callousness and greed. We must decide where the balance lies between healthy diversity and social failure.

Peter Marcuse is Professor of Urban Planning at the Graduate School of Architecture, Planning, and Preservation at Columbia University in New York City.

Domesticity

Our attitude toward home has changed.

By Witold Rybczynski

What a rich and meaningful word it is: *home*. Frenchmen, Italians, and Spaniards can only return to their houses, but we who speak English—or any of the north European tongues—can return to our homes. It is an important distinction this, between house and home, the theme of numerous maudlin country and western songs, but nonetheless true for that. It reflects a particular sentiment—a bourgeois sentiment—for the place where we live, to which we belong, for which we have affection.

"Make yourself at home," we say, and, of course, "welcome home." We don't get countrysick or citysick, we get homesick. A list of derivative words encapsulates the fondness we feel for home: homemade, homegrown, homebred, homespun, and home-brew, as well as homeward, homecoming, home-fire, homestead, hometown, and homeland. Even homely, which has lately acquired a pejorative sense, originally meant unpretentious, which was to say, suitable for home life.

Home is a world of the interior, of cozy firesides and intimate rooms, of easy chairs and privacy, of warmth and comfort. Especially comfort. It was not always so. Before the eighteenth century the home lacked almost all of these attributes. The late-medieval home, say a burgher's house, was large by modern standards, but it also contained many inhabitants. It was, first of all, a public place, a place for visitors, customers, and clients; also for guests, and travelers, for it was hotel and restaurant in an age that lacked these institutions. The home combined dwelling and workplace.

This pattern continued in central Europe for a long time. In Thomas Mann's *Buddenbrooks*, set in nineteenth-century Lubeck, several generations of the family live together in a large house that also includes offices and a warehouse on the ground floor. By then, the concept of pri-

Jean-Baptiste Mallet, *The Breakfast Room, with Lover at the Door*, 18th century, France. Cooper-Hewitt Museum, Bequest of Edith Sachs.

vacy had evolved to the point that family, servants, and employees lived and worked in separate quarters. This was not the case within the sixteenth-century home, where all—low and high—rubbed shoulders with easy familiarity.

This rubbing of shoulders would surprise us. Apprentices slept in the same bed as the children of the house. Servants, if they did not sleep with their masters, slept beneath them, on truckle beds; in any case, they slept in the same room. There were several persons to a bed, and there were also several beds to a room, for there were no individual bedrooms. A chamber usually included many beds, in which the entire household slept in what one can only conjecture to have

been unembarrassed intimacy. As manners became more refined—or at least altered—one senses the beginning of a need for privacy in the growing use of bed-curtains, although these may have been intended to prevent drafts as much as prying eyes.

The home had a few large rooms that served many functions: sleeping, eating, cooking, entertaining, and transacting business. Furniture was utilitarian rather than decorative, and was limited to beds, tables, and benches. Chairs were reserved for persons of rank—the head of the household, the teacher in the classroom, the abbot in the monastery—common people sat on benches or stools, or on the floor, as Indians and Arabs do to-

day. By the seventeenth century, with increased prosperity and improved craftsmanship, furniture became more varied, and more elaborate. Four-poster beds came to resemble small houses. Ornate chairs and armchairs became common, as did intricately carved cupboards and sideboards. Since the layout of the home had not altered appreciably, all these pieces were crowded into the principal room with little regard for what we would call arrangement—it had all the charm of a discount furniture warehouse on clearance day.

During the eighteenth century the domestic atmosphere changed appreciably. With the growing importance that was being attached to the family, the home, which had always been the place where one lived, became, in addition, an idea. This is a subtle distinction, but an important one. People became attached to their homes, and devoted to home life. This new sentiment required a new word—*domesticity*.

A growing consciousness of family and self produced a craving for privacy, first from the outside world, later from servants, and later still from family members. This manifested itself in various ways. Houses began to be subdivided into several rooms, some for social functions, and some for intimate family use. Corridors permitted architects to plan houses so that one no longer passed *through* rooms, but *beside* them. Different rooms acquired permanent uses—sleeping, eating, and entertaining—and the furniture within these rooms was given a permanent position, that is, it was arranged for everyday use and not only for architectural effect. Backstairs, passages, dumbwaiters, and bell-rooms kept the servants at bay. And even within the family, the house layout provided distinctions—libraries for gentlemen, withdrawing rooms for ladies, nurseries for children.

The home had lost its public character. But the desire for privacy not only produced a different atmosphere, it also engendered an appreciation of comfort. In England and France, the eighteenth century was the period of great accomplishments in furniture. Chairs became more easeful, better padded and shaped, and suited to relaxed postures. Sofas and ottomans encouraged lounging, armchairs invited conversation, and wing chairs coddled the reader. The wing chair also protected the sitter from drafts, reminding us that thermal comfort was also a consideration. Greater attention began to be paid to the design of fireplaces, which for the first time contributed warmth and not simply smoke to rooms. And rooms were in any case smaller and hence easier to heat.

The nineteenth century consolidated the technical gains of the previous hundred years. Gasoliers replaced oil lamps, and provided most of the advantages of electric light, albeit dirtily. Interior plumbing facilitated a higher standard of hygiene. Heating improved steadily. But more important than these technical changes were the changes that had not yet taken place. Throughout the first half of the nineteenth century Americans lacked something that they now take for granted—mass public entertainment. This was a world without professional sports, without vaudeville and, of course, without movies. The beach resort had not yet come into fashion; only the wealthy had summer houses. There were no weekends, let alone weekend cottages. What leisure there was—and there was considerably less than today—was domestic leisure. It was the period of parlor games and home theatricals. The bicycle, which would give mobility to young and old, was still in the future, so was Henry Ford's invention. Families stayed at home, and the home became an important social institution, perhaps *the* institution of the age.

Domesticity was inextricably linked, or so it seemed, with the woman's role in the home. During the eighteenth century the household had come increasingly under her dominion, and now her influence became apparent in the decor itself: antimacassars, cut flowers, chintz, and skirted furniture. It was she who exercised considerable skills in the management of these large households, presided over the education of the children and the welfare of the servants, and took the leading role in the preservation of the appropriate domestic atmosphere—she kept the home-fires burning, literally and figuratively.

By then, the home-fire was likely to require little tending. The early 1900s saw unimagined improvements in the home—due primarily to electricity. Household appliances such as vacuum cleaners, washing machines, electric irons, and hot water heaters, reduced the reliance on servants, and made the home an even more private family place. Electric lights, fans (eventually air-conditioning), and central heating improved comfort immeasurably. Telephones reduced isolation, especially in rural homes. Gramophones and radios augmented the simple pleasures of the fireside. By the 1950s, prosperity brought easeful domesticity within the reach of more people than ever before.

The twentieth century was a watershed in the evolution of domestic comfort—but, paradoxically, it left domesticity diminished. Americans began to look outside their comfortable homes. To the movie house and the beach—for their amusements; to the shopping mall for their social life; to the drive-in restaurant for their meals. The car gave mobility to parents and teenagers alike, indeed, to entire households. Home was where you lived—for a while—before trading-up. Hence the nostalgia for the homemade and the homegrown, for the very idea of home itself.

Domesticity no longer holds sway over the nation; this does not mean that it has disappeared. Modern experiments in collective living, whether in revolutionary Moscow in the 1920s or in "revolutionary" San Francisco in the 1960s, have all foundered. The consciously undomestic atmosphere of modern architecture never found public favor, anymore than did the charmless, and uncomfortable, furniture that was intended to accompany it.

The renewed interest in Victoriana,

James Jacques Joseph Tissot, *Hide and Seek*, about 1877. National Gallery of Art, Washington; Chester Dale Fund.

when it is not a fad, represents a fascination with the golden age of domesticity. Not that Victorian home life will ever return—too much has changed, above all, the role of women, in society as in the home, and the intrusion of the state into what had previously been domestic affairs. But the devotion to home and family appears as strong as ever. The bourgeois delights of domesticity have proved surprisingly resilient.

Witold Rybczynski is Professor of Architecture at McGill University in Montreal and the author of *Home: A Short History of an Idea.*

Housing Styles

Residence of Henry Delamater, Rhinebeck, New York; Alexander Jackson Davis, architect, 1844. Picture Library, Cooper-Hewitt Museum.

Residence of W.B. Douglas, Geneva, New York; Richard Upjohn, architect, 1861–63. Picture Library, Cooper-Hewitt Museum.

Gate Lodge, Poughkeepsie, New York. Picture Library, Cooper-Hewitt Museum.

Villa, Utica, New York. Picture Library, Cooper-Hewitt Museum.

Residence of J.J. Herrick, Tarrytown, New York; Alexander Jackson Davis, architect, 1855. Picture Library, Cooper-Hewitt Museum.

Residence of John Munn, Utica, New York; Alexander Jackson Davis, architect, 1854. Picture Library, Cooper-Hewitt Museum.

Residence of John E. Williams, Irvington, New York, 1850–69. Picture Library, Cooper-Hewitt Museum.

Residence of Darwin Martin, Buffalo, New York; Frank Lloyd Wright, architect, 1904. Picture Library, Cooper-Hewitt Museum.

Residence of Dean Richmond, Batavia, New York; William Kelly, architect, 1837. Picture Library, Cooper-Hewitt Museum.

Residence of Halsey R. Stevens, Newburgh, New York; Vaux and Withers, architects, about 1857. Picture Library, Cooper-Hewitt Museum.

Residence of Silas O. Smith, Rochester, New York, 1839–41. Picture Library, Cooper-Hewitt Museum.

Gate Lodge of Netherwood, residence of James Lenox, New Hamburg, New York; about 1840. Picture Library, Cooper-Hewitt Museum.

Sunnyside, residence of Washington Irving, Tarrytown, New York; Washington Irving and George Harvey, remodelers, about 1835. Picture Library, Cooper-Hewitt Museum.

The Armour-Stiner (Octagon) House, Irvington-on-Hudson, New York; early 1860s. Picture Library, Cooper-Hewitt Museum.

Residence of C.H. McCormick, Richfield Springs, New York; McKim, Mead and White, architects, 1881. Picture Library, Cooper-Hewitt Museum.

Domestic Architecture

By Mary Mix Foley

The houses of the United States are so varied that no generalization can apply to all of them. Our domestic architecture stems from a diverse European heritage, adapted to a range of continental climate and terrain, overtaken by a series of revival styles, complicated by the shifting and mixing of population during a long migratory settlement, and encompassing throughout it all the change from a handcraft society to a modern industrial nation. Within this many-faceted history, however, the regional dwellings of the earliest colonists had established patterns on which much of our traditional domestic architecture has been based.

We still recognize familiar types: New England's clapboard and shingle houses, particularly the saltbox, and the Cape Cod cottage, tightly organized around a heat-retaining central chimney block; the equally English wood or brick houses of early Virginia and Maryland, with their characteristic end chimneys and central passage through the house. There are also the graceful cottage with flaring Flemish eaves that was revived in the twentieth century as Dutch colonial; the solid, thick-walled stone houses of Pennsylvania, varied according to the traditions of German, English-Quaker, and Welsh settlers; America's most famous house, the log cabin, first built by Swedish colonists in the Delaware River Valley. And we have: the airy, galleried, southern plantation house, originally a French colonial type; and the California ranch house, based on a Spanish-Moorish tradition of adobe construction, with a linear, one-story plan and enclosed patio.

Like folk architecture everywhere, these houses had no "style" as such. Their appearance was the result of structural and functional necessity. Beauty was incidental. And yet they have an almost atavistic appeal.

The seventeenth-century New England farmhouse, with its gaunt, angular form, weathered clapboards, and diamond-paned casement windows, is an example of such utilitarian, but expressive character. Inside, an exposed timber frame, walls of whitewashed plaster or vertical planking, low beamed ceilings, and a huge cooking fireplace showed that structure alone, through pattern, texture, and natural color, could create an architecture of simple beauty and warm appeal.

Classical Architecture

Early in the eighteenth century, a radically new kind of house appeared here. It was a colonial version of the English Georgian style, itself a thoroughly anglicized rendering of the architecture of the Italian Renaissance.

Unlike its predecessors, the Georgian colonial mansion was formally symmetrical and rich in classical adornment, its every aspect studied for effect. The hipped roof and an improved fireplace design permitted larger rooms and more of them, balanced two on either side of a center hallway; it is the now-familiar center-hall colonial type. Structure was hidden beneath walls of painted paneling or patterned wallpaper; the fireplace embellished with a bolection molding, a mantel or full chimneypiece.

Such houses reflected the growing prosperity and sophistication of American colonists and their society. Such houses also illustrated a new kind of beauty: the elegance of classical proportion, formal symmetry, and applied ornament. The classical way of building lasted roughly from 1700 to 1860, changing during that time from Georgian colonial, with its baroque and Palladian emphases, to the federal period's fashion for delicate Adamesque ornament and, finally, to the Greek revival temple-form house.

Nothing could be a greater contrast to these formal, classical styles than the utilitarian folk houses that had preceded them. But the suitability of the earlier types to regional climate and patterns of living made them difficult to displace.

As a result, there occurred a marriage of opposites, a melding of the classical styles with regional vernacular. The gable-roofed Puritan homestead—stark and unadorned—dissolved into the white clapboard, green-shuttered house with modest classical doorway that we see in New England today. In the South, the Greek revival—aided by pre-Civil War prosperity—enlarged and transformed the simple plantation house into the imposing, white-pillared, antebellum mansion.

A small cottage might achieve the classical look with a portico of latticework, suggesting a "frieze" and "columns." Even the adobe ranch house was given porch posts of simplified classical design. Throughout the country, the imaginative interplay between high style and vernacular had created an architecture of variety and originality that nevertheless was tied together by classical themes.

The Victorian Period

This process of interaction did not end with the Greek revival. Even in the Victorian period, during which style was piled upon style, many of the old regional types persisted, using the decorative elements of each fashion mainly as trim. Still, at the same time, Victorian exuberance was inventing a new world and with it a new kind of house.

This was the period during which Americans industrialized their building process. Factories rolled out plate glass in larger sheets than had ever before been available. Foundries mass-produced cast-iron ornament as a substitute for laboriously handmade wrought iron. The steam-powered scroll saw translated carved stonework into wood, which rapidly took on a life of its own as Victorian "gingerbread." Even such a small item as the cheap, machine-made nail helped to revolutionize house building. It inspired the invention of the balloon frame, a continuous, nailed skeleton of closely spaced, lightweight wood members, superseding the mortised, tenoned, and pegged timber frame of the handcrafted house.

Against this explosion of the new, the old classical forms with their static rectangular plans could not hold. Victorian houses—from the early Gothic revival and Italianate styles, to the post-Civil War Eastlake, Queen Anne, Romanesque, colonial revival, and the Stick and Shingle styles that derived from them—were picturesque, that is, asymmetrically massed and broken by towers, bay windows, and projecting wings. Victorians were experimenting with new shapes and arrangements of rooms that were adapted to contemporary living patterns, but expressed through these flamboyant styles.

The most creative architects used large areas of glass to open selected walls to floods of light and beautiful views. Sheltered verandas and balconies, as well as open terraces, provided the pleasures of outdoor living that had become part of the Victorian mystique. Indoors and out were interwoven with each other in this new type of house.

If this sounds like modern architecture, that is because it very nearly was. With the further freeing of the plan, the further exploitation of structural potential, and the elimination of historical references—the path taken by Frank Lloyd Wright in his early designs—one can see the modern house emerging from its Victorian chrysalis.

Modern Architecture: The Wright Approach

Frank Lloyd Wright, one of the great pioneers of modern architecture, did not seek to invent a "style"—a term he disliked—but rather an approach that could create an indigenous American architecture as varied as the needs of its occupants and the regions of the country in which they lived.

Wright tied the house to its natural setting through the use of native materials and by a design that, of itself, tempered the local climate from which it offered protection. But by taking full advantage of modern resources and methods—or inventing them when necessary—Wright designed contemporary houses that were as germane to our times as folk architecture had been to the handcraft society of its day.

Modern Architecture: The International Style

A very different European phase of modern architecture arrived in this country during the early 1930s. It was brought here by pioneers of the style, notably Walter Gropius and Mies van der Rohe. The severe machine aesthetic that they had helped develop shared with Wright's work a rejection of historic style, a basis in twentieth-century technology, and a free-flowing interior plan—but not much more.

As its name implies, the goal of the international style was the creation of a universal, industrialized system of architecture, so simplified and generalized ("Less is more") that it could be used for any building, on any site, in any country, anywhere.

The "machine for living" that resulted was a flat-roofed, severely rectangular structure, broken, if at all, by a cylindrical counterpoint, or other minor geometry, and enclosed by a smooth, white stucco and/or glass wall surface resembling a continuous, tightly-stretched fabric. Rather than being integrated with nature, the house was calculatedly set off from its surroundings as a man-made, constructed thing.

Postmodern Architecture

Postmodernism, today's fashionable currency, represents a reaction against both phases of modern architecture. Charles Moore and Robert Venturi, who shocked

Popular Architectural Styles in American Homes

Carpenter Gothic — Italianate — Queen Anne — Stick — Eastlake

Craftsmen — Bungalow — Dutch Revival — Modified Cape Cod — Tudor

Contractor Modern — Neo Colonial — Split Level — California Ranch — Cape Cod Cottage

Prefabricated Levitt House — Prefabricated Western Rustic — Plantation Style Colonial — 3 Level Split Level — Brutalism

"Architectural Styles in American Homes," from *100 Years of Exterior Color*, 1983. Illustrations courtesy of Benjamin Moore & Co.

the architectural establishment with their new approach in the 1960s, brought back to the architectural lexicon a whole catalog of forbidden fruit: historical allusion, applied ornament, even elements from tract housing and the Las Vegas strip ("Main Street is almost all right"). Simplicity and good taste were out; complexity, contradiction, ambiguity, and "messy vitality" were in.

The goal was to return meaning to architecture by way of signs and symbols applied to a "decorated shed." But symbolism began to take surprising turns. The latest postmodern offshoot is punk, which deepens the split in American domestic architecture that has separated modern design from the traditional or conventional house. So far, traditional architecture has won handily, accounting for the great preponderance of houses built in this country in this century. A house that looks familiar has been, and continues to be, what the majority of American home owners want.

Today, there may be an unusual opportunity to forget shibboleths of all sorts and to improve the general quality of our domestic architecture.

A growing number of architects have abandoned self-consciously applied "signs," instead absorbing symbolism into architecture itself. If, without sacrificing the substance of modern design, architects can fuse its critical requirements with the symbolism of region and tradition, then an architecture of broad appeal and variety could be in the making.

This would be nothing new. Americans have been combining opposites ever since folk building absorbed the Georgian style in the eighteenth century. Perhaps such a synthesis, in whatever period, is the typical American house.

Mary Mix Foley is a former Associate Editor of *Architectural Forum* and the author of *The American House*.

Residential Interiors

Furnishings reflect taste and aspirations.

By Elisabeth Donaghy Garrett

R.J. Horner & Co., *Our American Homes*, probably 1890s. Cooper-Hewitt Museum.

Household furnishings are the nonverbal travel logbooks of family life at home—revealing with an inarticulate intensity the time of embarkation and suggesting the success of the voyage. Though mute as historical documents of this transit, these objects of daily use reify and personify the most personal aspirations and changing tastes.

The rigid hierarchy of the seventeenth-century world was readily apparent in the well-defined separation of interior domestic space into an informal utilitarian room—the hall—and a formal superior apartment—the parlor, which though functional reveled in display. The former might be cluttered with the accoutrements of the hearth, a homey bed, a table for dining, stiff-jointed stools and hard-seated benches, a resolute great chair from which the paternal master of the household might issue his authoritarian commands, and an oak-grained chest of which was sometimes asked "a double debt to pay / A bed by night, a chest of drawers by day."

The parlor display of material goods demonstratively proclaimed the worldly success and otherworldly favor of the puritan ethic. Here guests were received, here the master and mistress often slept and formal meals were taken. Here, too, were concentrated the textile stores of the family—some boldly in evidence, others stowed in parti-colored and relief-carved chests, but all bespeaking wealth and the luxury of supply. Among those displayed textiles the parental bed, osten-tatiously draped in yards of resplendent crimson, green, or yellow wool or linen, was supreme. There might also be curtains at the window, a carpet on a table, turkey work or leather-upholstered side chairs, and scarfs or cushions atop the weighty "court" cupboard conspicuously arrayed with silver and ceramics. Such parlor pageantry did not escape the prying eyes of the covenanted community, for social and humanitarian visits kept domestic doorways always ajar.

Furnishings in the eighteenth-century home confirmed this social openness and fastidious arrangement. Tea tables, card tables, and an abundance of versatile dining tables for the accommodation of two or four, or eight or twelve persons suggests active social interchange among living and doing people. The two rooms that jostled for supremacy in the hierarchical room arrangement of eighteenth-century interiors were each used as reception rooms—one for social calls, the parlor or drawing room; the other, the best bedchamber for humanitarian visits. The frequency of birth and the uncertainty of health meant that the best bedchamber was much in use by the family as well as by those kindly neighbors who sat for hours in a down-puffed easy chair watching at the bedside of the sick or who pulled the chamber chairs into a circle to celebrate successful delivery or bereave remorseless death.

If the eighteenth century was social, it was also compulsive about order. One example of this was the increasingly specific function of rooms (a systematized approach that paralleled the contemporary scientific attempt to categorize and classify all matter of nature). By the end of the century the dining room had splintered off from the parlor in the houses of the affluent as the dressing room secreted itself beside the bedchamber. New specialized forms—extension tables, sideboards, dumbwaiters, dressing bureaus, and washstands—made clear the use of the rooms. They further expressed the desire for regularity, convenience, and politeness—politeness in serving others with ease, or politeness in making oneself pleasant to others.

Order and regularity were further demonstrated in the Georgian interior by careful attention to clear spatial definitions through contrasts of materials and/or colors and an emphasis on precise linear borders. Paper or papier-mâché borders defined wall divisions; the stiles and skirts of chairs and tables were beaded, gadrooned, carved, inlaid, or brass-nailed; and window curtains and bed hangings were taped or fringed. This precision of line was reinforced by harmony of color: all furnishing fabrics in a room were to accord in hue if not material. Further, furniture was intended to complement the architectural elements of an apartment in both proportion and placement. Thus, when Charles Carroll of Carrollton ordered crimson silk-damask curtains along with a sofa and twelve matching chairs for his Annapolis home in 1771 he cautioned,

> As the dimensions of the Room is 20 feet square . . . a skillful upholsterer will suit the size of the Sopha & chairs to the Size of the Room—& be careful not to send them too large.

In these formulated interiors, looking glasses and tables stood in window piers, window seats in window embrasures, pairs of sideboards in niches, and pairs of sofas in recesses, or flanking or at right angles to the fireplace. Order was stated in this deliberative symmetrical placement of paired forms and maintained by the furniture being ranged against the walls and brought out into the room for use. In the parlor the prototypical dozen chairs, either slip-seated or upholstered over the rail, provided a ribbon of color along the walls, and servants were admonished in replacing them after use to keep their hand behind lest they knock plaster off the wall or nick the polished mahogany chair backs. Gateleg, drop-leaf, and hinged-top tables folded neatly away along walls and in corners. Casters of brass, wood, and leather facilitated transporting them about the room, yet one of the most oft-mentioned repairs in eighteenth-century cabinetmakers' account books is broken table legs. Table tops, though often covered with a cloth (typically bright green baize), were otherwise bare and ready to be moved about the room for use. These neat, uncluttered surfaces and the open space in the center of the room facilitated housekeeping, promoted the easy rearrangement of the furniture for a variety of uses—tea drinking, card playing, sewing, eating, reading—and prevented family members from tripping over furniture left out in these often dimly lit interiors.

Lighting was indeed scant in the pre-1850 home. The family was forced to pull their chairs around a single candle or lamp, which would be brought in from the kitchen at candlelighting. Artificial light was thus a cement that held the early family together, imposing a temporal regularity on its members, who were forced to gather to benefit from the single light source and to retire when it was extinguished. Furnishings were designed to take advantage of what little light there was. Furniture of dramatic grain, with bold brasses or gilded elements and a mirror-bright finish was much esteemed, whereas textiles could be distinguished by night either by their forceful patternings and contrasting trim or by the movement of their glossy, glazed, or watered finishes. Walls were similarly coated with glossy paints or wallpaper of dramatic design or satin-finish grounds. Not until the full-fledged adoption of gas and kerosene lighting ensured stronger illumination in the second half of the nineteenth century would mat finishes and dark fabrics of small motif be much admired.

Before the introduction of central heating, which allowed family members to scatter about the house with comfort, the widely divergent temperature variables of the North American climate likewise served as a bond. Room usage prior to the arrival of the furnace in the basement was calendrically prescribed. Family members moved about the house in a seasonal migration in the hope of escaping sultry heat or frigid blasts. Summer might find them grouped in an airy through-hall seated on cool, cane-seated or Windsor furniture, whereas a cozy, carpeted and curtained back parlor might offer refuge in the depths of winter, when water, ink, and wine froze about the house. This intimate room would have been furnished with utilitarian pieces evocative of the mundane: tables, chairs, and perhaps a sofa crowded about the hearth or airtight stove. There might be a desk and often a clock that ticked off the minutes, hours, days, weeks, and months of enforced confinement. A smattering of children's furniture—diminutive chairs, crickets (stools), a cradle—suggest the constant challenge to the much cherished family harmony as young and old sought to get on together. Privacy, though often desired, was simply not feasible until the warm, liberating breezes of spring allowed the family to escape to upstairs bedchambers and outside gardens.

Central heating and gaslighting promoted independence and privacy in the Victorian era as larger houses with more diversified rooms offered greater seclusion more days of the year. Evenly distributed heat and non-portable gas outlets also meant that mobility was no longer a determining factor in furniture design. Towering, immobile cliffs of veneer rose up as bedsteads in chamber after chamber and ponderous chests, cabinets, lounges, sofas, ottomans, and hassocks sprawled densely across drawing rooms, sitting rooms, libraries, boudoirs, and smoking rooms. Tables, now stationary, could be covered with all manner of bijouteries and, in fact, should be, for such collections evinced the individuality of the homemaker. With this accumulation of accessories the shelf ascended to a position of supreme importance in interior decoration and furniture design.

Multishelved étagères, corner shelves, curio cabinets, hanging shelves, and easels are passive forms that contrasted with the active forms of tea and card tables in an earlier setting. The forthrightness of the enlightenment interior had softened into the evocation of the Victorian, as the poetic, picturesque, and historical revival replaced the rational. Victorian furnishings became romantic ruminations on past eras that never existed but that offered escape from a troubled present racing forward with a speed that unnerved this confident age. The kaleidoscopic complexity and rich diversity of this Victorian world was translated into interior decor as walls became layered and faceted with a surfeit of ornament, and furniture arrangements came to be admired as independent compositional groupings rather than as units in a cohesive whole.

Despite the many differences, there are unifying themes that run as a leitmotif through the logbook of life at home in the United States. Whether one raised the forged iron knocker on a medieval door of fortress strength or sounded the cast brass knocker on a Palladian portal of sure proportion or whether one pressed the clamorous doorbell at a towering Victorian threshold, one entered a home imbued with a high level of expectation. The unabashed scramble for material goods and the belief that a decent sufficiency was the inalienable right of all meant that a greater percentage of Americans had mahogany tables on which to place plenteous food, had woven carpets on which to walk, and had upholstered sofas on which to relax, and they had more than any other people in the world. The leveling effect of this social equality mandated an art of moderation or, as one observer noted, "a pleasing uniformity of decent competence." This intrinsic reserve was in part an expression of Yankee taste and in part a response to necessity: the practical side of the American character had always favored a solid, plain style that, if also beautiful, must be useful; and the acute shortage of servant help, or the bungling carelessness of those who did serve, required a sturdy, forthright style free from superfluous ornament that would be easy to clean and more sanguine of survival.

The reliance on England or the Continent for the last word in taste was another constant. Seventeenth- and eighteenth-century Americans seemed, in the words of Henry Wadsworth Longfellow, "English under another sky," and their speech, costume, architecture, furniture, and cookery were those of the well-bred British provincial. The nineteenth century broadened its gaze to encompass the entire Continent of Europe for what Paul Bourget, a French observer of the American scene, called the "constant, timeless endeavor to absorb European ideas." This self-conscious dependence, this unimaginative aping has also been evidenced in the persistence with which we have "followed the Joneses." Late eighteenth- and nineteenth-century critics decried the sameness, the conformity of interiors and furnishings, and Victorians were often hard-pressed to distinguish their own houses from those of their neighbors—a most ironic dilemma in an era that pronounced the home to be the expression of one's individuality. A corollary of this monotony was the often-criticized primness and formality of the interior arrangements, where scarcely any object seemed meant for use. Thus, even in the twentieth century, the British commentator W. L. George might censure the American home, which seemed bare, untenanted, too real, too new, and he pined for that comfortable, frowsy feeling of the British country house, with its "compound of dullness, boiled mutton, an ill-cut lawn, a dog, a cat, and some mice to keep the cat amused."

"The true character of Americans is mirrored in their homes," wrote one who came to weigh the success of this grand American experiment. And, indeed, the history of American homes and furnishings is the saga of the American people. Though the players might be gone, some of the props have fortuitously survived, providing us with a glimpse into the private pages in those logbooks on life at home in a brave new world.

Elisabeth Donaghy Garrett is Assistant Vice President of Sotheby's and associate director of its American Arts Course. She is the author of the forthcoming book *At Home; The American Family 1750–1870*.

The Toxic House

Home can be a safer place.

By Debra Lynn Dadd

It is the American dream to have a house—a place of one's own where one can live with the peace-of-mind that one is safe from harm and that one's basic needs are met. A house is a place to raise a family, to express oneself, a place to feel secure. But all is not well in the houses of modern America. With recent developments in housing construction, and especially with the boom in "new and improved" artificial materials since World War II, the houses in which we live have become a major hazard to our health.

Indoor Air Pollution

Ten years ago, the phrase *indoor air pollution* had not yet been coined. Today architects discuss the problem at conferences, government agencies attempt to regulate it, and homeowners buy up test kits to find out just how high the levels of formaldehyde or radon in their homes might be.

Indoor air pollution was discovered quite by accident when researchers in Los Angeles were taking smog level readings. Since the recommended procedure during smog alerts is to stay indoors, one researcher thought to take an indoor reading. To his surprise, the pollutant levels were actually higher indoors. In 1984, the Environmental Protection Agency (EPA) did its first study to measure personal exposure (what is actually inhaled as opposed to what is ambient in the air). Compact air monitors were worn by 850 people nationwide as they went about their daily activities (including sleeping), while backyard monitors measured outdoor concentrations of the same chemicals. The results showed indoor personal exposure to be three to seventy times higher than outdoor levels. Even more remarkable was the fact that these measurements were taken in communities with heavy industry, where outdoor contamination would be at its highest. In 1987 the EPA targeted indoor air pollution as a top priority.

Indoor air pollution is known to affect health by damaging the tissue of the respiratory system and by poisoning the blood. It can cause emphysema, bronchitis, asthma, cancer, birth defects, and increased incidence of upper respiratory disease and heart disease. On a more subtle level, some people experience watery eyes, breathing difficulties, headaches, coughing, frequent upper respiratory problems, aggravation of chronic heart and lung disease, shortened life span, and general poor health. Exposure to indoor air pollution can also cause a breakdown of the immune system that appears as almost any symptom imaginable.

A number of simultaneous developments are responsible for indoor air pollution. The proportion of synthetic materials used in constructing and furnishing modern buildings has increased tremendously over the last twenty-five years. In 1963, it was still possible to buy a brand new suburban tract house with solid wood cabinets and wool carpets over a hardwood floor. Today, new homes are filled with artificial materials, most of which give off vapors with known toxic effects. Compounding this problem is the fact that ventilation in both new and old houses has decreased. Older buildings were generally drafty enough to allow an adequate rate of exchange between indoor and outdoor air, even in the winter when doors and windows were closed; since the late '70s, however, when the oil crisis spawned widespread interest in energy efficiency, old buildings have been weatherstripped, and new buildings have been constructed more tightly. This has reduced air exchange and allowed the buildup of indoor pollutants that at times reach levels higher than the maximum allowable outdoor standards. Our growing dependence on air conditioning has further exacerbated the problem. Whereas people once tended to rely on screen doors and open windows for ventilation, they now are more likely to turn on an air conditioner.

The easiest way to improve the air quality in a house is to open the windows and allow toxic pollutants to escape. If necessary, air-to-air heat exchangers can be installed to minimize heat loss. In West Germany, followers of *Baubiologie* (literally "building biology"—the study of the impact of buildings on the health of people, the science of holistic interactions between life and living environment, and the application of this knowledge in building houses) take a different approach. They build houses of porous materials (such as brick, stone, wood, and plaster) that allow the entire shell of the house to "breathe" and to expel pollutants. This ventilation by diffusion also has the advantage of absorbing and releasing excess moisture, which helps regulate indoor humidity.

Building Materials

Many building materials contain toxic substances that are potentially harmful not only to a building's occupants but to the factory workers who produce them, the construction workers who work with them, and even to the environment at large. It is essential when selecting building materials to consider the impact of our choices on the earth's plants and animals, its soil, its water, and its air.

If wood is to be used in a house, it should be real wood, without chemical preservatives or treatments. Particle board, which is frequently found in kitchen and bathroom cabinets, as subflooring, and inside doors, is not an acceptable substitute for real wood. All products made with particle board will release small quantities of formaldehyde, a substance that has been found to cause cancer in laboratory animals and is a suspected human carcinogen.

Formaldehyde emissions are greatest when a product is new, and they decrease with time, but it takes many years for formaldehyde to evaporate entirely. Even plywood, although made with a formaldehyde resin, is preferable to particle board.

The National Academy of Sciences estimates that 10 to 20 percent of the general population may be susceptible to irritating symptoms from exposure to formaldehyde at extremely low concentrations, causing coughing, swelling and irritation of the throat, watery eyes, headaches, rashes, disorientation, nosebleeds, and many other common symptoms.

While there are no warning labels on products made with particle board, there is a warning label required on sheets of particle board sold as underlayment: "WARNING: This product is manufactured with a urea-formaldehyde resin and will release small quantities of formaldehyde. Formaldehyde levels in indoor air can cause temporary eye and respiratory irritation and may aggravate respiratory conditions or allergies. Ventilation will reduce indoor formaldehyde levels."

In the past several years, new types of paints and finishes have come on the market that are much less detrimental to the health than standard house paints. One type, which is imported from West Germany, is made from 100 percent natural ingredients. Another type is made from low-toxicity synthetic ingredients that seem to be safe, even for people who are very sensitive. So far, these paints can't be found at the local hardware store, but they can be ordered by mail, and it would seem that the extra effort is worthwhile. A Johns Hopkins University study found over three hundred toxic chemicals and one hundred fifty carcinogens that may be present in paint. Among the more common ingredients of paint are ethanol, formaldehyde, glycols, kerosene, pentachlorophenol, phenol, trichlorethylene, and a number of different plastics, including acrylic, latex, phenol-formaldehyde resin, polyester, polyurethane, and tetrafluoroethylene. Spray paint has an aerosol propellant, which, in addition to having its own negative health effects, also makes it likely that tiny droplets of paint will end up in one's lungs, as well as on the wall.

The greatest danger from paints and finishes occurs while they are wet and during the initial drying period. Of the standard paints, the water-based latex variety is best, although "low odor" paints should be avoided—they are just as toxic, but without the warning smell. Painting should be done during warm dry weather to promote quick drying and so that windows can be left wide open to provide constant ventilation. Under normal conditions, water-based paints will be odor-free and relatively safe in about two weeks, but the process can be hastened by closing off the room and "baking" the paint. Make sure there are no plants, pets, or humans in the room, close all the doors and windows, turn up the heat full blast for two or three days and nights, and then ventilate.

The safest materials for floors or floor coverings are ceramic tile, brick, stone, concrete, hardwood, natural linoleum, or untreated natural fiber carpet. Probably the most toxic floor covering is that made from vinyl. Soft linoleum that comes in rolls is particularly dangerous. It is made from polyvinyl chloride, a plastic that emits fumes of vinyl chloride, a cancer-causing agent. Synthetic wall-to-wall carpeting is also toxic. In addition to being made from fibers that emit fumes, these carpets are saturated with flame-retardants and stain-resistors, and they harbor dust and mold, which makes them a nightmare for allergy-sufferers especially.

Electromagnetic Fields

Electromagnetic fields are electrical and magnetic fields generated by the sun, the moon, the earth and other planets, our bodies, and manmade electrical power

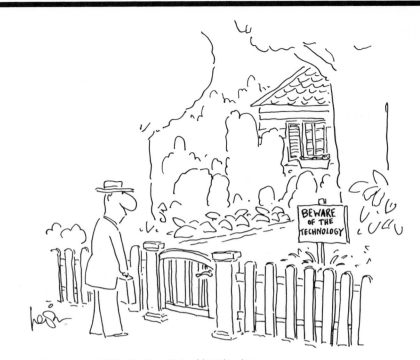

Drawing by Arnie Levin; © 1984, The New Yorker Magazine, Inc.

generating stations. The activity of every living cell in our bodies is regulated by the flow of electromagnetic fields. Our metabolism is geared to the background levels of radiation and electromagnetic energies from the earth and the cosmos—the earth's electromagnetic field pulses at the rate of 7.83 hertz, our body's own bioelectrical system pulses at about the same rate.

The installation of electricity in American homes, around one hundred years ago, revolutionized home environments. Quickly Americans encased themselves in invisible cocoons of electromagnetic energy pulsing at 60 hertz. This was thought to be perfectly safe. Now researchers are not so certain. While virtually all experts say no proof exists that exposure to the electromagnetic fields of the electrical wiring and appliances in our homes (or from nearby power lines) poses any health threat, accumulating scientific evidence has convinced many that there is cause for concern. Laboratory studies on animal cells have clearly

shown that electromagnetic fields from 60 hertz alternating current emit radiation that can interact with individual cells and organs to produce biological changes. Verified epidemiological studies found that children who live near ordinary neighborhood electrical distribution lines were twice as likely to develop cancer as those who did not. Results of such studies are encouraging a major worldwide research effort.

Several things can be done in the design and construction of a house to reduce exposure to manmade electromagnetic fields. Site the house as far as possible from main electrical distribution lines for the neighborhood. Install shielded wire. Incorporate design features that minimize the need for electricity—such as windows and skylights to reduce the need for artificial lighting, climate responsive heating and cooling to reduce the need for electric heating and air conditioning, and, if the inhabitants of the house are willing, such things as a solar cooker instead of a stove, and a root

cellar to replace the refrigerator.

In addition to the possible dangers from manmade electromagnetic fields, the effects of magnetic field disturbances from within the earth must also be considered. Within the earth's geomagnetic field are locations where minute changes exist in its electrical conductivity. These areas of change, known as geopathic zones, are brought about most frequently by geological fault lines and fissures in the earth's crust and by underground water (particularly wells). Recent research indicates that there is a definite connection between the presence of magnetic field disturbances of the earth and a higher incidence of cancer, endocrine diseases, infant mortality, insomnia, lack of concentration, hormone imbalances, and a variety of other conditions. Before deciding on a building site, have it evaluated for geopathic zones. The ancient arts of geomancy and Chinese *feng shui*, which are sensitive to the earth's energies and focus on techniques of proper placement of houses in the landscape, as well as on the proper placement of furnishings within houses, are being revived for this purpose in the West as well as in the Orient.

The Nontoxic House

As we become more aware of the hazards of our modern houses, many people are exploring alternatives that are healthier. What is emerging are houses that are not only "nontoxic," but are more in tune in all ways with the natural environment of which they are a part. While still retaining some modern conveniences, a new genre of house is appearing that brings us back to the basics of how a house was built before it was "new and improved." Such a house is ideally placed in the landscape, made of natural, local materials, designed for maximum energy efficiency, aesthetically pleasing and functional, well built, and safe for its inhabitants.

Debra Lynn Dadd is the author of *Nontoxic and Natural* and *The Nontoxic Home*, and editor of *The Earthwise Consumer* newsletter.

Federal Programs

By Sam Bass Warner, Jr.

Ever since the founding of the United States in 1781 the federal government has played a vital role in the provision of the nation's housing. It has, however, mostly confined itself to a supporting role in which it has assisted private builders by opening up cheap land and by establishing and maintaining protected sources of mortgage money.

The exceptions to this supporting role have been the direct construction of housing during wartime (first undertaken in World War I) and the funding and supervision of municipal housing authorities (begun in 1934) to build projects for low–income families. These public housing projects today constitute only 1.5 percent of all the housing in the United States (1.3 million units out of 88 million units in 1980).

A home, whether it be a freestanding house or an apartment, is always a combination of three elements—the land upon which it stands, the invested capital and mortgage loan that finances it, and the design, labor, and materials that bring it into being, or maintain it. In the past the federal government has devoted most of its energies to two of these three elements: the land and the mortgages.

The reason for this focus lies in the nature of American politics. Strong coalitions of small men and large, of landowners, developers, farmers, home owners, builders, and bankers can be formed to press for cheap land and cheap money. Such policies benefit all the members of the coalitions, even though they do not benefit each member to the same degree. Federal construction, however, has always been viewed as encroaching upon the private dealers in land, on the private builders, the private bankers, the private real estate dealers, and the private landlords. Therefore, except for grudging acquiescence during wartime, programs for federal construction of housing have been bitterly fought and deeply compromised.

During the nineteenth century the orderly rectangular survey of the Western frontier and the easy terms of sale of the public domain provided settlers and town builders with an abundance of cheap land. Today many an American city and suburb owes its wide streets and orderly house lots to the old federal survey conventions.

In addition, in 1862 Congress offered generous land grants to railroads, thereby opening up millions of acres for farms and homes. Almost a century later, in 1956, Congress repeated its railroad work. That year it authorized the construction of the interstate highways within and between American cities. The new expressways brought vast tracts of open land into the orbit of United States cities and metropolitan regions and thereby made it possible for Americans to live in their favorite style, the detached single-family house.

Were it not for these massive and long-sustained federal land programs most residents of cities and towns in the United States would be row house dwellers or apartment dwellers like their opposites in Europe. Indeed, today, unless some fresh land policies are instituted by the states and the federal government to free up metropolitan land markets, more and more of the nation's families will be forced to return to housing patterns of the eighteenth and nineteenth centuries.

Beginning with the Great Depression

and continuing until the most recent measures to control inflation—that is, from the founding of the Home Loan Bank Board in 1932 until the deregulation of savings bank and mortgage interest in 1980—the federal government has been a major contributor to home finance. President Hoover set up a federal banking system for savings banks and encouraged the local establishment of Federal Savings and Loan Associations so that the supply of cheap mortgage money might be increased, private building stimulated, and carpenters and masons put back to work. However, the depression was so severe that the entire banking system collapsed soon thereafter. To put the savings banks back on their feet President Roosevelt added two new institutions, an agency to purchase the mortgages taken by private banks (Home Owners Loan Corporation), and an agency to guarantee the mortgages of middle-income home buyers (Federal Housing Administration).

Subsequently, many programs were added to this basic federal financial structure. No-down-payment guaranteed mortgages were given to veterans of World War II, and from 1959 on there followed a spate of innovations that targeted special populations: in 1959, financing for housing for the elderly (Sec. 231 loans); in 1959 and 1961, below-market interest loans for builders providing housing for persons displaced by urban renewal and for persons too prosperous for public housing projects but too poor for decent market housing (Sec. 221(d)(3)); in 1965 and 1968, rent supplements for the landlords of such families (Sec. 236) and 1 percent mortgages for such families if they bought a house (Sec. 235); in 1968, mortgages for developers of suburban new towns, like Reston, Virginia; and in 1974, a revised and reduced rent subsidy program (Sec. 8).

Today all these additions have been dis-

First home built with a Federal Housing Administration mortgage, Alexandria, Virginia, 1934. National Archives.

Starrett City, Brooklyn, New York, under construction, about 1974. Courtesy of Division of Housing and Urban Renewal, New York. State/Skyviews Survey, Inc.

to its cheap land supply and financial aid: the provision of public housing and the clearing of structures from expensive inner city land.

The first program, begun in 1934 during the Great Depression, recognized that given the wages paid for the bottom jobs and given the certainty of periodic unemployment, low-wage Americans could never be supplied with decent housing by private builders. At the same time no one contemplated assisting the poor to help themselves by allowing them to build shacks and shanties as they did in the rural United States. There was no way in 1934, as there is no way in 1988, for the poor to get access to urban land. Therefore the federal government established a special agency—the Federal Housing Administration—to supervise and to subsidize city authorities that wanted to erect and manage public housing.

Two qualities have marked public housing ever since its beginnings. First, because private interests have seen public housing as a threat to themselves they have relentlessly opposed it. In doing so they have forced the federal government to accept the principle that public housing must always be built at standards below the common understanding of satisfactory open-market designs. That is, if you are a project American not only must you wear the cheapest copies, you must live in one.

Second, the supporters of public housing—the social workers, architects, building unions, and the like—hoped that the new federal projects would be an improvement on the mean streets of small houses and tenements that characterized the city's slums. They looked to Europe, especially to England and to Germany, where after World War I municipal authorities erected large clusters of housing with a good deal of open space about. Adapting such precedents to the United States, the Federal Housing Administration authorized "projects," not scattered units of a building or two. The unintended consequence of these plans has been the building, in most cities, of large, ugly, and isolated public housing clusters that have contributed to the isolation and the segregation of Afro-Americans and the poor.

Only in small cities where the programs involved a few units was this project-enforced isolation escaped.

Urban Renewal, begun in 1949, was the federal program designed to assist cities to rebuild their old inner areas. It was originally conceived as a program to replace slums with subsidized low-rent and middle-income housing. The continuing migration of well-to-do taxpayers and downtown customers, however, redirected the program. In 1954 a coalition of mayors, store owners, and real estate interests transformed Urban Renewal into a program of inner-city land clearance to support the private construction of new offices, stores, and luxury housing. Although Urban Renewal did not displace nearly so many families as the Interstate Highways, its removal of the poor and the working class for the benefit of the prosperous forced its ultimate abandonment in 1973.

Today federal policy is at a standstill. Public housing remains useful and in heavy demand, but it also remains politically controversial. The sheltered pools of federal home finance have been abandoned, and now interest rates along with the prices of land, labor, and materials have bounded upward. Indeed so rapid has been the housing inflation that no longer can a majority of American families afford to purchase or rent new construction. At the bottom of the housing market, the poor, especially today's female-headed households, are doubling up again. It seems likely that the nation, which so recently experienced the pleasures of bountiful housing, will again develop active housing coalitions to demand support for the private housing market.

At the moment it is impossible to predict just what those coalitions will achieve. Yet, given the precedents of the previous two centuries, the best guess is that new federal housing policies will address the supply of cheap land and cheap money.

Sam Bass Warner, Jr., Professor of History at Boston University, is the author of *The Urban Wilderness: A History of the American City* and *Province of Reason*. His latest book is *To Dwell Is to Garden, A History of Boston's Community Gardens.*

continued or severely cut back and a tax issue has moved to the forefront of federal financial aids to housing. The income tax had always allowed a deduction of interest payments for taxpayers who itemized their returns, and this deduction acted as a subsidy to the wealthy who purchased at the top of the housing market. Then during the 1970s the pace of inflation carried middle-income families into heavy tax brackets and the income tax itself became a significant federal housing program.

Taken all together, the federal mortgage guarantees, the direct loans and subsidies, and the tax deductions financed the nation's longest and largest housing

boom. Between 1950 and 1980 private builders constructed forty-six million housing units or 48 percent of the current housing stock. The new interstate highway land and the sheltered mortgage money and tax benefits enabled Americans to take up their present form of dispersed metropolitan living. As they did so, most of the overcrowding and doubling up of families ended, and much that was old and mean was abandoned or burned. At the housing peak a few years ago Americans enjoyed an abundance of space and shelter that no population had ever before possessed.

The federal government also undertook two programs that were exceptions

How Americans Live

What does the latest census reveal?

By Larry Long

People who count things, as the U.S. Census Bureau does, sometimes pause to observe milestones, and a big one occurred in the United States in 1987. In the spring of 1987 somewhere in the United States the last nail was hammered, the doors were hung, and the paint dried on the nation's one-hundred-millionth housing unit. That is as many places to live as there were people in the United States in 1914. Only nine other nations have as many people as the United States has housing units.

No one can pinpoint which housing unit bears the distinction of being the hundred millionth, but it was probably located in the South, because that is where one half of the nation's housing has been built since 1980, when the last national census inventoried our housing. Statistically speaking, the hundred-millionth unit was probably a single-family dwelling—maybe a brick rambler in the suburbs of one of the South's growing metropolitan areas, but perhaps a duplex, an apartment, or a mobile home. Maybe it was somebody's vacation home.

Like other housing units, the hundred millionth can be thought of as the sum of its parts—the building materials used to construct it and the utilities, supplies, and services that maintain it. Or it can be thought of as a financial asset, a mortgage, or a stream of rental payments. Not ordinarily given to romanticism, demographers usually see a house as somebody's home and want to know who lives in it, their family status, if children are present, and other social and economic characteristics of the occupants. The Census Bureau attempts to satisfy these and related views of housing by conducting a count of all housing in the decennial censuses (years ending in zero), and in continuing surveys based on representative samples of housing units. These approaches typically obtain information about a housing unit by interviewing its occupants, but building managers and others may be consulted about the status of vacant units and some characteristics of occupied units.

Counting Heads and Homes

Counting the population of the United States goes back to 1790 and a constitutional mandate to apportion each state's seats in the House of Representatives according to its number of inhabitants. Enumerating the population means identifying every housing unit and everyone who lives in each unit as well as various group quarters such as dormitories, military barracks, and other institutional settings. The 1980 census counted over eighty million occupied housing units, where 221 million persons lived at an average of about 2.8 persons per unit. Nearly six million Americans were counted in group quarters. Homeless persons who are found in shelters on nights when census enumerators canvas temporary living quarters are counted as part of the group-quarters population.

In 1940 the first housing census was conducted in conjunction with the population census. The initiation of new census questions on housing was strongly motivated by concerns during the Great Depression about the number of Americans who lived in substandard dwellings and were ill housed. At first the Census Bureau tried to train temporary census workers to evaluate the overall quality of housing and identify poor housing in categories like "dilapidated" or "deteriorated," but such distinctions proved to be inconsistent among raters and were supplanted by objective measures of specific conditions like presence of complete plumbing facilities and measures of overcrowding.

By the mid-1980s about 98 percent of occupied housing units had complete plumbing facilities and private kitchens, and only about 3 percent averaged more than one person per room, a figure sometimes used as a measure of overcrowding. These approaches to measuring housing quality have been supplemented in recent years by asking respondents about the reliability of equipment in their units (for example, the heating system) and their assessment and satisfaction with the unit, the neighborhood, and public services.

One important issue in recent censuses of population and housing has been to determine the particular housing unit to which individuals are to be assigned. Affluence means that more people own or rent more than one residence, and some retired or semiretired persons are "snowbirds" who spend summers in the north and winters in Florida or other southern or western locations. Such persons may have important reasons—tax or others—for picking which residence they want to claim as their usual or permanent residence, regardless of census instructions. Where they are counted matters to localities, which may receive federal or state funds in proportion to population, and to states, which may gain or lose representation in Congress as a result of where the snowbirds are counted.

Traditionally censuses have included questions to identify persons only temporarily present or temporarily absent from a household; in the 1980 census (conducted as of April), about one out of every twenty-eight households in Florida was found to consist entirely of persons with "usual" residence elsewhere, probably a "permanent" or preretirement home in another state (the other state they most often reported was New York). It has become a contentious issue that is not fully resolved whether for census purposes all persons can or should be assigned to one and only one housing unit that is their "usual" residence.

Growth of Population and Housing

The housing stock has been growing faster than population in recent years. During the 1970s, population growth slowed as a baby bust succeeded the baby boom that had lasted from the late 1940s to the early 1960s, but the growth rate of households, that is, occupied housing units, increased. From 1970 to 1980 population grew by 11.4 percent, but households grew nearly 27 percent. From 1980 to 1985 the differences narrowed somewhat, but households still grew faster than population—5.4 percent for population and 8.8 percent for households. If housing grows faster than population, then obviously the average number of persons per housing unit drops. Just before World War II, the average population per household was 3.67; by 1974 it dropped below 3.0, and today stands at 2.67.

These declines in average household size derive in part from demographic and social trends like low fertility and high divorce rates, which make two small households out of one. Declining household size also reflects a measure of affluence that allows many persons not to have to share housing with others. Fewer couples live with elderly parents, and more persons live alone. One-person households continue to grow, from 17 percent of all households in 1970 to 24 percent today. Married-couple households have dropped from 70 percent of households in 1970 to 58 percent today.

More housing units are occupied by a single person partly because young persons continue to postpone marriage. Age at first marriage reached a low point in the 1950s (just over twenty for women and between twenty-one and twenty-three for men), as young persons at that time encountered a rapidly expanding economy and, early in life, formed families and looked for housing in which to raise their children. The result was the baby boom of the 1950s and early 1960s.

But as the baby-boom children reached adulthood, they flooded a rather sluggish economy with large numbers of job seekers, so that the relative income position of the baby-boom children has been less favorable than that of their parents at a similar age. For these economic reasons, and maybe because of changes in attitudes toward marriage and family, the average age at marriage has been rising—to about twenty-three for women and nearly twenty-six for men by the mid-1980s.

Young adults have become increasingly likely to be found in their parents' homes rather than in their own homes or apartments. In 1960, 43 percent of persons eighteen to twenty-four years old were living with one or both parents; by 1985 nearly 54 percent of this age group were living in their parents' home. After finishing high school more persons continue to live with their parents, and more seem to move back in with their parents if they lose a job, if their marriage breaks up, or if something else makes independent living impossible to afford. If living arrangements of 1960 had continued to the present, there would be nearly three million *fewer* eighteen-to-twenty-four-year-olds living with their parents. This is a major change in the housing arrangements of young persons, equivalent to the entire population of Chicago packing their bags and going home to mom and dad.

Elderly persons have become less likely to live with their adult children or other relatives, and they increasingly maintain independent residence. Many live alone. The percentage of persons sixty-five years and over who live alone rose from 19 percent in 1960 to 30 percent in 1985 (excluding those in group homes for the elderly). The surveys from which these figures come do not cover institutions, but the 1980 census reported that 7.2 percent of men and 12.5 percent of women seventy-five years old and over lived in institutional settings. The figure is higher for women partly because women outlive men, and more survive to very advanced ages.

Year-Round Housing Units in the United States

Distribution by Occupancy

Vacant (10.3%)
Renter-occupied (32.4%)
Owner-occupied (57.3%)

Distribution by Building Type

Mobile homes (4.3%)
50 or more units (5.0%)
5-49 units (11.2%)
2-4 units (12.4%)
Single-family (67.1%)

Home Ownership and Its Affordability

The boom in housing construction after World War II made us a nation of home owners as the percentage of households owning their own home passed the 50 percent mark, a major milestone. The percentage of households owning their residences rose rather steadily until sometime around 1980, peaking at close to 65 percent of households. Since then, home ownership has declined and seems now to be hovering at below 64 percent. This may seem like a modest decline in a statistical series that cannot increase forever, but it means that there are about one million more renter households than would have been expected if the overall home ownership rate had stayed at its peak.

Demographic trends have contributed to slowing the growth in home ownership. The aging of the baby boom into young adulthood in the 1970s meant that many households were just recently formed and were at ages when renting is common. The unusually large numbers of persons in their twenties made for tough competition for the career jobs that are often required by mortgage lenders. The large size of the baby-boom generation has worked against its getting on the home ownership bandwagon as quickly as its parents did.

Also working against the further expansion of home ownership are some changes in the composition of households and families. More households consist of single persons, and more families consist of single parents; both groups tra-

ditionally have had fairly low home ownership rates. Single-parent families typically have lower incomes than two-parent families, partly because the latter increasingly have two earners. Other things being equal, these changes in the demography of households act to hold down the percentage of households owning the housing unit they live in.

The same changes depress common measures of the affordability of housing. Housing affordability is most often assessed by taking into account average selling prices of homes in a given year, average (usually the median) household income for that year, and a judgment about the monthly mortgage that the median household income can support with existing mortgage rates. In recent years such calculations have often suggested that the average family can no longer afford the average home that is for sale. Some of the decline in the index comes from the above changes in the composition of families and households, which hold down measures of average incomes. More families at young ages and more single-parent families acted to hold back "average" family income in the 1970s. Even among two-parent families, home ownership has sometimes been made possible only by more working wives and by more of the family's income going to housing. In one sense, more of the family's income can go to housing because of fewer children per family, but the relationship may go in the opposite direction and families may have fewer children so that they can afford their housing aspirations.

These demographic trends generally work independently of the prices of land, construction materials, and the other variables that influence the price of homes. They are part of the big picture of how much housing gets built, where it is built, how it is used, and the many other questions that censuses are called upon to answer.

Larry Long is Chief of the Demographic Analysis Staff at the Center for Demographic Studies, Bureau of the Census, Department of Commerce.

The Homeless

Its effect on housing is complicated.

By Patricia Carlile

Sol Eytinge, *The Hearth-stone of the Poor*, 1876. Kubler Collection, Cooper-Hewitt Museum.

The federal government can provide leadership and significant resources to end homelessness, but the hands-on solutions have to come from the community—they must be community based. We must help the homeless gain control of their lives, help them find and hold jobs, help them regain hope and leave life on the streets behind. We must make a long-term commitment to a comprehensive approach, providing combined services that meet the diverse and desperate needs of those who have been left behind. As Secretary of Housing and Urban Development Jack Kemp has said: "All of us must work together to end this tragedy: all levels of government, the private sector—profit and nonprofit—neighborhood-based organizations, and individual citizens." The time has come to look beyond emergency shelter.

The following information represents the best current assessments of the size and characteristics of the homeless population:

1. The limited number of studies that have attempted to estimate the size of the homeless population nationwide has found that overall numbers are smaller than widely cited estimates of millions. The number of homeless persons increased substantially between 1983 and 1987, the last year in which data were collected for nationwide estimates by such groups as the National Alliance to End Homelessness and the Urban Institute; the best estimate for the size of the homeless population for 1983 and 1984 is between 250,000 and 350,000; the best estimate for 1987 is between 500,000 and 600,000.

2. The homeless population is mostly male (70 to 80 percent), is comprised principally of single adults (almost 90 percent), and has a median age of thirty-six years.

3. The average monthly income of homeless persons is very low, less than $175 per month.

4. Recent data on employment and program participation found that approximately 80 percent of the homeless population is unemployed, although many of these people work on occasion. Roughly 20 percent receive state-administered and state-financed general assistance; 10 percent receive Supplemental Security Income (SSI) benefits, principally funded by the federal government; and approximately 6 percent receive assistance from the Aid to Families with Dependent Children (AFDC) program, funded by both the federal and state governments.

5. While the ethnic composition of the homeless population varies according to the ethnic composition of particular locales, minority groups contribute heavily to homelessness, in proportions far beyond their share of the overall population.

6. Family members constitute 20 to 25 percent of the homeless population and comprise a larger proportion of those using services. Although families have been among the fastest-growing components of the homeless population, recent evidence suggests that this trend is slowing, and according to a 1988–89 Partnership for the Homeless survey of five hundred public and private social service agencies, in some places it has stopped growing altogether. Most of the homeless families are headed by single parents, usually female. Findings from the 1988 National Survey of Shelters for the Homeless indicate that domestic violence is a contributing factor to homelessness, involving 50 percent of the families in family shelters. Regarding homeless youth, a General Accounting Office study based on a national sample found that on a given night there were 68,000 homeless youth age sixteen and younger who may be members of families that are homeless.

7. Among homeless persons, there is a heavy prevalence of alcoholism and/or drug abuse (30 to 40 percent), severe mental illness (approximately 30 percent), and a variety of acute and chronic disease and nutritional problems. Recent studies supported by the National Institute of Alcohol Abuse and Alcoholism suggest that 35 to 40 percent of all homeless persons have had, or currently have, alcohol problems, and that 10 to 20 percent have a problem with other drugs such as cocaine, crack, and heroin. In addition, roughly 10 to 20 percent of the homeless population is estimated to have both serious mental illness and a problem with alcohol and/or other drugs. Recent studies supported by the National Institute of Mental Health suggest that approximately one third of the population of single homeless adults suffers from serious mental illnesses such as schizophrenia, severe depression, manic-depressive disorder, and other major mental disorders. Research also has documented the prevalence of emotional problems among homeless families and children.

8. Approximately two thirds of the homeless population have had spells of prior institutionalization in jails, prisons, mental hospitals, or alcohol or other drug detoxification and treatment centers. Educational levels generally are low, and supportive personal relationships are lacking.

The Response—Federal Programs Highlights

There are two major types of federal programs for the homeless population: those that specifically target homeless individuals and families and those that primarily serve a larger population that includes the homeless population. In order to provide the homeless with the assistance they require, both types of federal programs need to work effectively together. In addition, this federal effort needs to be coordinated with state, local, and private initiatives.

Programs targeted to the homeless population have been expanded substantially in recent years and currently provide a wide range of assistance, including health care, emergency shelter and services, transitional housing, mental health and substance abuse treatment, and nutrition. In fiscal year 1989, their funding totaled $496 million, a 32 percent increase compared with fiscal year 1988. For fiscal year 1990, President Bush proposed that their funding be increased by 64 percent, to approximately $812 million.

Federal funding for programs that provide assistance to disadvantaged low-income families and individuals is also substantial, although it is difficult to tell exactly how much of this funding is used to assist the homeless population. In Health and Human Services alone, funding for programs to help low-income persons was more than $60 *billion* in fiscal year 1989. Unemployment compensation, Medicaid, Food Stamps, Aid to Families with Dependent Children (AFDC), Maternal and Child Health Block Grant, Education for Disadvantaged Children, Job Training Partnership Act (JTPA), Community Development Block Grant, and Low-Income Housing Assistance all fall within this category of programs.

In November 1989, President Bush announced a three-year initiative—Homeownership and Opportunity for People Everywhere (HOPE)—to increase home-

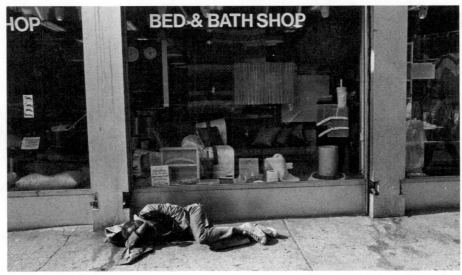

© 1987 Philip Greenberg.

ownership opportunities for low- and moderate-income families and to create jobs and entrepreneurial activity in the nation's distressed urban and rural communities. As part of this endeavor, $728 million is targeted for additional federal housing assistance for the long-term homeless population. These HUD funds are to be matched dollar for dollar by states, localities, and nonprofit organizations to provide social and health care services for the homeless.

HUD is one of seventeen federal agencies that sits on the Interagency Council on the Homeless, which provides federal leadership for activities to assist homeless individuals and families. Major activities include (1) planning and coordinating the federal government's actions and programs to assist homeless people, and making or recommending policy changes to improve such assistance; (2) monitoring and evaluating assistance to homeless persons provided by all levels of government and the private sector; (3) ensuring that leadership and technical and professional assistance are provided to help community and other organizations effectively assist homeless persons; and (4) disseminating information on federal resources available to assist the homeless population.

The National Response—An Overview

The national response to homelessness is growing, with support from all levels of government and the private sector.

Preliminary data from 1989 suggest that the fifty states and the District of Columbia have continued to increase their financial commitment to providing assistance to the homeless population. Programs providing emergency health care, social services, emergency shelter, and transitional housing to homeless individuals and families received $430 million in 1988 (from states). In 1987, $240 million was spent by the states for the same type of programs. These figures exclude state funds spent to match federal funds. States have also established mechanisms to coordinate state policy and funding of assistance for the homeless population, and have, for example, formed councils or agencies to address the problem of homelessness.

The nation's first response to increased homelessness in this decade was by community groups, principally charitable nonprofit organizations. Much credit is due to the individuals, organizations, and communities that led in this effort. Their assistance continues, although its nature

is shifting along with the changing character of the homeless population. Most of the early effort was in the form of emergency services. There is now an emerging, although still limited, recognition of the need for services to prevent homelessness. Existing shelters have expanded both in capacity and in types of services offered, adding health care and other supportive services. Community programs have begun to include more permanent solutions such as long-term housing, skills training, and specialized treatment.

Finally, private-sector for-profit organizations continue to assist homeless persons through efforts by individual companies and associations. For example, the Foundation Center, a national nonprofit service established by foundations to provide information to those seeking grants, reports that, in 1986–1987, 308 grants from 120 foundations were awarded for homeless services. These grants, totaling more than $12.7 million, covered such areas as shelter, housing, legal rights, advocacy, food services, and health care and services to the children of homeless people and to homeless youth. In 1987–1988, the total value of grants for homeless services rose to $28.5 million. This included 444 grants awarded by 133 foundations. Grants were awarded to thirty-seven states with more than half of the funding going to California, Colorado, the District of Columbia, Illinois, Indiana, Massachusetts, Michigan, and New York.

Despite the many and varied efforts by individuals and organizations across the country, the tragedy of homelessness continues. Unfortunately, there are no easy solutions to this multifaceted problem. More resources are needed; the delivery of assistance must be improved and streamlined; and comprehensive approaches to helping individuals become self-reliant are needed. Based on our experiences to date, ending this problem will require a concerted effort, involving federal, state, and local government, and the private sector.

Patricia Carlile is Executive Director of the Interagency Council on the Homeless.

Homelessness

Donald M. Fraser
Mayor, City of Minneapolis

Just as we can call the kids who drop out of school "drop-outs," because the school system's resources aren't large enough or adaptable enough to fit their individual needs, so can we call the homeless "push-outs" from society. As employment standards go up, as cheap SRO housing is torn down for new development, as the number of marginal jobs that pay a living wage shrinks, as long-term income assistance is reduced, people are pushed out from the mainstream of community life to join the ranks of the homeless. Added to their number are those who are pushed out from shrinking institutions for the mentally ill, lacking surveillance of follow-through on their long-term treatment plans.

The word "homeless" is applied to so many different kinds of people with so many different personal histories and problems, however, that we can't get a handle on the problem. We base our counts on surveys of people who use the emergency shelters. They tend to be white males below the age of forty with a history of chemical dependency and/or mental illness. Perhaps that only suggests that our community systems are more adaptable and better able to accommodate the homeless who fit other descriptions, such as battered women or runaway youths.

The best general solution to problems of the homeless is to focus on programs that will ease the transition from homelessness back into a life where people can think further than the next meal or next night's shelter. These programs would also shore up support for those who would otherwise join the ranks of the homeless.

In Minneapolis, we've been working on a program called "More than Shelter," which combines private and public funds

Shanties on Eighth Avenue, 1860s. Kubler Collection, Cooper-Hewitt Museum

to expand board and lodging facilities, SROs, and transitional housing. Two or three homeless people are accommodated in each transitional apartment for up to six months until they can secure employment and find more permanent housing. You can't find a job unless you have an address, a place to leave your goods, and a place to clean up. Transitional housing provides those resources.

But our local initiative is paltry in comparison with the need for guaranteed relief for the homeless who are pushed out from society against their will. The federal government provides housing for senior citizens, for the handicapped, and for single-parent families. HUD should also provide housing for non-elderly singles. Why should any adult be left out of the social contract who wants to be counted in?

Homelessness is not a new phenomenon. Bums, vagrants, chronic inebriates—symptoms of our failed hopes— have swelled or diminished in number depending on social and economic conditions. Many of those now on our streets, for example, are veterans of our self-punishment inflicted by the Vietnam War.

Perhaps it's just as well that gentrification of our downtowns, by eliminating "flophouses" and "skid rows," has made the plight of the homeless more visible and therefore discomforting to the nation's policymakers. Maybe out of this we'll finally understand that there's a federal mandate to pull everyone into the social contract. The first approach to prevention would support early childhood and youth development programs plus income and housing assistance for adults to avert "push-outs," from school or from adult society.

Clarence "Du" Burns
Mayor, City of Baltimore

Homelessness is an indictment against our democratic society, as well as against all humanity that claims to be civilized. If we throw our hands up in despair and cry out "Nothing can be done," we are saying, in effect, that homelessness is an integral part of civilization. I am positive we do not want even to imply that. Adequate shelter must be perceived as a national priority and as a right, not a privilege. We provide adequate housing for monkeys, lions, elephants, horses, etc. Certainly we can find the wherewithal to provide adequate housing for humans. It is not only a matter of funding, but also of will.

Christopher S. Bond
United States Senator, Missouri

The homeless are not really helpless. They manage to survive under the most dire conditions. Our communities must look for ways to transform that kind of tenacity into skills that will enable the homeless to make decent lives for themselves.

Raymond L. Flynn
Mayor, City of Boston

Homelessness in America is as preventable as it is tragic. It is a result of inadequate national policies in the areas of affordable housing, mental health, welfare reform, and job training. It is difficult to experience the American Dream when you and your kids are sleeping in a car or on a subway grate. If this nation were willing to invest at the necessary levels in these four areas of basic public policy, we would see a drastic reduction in the num-

bers of individuals and families who are denied the basic need of a roof over their heads, and the basic right to dream.

Lewis C. Murphy
Mayor, City of Tucson

We must define what we mean by "homeless." Tucson, by virtue of its year-round outdoor climate, has a considerable problem with transients; by this I mean those who voluntarily maintain a life-style of living off society while traveling from place to place. Tucson has also the chronically mentally ill, those who in another day would have been institutionalized for care; many of these also are transient in character. We also have the chronic substance abusers, some of whom are transient, many of whom are resident. Finally, there are the homeless, most of whom have come from elsewhere, but who are being provided for to the extent we can.

I am not sympathetic to the transient who will not work for what he gets. I am sympathetic to the others, and I think a responsible society should care for them in some fashion. We are trying to do that in Tucson. The state also is trying to come up with a workable program to treat those who are chronically mentally ill.

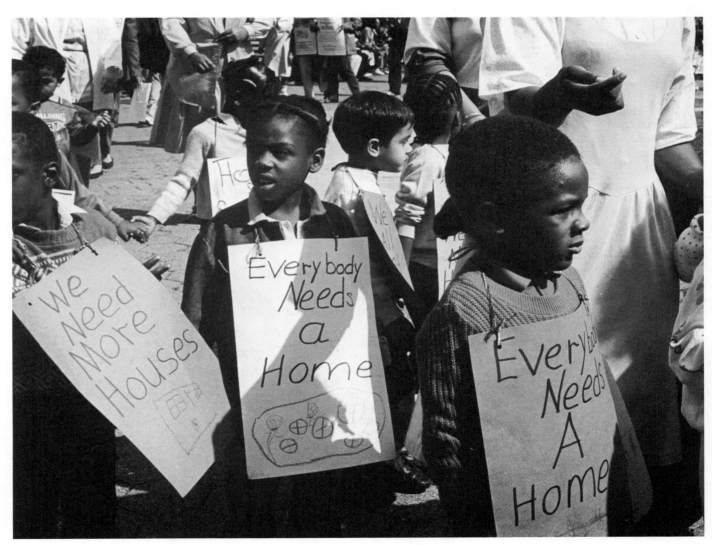

Rallying in support of public housing, New York. Community Service Society of New York/Teresita I. Batayola.

Sidney J. Barthelemy
Mayor, City of New Orleans

Every human being in this country has a right to safe and adequate shelter. It is the responsibility of city, state, and federal government to protect the future of this country by saving our children, saving our citizens from the degradation of life on the street. Through citizen action and communication between cities, we will not only address the issue of homelessness but effectively combat the socioeconomic factors that contribute to it. Through the marriage of government, business, and social service agencies, we can enrich the lives of the homeless and let them know that they have not been forgotten.

Claiborne Pell
United States Senator, Rhode Island

Even the most noble intentions can produce tragic consequences. The homeless of America represent the unfinished business of an enlightened people.

George V. Voinovich
Mayor, City of Cleveland

Homelessness is a symptom of the need for jobs, for housing, for better mental health care, and for a welfare system that works. Providing shelter for the homeless is only a first step.

Richard Arrington, Jr.
Mayor, City of Birmingham, Alabama

The problem of the homeless does, despite inferences to the contrary, have a solution. It is my judgment that this problem must be attacked institutionally by the local, state, and federal governments. Urban areas must set this issue as a real priority by leveraging available local, state, and federal funding. Indeed, our national goal should be the generation of affordable housing for all who would avail themselves of such a basic right. Recent efforts on the part of Congress indicate that our national leaders are willing to place additional resources at the disposal of us all for the purpose of eliminating the many problems associated with being among the homeless. Additionally, more local job development must take place in order for us to make a substantial dent in the intensity of the problem of the homeless in America.

James J. Blanchard
Governor, State of Michigan

Few would argue that we need more shelters to house the homeless, but the homeless family, the low-income elderly couple, and the displaced single person need more than a temporary solution. The extent and seriousness of homelessness will increase unless specific public policy initiatives, resource investments, and long-range planning are undertaken immediately to address the problem. We must make a commitment, at every level of government, to ensure that decent and affordable rooming houses, apartments, and homes are available for people at all incomes, in all parts of this country.

George Deukmejian
Governor, State of California

Homelessness is perhaps the most pressing social problem of the decade. My administration has worked diligently to address the serious challenges surrounding this important problem and has several programs that can assist the homeless, including the recent landmark welfare reforms embodied in the Greater Avenues for Independence Program.

Improving the condition of the homeless requires that the public and private sectors work together. This is especially important at the local level, where citizens are closest to the problem. Through this cooperative effort new ideas and long-term solutions can be developed.

I strongly encourage individual citizens, government agencies, private organizations, and businesses to examine the plight of the homeless in their communities and to donate whatever time, resources, ideas, or other assistance they can so that the homeless may successfully reenter society and become self-sufficient, contributing citizens.

George Bush
President of the United States

For two-hundred years, our society has been based on the idea that citizens can depend on their fellow citizens for assistance. However, when this is not enough, I believe it is imperative that government, beginning at the level closest to the people, step in to ensure that all Americans receive proper and sufficient care. The problem of the homeless in America is one of our most pressing domestic concerns, and this administration is unalterably committed to ensuring that all its citizens have, at the very least, a place to live and food to eat.

Dennis E. Eckart
United States Congressman, Ohio

Cities across the country report that homeless people—including families and children—are routinely being turned away from emergency shelters due to lack of space. Many of these people are part of a group of the "new poor," having lost jobs and been unable to find employment that will support a family. Unlike the stereotypical "skid row" derelict, today's homeless make up a diverse group including the mentally ill, evicted families, abused people, and cast-off children. Although HUD claims that the number of homeless in the United States is between 250,000 and 350,000 people, more realistic statistics put the number of homeless at closer to two million.

Clearly, the need to address this problem is vital to the health and well-being of the homeless as well as to that of our society as a whole. It is imperative that we, as a collection of communities and states that make up our nation, join in a partnership to address the needs of the people who need us most, the homeless.

Bob Graham
United States Senator, Florida

The contrast between the rich abundance of this country and the wretched existence of our nation's homeless is stark and compelling. America cannot be both a land of boundless plenty for some and a cold and hopeless dead end for others. We have a personal responsibility to be charitable, to share in prosperity with those less fortunate. We have a national responsibility to provide access to basic human necessities—shelter, food, medical care—for all Americans. That goes beyond a social or political imperative. It is a moral imperative. Adequate shelter is a right every American citizen is entitled to.

Evan Mecham
Former Governor, State of Arizona

Providing homes for the homeless is not a problem that can or should be dealt with on the national level. Massive projects funded with federal money, supposedly to provide housing for the urban poor, have for the most part been tragic failures. But what other alternatives are available?

As we seek to do more for ourselves at the state and local level, we free our programs from the crushing weight of a federal bureaucracy. The difference in costs between federal and local funding can well be the difference between success and failure. Instead of providing for people, we should teach people how to provide for themselves. If you give a hungry man a fish, you can satisfy his hunger for a day. Teach him how to fish, and he will never be hungry again.

Edward I. Koch
Former Mayor, City of New York

The number of homeless people has risen dramatically nationwide in the past few years. Last winter, New York City sheltered over twenty-six thousand people on an average night. This includes fifty-five hundred families, with nearly eleven thousand children.

From *Shopping Bag Ladies: Homeless Women Speak About Their Lives,* by Ann Marie Rousseau (New York: Pilgrim Press, 1981); photograph by Ann Marie Rousseau.

The problem of homelessness is not new. What is new is the failure of the federal government to help fund low-cost housing. The City of New York is committed to providing a permanent, long-term solution to this crisis. The city's economic recovery has enabled us to announce an ambitious $4.2 billion ten-year capital housing plan. But the plight of the homeless is not just a New York City crisis or an urban crisis. It is a national crisis, and it requires the federal government to resume its financial commitment to housing.

Mario M. Cuomo
Governor, State of New York

Despite the best efforts of state and local governments across our country, homelessness has become a national crisis in scope—a crisis for which the federal government must finally accept responsibility, just as it has been responsible in part for creating the conditions that led to it.

The homeless cannot—and should not—be the sole concern of private charities or any single level of government. We need a true partnership, one that takes advantage of the federal government's awesome resources, state and local governments' efforts and expertise, as well as the grassroots involvement of private charities.

I applaud the current bipartisan effort in the United States Congress to begin this journey toward a sound national policy for the homeless. These efforts can change this country's course from denying federal responsibility for homelessness to one of national enlightened action by providing the means for a joint solution to this problem.

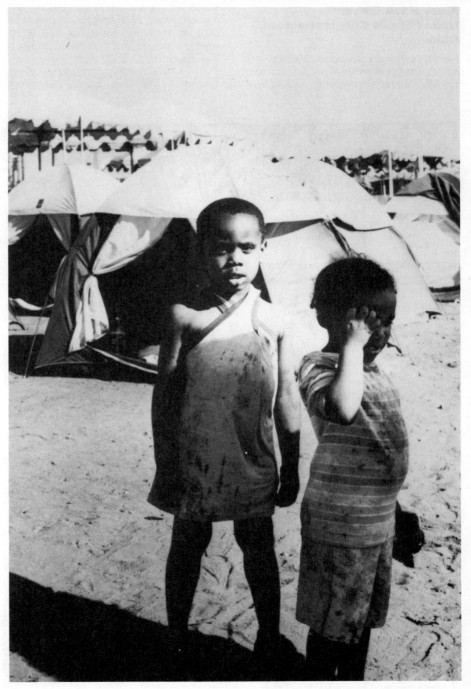

Urban Campground, Los Angeles—First Arrival, July, 1987 (Jacobi and Shameka upon arrival at the "Independent" section of the Urban Campground); photograph by Mary Ann Dolcemascolo.

Mary Rose Oakar
United States Congresswoman, Ohio

Homelessness is a national disgrace for a country as great and prosperous as America. We must challenge ourselves to overcome inertia and shortsightedness and move forward with enlightened ideas for bringing together architects and developers, planners and financiers, business and government. They must unite in commitment to eliminating homelessness by designing and constructing permanent housing that is affordable, safe, and decent, where people can live with dignity and self-respect. It is imperative for national and local authorities to work cooperatively to develop comprehensive programs to help the homeless.

As the sponsor of the National Transitional Housing Program through which homeless and deinstitutionalized mentally ill persons receive social, medical, and occupational counseling to enable them to reenter mainstream society, I know that this and emergency shelters can only be an interim solution. As a compassionate nation, it is our moral duty to help the homeless through long-term solutions that provide permanent housing, not to accept overcrowded and understaffed shelters as the best we can do.

John Breaux
United States Senator, Louisiana

Homelessness is one of the great tragedies in America. People in the most advanced country in the world should have a decent place to live. The federal government must develop and enforce a housing policy that is committed to fulfilling the promise made by Congress in the Housing Act of 1949, which declared as its purpose "the realization as soon as feasible . . . of a decent home and a suitable living environment for every American family."

Guy Hunt
Governor, State of Alabama

The problem of the homeless is a real and tragic problem that must be effectively addressed by state and local governments. Our society must be a caring people who are aware of those in need and a people who help meet those needs. In Alabama, it is my intention to be involved in efforts to help the homeless in our state.

Ernest F. Hollings
United States Senator, South Carolina

In the wake of the Reagan Administration's radical cuts in federal housing programs, the problem of the homeless has reached an acute stage. The "truly needy" have become the truly desperate. This is a national shame that requires urgent attention at all levels of government.

Michael S. Dukakis
Governor, The Commonwealth of Massachusetts

I find it unacceptable that in 1990 in this great country of ours, there are literally thousands of men, women, and children wandering the streets of our cities and towns with no place to go, no place to call home. This country can solve the problem of homelessness, but to do so will take leadership and commitment at *all* levels of government. After World War II, this country faced a major housing shortage; at that time, working together, federal, state, and local governments produced thousands of units of affordable housing. We can and must do that again.

Timothy E. Wirth
United States Senator, Colorado

The question of what to do about the homeless people across our nation is a very troubling one. Americans are, in general, a compassionate people. We want to help when we see someone down and out. Unfortunately, the ranks of the homeless have increased at such an unprecedented rate that our response, however well-intended, has seemed little more than a classic example of "way too little, much too late."

Bob Martinez
Governor, State of Florida

As Governor, I recognize the responsibility to provide for those Floridians who cannot provide for themselves. I remain committed to families and single-parent households with dependent children, elderly and disabled Floridians who need temporary public financial assistance for food, shelter, and medical care.

Albrecht Dürer, *The Nativity* (The Small Passion), 1509–11. Cooper-Hewitt Museum, Gift of Leo Wallerstein.

William P. Clements, Jr.
Governor, State of Texas

The first step in solving the problem of the homeless requires that local, state, and federal officials lay a quality economic foundation. This will provide a framework for jobs, which in turn provides a stable habitat for us all.

Bernie Simon
Mayor, City of Omaha

In a society concerned about the health and well-being of all its citizens, America's growing problem of homelessness is a national tragedy. Local communities must develop integrated programs that provide services in a dignified and effective way to people in need. The federal government must understand that homelessness is a national problem and must provide resources so that communities can truly house the homeless.

Bill Bradley
United States Senator, New Jersey

The problem of homelessness is a source of great national shame. The Department of Housing and Urban Development estimates that there are 250,000 to 350,000 homeless in the United States, a figure that critics argue is very low. Moreover, we cannot afford to delude ourselves with the notion that the homeless are primarily a group of alcoholic men who have chosen their life-style and do not wish to be a part of society's mainstream. In fact, the homeless population is composed of many different groups. These include alcohol and substance abusers, the deinstitutionalized chronically mentally ill, the elderly poor, and unemployed single men and women. Recently, the largest increase has been in families with children. In Trenton, New Jersey, it has been estimated that families with children comprise 50 percent of the homeless population. The national average is nearly 38 percent.

Very few of the homeless choose to live in the streets. Rather, homelessness

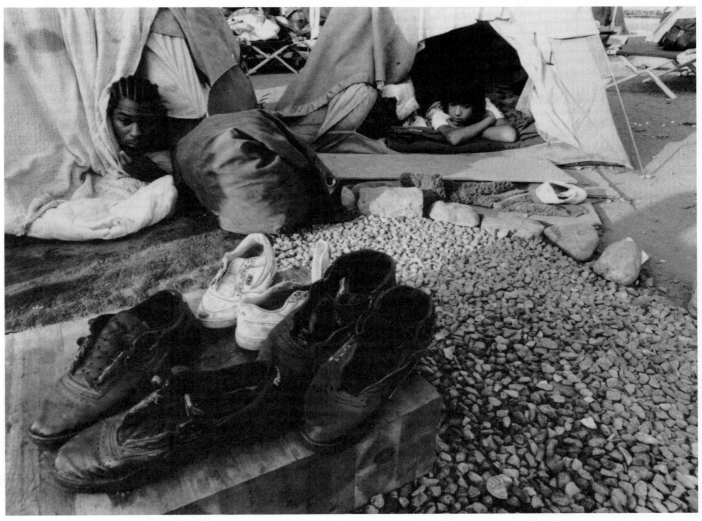

Urban campground for the homeless ("Tent City") in Los Angeles, August 27, 1987. Reprinted from *Homeless in America: A Photographic Project,* Courtesy of the National Mental Health Association and Families for the Homeless; © Eugene Richards/Magnum Photos.

stems from a variety of factors: unemployment, social service and disability cutbacks, lack of aftercare services for the deinstitutionalized mentally ill, and housing shortages in urban areas.

The federal government can and must take a leadership role in responding to the needs of the growing homeless population. For this reason, I have worked with a coalition of senators to develop comprehensive homeless legislation. Among

other things, this legislation expands and improves short-term shelters; provides additional certificates to help homeless families pay rent; provides funds for the acquisition of and operation of temporary housing with special support services; expands grants for food and bedding; and enables homeless people to know of and receive all services for which they are eligible, including guaranteed education of homeless children. In addition, the

package establishes a council to coordinate and evaluate federal programs, provide information, study, and report to Congress on the problem of homelessness.

In the final analysis, it is true that societies are measured by the care they afford their neediest citizens. I believe we must act to assist these unfortunate people. I am pleased that the Congress has acted to address this national problem.

Reform Movements

Did they succeed or fail?

By Allen F. Davis

The settlement movement was an idealistic protest against an urban, industrial world of poverty, alienation, and despair. Settlement workers, who were mostly young and well educated, felt a responsibility to bridge the gap between social classes. They went to live in the slums of industrial cities as much to learn as to teach. Many of these early settlement "residents" felt cut off from the excitement and reality of the metropolis and alienated from a world of work and meaning.

The first settlement in America was Neighborhood Guild, founded in 1886 by Stanton Coit in a crowded immigrant area on the Lower East Side in New York, but probably the most famous was Hull House, started by Jane Addams and her college classmate Ellen Starr on the West Side of Chicago in 1889. Lillian Wald's Henry Street Settlement in New York, South End House in Boston, and the College Settlement in Philadelphia all played important roles in the settlement effort to humanize the industrial city.

But there were others as well, for the movement spread rapidly. There were seventy-five settlements in 1897, and over four hundred in 1910. Not all the settlements were centers of reform, but the best and most prominent made important contributions to the social justice movement in the United States.

Early settlement workers were influenced by Toynbee Hall, the first settlement in London, and by a group of British reformers, including John Ruskin and William Morris, who rebelled against the drabness and lack of beauty in the modern city. The settlement workers went to live in the slums not to live like the poor, but to use their base in an urban neighborhood to change society.

The settlements were not charities, nor did the poor live in the houses, but many settlements with their communal dining halls, their clubs, classes, and constant activity, became convenient and exciting places to live. The settlement workers, especially in the early years, were optimists who believed that reform was possible. They were also environmentalists who thought that poverty was caused not by heredity but by the particular urban situation. They had faith that if one could provide the poor with better houses and better schools, one could make better people and a better society.

Nothing troubled the settlement workers more than the poor housing and overcrowded conditions that they saw all around them. They were shocked by the "pale, dirty, undersized children" and the dark, damp rooms where whole families existed. One New York settlement worker found eleven people living in two rooms, and another discovered a tenement room on a hot summer day "crowded with scantily-clothed, dull-faced men and women sewing upon heavy woolen coats and trousers."

The settlement workers did not invent housing reform. There had been many attempts to improve urban housing before they arrived on the scene, such as model tenement projects and experiments dubbed "philanthropy plus five percent," because the charitable gentlemen who invested in the projects took a modest return in order to assure reasonable rents. Many of these reform projects also employed "friendly visitors" or rent collectors to help the worthy poor learn how to practice thrift, industry, and neatness. The upper-class visitors usually had a paternalistic attitude toward the poor, and they were especially upset when they found beer bottles or strange men in the model apartments. The settlement workers did not avoid paternalism, but because they actually lived in a working-class neighborhood, they often had a better sense of the problems faced by the slum dwellers and a greater empathy and understanding of their difficulties.

The housing reformer most closely associated with the settlement movement in the 1890s was Jacob Riis, the Danish-born journalist, photographer, and author of *How the Other Half Lives* (1890). Riis taught the settlement workers how to express their moral indignation over the slum housing conditions by writing carefully crafted articles describing how real people lived and died in the tenement districts. He also demonstrated the power of the photograph and the lantern slide in convincing people that reform was necessary.

Riis joined forces with settlement workers in many reform campaigns and later founded a settlement house himself. His ideas about the importance of the neighborhood and the need for neighborhood parks and playgrounds fit exactly with the settlement goal of building a sense of community in the city.

Another housing reformer who worked with settlement residents was Lawrence

Jacob A. Riis, *Tenement Backyard*. Jacob A. Riis Collection, Museum of The City of New York.

Veiller, a graduate of City College in New York, who had been a resident of New York's University Settlement on the Lower East Side. Veiller was a technical and scientific reformer who believed that the housing problem could be solved if only the right kind of restrictive legislation and the proper housing codes were passed. He organized a housing exhibit in February 1900 to which many settlement workers contributed, not only those from New York, but also from Boston and Chicago. The exhibit demonstrated through photographs, charts, and statistics just how dangerous working-class housing was in urban America.

The most influential part of the exhibit was the model of one block in New York that contained thirty-nine tenements housing 2,781 people. There were only 264 water closets; only forty apartments had hot water; and there were no bathtubs for the entire block. The exhibit led directly to the appointment by Governor Theodore Roosevelt of a tenement house commission, and to the passage in 1901 of a New York housing law. The law would prove to have its flaws, but the settlement network used it and the exhibit to promote reform in other cities and states.

Settlement workers were part of a statistical generation that believed that if the American people were told carefully documented truth, they would support social change. But settlement workers always combined their statistics with moral outrage. They promoted housing reform, first in their neighborhoods, then in the city, and finally in the state and the nation. They also tried to improve living conditions on a more personal level.

The settlement houses themselves, with living rooms filled with carefully selected furniture, books, and prints, were models for immigrant families to follow. Clubs and classes also taught neighborhood women how to be efficient and orderly housekeepers. Settlement workers recommended uncluttered woodstained furniture, iron beds with mattresses, unupholstered chairs, and shelves rather than bulky sideboards. Influenced by the Arts and Crafts movement of the late nineteenth century, the reformers tried to promote simple rooms free of "dust-collecting and germ-ridden carpets, drapes, and wallpaper."

They also tried to get the immigrant slum dwellers to separate their living functions into bedrooms, living room, and kitchen. But many of their neighbors rather enjoyed living in untidy disarray. Separation of living functions in overcrowded tenements was impossible in any case, making it difficult for the reformers to teach the middle-class virtues of cleanliness, neatness, and order.

If the settlement workers were sometimes baffled by their neighbors, they did appreciate the dangers of living in overcrowded, badly ventilated tenements. Their investigation of housing conditions often was related to their campaigns for parks and playgrounds and for better schools. Housing reform also led to campaigns to prevent child labor, to outlaw sweatshops, and to try to prevent tuberculosis. Housing reform ultimately also involved settlement residents in politics, as they recognized that poor housing was a political problem and concluded that they could not accomplish their goals at the local level.

It was no accident that settlement workers played important roles in the organization of the National Housing Association in 1910, and that settlement workers led the fight for federally funded public housing. It was the housing shortage during World War I, however, that triggered the first experiments in public housing. The government took over or built a dozen housing projects, and Lawrence Veiller drew up the "Standards for Permanent Industrial Housing Developments" that were followed in all federal housing. When the war was over, however, the projects were abandoned and it was not until the depression years that public housing got another chance.

Mary Simkhovitch of Greenwich House in New York was one of the most important leaders in the public housing movement. She had become discouraged, as had a great many reformers, about the slow progress in improving housing. In 1931 she helped to organize the Public Housing Conference in New York. The next year the organization became na-

Hull House Dining Room. Jane Addams Memorial Collection, The University Library, The University of Illinois at Chicago.

tional in scope; Simkhovitch became its president, and another settlement worker, Helen Alfred, its secretary. The group tried without success to get a public housing provision written into the Federal Relief and Reconstruction Act of 1932.

After Franklin Roosevelt was elected, however, Simkhovitch and a few others approached Senator Robert Wagner, Harold Ickes, and Eleanor Roosevelt (all of them friends of the settlement movement) and convinced them that public housing was the only solution to the nation's tragically underhoused urban residents. They obtained a public housing provision in the National Industrial Recovery Act, convinced Ickes to include public housing in PWA projects, and most important of all, helped to draft the bill that became the Wagner-Steagall Housing Act. Simkhovitch served on the advisory committee in the Public Works Administration and on the New York Housing Authority. Her work for public housing was the capstone of a long career as a settlement worker and as a promoter of social legislation.

Other settlement workers around the country in cities large and small also fought for better housing from their outposts in the slums.

Public housing, like housing codes and model tenements, did not prove to be the solution to the housing problem, and overcrowded, unsafe housing and slums still exist today. In fact, it is possible to walk through a poor section of any great American city and conclude that one hundred years of housing reform have been a failure. Yet some housing has been improved, and some people have been able to move out of the worst slums.

The settlement workers were always idealists—sometimes naive, occasionally impractical—but their dreams of better housing for all the people, and a sense of community in the city, are worth remembering today—even in a world that appears more complex and more sinister than it did to the early settlement reformers.

Allen F. Davis is Professor of History at Temple University in Philadelphia and author of *Spearheads of Reform: The Social Settlements and the Progressive Movement, 1890–1914.*

Segregation and Discrimination

Fairness must be our goal.

By Gary Orfield

Housing discrimination seems like an anachronism, something that was supposed to have been solved long ago. It has been nearly two decades since Congress enacted a federal fair housing law and almost thirty years since the Supreme Court outlawed the restrictive covenants that once made it almost impossible for blacks to buy or rent outside the ghettos. Incidents of overt discrimination, violence, and intimidation against blacks who move into white areas are an embarrassing echo from what we think of as an earlier era, when old men marched around in sheets for a Ku Klux Klan parade in some distant small town in the South.

Housing segregation is illegal, and most Americans say that they would not object if someone from another race moved onto their block. The great majority of Americans, according to national surveys, believes that the housing markets are open and that any family with the necessary money can buy the house it wants. Since few blacks prefer segregated housing, and there are significant numbers of black families that can now afford housing in virtually any neighborhood, these attitudes should produce increasing integration.

Anyone who lives in a large city today, however, knows that something is wrong. The ghettos remain, conditions inside the ghettos are becoming worse, and their boundaries are still rapidly expanding. These facts, which are painfully visible, can be reconciled with public beliefs about fair housing laws only by assuming either that blacks remain segregated because they do not have adequate money or by assuming that they choose to remain segregated. The best available evidence, however, suggests that neither of these factors can account for more than a modest fraction of the segregation in our cities.

One might also believe that there has simply not yet been time for enough

moves to take place to show the long-term impact of fair housing. But on average, three families have lived in the typical United States housing unit since fair housing became law. Segregation has not merely continued where it was present before fair housing laws, it has been reinforced by the decisions of two decades of home seekers.

If neither explanation works, there are some large questions that must be answered to explain the conflict between public beliefs about fair housing and the evidence that segregation remains the dominant reality. Why do the ghettos continue to grow today? What difference does it make that cities remain segregated? Is there any way in which fair housing laws could become more effective?

The 1980 census, taken twelve years after the federal open housing law was enacted, shows little change in the basic pattern of segregation since 1960. In fact, segregation in major metropolitan areas increased during the 1960–70 period and fell only very modestly between 1970 and 1980. Segregation of blacks remains most intense in the older industrial cities. It is reflected in school segregation and other aspects of racial inequality. Illinois and New York lead the country in school segregation for blacks and Hispanics in the mid-1980s because they have vast expanses of residential segregation in their urban areas and because their school desegregation plans are far too limited to overcome the effects of those neighborhood patterns.

The only national study of housing discrimination, conducted in 1978 by the Department of Housing and Urban Development (HUD), found that black families were very likely to encounter discrimination in the course of a typical housing search. Since that time, studies in several housing markets, including Boston and Washington, D.C., have also shown high

levels of continuing discrimination. Recent research on mortgage lending in several parts of the country has shown a continuing pattern of unequal treatment of minority and racially changing communities by lending institutions, and a great shortage of housing capital in the ghettos. Minority families continue to perceive discrimination, and there is clear evidence that discrimination continues to be a major problem.

Hamilton Avenue, Paterson, New Jersey from *Urban Landscapes*, by George A. Tice (New Brunswick, New Jersey: Rutgers University Press); photograph by George A. Tice.

Children growing up in ghettos experience less opportunity for education and employment and are exposed to far more serious threats of violence, crime, and other problems than those growing up in typical suburban neighborhoods. Ghetto schools offer a much less demanding curriculum and level of competition. Most new jobs in most metropolitan areas are

in the outer suburbs, areas that are inaccessible by mass transit from central city minority communities. There, many households have no cars and many of the cars that are available are not reliable for long-distance commuting.

There is good evidence that children growing up in ghettos are more likely to live in ghettos as adults and that children educated in an integrated setting are more likely to find jobs in the growing sectors of the economy that require working with white clients or customers. Segregation in housing affects the kinds of opportunities available to people in urban society and affects the possibility of creating an integrated society in the future.

Segregation is a problem not only for blacks but also for the larger Hispanic communities. Hispanic barrios are becoming larger and more isolated from white communities as the Hispanic population soars in metropolitan areas. Hispanic segregation is not as extreme as that affecting blacks, and a considerably larger fraction of middle-class Hispanics lives in integrated areas. Still, those living in virtually all-Hispanic neighborhoods have many problems that are similar to what was experienced a generation ago in black ghettos, which were then absorbing a huge migration from the South.

One obvious parallel is the serious overcrowding of schools in the Hispanic areas of Los Angeles, Houston, New York, Chicago, and other cities. These problems are certain to become more apparent in coming years. Although we know much less about the dynamics of residential discrimination against Hispanics, research in Dallas and Denver has found that Hispanics there have faced problems of discrimination that have been at least as severe as those facing local blacks. In the future, as Hispanics become the largest minority group in many American cities, it will be essential to devise fair housing

48

policies that address both forms of discrimination.

Although the record is not impressive, there is no reason to conclude that fair housing cannot be achieved. So far, in fact, there has been little serious enforcement. All recent secretaries of HUD have complained of the extremely weak enforcement provisions of the federal law. After HUD investigators prove a violation and determine that a landlord will not negotiate a settlement, under the current law they can do nothing except refer the case to the Department of Justice, which may eventually decide to file a lawsuit. Only a handful of cases is filed each year by the Justice Department, even though HUD research suggests that there are millions of fair housing violations annually.

Congress has done nothing to add teeth to the law, in spite of years of reports on its weaknesses. An enforcement bill passed the House of Representatives in 1980 but was filibustered to death in the Senate. A new bipartisan enforcement bill was introduced early in the Hundredth Congress, in 1987. Enactment of a stronger bill would, for the first time, produce a serious deterrent to discrimination in the housing market.

There is another reason to think that the present pattern can be overcome. More communities than ever before have managed to remain integrated in recent years. Throughout the United States most census tracts in which more than one-tenth of the residents were black have become overwhelmingly black by the next census. These statistics have tended to reinforce the white fear that integration was merely a brief transitional stage between white and black occupancy. So long as white residents and realtors have believed that transition was inevitable, they have tended to act in ways that have produced self-fulfilling prophecies. The record became much more encouraging, however, in the 1970s and 1980s.

The increasingly rapid spread of ghettos, after fair housing laws were enacted, and the decreasing population pressure on integrated neighborhoods, after black migration to the North stopped and the black birthrate declined, brought a new

Jean-Michel Folon, *Seul*, © 1972. Courtesy of John Locke Studios, Inc.

set of circumstances to housing markets. Black population in the suburbs increased rapidly, raising the question of whether it would be possible to break the tradition of urban ghettoization in a very different setting.

A final important trend was the increased willingness of many whites to accept black neighbors. Whatever the reason, there was a substantial increase in the number of stably integrated communities by 1980, clearly demonstrating that resegregation was not inevitable.

After a generation of commitment to the idea of fair housing, it would be easy to conclude either that the movement

had been a success, because most people believe that the problem no longer exists, or a failure, because segregation remains very intense in many housing markets. Either conclusion, however, would be wrong.

The movement for open housing has had positive effects, but a great deal more must be done before any fundamental breakthrough can be achieved. At the same time, it would be foolish to concede defeat on a question of basic importance to the future of American society and race relations at the very time that so much evidence testifies to the possibility of success.

What is most needed now are serious enforcement tools with real sanctions, along with assistance to the growing number of currently integrated communities. Then those communities can consolidate their achievements and help move housing markets toward a situation where both minority and white home seekers have a substantial array of integrated as well as racially defined communities to choose from.

Gary Orfield is Professor of Political Science at the University of Chicago and author of *Fair Housing in Metropolitan Chicago: Perspectives after Two Decades.*

Design for Special Needs

What are the considerations?

By Ronald L. Mace

Today there is a large and growing population with disabilities or disabling conditions of aging who have great difficulty using most of the housing built in the United States. Unable to find appropriate housing, many disabled and older people live in houses that limit their independence and, when their abilities change, are forced to give up their homes prematurely to live in institutions or nursing homes. The problems experienced vary depending upon the design of the house and the type of disability the occupant has. Some problems are common among different types of disabilities and some are unique to people having a specific type of disability.

Hundreds of different disabilities and combinations of physical and mental disabilities make the issues complex, even for specialists. To simplify, we will discuss three broad categories of disabilities that affect the design and marketing of housing: mobility impairments, visual impairments, and hearing impairments. People with mobility impairments have problems with the greatest number of housing features, followed by people with visual impairments, and then those with hearing loss. Included in the mobility-impaired group are people who walk with difficulty and who cannot easily climb steps. Also included in this group are people who cannot bend or reach very far, people who have hand dysfunctions that prevent grasping knobs or manipulating controls, and people who have hidden disabilities such as arthritis and heart disease, which limit activity and reduce agility and stamina. This category, of course, includes people who cannot walk at all and who must use wheelchairs. The visually impaired group includes people with limited sight as well as those who are blind. They have difficulty with activities such as reading instructions on appliances, seeing where controls are set, or setting devices like thermostats. People who

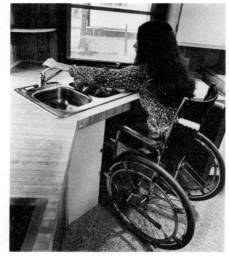

Kitchen counter and sink designed for use with wheelchair. Photograph courtesy of Barrier Free Environments, Inc., Raleigh, North Carolina.

have hearing problems may have limited hearing and need good acoustics or aids to hear everyday sounds, or they may be deaf and unable to hear doorbells, fire alarms, and the evening news.

The most frequently noted problem features in conventional housing are the single step or steps at dwelling entrances and the narrow bathrooms doors. These two features prevent a great many mobility-impaired people from living in available houses and from visiting friends or neighbors. Other problems for mobility-impaired people include: limited maneuvering space, particularly in bathrooms and kitchens; light switches, faucets, receptacles, counter tops, thermostats, shelves and closet rods mounted too high or too low or too far away to reach; raised thresholds; narrow doors to other rooms; and doorknobs, faucet handles, and appliance controls that are difficult to grasp and operate.

It is interesting to note that almost

every one of these problems can be resolved with simple planning and selection of conventional products. These solutions create no additional cost and no noticeable change in appearance. Wider doors can be substituted for narrower, flat thresholds for raised ones, controls and switches can be placed lower on walls, and receptacles higher. Shower and tub controls can be placed off center near the outside of the fixture for easy reach. Appliances can be selected that have contrasting graphics and click stops on the controls. Thermostats with large and/or lighted numerals can be specified.

Through careful design and placement on their sites, houses can be constructed without steps at entrance doors thus at least improving access to ground floors. Some knowledgeable designers raise garages and outside walks to the house floor level to let vehicles climb the heights rather than the people. Maneuverable space in bathrooms, needed by those who use walkers and wheelchairs, and not perhaps by others, can be provided if and when needed, and without increasing room size, by installing removable vanity cabinets or recessed and wall supported counter top lavatories.

It is also interesting to note how every home occupant, disabled or not, benefits from these more usable features. Everyone can better read and understand good graphics on appliances. Click stops and audible and visual signals provide redundant cuing that ensures that any user will know the status of controls. Wider doors make it easier to move furniture and appliances and they help to prevent damage to expensive belongings on moving day. Entrances without steps are safer for everyone, particularly in ice and snow and during emergencies. Extra space in bathrooms for people who need it is a marketing plus for others, who may like to place bookshelves or furniture in these usually austere spaces. Houses having

these features do not look different, nor do they cost significantly more, yet they are rarely included in conventional housing. This is because builders generally do not know what is wrong with their housing. They have not heard complaints from a significant market segment and they believe that accessible housing will be vastly different and special, more expensive, less profitable, needed by only a few people, and avoided by others.

Some special accessible housing that has been required by laws and by building codes has reinforced these negative ideas. Accessible housing laws almost always require a small percentage of rental units (usually 5 percent) to be designed for wheelchair users. Whereas special units for wheelchair users sound like a reasonable idea, it must be noted that wheelchair users are a small percentage of the total disabled population. The standards applied have been relatively poor and have specified some clinical features, such as stainless steel grab bars in bathrooms, that most people dislike and do not want to live with. Builders have not been able to rent all special units to wheelchair users, and many other people, including some disabled people, have avoided them.

A more enlightened approach to required access in housing has evolved in recent years in response to these problems. Called "Adaptive Housing," this approach specifies that some common access features will be fixed and installed at construction time and that others be made adjustable, and a few other specific features could be added or removed when needed by particular occupants. For example, wider doors, level entrances, and easily reachable controls would be permanently installed, but closet rods, shelves, and some counter-top segments would be made adjustable in height. In addition, grab bars could be added (provided walls are reinforced to support them) and some base cabinets can be removable to increase maneuverable space in bathrooms and kitchens for people in wheelchairs. This concept is producing greater numbers of usable dwellings that can be better adapted to almost any occupant's needs and marketed to the general public. The concept is thoroughly outlined and illustrated in a new manual from the United States Department of Housing and Urban Development titled *Adaptable Housing: Marketable Accessible Housing for Everyone*.

Perhaps the most significant reason for the lack of universally usable housing is the misconception by builders that there is no market or only a small market. The housing industry has done a reasonable job of designing for and marketing to young, able-bodied adults. Builders have not perceived young disabled adults and older people as being a part of the market for their houses. By repeatedly building the same conventional housing, builders have inadvertently excluded disabled and older people from living in their houses. For appropriate housing, disabled people have had to turn to special housing programs and care-givers rather than to the housing industry. Information for builders has been limited. Market research directed to the general housing market and focusing on home size, price, aesthetic and trendy features has missed the more pragmatic and functional needs of disabled and older people. For a variety of social, psychological, and economic reasons disabled and older people have not come forth and made their needs known. Information from care-givers, who serve only the most severely affected and needy of these groups, has often resulted in much needed but special programs and more institutional forms of housing. Their information has been recognized in the industry as special and appropriate for special groups in special locations but it has done nothing to change general housing design practices.

Being disabled and old are not popular conditions in our society. No one wants to be singled out and identified as either. People are often embarrassed and reluctant to call attention to their needs. Some do not know what is possible and therefore do not know what to say. Others do not know who to tell and are never asked. When housing is inappropriate most people prefer to "make-do" rather than to make changes. They "get by" by altering their life-styles to eliminate activities that are made difficult by the design of their homes. Some create makeshift adaptations to their homes; others give up and rely on others for assistance in doing everyday tasks. This poor communication between disabled users and housing producers deprives the industry of valuable information. It prevents knowledgeable change from taking place and perpetuates the design and marketing of housing that is not suitable for all users. As pressure for improved housing grows, disability specialists and design researchers are busy improving the flow of information.

Many builders, noting change in our society, are asking, "Is there a market for more broadly usable housing and how large is it?" The size of the disabled and older population depends upon how you define disability. The numbers by any definition are large and growing. The number most frequently cited by government agencies and advocacy groups is thirty-six to thirty-nine million people. This number is derived from statistics of government benefit programs such as Social Security Disability, veterans benefits, and from recent census data. Although this number includes those who can easily be identified as having significant disabilities that affect daily activities, many people place the number much higher. They cite the narrow focus of the census data on employed disabled people only. The fact that a great many disabled people do not receive benefits means they would not be included in the thirty-six million figure. Some manufacturers of aids and appliances used by disabled people, such as canes, crutches, back braces, and incontinence supplies, place their market at seventy to eighty million. If one includes common conditions of aging—such as reduced eyesight and limited hearing, arthritis, and hidden disabilities such as heart disease, which restrict agility and stamina—the numbers grow extremely large. Almost everyone has family members or friends or acquaintances who have disabilities. It is easy to see that hardly anyone goes through his or her entire lifetime without having some type of temporary or permanent disability. Most people who wear eyeglasses, who have arthritis, who cannot reach very high or who have difficulty climbing stairs do not consider themselves disabled. They would probably not respond to a survey on disability, yet they have limitations in some activities and frequently must depend on aids and support devices such as glasses, hearing aids, and canes. For this reason we will never know exactly how many disabled people there are. We do know the numbers are larger than most people imagine. We also know that we need not identify and label people in order to design housing that responds to changing needs throughout the lifespan.

Housing so far has not kept pace with other changes. Disabled people come from every socioeconomic strata. Those who are financially self-sufficient have generally been able to acquire housing and other services and to live well albeit restricted lives. Inability to work and lack of educational and employment opportunities caused by inaccessible buildings and discriminatory program practices have kept many other disabled people in the low-income category and thus made them less attractive as a market for housing or any other services. Legislation is changing this situation for all disabled people who can participate. The Rehabilitation Act of 1973 requires all programs receiving any form of federal assistance to be made accessible to all qualified disabled people. The 1968 Architectural Barriers Act requires all buildings receiving federal money for construction or leasing to be accessible to physically disabled people. The Education for Handicapped Children Act (PL 94–142) of 1975 requires school systems to educate disabled children in the same settings as nondisabled children. In addition, the recently approved amendment to the Fair Housing Act of 1988 eliminates the common practice of denying disabled people housing opportunities because of their disabilities. These laws and other federal and state laws are opening new opportunities for disabled people to become educated and employed and to participate actively in society.

The deinstitutionalization movement is removing many disabled people from large institutions and requiring that they be served with housing and support services in their local communities. Nationwide independent living programs are establishing centers where disabled people can find assistance or learn how to get the services they need to live independently in their communities. These trends are adding to the pressure for a broad variety of accessible and more usable housing in every price range and location.

Increasing numbers of disabled people, greater awareness of common needs in housing, new laws, improved attitudes, and new technologies are creating many changes in our social system. In the matter of housing, these changes are defining a need for at least two types of accessible housing: (1) a percentage of special housing designed specifically for people who have particular types of disability, and (2) large numbers of conventional housing available on the open market in every price range, style, and location. These conventional houses would include common features that make them more universally usable and convenient for everyone. Some special housing will always be needed for those severely disabled people who cannot be independent and who need unusual features and/or special services. This housing needs to be better designed than the minimums specified in building codes and standards. Most special housing is developed as part of special housing programs and is managed by care-giving organizations. Conventional, universally usable housing is not currently produced and will require changes in the design of market-oriented housing. These changes are taking place as understanding of the market potential increases and as technology, new standards, and new products make it easy to create more universally usable housing.

Ronald L. Mace, FAIA, is an architect and specialist in design for disabled and older people. He is President of Barrier Free Environments, Inc., in Raleigh, North Carolina.

Family Patterns

Domestic ideals are always changing.

By Gwendolyn Wright

For generations now, Americans have tended to see their homes as statements about themselves. Similarities in such self-definitions have paralleled basic trends in housing design as patterns of family life and housing style have evolved together over time. In fact, builders, decorators, and authors on domesticity have often explained design innovations in cultural terms, describing, for example, how the open plan keeps the family closer together or how wood and stone walls suggest family stability.

Even reformers, whether conservative or radical, have used domestic architecture as a way to represent the improvements they wanted to see. New styles for facades, rearranged floor plans, and innovative site plans would, they believed, reinforce a different structure of family life, eventually leading to basic alterations in national character. In looking at the housing patterns of American cities, suburbs, and rural areas, then, we see documentation of both the changing realities and the changing ideals of the residential life within.

Nonetheless we need to exert some restraint in making such cultural connections. The definition of household has to be expanded to include many variations beyond that of the nuclear family, variations that have always existed. The commercialization of domestic architecture and domestic advice in this country over the last two centuries also precludes any simple notion of families or individuals directly expressing their own predilections.

We see personal expression, of course, and definite group preferences within a larger portrait of American domesticity. But we also see a network of other forces affecting built form and cultural form alike. Large-scale builders and developers dominate the available moderate-cost market in many areas; advertising and advice literature dictate what is fashionable and even what is deemed acceptable; government bureaucrats, from the local to the federal level, issue regulations about the size and accoutrements of dwelling units, and about who can live where.

Houses can offer us a chronicle of American family life for an individual family, for different groups within the society, and even, to a certain extent, for a prevailing national image of the "average" family. Yet the history of housing patterns attests to the difficulty of choosing for ourselves how we want to live. To say that our dwellings reflect American family life points up the fact that images of both have constantly been manipulated, each in terms of the other.

One can trace a fascinating overview of how trends in domestic architectural design have responded to trends in American family life, and vice versa, in actuality and in imagination. Middle-class housing has consistently represented the national norm for people of all classes.

The cottages in the United States before the Civil War, for example, whether in town or countryside, testified to an increasingly romantic concept of the woman's domestic role. Gothic tracery over a window reinforced the Christian beliefs of the family who lived there, just as the steep pitch of the roof and the tiny front porch spoke to them of the comforts and security that home provided. Andrew Jackson Downing, the preeminent designer in this Gothic revival mode, called such evocations "expressions of purpose," and he adamantly hoped that architectural reminders of domestic virtue could counter Americans' restless mobility.

While the revival styles of such cottages introduced new ornamentation to facades and interior walls, most of these antebellum dwellings were still relatively plain and straightforward. In many ways they paralleled the purported visual mes-

"Coffee and Cigars in 16-B," bachelor library; Michael Hare and John B. Manzer, architect and designer, for "America at Home," about 1940. Picture Library, Cooper-Hewitt Museum. Richard Averill Smith.

sages of urban row houses during that period. Each dwelling unit provided a private retreat for family life, but there was little effort to assert individuality or status. Houses were seen, by and large, as part of a relatively egalitarian and self-consciously simple community of families—whether the neighbors lived far away or just alongside.

This attitude toward architectural and social restraint disappeared after the Civil War. During the second half of the nineteenth century, a new focus on each family's particularity—its status in society, its tastes and interests, all purportedly expressed through domestic architecture—came to the fore. Elaborate ornament on facades and intricate floor plans testified in their minds to the individuality of those who resided within. Even the names of rooms showed this effort to give a personal fit—music rooms, dens, reading nooks, and later, the sumptuous Turkish corner for lounging. Decoration, too, could give a message, for the right combination of artistic purchases and handmade "household elegancies" demonstrated the domestic prowess of the woman of the house.

Such homes were intended to shelter delicate women and children from the dangers of the city and to provide men with a retreat from the pressures of business. Associations between women, home, and nature generated interest in natural materials—rough stone and clapboard, often juxtaposed on the same facade, and the colors of autumnal forests.

In fact, however, the very act of keeping the home up-to-date kept middle-class women in contact with the commercial city. Department stores such as Marshall Field in Chicago sold items once made at home, and their professional interior decorators as early as the 1890s offered suggestions about the latest fashions for accentuating personal expression. The impetus to fill up every room with "interesting and instructive" objects generated many shopping trips. Only the commodious and relatively open kitchen in the back of the house confined itself to a certain straightforwardness.

The turn of the century saw a reaction against this vision of domesticity, prompted in part by women's demands for a life outside their homes as well as by new architectural styles. Simplicity and efficiency became the key words for housing: facades and interior spaces were pared down and regularized, walls were stripped to smooth surfaces, and unnecessary bric-a-brac was removed. The bungalow was the most widely used term for the smaller, economical dwelling of the time. The informality of its open plan often provided for dining only in an area off the living room or a built-in nook in the kitchen; these responded well to families that spent less time together. Houses often appeared in planned clusters of almost identical dwellings, sometimes grouped around an off-street common court.

The tendency toward simplification and uniformity intensified in these early years of the twentieth century, when a new generation of home economists promoted the concept of the "scientific"

dwelling, as rationally planned and efficient as a laboratory, especially in the kitchen. Feminists lauded the new trend, believing that this kind of environment could give women more time for themselves. Conservatives praised it as well, convinced that the only way to preserve the family and the single-family home was to treat housewives as trained professionals in modern workplaces. Indeed, these uncluttered bungalows did require less time to keep clean, but the idea that the appearance of a house could by itself transform gender roles proved illusive.

We can see antecedents of the architecture and of the cultural conflicts associated with the progressive bungalow in the urban apartment hotels of the 1880s and 1890s. There upper middle-class families, as well as single professional women and men, had their private accommodations within a larger, technologically advanced, semipublic complex. Kitchens and servants' rooms, restaurants for entertaining, and lavish lobbies supplemented the compact rooms of the busy household. Many female residents praised the conveniences, but traditionalists worried about the implications of such amorphous privacy for the family ideal they wanted to protect.

The number of apartment buildings continued to rise, all the same, but by the early twentieth century they had come to be identified with a somewhat racy, unstable pattern of residency. As a consequence, apartments lowered property values in single-family residential neighborhoods, and residents there began efforts to prevent their construction.

The suburban housing boom during the 1920s truly celebrated the romantic, privatized ideal of home, family, and women's role. Emily Post and some decorators described a "sex psychology" approach to home decorating that exaggerated gender stereotypes. The frilly bedroom alluded to a sensuous femininity but, other than passing references to the dark-hued, leather-furnished den, decorators did not really seem to consider the home a province for men.

Few houses provided extra rooms, in any case, since new plumbing standards and higher construction costs kept sizes

quite small; cozy became a favorite description to make tight spaces seem pleasant. Historical allusions abounded on the facades of tiny Spanish haciendas, diminutive French chateaux, and Cotswold cottages topped with imitation thatch. Whatever the ostensible styles of their houses, many anxious suburbanites turned to the legal tactics of zoning and the restrictive covenant to prohibit nonresidential uses and families of minority backgrounds.

The focus on family closeness and neighborhood homogeneity became even more pronounced in the dramatic suburban expansion after World War II. The standardization that had hitherto been hidden behind various historical facades now came out into the open; thousands of identical dwellings went up simultaneously in new developments. To be sure, the ideal of personal expression through the home had become entrenched in American culture, and residents took great pains to redecorate and landscape their homes in individualized ways. Yet the real focus for many of these families now shifted to the back of the house, where large picture windows and sliding glass doors opened out onto a patio or a backyard with its barbecue. The themes of nature and familial privacy had been synthesized.

Convenience remained important, now embodied in built-in equipment and open floor plans, so that mothers could easily watch over their children while working in the kitchen. A new room suddenly emerged to serve this casual, child-centered world. The space was first called the don't-say-no room, then the multipurpose room, but when a 1947 *Parents' Magazine* model-house plan used the term *family room*, it was adopted generally to convey both the suburban ideal and day-to-day fun. Linoleum floors facilitated hobbies and teenage dancing, while comfortable furniture allowed easy television viewing. Both tract developers and architects celebrated this setting during the baby-boom era.

The burgeoning suburbs had a definite sociological profile that did not fit all Americans. That profile indicated younger residents, a high fertility rate, and fewer

working women than in the central cities. Yet the suburban home, more than ever before, came to be seen as the epitome of the "American dream." Television and advertising promoted this one-dimensional national image, as government agencies followed suit with highway building and tax credits for home mortgages, all designed to promote suburban homes for nuclear families.

Of course, other kinds of housing for other kinds of residents did appear in cities. Both the private market and public housing agencies erected high-rise apartment buildings with small, standardized units, although the amenities of public housing were constantly cut back by Congress. In both cases, it was assumed that families with children should move to the suburbs. That explained the sparse facilities and minimal dimensions of even many luxury units.

Today's housing choices often seem constrained in comparison with the comfortable domestic arrangements of previous generations. And the idealistic optimism that those generations projected about their home life is rare. Yet in many ways it is not so much the objects that are being called into question as a set of premises: the notion of a perfect fit between home and family, an image of the home environment as a cocoon that ensures harmonious family life, the suggestion that we all need the same kind of housing.

Without doubt, we now have more people who need decent homes—or any homes at all—than at any time since the 1930s. Perhaps that stark realization by itself can lead those of us who have some choices available to challenge the myth of an ideal home that reflects and reinforces an ideal image of the family. If we now acknowledge a diversity of family patterns, we also need to build, to reuse, and to demand many different kinds of homes.

Gwendolyn Wright is Director at the Temple Hoyne Buell Center for the Study of American Architecture at Columbia University and author of *Building the Dream: A Social History of Housing in America*.

Self-identity and the Home

The one reflects the other.

By Clare Cooper Marcus

"Home is where the heart is . . . home-town . . . homeboy . . . home cooking . . . homeroom . . . homebody . . . home run . . . home base . . . Make yourself at home . . ."

Our language is replete with allusions to home—that nurturing, secure place where our lives began, and where our thoughts sometimes return with nostalgic yearning. Whether it be our parental home, a treasured neighborhood or village, our country of birth, or our current apartment, "home" has a universal ring of safety, familiarity, and comfortableness, in contrast to the real or imagined alienation of the city, of foreign shores, or of an institutional setting.

Although home implies at the very least a roof over our head and shelter from the elements, its role in our lives is far more profound than that. For it is often the sole location where we can put down roots, mold our surroundings, furnish, decorate, and beautify a place as a reflection of who we are. Although self-identity is also expressed in the way we dress, in our occupations, the friends we keep, and the recreations we pursue, and although self-identity and social identity are closely interwoven, for most of us the dwelling remains the most significant—and perhaps the most accurate—mirror of who we are.

In childhood, home is inextricably bound up with parents, particularly mother. Here we learn to take our first steps, to explore the world with all our senses, and to play games—peek-a-boo, hide-and-seek—where we experiment with notions of separation and return. With little sense of who we are separate from parents and family, we play close to home and eye the world outside from the selective comfort of front porch, bedroom window, or treetop hideaway. We experiment with creating our own child-like homes—be they cubbies, dens, forts, or tree houses—learning our first lessons in seeking privacy and in molding a little corner of the world to suit our needs. Playing in a "house" of our own making, coming and going from the parental home, we start to experience those dialectic opposites that encapsulate the essence of home—inside-outside, familiar–strange, private–public, rest–movement.

With the onset of adolescence, marked changes occur in our relationship to the parental home, paralleling an emergent sense of self-identity and social identity. Posters are pinned up on bedroom walls, new fashions are tried out, loud music is played, and parental taste in everything from dress to home decor is called into question. The playroom or living room is abandoned in favor of the young person's bedroom, a home within a home, a place to experiment in private with new roles.

If this room is shared with a sibling, it may be a time for territorial rituals as each attempts to demarcate "my space." In other cultures, young people prove themselves through learning to hunt, taking on work assignments, or participating in initiation ceremonies; in this culture, the control and personalization of space is a significant rite of passage into adulthood.

In times gone by young adults in Western society would frequently stay at home until marriage; there was no transition place between parental home and home created with a partner. In modern times, the rented apartment, shared house, dorm room, or wandering lifestyle-with-backpack have become the norm for young and not-so-young adults. Dwellings available are usually mass-produced for a changing cast of residents. The student room or bland studio apartment becomes the backdrop for emerging environmental expressions of self-identity. Studies of satisfaction with student accommodations indicate that the more the residents are allowed to alter their rooms (paint, move furniture, put up pictures), and the more homelike the image of the building (low-rise, semi-private entries, lack of long corridors, materials locally associated with "home"), the more satisfied residents are with their accommodation, and the greater care they take of the environment.

At any stage in the life cycle, but particularly in adulthood, we invest meaning in a place when we are permitted to "appropriate" and care for it. Low-income residents of subsidized housing who have small yards added to ground-level dwellings are noticeably more interested in personalizing the environment and feel more inclined to care for the *shared* spaces (sidewalk, footpath, landscaping) just beyond their domain. Studies indicate that burglaries are actually less frequent in dwellings with cared-for yards.

Where people are *not* permitted to change or care for their home environments—through "hard" architecture, poverty, management regulations, and so on—an important avenue of self-awareness is closed. Indeed, in settings where individuality is deliberately downplayed to heighten the importance of the group or of higher motives—for example, in the military or in religious orders—it is noticeable that self-identity, via personal styles of clothing and the creation of a

"While we're at supper, Billy, you'd make Daddy and Mommy very happy if you'd remove your hat, your sunglasses, and your earring."

Drawing by Ziegler; © 1985, The New Yorker Magazine, Inc.

Photograph by Daisy Taylor.

Photograph by Lauren Taylor.

personal "home," is precluded.

The Shared Home

If and when an adult decides to *share* his/her living space with another—lover, partner, spouse, roommate—compromises have to be made regarding whose "self" gets translated into form. In earlier times, the stay-at-home wife/mother often made most decorating and furnishing decisions; a woman's self-identity was (seemingly) expressed via the home, her husband's via his work. With the evolution toward gender-equality, with the increasing movement of women into the work force and with the (not quite so apparent) increase in male involvement in housekeeping and child rearing, the home has become less of a woman's domain, more of a shared responsibility.

For many couples, the shared experience of house remodeling is a significant act of bonding, to each other and to the place. But for some, conflicting values previously masked by the gendered domains of home and work become painfully manifest. Architects working with private, house-seeking clients are well aware of the potential for conflict as couples, whose relationships may be shaky to begin with, seek to "stabilize" them via the design of a "dream house." For some, the conflicts of values—explicit in contrasting programs for the architect—can lead to separation and/or divorce. The subsequent division of the material symbols of home can be as traumatic as the divorce itself. Ironically, the condos and swinging-singles complexes that punctuate the urban landscape have become ideal "landing places" for recently separated spouses. Fully furnished apartments (sometimes with maid service) provide an instant "home," precluding the need, while in transition, to seek self-identity in the dwelling.

For others, too, in these mobile times, the "instant home" has become a reality. Developers have always advertised that they are selling "homes," when in fact they are dealing in houses. However, high-income corporate buyers in suburban California can now buy large houses that may, indeed, be perceived as "homes," for they are sold fully furnished down to sheets, pots, and serving spoons. The busy executive—whose self-identity may be entwined more with business, profession, and living in the right location than with the house per se—is willing to pay anonymous others to transform dwelling into "home."

Meanwhile, when on the road, he or she can choose to stay in a "home-hotel," where architectural form and interior decor render the boundary between "house" and "hotel" even more fuzzy. Thus, for some, the need to find self-identity in the home is becoming less critical, while the need to express self in the workplace, and perhaps, in office decor may be rising in importance.

Aging and Self-identity

As more research emerges on the psychological needs of elderly people, it becomes apparent that staying in the family home, surrounded by the memorabilia of a lifetime, is crucial to maintaining good health and a positive feeling of self-worth. When the environment in congregate housing is entirely devoid of messages that reflect back to a person, who he or she *is*, a critical component of self-identity is lost. As among students in congregate housing, elderly residents seem most satisfied the more they can personalize their environments through furnishing, decorating, gardening, and so on. Many residents in geriatric nursing homes are particularly upset by the non-homelike hospital atmosphere, and will frequently tell themselves (and relatives) that their stay is temporary until the treasured time that they can go "home again."

The last two decades have seen quiet but remarkable transformations of some institutions into more homelike settings. Old Victorian houses and other unwanted mansions have been successfully transformed into halfway houses for recovering alcoholics, runaway teenagers, or model prisoners. The key to having these settings experienced as homes is a subtle combination of exterior form, building materials, room sizes, relaxed management style, and the ability to modify and personalize one's own space. Places to give birth (alternative birth centers) and places to die with dignity (hospices) have similarly created more homelike settings in otherwise institutional medical environments.

Home can be a room or dwelling to which we return every day; it can also be a state of mind. To feel "at home" is to feel comfortable, at ease, relaxed, perhaps surrounded by those few who truly understand or care for us. To be homeless is not only to be deprived of basic shelter, it is to be stripped of any place in the world where one can truly feel "at home." For the wandering holy man, being at home in the world at large may be the ultimate experience of detachment. But for most of us less evolved beings, a permanent dwelling where we can put down roots is both a necessary component of physical security and a significant psychosocial expression of who we are.

Clare Cooper Marcus is Professor of Landscape Architecture at the University of California at Berkeley and author of *Housing As If People Mattered.*

Dreams and Visions

Cinderella Castle, Walt Disney World Magic Kingdom, Orlando, Florida, 1986. Copyright 1986, The Walt Disney Company.

The Royal Pavilion, Brighton, England; remodeled and expanded for the Prince Regent, later George IV; John Nash, architect, 1815–1821. Picture Library, Cooper-Hewitt Museum.

Neuschwanstein Castle, Bavaria, Germany; built for Ludwig II of Bavaria; Edward Riedel, Georg Dollmann, Julius Hofmann, architects; begun 1869–work ceased 1886. Picture Library, Cooper-Hewitt Museum.

The Pineapple, Stirlingshire, Scotland; built for the Earl of Dunmore; 1761. Courtesy British Tourist Authority.

Casa Milà, Barcelona, Spain; Antonio Gaudí, architect, 1906. Courtesy Càtedra Gaudí.

Das Hundertwasser Haus, Vienna, Austria; Friedensreich Hundertwasser, architect, 1983–85. Courtesy Joram Harel. Copyright Peter Dressler, Vienna.

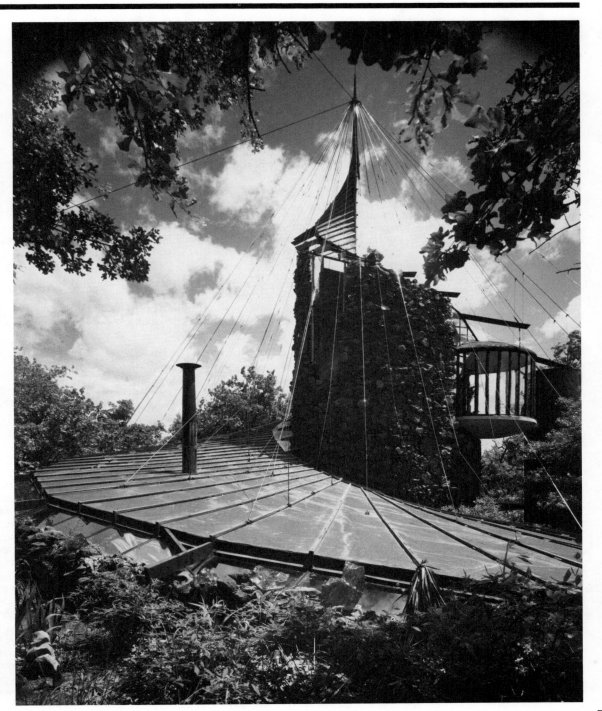

The Bavinger House, near Norman, Oklahoma; Bruce Goff, architect, 1950–55. © 1980, Julius Shulman.

Territoriality

By Elizabeth Mackintosh

"That's Daddy's chair and no one else can sit in it!" "This room belongs to Susan! Please knock!" "My place is the one with the purple shutters and the red geraniums in the window boxes." "Excuse me, are you looking for someone? I live here." "Those people have no business being in our building. I'm going to keep an eye on them and call my neighbor if I need to." "No trespassing—Playgrounds and Facilities for Exclusive Use of Residents and Registered Guests."

These are examples of "territoriality" in housing. We usually think of territoriality in terms of animals establishing or defending their territory: a colorful cardinal singing from the top of a tree; a huge elk locking horns with a challenger. But the concept of territoriality is increasingly helping psychologists, urban planners, architects, and housing managers to understand how people function in and around their homes. It is also helping them to design better apartments, housing complexes, and open spaces.

People exhibit territoriality when they define and control a particular space, when they lay claim to an area and defend it against intruders. Animals establish territories to regulate resources, to mate, to rear their young, and to maintain a hierarchy or organization within the species. For the most part, animal territorial behavior is biologically based, but it can vary with changing environmental conditions. Territoriality in humans is much more complex.

In addition to a biological need for a minimum amount of space, free from physical discomfort, people have social and cultural needs. They need a place that is secure from outside threats. They need privacy and intimacy, and a place where they can socialize and express their identities. The basic premise of territoriality is that, to the extent that people can control, use, modify, and personally mark a space, they will feel an attachment, commit-

ment, and responsibility for it. They will, therefore, take good care of it, defend it from outsiders, and enjoy it.

It is useful to look at housing territories on a hierarchy of levels ranging from private to public:

1. Private: used only by the residents, such as a home or a bedroom;

2. Semiprivate: used by a group of residents, such as space directly adjacent to a home—hallway, lobby, or communal open space;

3. Semipublic: used by residents and nonresidents, such as the sidewalk outside a house or an apartment building, the plaza or sitting area open to the public;

4. Public: used by the entire public.

The more private a space is, the more control a person has over it. Individual self-expression is greatest in private spaces. Such environments usually have the most importance for people and are defended more vigorously against intruders.

Territoriality in Private Spaces

The traditional and ultimate expression of territoriality in housing has been the ownership of a single-family house. One controls both the interior and exterior appearance and the access to outdoor and indoor space. However, as many other housing types become more common (row houses, high-rise apartment buildings, rentals, condominiums, and cooperatives), it is important that we understand how territoriality may be promoted in these other housing types so that residents' satisfaction is maximized, the housing is well taken care of, and vandalism and crime are held down to a minimum.

Transforming a house into a home creates a personal bond between the resi-

Drawing by H. Martin; © 1985, The New Yorker Magazine, Inc.

dent and the dwelling unit. As studies of rental housing units and student dormitories have demonstrated, allowing residents or students to personalize and modify their spaces leads to a commitment and better upkeep of the space. Participation in management decisions about the space has similar results. People feel more pride in their dwellings when they can make some changes—painting, adding shelving, or making a garden, for the exteriors of dwellings also can be individualized to promote residents' identification with their homes.

Within the home, households and families develop varying territorial systems and styles to facilitate their social functions. A study of lower middle-class families found two types: (1) families with firm boundaries, who closed doors frequently, were more formal, used dining rooms more often, and had less role-shar-

ing and interaction; and (2) families that left doors open more frequently, were informal, ate and entertained in the kitchen, and had more sharing and interaction among members.

Parents vary on how much freedom they will permit their children within the home. Generally, the higher the educational level of the parents, the fewer the restrictions placed on children's use of space within the home. In some cultures the living room is kept as the "best" room, is reserved for adult use and is off limits to child play. In contrast, other groups use the living room as a family room. Problems arise when homes do not match territorial needs or expectations: not enough bedrooms for everyone, no separate dining rooms or no family rooms.

Some approaches to solving territorial conflicts, as found in a study of families in moderate income multifamily housing, are: (a) people use different rooms for different activities at different times; (b) the dominant family members make others do the same activity; or (c) individuals cooperate by using headphones so that two different activities can take place in the same room.

In an effort to achieve territory for each family member, some middle-class families in two-bedroom apartments give the master bedroom to their two children and divide it in half with a partition. Houses and apartments with demountable partitions permit residents to have flexibility in space use and thereby satisfy changing territorial needs.

Semiprivate and Semipublic Spaces

The concept of territoriality has received the most attention as it relates to semiprivate and semipublic spaces. In 1972 Oscar Newman postulated that territorial definition, reinforced with surveillance opportunities, was the main ingredient of "defensible space"—an environment that is brought under the control of residents who defend it and deter crime. Areas that are "no man's land," where responsibility for the space is unclear and access cannot be easily controlled, do not foster territoriality and are therefore vulnerable to crime. Among such places are long hallways that are shared by many residents in high-rise buildings, buildings with multiple entrances that are easily accessible to nonresidents, and large outdoor spaces adjacent to apartment buildings that are not clearly associated with a particular building or group of buildings. Research has found that in buildings that are smaller and lower, residents have more to do with their neighbors; they question strangers more readily, take more responsibility for their buildings, and therefore experience less vandalism and crime than residents in larger and taller buildings do.

Territorial definition can be achieved in many different ways, varying from symbolic demarcation, such as painting row houses different colors, to "soft" barriers, such as low hedges or short fences, to

Public housing projects, Long Island City, New York, 1988. Phoebe Barnard.

"hard" barriers such as ten-foot high chain-link fences. Surveillance of space that enhances territorial control can be achieved by the location of windows, dwelling entrances, seating areas, activity centers (parking, playgrounds, laundry rooms), or pathways adjacent to a particular space. Less "natural" surveillance techniques are guards, doormen, and electronic equipment.

New zoning regulations, called the Quality Housing Program, which were approved unanimously in June 1987 by the New York City Planning Commission, include security and safety requirements based on the principles of territoriality. Under these regulations no more than fifteen dwelling units per corridor can be serviced by a common elevator and/or stair so that neighbor recognition is pro-

moted and strangers on a particular floor can be easily identified by residents. Open spaces must be fenced and visible from the public spaces within the building. Stairs and elevators should be visible from the street, and doors to dwelling units should be placed so they are visible from the elevators.

Social and cultural characteristics also influence residents' territorial behavior in semiprivate and semipublic spaces. A homogeneous group of residents will have fewer misunderstandings and conflicts over spaces than a more varied population. For example, sociologists contend that for working-class residents the boundary between the dwelling unit and the immediate environment is quite permeable, that is, social life occurs in a continuous flow between apartment and

street. In contrast, middle-class residents view their territory in less fluid terms, with firmer boundaries based on access. Anthropologists have observed that different cultures prefer different amounts of distance between people and that they have different expectations of their neighbors. People accustomed to close neighborly relations are surprised by those who do not seem as friendly and warm as expected, and they consider them cold. For Anglo-Saxons, Latins come too close when talking and the Anglo-Saxons draw back.

In large cities such as New York City, where land is scarce, competition for public open space is fierce, and the lack of affordable housing is a major problem, difficult political and urban-design decisions must be made that affect people's satisfaction of territorial needs. For example, housing complexes built in the 1940s, when land assemblage was relatively easy, are designed with large open spaces entirely for their residents' use. These fort-like complexes with outdoor spaces surrounded by buildings, permit no outsiders ("No Trespassing") and satisfy residents' territorial needs. On the other hand, newer housing complexes built in the 1970s have constructed ground-level outdoor space for the use of both residents and nonresidents in an "open" plan. Local workers, as well as people in nearby housing that has no facilities, enjoy such seating and play areas while residents complain about the invasions of their territory and restrict their own children's use of such spaces.

An awareness of people's territorial behavior is already helping us to regulate, manage, and design better housing. As population and housing trends bring about different housing forms and coping strategies, such as time-shares, temporary housing for the homeless, and doubling and tripling up in small apartments, we should apply the powerful concept of territoriality to improve these other environments.

Elizabeth Mackintosh is a Senior Planner and Housing Coordinator in the Queens Office of the New York City Planning Department.

Communal Amenities

They are an enticement to tenant action.

By Robert H. McNulty

Hard times are here for local housing agencies. From Maine to California, seventy thousand public housing units stand boarded up. One to two thousand more are demolished every year. In the meantime, federal subsidies for public housing have shrunk dramatically. For 1981, the budget allowed $30 billion for construction of such housing; by 1986, only $10 billion was allotted for all the cities in the nation. In New Jersey, the waiting list for housing is ten years long; whereas in New York City, the homeless numbered twenty-five thousand in 1986, almost twice the 1983 figure. The shortage is

made immeasurably worse by the problems that have always plagued public housing: the vandalism and crime that make maintenance continual uphill work, the pervading squalor that feeds on residents' frustration and despair.

As a palliative to the ills of public housing, tenant management has attracted recent notice. The concept of tenant management is not new. Early experiments, some before World War II, had shown that good things begin to happen when tenants take responsibility for their own housing. The sense of social control, of having some say in one's destiny, can

bring liberation from the numbing hopelessness that often accompanies poverty.

But what can act as an incentive to bring the housing residents together? If these people are able to organize, to form groups to improve their lives, why have they not already joined to combat the conditions in which they live?

Some attraction must be offered to make them want to work together. To bring them together—at least long enough for tenants' groups to form and to gain authority—some enticement must be held out to them. And this enticement must be considerable to overcome a long-standing passive acceptance of decaying shelters, where the criminal and the vandal are a common sight.

Amenities can serve as an important part of that enticement. In recent years, in many of the more striking cases when tenant management has had notable successes, tenants have joined together in the hope of adding—in addition to safety, health, and practical concerns—more spaciousness, more beauty, more grace to their everyday lives. These people in economic straits have chosen to join together to seek, among other benefits, the amenities that will enlarge the quality of their lives.

The name of Bertha Gilkey should be remembered as a pioneer. She began her work in the early 1970s in response to redevelopment plans for the decaying project in which she lived—Cochran Gardens. The thirteen ugly, box-like buildings situated on a bleak stretch of land near downtown St. Louis were slated for the wrecker's ball. Under Gilkey's prodding, a small group of tenants elected a tenant affairs council board, which agreed to work without salary. Gilkey then arranged for training in management, which was supplied by the housing authority. The Cochran Gardens Management Corporation (which still exists as a nonprofit private group) eventually worked as a 25

percent partner with the developers: Richard Baron, a former defense lawyer, and Will Thomas, a strong proponent of tenant participation. Suggestions for changes in living conditions in the Cochran development have always been brought forward by the tenants themselves. It is interesting that among the more prominent of the changes has been the provision of significant private outdoor spaces. These include individual spaces such as porches at doorways and stucco-walled balconies at windows. Such semiprivate spaces as a plaza park and a running track have also come into being. Another of their projects, intended to give children a "sense of place," involved installing scale models of the Cochran complex at a nearby elementary school.

Another group in the 1970s that deserves to be more widely known was the A. Harry Moore project, a complex of twelve-story buildings put up after World War II in Jersey City, New Jersey. By 1975, ten of the site's fourteen urine-drenched elevators were inoperable, the utility systems were deteriorating, and public areas were vandalized and debris-ridden. Of the twenty-three hundred tenants, 80 percent were children, in families headed mostly by single women, with 80 percent of the residents black and another 15 percent Hispanic.

Here, the impetus for change came from a grant from the National Endowment for the Arts. The grant had been solicited by Robert Rigby, the executive director of the Jersey City Housing Authority. His specific purpose was to start a tenants' group that would improve living conditions in the buildings. Rigby began with a door-to-door search for volunteers for a project-wide tenants' council. This council then drove a bargain with the housing authorities: the stairwells, doors, mailboxes, and lobby walls would all be repaired in a sample building to see

West Broadway Renewal, South Boston, Massachusetts, 1986. Courtesy Goody, Clancy & Associates. Clemens Kalischer.

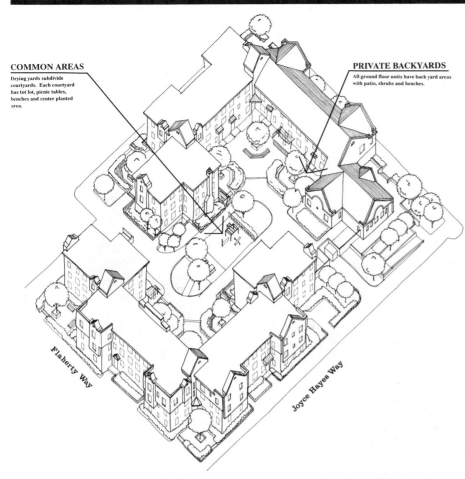

COMMON AREAS
Drying yards subdivide courtyards. Each courtyard has tot lot, picnic tables, benches and center planted area.

PRIVATE BACKYARDS
All ground floor units have back yard areas with patio, shrubs and benches.

Flaherty Way

Joyce Hayes Way

Lafayette Gardens, Jersey City, New Jersey, 1987. Housing Authority of the City of Jersey City.

whether the tenants' group could prevent vandalism and maintain the improvements. Not only did the tenants do so, but, in addition, they protected the new murals that members of their group created on the formerly graffiti-ridden plaster walls of the public areas.

Rigby, commenting on this, said, "Given half a chance, and a bit of support, housing for poor persons—even high-rise, high-density housing—can be not only decent, safe, and sanitary, but, more important, can generate a functional sense of community that resounds with the difference between surviving and living."

Another success story that involved public art also happened in Jersey City. The five-hundred-unit Lafayette Gardens, a 1941 project that is the oldest public-housing site in the city, was renovated with the help of a tenants' group in 1985. In this enterprise, an award-winning sculptor, Melvin Edwards, was brought in to install a playful metal sculpture in a small plaza in front of the building. In the somewhat featureless surroundings of the site, the sculpture acts as a "place-maker" and has brought a sense of local pride to public housing authorities who, in this case, have been the patrons of the

work of art.

Another interesting case is that of the West Broadway Task Force in South Boston. This group is one of the strongest tenants' groups in Massachusetts. Like others mentioned here, the West Broadway Task Force has formed a partnership with the authorities, being an equal party to a design contract with the Boston Housing Authority and the Commonwealth of Massachusetts. The "amenity" was the creation of a people-scaled neighborhood. The original planning of the site had featured four giant super-blocks, each with twenty-seven identical three-story walkups. The effect was dreary and inhuman; nothing about the vista gave the residents a sense of home. The depressing superblocks were broken up by taking down the most deteriorated buildings, and, in the new layout, four "urban villages" were formed. The prevailing street grid and block pattern of the surrounding neighborhood was re-established on the site, thereby blending the development into the overall plan of its nonpublic housing neighbors. This project was a joint venture carried through by Lane, Frenchman and Associates, of Boston, with Goody, Clancy & Associates. The firms solicited ideas from the tenants' group and determined preferences for trees, play areas, and other amenities. The residents also wanted private spaces outdoors: front and back porches, rear courtyards, and other private and semiprivate areas where traffic was banned. One of the improvements most enjoyed by the tenants was a new main street, which not only gave focus to the new neighborhood but was the site of expanded community facilities.

In Washington, D.C., the Kenilworth tenants' group has emphasized amenities that have created jobs for the residents. In this case, tenants wanted a health center, a day-care center, a food cooperative, and a maintenance shop. These mandated an employment office as well; and now thirty-one residents of the development are fully employed in running and staffing a range of on-site services that are geared to self-improvement. The success of the venture is striking: in 1982, 76 percent of the occupants were on wel-

fare, whereas in late 1986, only 26 percent were supported by public assistance. This economic gain has come from a rising quality of life. (This is the factor that Partners for Livable Places has termed "the Economics of Amenity".)

These projects in which tenant councils have successfully enriched the lives of residents are the more pertinent now because of the current groundswell for tenant management. The concept is fast gaining adherents in the private as well as in the public sector. In 1985, for example, the Amoco Corporation, with the help of the Ford Foundation, awarded a grant to the National Center for Neighborhood Enterprise to bolster tenants' groups in fifteen cities (including an Indian housing authority in Utah). In June 1986, the House of Representatives, by a margin of 419 to 1, passed legislation that provides $1.5 million in technical aid to fifteen tenants' groups. The bipartisan appeal of the idea is hardly surprising given the conservative mood of the country, and the present pressure against government hand holding.

This does not mean that tenant management can be a panacea for all the troubles of public housing. Neither this nor any other solution will fit all cases. Among the obstacles to tenant management is the frequent inability of tenants to organize, and the resistance of many housing authorities. As Robert Rigby has said, "It's not for everyone, everywhere."

In the situations where tenants are able to organize for their own good, however, it is interesting to note what factors they want. They choose practical matters: they choose security, physical safety, health. But they also look for factors that lie beyond the force of necessity. Tenant management councils insist—often from the very start—on open spaces, public art, trees, plazas, and public facilities such as day-care centers and markets. They insist on quality-of-life factors. They choose amenities.

Robert H. McNulty is founder and President of Partners for Livable Places in Washington, D.C. The nonprofit organization works to advance the economic and social resources of design and planning to improve communities.

The Neighborhood

It gives warmth to the urban experience.

By August Heckscher

That neighborhoods exist within the great metropolis is in itself a somewhat surprising idea. It not only goes against the evidence of our eyes—the sight of endless and largely undifferentiated areas of streets and housing—but also against the values of many city dwellers. They seek not the friendliness and support of the village but the freedom, the anonymity, the absence of close ties that have always been associated with city living.

Nevertheless, urban planners have long used the neighborhood as a guiding ideal. At the turn of the century they conceived it as a bounded area, free of through traffic, consisting of a citizenry more or less homogeneous in income level, ethnic background, and economic and cultural interests. More recently they have defined the neighborhood in looser and less categorized terms.

Conforming to what the average citizen perceives and feels, planners have continued to recognize neighborhoods as building blocks in the urban structure, but have described them in ways that blur the village metaphor. No longer set apart and necessarily homogeneous, neighborhoods are now conceived as entities that for different reasons and in various ways endow those who live there with a sense of common interest. The unifying factor may be something as relatively amorphous as a historical name or a tradition inherited from an earlier generation. It may be an architectural style, a transportation facility, an isolation enforced by topography. Usually economic and ethnic affinities play a part, but they are not by any means the sole determinants. Indeed the very fact that people of differing backgrounds must talk and argue together in arriving at solutions to local problems may be in itself a powerful bonding element.

The sense of neighborhood is nurtured within communities having a record of stability, but more often the pressures of change are what bring people together. In developing a parapolitical system of defense they not only resist invaders of various kinds but grow closer together. Thus in today's urban neighborhood (at least outside a single dwelling or a block) social contacts are not the primary consideration. Such contacts may be as wide as the city itself and as varied as all the facets of its population. What is valued is the consciousness that in working together the neighbors may preserve a habitable environment from massive development by outsiders or from the destabilizing effects of sudden incursions by new groups.

•

Viewed in these terms, the neighborhoods of a city like New York repre-

View along Lee Avenue, Williamsburg, Brooklyn, New York. Jack Manning / New York Times Pictures.

sent a lively and constantly shifting panorama. They range from those with literary and artistic traditions (like Greenwich Village or Soho) to those of long-standing ethnic character (like Harlem or Howard Beach); they include areas marked by economic factors—prevailing poverty or prevailing wealth—and those identified by a similar housing stock, like areas of brownstones in Brooklyn or of art deco apartment buildings in the Bronx. Some of these neighborhoods appear to be improving, others to be declining. The

and frightened middle-class into the shelter of Co-op City), a scene of devastation was left—to be restored gradually by newcomers moving in to benefit from the physical advantages that first gave the area its distinction.

Gentrification is the word commonly applied to this process of economic renewal. It is a misnomer except in those cases where large-scale developers endeavor to transform at a stroke the nature and composition of a community. Elsewhere it is not the "gentry"—if such a

neighborhoods other than the traditional Chinatown; Indians and Pakistanis are moving into Flushing as Greeks have moved into Astoria, while Brighton Beach is no longer the same neighborhood in which Neil Simon grew up but an enclave of Russian émigrés. It is impossible in talking of such neighborhoods as these to use the word decline, though the evidence of change is undeniable.

Neighborhood-watchers become expert in detecting small signs of how the local winds are blowing. Professor Louis Winnick, of the New School for Social Research, is embarking on major research in this area. For him, he tells me, the telephone book can reveal an unexpected number of names characteristic of a certain nationality. Storefronts are particularly sensitive indices. Being free of rent control, they reflect the emerging market, so that the cost of nearby apartments will scarcely have begun to rise before everyday services show signs of giving way to the satisfaction of more exotic and more expensive desires.

The open spaces of the neighborhood tell their own story. Here the inward life of the local population is revealed to the passerby. The degree of community spirit and organization is apparent. Indeed the small park is often seen as being in itself not only the symbol of an improving neighborhood but the fulcrum by which the whole burden of local shortcomings is lifted.

As park commissioner in the late 1960s I was subject to the pressures of local groups who were convinced that neighborhood revival could be assured by the redesign and reconstruction of its most prominent playground. But instead, it turned out that these parks and playgrounds were still invaded by vandals and disfigured by graffiti, in proportion to the degree of deterioration in the surrounding neighborhood—its housing, its streets, its schools and services. It would have been comforting had a new park by itself been able to turn the tide of decay; at best it was one tool in achieving a large goal.

Another tool has been historic preservation. The pride that people develop in their older buildings, their wish to save them at all costs, is part of a natural im-

East 93rd Street, between Fifth and Madison Avenues, New York, 1988. Phoebe Barnard.

pulse to upgrade the environment. This is true even when the buildings have little enough to do with significant past events, or have little in the way of unique architectural merit.

•

The good city is distinguished in the end by the way in which it satisfies both the citizen's craving for the excitement of metropolis and also the desire for the neighborliness of a small community. It is well governed when the politics of the community meeting and the local planning board are at least as lively as the politics of city hall. The neighborhood—hard as it is to define and erratic as its course sometimes appears—remains an essential ingredient of the urban experience, the one that gives life much of its humanity and warmth.

August Heckscher, former Park Commissioner of New York City, is Chairman of the East Side Neighborhood group CIVITAS and author of *Open-Spaces-The Life of American Cities*, a Twentieth-Century Fund Study.

Mott Street, Chinatown, New York City. New York Convention and Visitors Bureau.

main fact about virtually all of them is that they are in the midst of change. As the city grows and alters they retain their sense of apartness and yet continuously assume a new status and character.

The process of change can produce dismaying results. There is, as Adam Smith said, a great deal of ruin in any nation; and this is certainly true of the modern city. Neighborhoods on the West Side of Manhattan—once highly developed with magnificent housing, noble institutions, and open spaces—have only now revived after a long decline. The Grand Concourse in the Bronx is a more recent example of an area that has decayed before our eyes. Its revival is far less evident, yet here, too, signs of upgrading can be discerned. As groups moved out (in this case the harried

group exists at all in this country—that take over, but a mixture of the wealthy and less wealthy, of new citizens and the more established, of yuppies and senior citizens. The search for less expensive housing draws divergent groups, and the mix creates a new neighborhood in the footprints of the old.

A change sometimes perceived as beneficial and sometimes as destabilizing is provided by the waves of new immigrants arriving year by year. Since 1965, when the United States liberalized its immigration laws as many as one hundred thousand immigrants have been coming into New York City annually (we do not know precisely how many of these remain), and their effects can be seen in many areas. Asians are now settling in

Revolution in Urban Development

Will the old city disappear?

By Melvin M. Webber

Cities have traditionally concentrated around the spot where the original town settlers first built their homes and shops. In the future, they are likely instead to be geographically dispersed across the countryside.

In the early days, most merchants and industrialists tried hard to locate close to the spot of initial settlement, the town center. The concentration of interdependent firms made them accessible to each other and to their suppliers and the customers they depended on. Each succeeding generation of families also tried hard to locate their homes close to the town center. Because most jobs were concentrated there, they had access to many job opportunities, and they could limit the time and cost of getting to work.

With everyone seeking to locate in the center of town, competition for building sites there pushed land prices there persistently higher; and high land prices compelled high densities and then high-rise buildings. Despite Americans' traditional preference for single-family houses on the ground, few center-city dwellers have had that option. For most people living near the cores of the biggest cities, the only viable choice has been multiple-family dwellings of one type or another.

Even though families tried to locate near the center of town and were willing to accept some degree of crowding, the expanding urban populations inevitably meant that most people would nevertheless live at considerable distances from the center. Indeed, every town and city has been suburbanizing ever since it was settled, growing ever outward to accommodate more and more inhabitants.

For most American cities in the eighteenth and nineteenth centuries expansion was slow, limited by the speed of available transportation systems—walking for most, horse-drawn vehicles for some. Later, faster electric trolleys permitted people to live farther away and still get to work on time, but not very far away. When automobiles became available in large numbers in the 1920s, new suburban settlements quickly surrounded the old cities. Then it became possible to get to work in the center within a half-hour, even if one lived twenty miles out. During recent decades a series of dramatic technological and institutional changes have coalesced to accelerate that expansion—to trigger a virtual explosion of urban settlements, dispersing their parts into what we used to call the hinterland. These changes are:

1. The conduct of business and industry has been changing. Expanding managerial activities, information-processing, and specialized professional services have combined to displace mills and factories with offices as the primary places of work. Now, somewhere between half and two-thirds of all employed persons work in offices. Some of them are involved in managerial and other professional roles that require skilled judgment and frequent intercourse with other specialized persons. However, the vast majority today are engaged in routine paper-handling or computer-processing activities that resemble routine production activities long associated with factory work.

2. Manufacturing has been declining—from a third of all jobs in the United States at the end of World War II to less than a quarter today. Moreover, many industries that survive are largely freed from sites adjacent to sources of raw materials. Today, many manufacturers are more dependent on specialized knowledge than on ore and coal. Virtually footloose, a growing number of factories are able to follow their workers to wherever the workers prefer to live—an absolute reversal from early industrial patterns.

3. Women have been going to work in ever-increasing numbers. Well over half the nation's women are working or seeking work. Nearly two-thirds of married women between the ages of twenty-five and forty-four and living with their husbands are in the labor force. (Twenty-five years ago only a third of them were.) Moreover, nearly two-thirds of married women living in conventional nuclear families, with husbands and children aged six to seventeen, are now in the labor force.

4. Automobiles, airplanes, telephones, and now communication satellites and computer networks have made nearly

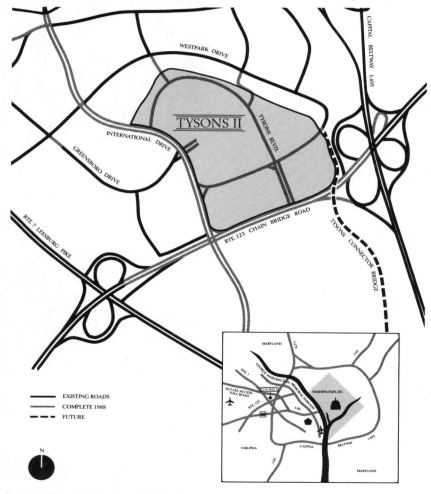

EXISTING ROADS
COMPLETE 1988
FUTURE

N

Tysons II, McClean, Virginia; Homart Development Company and Lerner Enterprises, 1988.

everywhere immediately accessible to everywhere else, thus vitiating many locational advantages that once attached to certain cities and to certain city centers.

Any one of these changes would have been enough to generate a revolution in urban development. Together, they are making for new kinds of cities without precedent.

The early suburbs were largely made of houses and related consumer retail and service establishments. Suburbanization of residences is no doubt a direct expression of the American family's preferences for space and amiable environments for child rearing, further encouraged by rising rents and degrading environments in the city centers. Federal Housing Authority financial incentives and the mobility fostered by the highway-building program made home ownership both attractive and prudent in those new single-family housing developments. Retail outlets and consumer services immediately followed the consumers to the suburbs, thereby helping to assure decent living arrangements at the city's edge. But still, large proportions of suburbanites had to commute long distances to the central business districts.

In years during and after World War II, the suburbs became home for numerous factories as well. Changes in production processes called for single-story factory floors spread over large areas, and large cities could be found only well outside the built-up, high-density districts. Besides, since most suburbanites came to work by car, employers had to provide extensive parking areas, themselves calling for large sites, preferably at low cost, and so, necessarily, far out of town.

All this occurred while corporations and business-service firms continued to cling to the city centers, creating that most visible urban symbol of the century—the high rise skyline. In the 1950s and 1960s, a few bold firms did move their headquarter offices to places such as Westchester County, but they were exceptions—at most, portents of things to come.

In recent times, however, a great many companies have become aware of the four fundamental changes that have unobtrusively been evolving over the decades, slowly accumulating force enough to provoke a virtual revolution in their industries:

1. The mass-production workplace has gradually been shifting from the factory to the office.

2. Knowledge has been replacing bulk commodities as the raw material for many industries, especially the new ones.

3. Suburban districts have been amassing a huge untapped resource—an unexploited labor pool of underemployed women.

4. Automobiles, telephones, and computer networks have freed offices from their tether to central business districts, making them as footloose as modern factories.

Those discoveries unleashed a cadre of land developers who are now building gigantic office complexes on previously vacant land at the metropolitan edge and beyond. Tens of thousands of office jobs are being relocated out of central cities to these sites. Two, east of San Francisco, are projecting thirty thousand jobs by 1990. Tysons Corner, outside Washington, D.C., already holds twenty-five thousand jobs. Throughout the country, office buildings surrounded by extensive parking areas are sprouting near the single-family housing projects that supply workers to them. Although less visible than the skyscrapers downtown, these office parks are fast becoming successors to the high-rise central business districts, and the mark of the future city. More to the point, by moving jobs out where the job holders live, they may be signaling the dissolution of the last force that has been holding the traditional city in place.

That is the big city news for the 1990s. The glue that has held cities together throughout human history is being dissolved. Even when tens of millions of people were gathered into the large metropolitan areas, they have always been compelled to cluster around the city center; even the extensive suburbs have had to wrap around the old city and within commuting distance of it. But that requirement is fast disappearing.

Especially in the new cities of the West and South, the compounding effects of these four trends are permitting a scale of spatial dispersion that was never before possible. With real-time accessibility permitted by the new transportation, by telecommunications, and by computer technologies, even the most specialized corporate executives are free to abandon the high-rise city center in favor of the countryside where many of them prefer to live. Their employees, both male and female, need no longer suffer the discomforts and costs of the long commute into the city center. They too can live and work in the exurbs. Given the average American's manifest preferences for a single-family house cum garden, it seems reasonable to expect that the long-term centrifugal move away from the old city center will accelerate, now that office jobs also are leaving.

The signs of the new urban patterns are everywhere. Resident populations in old center cities in the East have been falling for three decades, while populations in small and middle-size settlements well outside the old commuting range, even in such seemingly nonurban places as Vermont, the Rocky Mountains, the desert of the Southwest, and the foothills of the Sierra Nevada range have been expanding. Equally striking, many of the migrant companies are engaged in highly specialized activities, just the sorts that require intimate contact with suppliers of diverse business and technical services. They have been able to locate far away from the old-style cities precisely because their employees want to live in those outlying places and because they can stay intimately connected to suppliers and customers through the now-ubiquitous transportation and communication links.

Do these signs suggest that the old cities will disappear? Not in the near future, of course. There is far too much investment in buildings, institutions, and public infrastructure for the old cities to be abandoned. But the incremental growth is likely to be very largely outside, and at much greater distances than ever in the past. Hence, the recent construction boom in central cities is likely soon to end. Tremendous oversupply of office space in some cities (Houston especially) has already put a stop to construction there, and others are fast exceeding their markets, too.

In place of the old city, we can expect to see a wide array of new settlement types, developed at low densities, mixing high-rise and low-rise buildings in environmentally amiable settings, readily accessible to recreational areas and having desirable climates, typically in scattered locales with a relatively small population in each. Residents will no doubt continue to demand high-quality educational, health, and other urban services of the older cities and the older suburbs; but these, too, will no longer depend on high density and close physical proximity. They depend on good environment and fiscal adequacy, however; and the simultaneous migration of employers and employees should help to assure adequate local tax revenues and hence mutual support.

And so it seems that the age of the high-density cities may be coming to an end, to be succeeded by a diverse and dispersed pattern of settlement. Can it be stopped? Probably not. The engines propelling it are driven by powerful forces that are outside the control of anyone. Does it portend a loss of the cultural richness long associated with the city and city life? Probably not. The new-found capabilities for travel and communication permit even the most dispersed populations to be closely connected and to enjoy the intellectual and material produce of the society. Indeed, compared to many living in the midst of the old urban centers, exurbanites must surely enjoy far greater opportunities, suggesting that spatial patterns of cities do not determine the important qualities of peoples' lives. But whether the emerging new cities are to be condoned or condemned—well, perhaps, it's just too early to tell.

Melvin M. Webber is Professor at the Institute of Urban and Regional Development of the University of California at Berkeley.

Cityscapes

La Promenade des Anglais, la Baie des Angès,
Nice, France. Editions S.E.P.T.

Paris, France.

Fifth Avenue, New York City.

Causeway Bay Typhoon Shelter, Hong Kong. The Lux Company.

Amsterdam. © J.G. van Aqtmaal.

The Market in Campo dè Fiori's Square, Rome, Italy, Edzion: Ragoli.

Grand Canal, Cà d'Oro, Venice, Italy. Picture Library, Cooper-Hewitt Museum.

Basel, Switzerland. Franco-Suisse Editions.

Planned Communities

By Robert A.M. Stern

The story of American urbanism, like that of American architecture, is the story of beginning anew. The vastness of the continent has from the first opened the possibility of continual change: if one place grows old or dull, we can get away, hit the road, begin again. But while a healthy dose of wanderlust has helped to define our national character, the dream of creating new, more perfect places to live in has often not been left to chance but rather to a disciplined, predetermined, carefully articulated plan. This has been particularly true in regard to the suburb, which is a fundamental reflection of the American search for an ideal community in nature, set within arm's length of the city—a *rus in urbe*. Ironically, these planned suburbs have for the most part employed naturalistic plans and vernacular architecture to create the illusion of country villages set in picture-perfect landscapes, all calculated to convey a sense of an organically integrated natural and man-made history developed over time.

In 1853 Llewellyn Haskell, a friend of the architect Alexander Jackson Davis and an ardent supporter of proposals to create Central Park, established Llewellyn Park, a residential enclave in West Orange, New Jersey, that crystallized the ideals of the planned suburb. At the core of the development ran a fifty-acre linear strip of common parkland known as the Ramble, which served as the community's spine. A road called the Park Way—the first use ever of this term—ran along one side of the Ramble; other streets branched out to the house sites, which were laid out in a largely unmanicured landscape that flew in the face of conventional mid-Victorian practice. Covenants not only protected the Ramble but also, to help preserve the area's pastoral character, stipulated that no house be on less than one acre.

The absence of any commercial facilities and the nearly two miles from its

Forest Hills Garden, Queens, New York; Grosvenor Atterbury, architect 1912. Picture Library, Cooper-Hewitt Museum.

entrance to the nearest railroad station prevented Llewellyn Park from functioning as a fully developed planned suburb, a distinction that belongs first to Frederick Law Olmsted and Calvert Vaux's Riverside, Illinois (1869). As in the case of their design for Central Park, Olmsted and Vaux's town plan of 1869 was both idealistic and practical. Olmsted thought that the gridiron plan, though sensible from the point of view of real estate development, too much suggested the city rather than the country village. In a brilliantly pragmatic move—one that became a standard of suburban planning—he modified the grid by curving it, thereby providing both easily divisible real estate and the illusion of a naturally evolved rural settlement pattern. Olmsted then took his

pragmatism one step further, turning the site's principal deficit into an incomparable advantage by transforming the useless flood plains of the Des Plaines River into parkland. Olmsted also designed a landscaped roadway, with separate lanes for pleasure and commercial vehicles, to connect Riverside to Chicago. Olmsted called this road, which was unfortunately never built, the "park way," a term he may have picked up from Llewellyn Park.

Riverside was not just a residential enclave, but included shops, schools, and a town hall. Yet it was an evocation rather than a bread-and-butter realization of an autonomous community, for none of its inhabitants did any of their useful work there. A dream town without an economy, Riverside was a village that could

never have actually existed in the past. As both a practically laid out, independent village and a brilliantly designed stage set for enacting the Good Life in industrial America, Riverside set the standard for future suburbs.

The concept of the railway suburb was initiated at Riverside; it reached its design apogee nine miles from Manhattan, at Forest Hills Gardens, which was begun in 1909. The community's developer, the Russell Sage Foundation, hired the Olmsted Brothers as planners and Grosvenor Atterbury as architect. The foundation intended Forest Hills Gardens to be a suburban village for wage earners that would not only satisfy the needs of its inhabitants but serve as a paradigm for future similar ventures elsewhere. But, like its

English prototype, the Hampstead Garden Suburb outside London, Forest Hills Gardens was an aesthetic triumph but a failure at social reform: the proximity to central London in the one case and to Manhattan in the other rendered the property values too high. Almost as soon as the developments commenced, they became upper middle-class preserves.

Forest Hills Gardens' railroad station was designed by Atterbury as the gateway to the community. Homebound commuters arrived at Station Square, a brick plaza bordered on one side by the railroad embankment and on the other three sides by continuous arcaded buildings that housed apartments, shops, and the Forest Hills Inn, whose tower dominated the square and provided a visual focus for the community. Beyond Station Square, houses were laid out along streets arranged in a modified grid that incorporated long curving avenues. Forest Hills Gardens was an idealized metropolis in miniature; passing through the suburb from Station Square to Forest Park at the community's edge suggested a metaphoric journey from town to country.

The planned suburb constitutes one of the most significant contributions to American urbanism as it serves to make real our most extravagant and lyrical fantasies. But in even the most lovingly crafted suburb, the pressures of the workaday world create compromises. Resort villages, unfettered by many of the practical considerations of daily life, constitute some of our most perfectly crafted, architecturally consistent planned communities while rendering the dream landscapes of mountaintop and seaside into easily inhabited arcadias. Ever since industrialization provided Americans with sufficient prosperity and leisure time to travel, they have taken the suburb with them on vacation.

One of the most thoroughly planned suburbs designed to accommodate leisure-time activities was Tuxedo Park. In 1885, Pierre Lorillard III, finding himself unexpectedly excluded from the list of the Four Hundred socially elect, fled the established summer resort of the group, Newport, Rhode Island, to create his own

exclusive but informal resort suburb located in the Ramapo Mountains, only forty minutes by train from New York City. Not exactly a screaming populist, Lorillard developed Tuxedo for two hundred families, described by one observer as "a guide to Who is especially Who in the Four Hundred," as Cleveland Amory relates in *The Last Resorts*. Lorillard succeeded in establishing his planned community as the cutting edge of snobbery. The laws of American etiquette were laid down there by Emily Price Post, a resident of Tuxedo and the daughter of its principal architect, Bruce Price. Even the style of the short dinner jacket without tails that was introduced by Lorillard's son has come to be adopted everywhere, bearing the name of Lorillard's retreat.

To underscore the informality of his natural retreat, Lorillard, with the assistance of James Smith Haring and Ernest W. Bowditch, devised a scheme that incorporated a network of looping roads related to the land's natural contours. The

architecture at Tuxedo Park was, like the plan, intended to harmonize with the site and was modest in scale and character. A stone lodge and gatehouse opposite the town's railroad station were designed by Price. Price's houses, intended primarily for young, rich couples, were small and designed to harmonize with the surrounding landscape; the cottages were constructed of rough-hewn stone, brick, and wood shingles stained varying shades of russets and grays.

In our time planned communities have largely given way to the ubiquitous spread of land subdivisions—an oozing "slurbia"—and lifeless "condo villages" that possess few, if any, traditional town facilities. Living in such a development one could, like being in a fast-food restaurant, be *anywhere*.

In the late 1970s one developer sought to build a resort community that would be architecturally and urbanistically richer than the sprawling condos that litter Florida's landscape. Robert Davis owned

eighty acres of land on the Florida panhandle fronting the Gulf of Mexico. The site was just about the right size for a profitable condominium development, but it was also right for a small town. Davis chose the latter, calling his town Seaside. He has worked with two young architect-planners, Andres Duany and Elizabeth Plater-Zyberk, to establish a coherent sense of place, devising a master plan and zoning code that were completed in 1983; the town that they project will be substantially built within ten to fifteen years.

A town center, with shops, offices, workshops, and a conference center that doubles as a town hall, will focus on two connected public squares. Streets, ranging from wide tree-lined avenues to narrow alleys, are laid out in a modified grid. A principal street, lined with large lots radiating out from the town center to the tennis club at the edge of the development, is zoned for a mix of private houses, small apartment buildings, and inns.

After conducting a study of small southern towns, the planners concluded that a vital and authentic town character could not be established by a single architect. Private buildings are commissioned by individual citizen-buyers but are subject to the building code, which encourages, and in some cases requires, the inclusion of elements of regional architecture, such as front porches, white picket fences, painted wood siding, and roofs made of wood shingles or metal and sloped at a specified low angle.

Seaside's slogan is "A New Town. The Old Ways." Although the houses may evoke memories of simple summertime life before air-conditioning, condos, and time-sharing plans, Seaside is not a nostalgic pipe dream. It is a very real attempt to realize the full potential of the suburban dream by reconnecting late-twentieth-century Americans with their own great traditions of urbanism.

The Sward House, Seaside, Florida; Deborah Berke and Associates, architects, 1985; photograph by Steven Brooks.

Robert A.M. Stern, a practicing architect and a Professor at Columbia University, has dedicated much of his career to housing. His books include *The Anglo-American Suburb*, *Pride of Place*, and *New York 1930*.

Retirement Havens

By Peter A. Dickinson

With increased leisure or retirement time, home can become a recreation and entertainment center, an office and convalescent ward. In determining housing needs and desires, how one is old is more important than how old one is.

For instance: if the housing desired is for active retirement living, it should allow activities to be enjoyed inside and out. The structure should be as trouble-free as possible, attractive and roomy enough to entertain business and social friends. For such uses the following might be considered: detached housing, retirement hotels and clubs, shared housing, adult communities, mobile homes or "granny flats."

If more privacy is desired, housing might be a snug harbor to which one can retreat and relax in security, and where one can read, watch television, work on hobbies, listen to music, and rest without being bothered. There, one would need adequate lighting, furniture, and household equipment for protection and comfort. Such requirements might be provided for in apartment houses, town houses, co-ops, condominiums, or congregate housing.

If convalescence is a possibility, since accidents and illnesses happen at any age and stage of living, housing may have to include the provision of medical attention. Often the choice between remaining at home or moving to a hospital or nursing home depends on whether one's housing is adequate for convalescent needs. For this requirement one can consider multi-type high rises or life-care residences.

One point is certain: Whatever one's housing needs today, they will change tomorrow, when children leave home, when there is a death in the family, when the breadwinner changes jobs or retires. So one must keep an open mind about housing and think of needs when and if there is a change. It is not where one lives but how one lives that dictates housing needs and desires.

What to Look for in Retirement Housing

In terms of general layout, housing should include the following features:

- All rooms on one floor. No thresholds or walking hazards.

- Doors and halls wide enough to accommodate wheelchairs.

- Lighting. Perhaps three times as much lighting as for younger families, including good lighting in all hallways, near stairs, and in dark places.

- Nonslip surfaces. Unglazed ceramic tile or unwaxed vinyl in kitchen, bathroom, or near other hazardous areas.

- Railings and supports. Handrails by any stairs or inclines, grab rails or supports in bathroom, kitchen, or near other hazardous areas.

- Heating and cooling. Central heating and cooling to ensure seventy to seventy-five degrees Fahrenheit in each room.

- Sound control. Some provision to muffle outside noises and to enhance indoor acoustics.

- Safety and alarm devices. Smoke detectors, burglar alarms, medical emergency calling systems, telephone reassurance.

In short, housing should be suitable for comfortable living when one is either healthy or sick.

Room-by-Room Requirements

- Bedrooms. There should be one or more bedrooms, or a sleeping alcove, to allow privacy and to permit sick care. There should be enough room around the bed so that it can be made up easily, and there should be a direct line, with no obstacles, between the bedroom and bathroom.

- Bathrooms. Doors should be wide enough and bathroom fixtures arranged so as to accommodate a wheelchair. There should be grab bars or strong rails to help when getting in and out of the bathtub. All fixtures should be strong enough for support.

- Kitchens. This room should be large enough and pleasant enough to eat in. Within the work area, the best arrangement is a continuous flow from refrigerator to sink counter to range to serving area. Cupboards should not be over sixty-three inches from the floor, and storage bins twenty-seven inches, in order to eliminate excessive reaching and stooping.

While much of the housing that is built today incorporates many of these features, the housing that is best suited to retirees consists of some form of congregate housing—apartment housing complexes in which retirees pay what they can afford. Sponsoring agencies pay for most of the operating expenses.

This type of housing is common in West Germany, Austria, and Switzerland. Another retirement housing concept has been pioneered in Australia and France; it is called Elder Cottage Housing Opportunity (ECHO). Known in Australia as the "granny flat," these units are small portable cottages that are placed next to a larger house, often that of a son or daughter. Residents pay a modest nominal fee of about fifteen dollars a month. When the occupant moves away or dies, the

A retirement community with varied housing types. Peter A. Dickinson.

entire building can be moved elsewhere for another retiree.

The United States may be the leader in life-care housing. Already about seven hundred retirement communities across the United States provide some form of continuing care for about two hundred thousand residents, and the American Association of Homes for the Aging expects the number of these centers to double in the next decade.

In a typical setup, retirees, who must be healthy when they move in, pay entry fees ranging from about twenty-five thousand dollars to over one hundred thousand dollars. Then they pay a monthly service fee ranging from about six hundred dollars to over a thousand dollars a month. In return, residents receive everything from meals and utilities to housecleaning and recreation. They also receive some medical or nursing-home care at no extra cost. This can translate into substantial savings, since the average monthly charge at a traditional nursing home is more than eighteen hundred dollars. Some of these retirement communities offer at least partial refunds if a person dies or moves away.

Where Do Retirees Live Now?

About half of the nation's twenty-eight million retirees aged sixty-five or older live in eight states: California, New York, and Florida (each with more than two million), Pennsylvania, Ohio, Illinois, Michigan, and Texas (each with more than one million). States with the largest percentages of retirees (13 percent or more) include Florida (18.3 percent), Arkansas (14.3 percent), Rhode Island (14.3 percent), Iowa (14.1 percent), Pennsylvania (14.1 percent), Missouri (13.6 percent), South Dakota (13.6 percent), Massachusetts (13.4 percent), Nebraska (13.4 percent), Kansas (13.3 percent), Maine (13.1 percent), and West Virginia (13.0 percent). All told, almost 12 percent of the population of 240 million is sixty-five or older.

Are they living in ideal places? I define a Retirement Eden as a place one would love to visit and would like to live in. It should be a haven where one could be

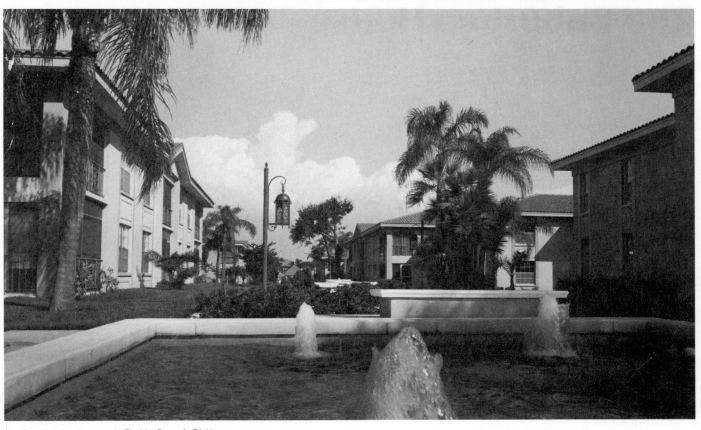

A retirement development in Florida. Peter A. Dickinson.

happier, healthier, and wealthier. And it should be a place where one could make money as well as save it.

Six Yardsticks Measure Retirement Edens

- Climate and environment. Places where, on most days, the temperature is sixty-six degrees Fahrenheit and the humidity is 55 percent. This climate allows body chemistry to function without strain. The more days like this, the better the people feel.

- Cost of living. Places where retired couples can live modestly on a spendable income of around fourteen thousand dollars annually, not including taxes, and

a single person on around ten thousand dollars and where they pay 9 percent or less in state and local taxes.

- Availability and cost of housing. Places where a variety of two-bedroom units can be found from about fifty-five thousand dollars.

- Medical facilities. Places where semiprivate hospital rooms cost less than $275 daily (the national average) and where there is at least one doctor per 750 residents.

- Recreation and culture. Places where someone interested in books, music, or art would feel comfortable.

- Special services for seniors. Places where there are transportation pro-

grams, hot meal programs, and other services and facilities for older people.

We are not likely to find places that are perfect in all respects, and these standards do not have to be met fully. Also, one person's retirement heaven is another's hell. Some like mountains, others valleys; some like pine trees, others palm trees. Yet for every fact there is a fantasy—some eight hundred Retirement Eden possibilities are available throughout this country.

Peter A. Dickinson is the founding editor of *Harvest Years* (now *Fifty Plus*) and *The Retirement Letter*, and author of *The Complete Retirement Planning Book*, *Sunbelt Retirement*, and *Retirement Edens: Outside the Sunbelt*.

The Suburban House
It symbolizes the American dream.

By Kenneth T. Jackson

It is almost a truism to observe that the United States has become a suburban nation. The 1980 census revealed that more than 100 million people, or more than 40 percent of the national population, lived in suburbs, a higher proportion than resided in either rural areas or central cities. The largest communities have been losing out not only relatively but also absolutely. Of the nation's twenty-five largest cities in 1950, eighteen lost population over the three following decades.

Meanwhile, the suburban house has become the quintessential physical achievement of the United States; it is perhaps more representative of its culture than big cars, tall buildings, or professional baseball. Suburbia symbolizes the fullest, most unadulterated embodiment of contemporary life-styles; it is a manifestation of such fundamental characteristics of American culture as conspicuous consumption, a reliance upon the private automobile, upward mobility, the separation of the family into nuclear units, the widening division between work and leisure, and a tendency toward racial and economic exclusiveness.

The term *suburb* has never had a precise meaning. But implicit in the suburban concept are four residential characteristics that have so far been virtually unique to the United States. They can be summed up as follows: affluent and middle-class Americans live in surroundings that are far from their work places, in homes that they own, and in the center of lawns that by urban standards elsewhere are enormous. This uniqueness thus involves population density, home ownership, residential status, and journey to work.

The first distinguishing element of suburban residence in this nation is low population density. With their broad streets and expansive lawns, American suburbanites are scattered, even in the largest conurbations, at average densities of fewer than ten persons per acre. Such sprawl results from the privatization of American life and the tendency to live in a fully detached house. Of the 86.4 million dwelling units in the United States in 1980, about 57.3 million, or two-thirds, consisted of a single family living in a single house surrounded by an ornamental lawn. More crowded urban conditions are common in other nations.

The second distinguishing feature of the suburban housing pattern is a strong penchant for home ownership. This characteristic can best be expressed statistically. About two-thirds of Americans own their dwellings, a proportion that rises to three-fourths of AFL/CIO union members, to 85 percent of all two-person households headed by a 45 to 64 year-old, and to 95 percent of intact white families in small cities. Overall, the American rate is double that of Germany, Switzerland, France, Great Britain, Sweden, and Norway and is also many times higher than that of such socialist nations as Bulgaria and the Soviet Union, where private ownership is technically illegal.

The third and most important distinguishing characteristic of the American housing pattern is the socioeconomic disparity between cities and suburbs. In the United States, status and income correlate with suburbs, the area that provides the bedrooms for an overwhelming proportion of those with college educations, of those engaged in professional pursuits, and of those in the upper-income brackets. Despite hopes and claims of a great revival in American cities in recent years, the 1980 census revealed a widening gap between residents of central cities in metropolitan areas and those of their surrounding suburbs, not only in income but also in employment, housing, living arrangements, and family structure. In 1970, for example, the median household income of the cities was 80 percent of that in the suburbs. By 1980 it had fallen to 74 percent. Even Boston, widely proclaimed for its downtown renewal and resurgence of middle-class housing, suffered a relative loss of median household income.

The situation in other nations provides a striking contrast. Whether one considers the Union of South Africa, where the oppressed black population has a long rush-hour journey to work while the inner city is reserved for the gracious homes of the privileged white minority; or Paris, where the "red suburbs" have long had a tendency to vote Communist; or South America, where slums and squatter settlements surround the great cities, high socioeconomic sections tend to be at the center, not on the suburban periphery.

The fourth and final distinguishing characteristic of the United States residential experience is the length of the average journey to work, whether measured in miles or in minutes. According to the 1980 census, the typical American worker traveled 9.2 miles and expended twenty-two minutes each way in reaching his place of employment at an annual cost of more than $1,270 per employee. In larger metropolitan areas the figures were much higher. Precise statistics are unavailable for Europe, Asia, and South America, but one need only think of the widespread practice of going home for lunch, often for a siesta as well, to recognize that an easier connection between work and residence is more valued and achieved in other cultures.

A brief essay cannot possibly account for the popularization of the detached suburban house in the United States. I would argue, however, that economic factors have been paramount and that both the creation of a suburban ideal and the persistence of racial prejudice have had a secondary role. Obviously, the American people have long had a distrust of urban life and of communal living. The dream of a detached house in a safe, quiet, and peaceful place has been an important part of the Anglo-American past and a potent force in the development of suburbs. In the 1850s, for example, Ralph Waldo Emerson celebrated the benefits of suburban living in rhetoric with a very modern flavor: "The aesthetic value of railroads is to unite the advantages of town and country life, neither of which we can spare." In comparison with German, Dutch, Japanese, Italian, and Spanish cultures, for example, Americans have never placed a high value on urbanity and group interaction. As Gwendolyn Wright has observed, "The dream house is a uniquely American form because for the first time in history, a civilization has created a utopian ideal based on the house rather than the city or the nation."

The suburban ideal is not unique to natives of the United States, however. A professed reverence for country life is common to many peoples and cultures. Immigrants from many lands exhibited a similar propensity for detached housing, and Polish, German, and Irish-Americans occasionally had higher home ownership rates in some cities than persons born in the United States. The private dwelling, therefore, is a more universal aspiration than suburban historians have previously been willing to admit. Was it not Voltaire who in the eighteenth century said that the serene ideal of human existence is to cultivate one's garden? What was important is not that American expectations and attitudes about houses differed from those of Europeans, for they appear not to have differed. Rather, the significant fact is that in the United States the average family was more able to realize its dream of a private home.

Similarly, no discussion of suburban housing can ignore the overriding significance of race. In comparison with the relative homogeneity of Denmark, Germany, Japan, or England, the cities of the

United States have long been extraordinarily diverse. In suburban terms, this provided an extra incentive for persons to move away from their older domiciles—fear. After the mass migration of blacks from the South gained momentum during World War I, and especially after the Supreme Court decision in 1954 that school segregation was unconstitutional, millions of families moved to houses in the suburbs "for the kids."

Economic causes have been more important than skin color in the suburbanization of the United States, however. Practically every American complains about the high cost of housing, but the simple fact is that the real cost of a suburban house in the United States has been relatively low and affordable in comparison with housing costs elsewhere in the world. There are essentially five components to this interpretation.

The first element has been per capita wealth. In material terms, the American people were the wealthiest in the world between 1790 and 1970. In 1949, for example, the American republic, with about 7 percent of the earth's population, had 42 percent of its wealth. Sweden, West Germany, and Switzerland, as well as oil-producing Kuwait and Saudi Arabia, have recently overtaken the United States, but their prosperity is a post-World War II phenomenon, and the notion of abundance has not been burned into their national psyches. As a "people of plenty," Americans could afford the economic inefficiency of the suburban house. In contrast, the Japanese have experienced centuries of scarcity, and their national psyche abhors waste. Even the droppings of humans are recycled as fertilizer on the tiny farms of that island nation.

The second component of low-cost suburban housing has been inexpensive land. Although purchasers have rarely regarded real estate as cheap, a broader view would reveal that the most fundamental difference between the United States and its industrial rivals was that American real estate was affordable and available whereas elsewhere it was expensive and scarce. Building lots in North America typically have been priced from one-fourth to one-half of comparably

sized and located parcels in Europe and Japan.

The third component of affordable price has been inexpensive transport, which has brought suburban home sites within easy commuting range of workplaces. Although the omnibus, the steam railroad, the subway, and the automobile were all developed first in Europe, it was in the United States that they were most enthusiastically adopted and where they most immediately affected the lives of ordinary citizens. Especially before World War I, the subways, commuter railroads, elevated trains, and electric trolleys of American cities were faster, more frequent, more efficient, and more cost-effective than transportation options elsewhere in the world. Even in 1987, the cost of operating an automobile remained cheaper in the United States than in other advanced nations. As Homer Hoyt, the nation's most distinguished demographer, noted thirty-five years ago, "The location, size, and shape of our cities has thus been a function of the transportation system prevailing during its main period of growth."

The fourth component of low-cost suburban housing has been balloon-frame construction. The development of an inexpensive and peculiarly American method of building with 2-inch by 4-inch wood studs brought the price of a private dwelling within the reach of most citizens. Such structures are uncommon in other countries, in part because their citizens regard the balloon-frame as flimsy, and in part because they lack the timber resources of the heavily forested United States.

The final component of low-cost suburban housing has been the role of government, particularly at the federal level. The prevailing myth is that the postwar suburbs blossomed because of the preference of consumers who made free choices in an open environment. Actually, because of public policies favoring the suburbs, only one possibility was economically feasible. The result, if not the intent, of Washington programs has been to encourage the ownership of a suburban house. FHA and VA mortgage insurance, the highway system, the financing

Ranch-style home, Levittown, New York, abut 1950. National Archives.

of sewers, the placement of public housing at the center of ghetto neighborhoods, and the location of federal agencies and offices of the Department of Defense, to name only the most obvious examples, encouraged scattered development in the open countryside. Whereas it was a national purpose to build subsidized highways and utilities outside of cities, it was not national policy to help cities repair and rebuild aging transit systems, bridges, streets, and water and sewer lines. Similarly, tax benefits for home owners result in a staggering subsidy for the suburban house. Suburbanization, therefore, was not a historical inevitability created by geography, technology, and culture, but rather the product of government policies. In effect, the social costs of suburban houses have been paid by the general taxpayer rather than by the home owner.

These five economic factors, along with racial prejudice and a pervasive

fondness for grass and solitude, have made private and detached suburban houses affordable and desirable to the middle class, and they have produced a spread-out environment of work, residence, and consumption that has thus far been more pronounced in the United States than elsewhere. The residential behavior of the American people, therefore, can be viewed primarily as the result of market forces and government policies. Some suburban families may have acted out of ignorance or irrationality, but most have moved to a single-family house because it maximized their utility from a stable set of preferences. In other words, the suburban house was a good deal.

Kenneth T. Jackson is the Mellon Professor of the Social Sciences and Professor of History and of Urban Planning at Columbia University. He is the author of *Crabgrass Frontier: The Suburbanization of the United States.*

Country and City

A modest suggestion may save both.

By Henry Hope Reed

A half century ago, the automobile, the wide highway, the government-guaranteed mortgage, and the forty-hour week produced the multitude of suburbs that is so much a part of today's United States. Then followed the migration to the countryside of one-story factories, corporate headquarters, laboratories, and research centers. Today we see a new pattern of landscape—one scattered with churches, schools, shopping centers, government agencies, and service outlets. No longer do communities cluster at a railroad station or around an old development. The clustered community in the traditional sense appears to be no longer a necessity. The commuter goes from a country residence to an office that is also in the country. How often have we heard, "I have not been to the city in six months to a year"?

Admittedly the migration to an all-green setting is not altogether new. Llewellyn Park in the Orange Mountains of New Jersey is an early example of the suburb dating from the 1850s. Harriet Beecher Stowe pointed out in the same decade the rewards of living in the country, which were made possible by the railroad. Automobile and highway have simply scattered such settlements farther into the countryside.

This new countryside bears no relation to that of the poets from Virgil to Pope. They sang of farmland and husbandry, of fields of wheat and herds of cattle. For centuries people were tied to the land. The object was to flee it for the city, the place of freedom. An old German saying is *Stadtluft macht frei* (City air makes you free). If persons of means went to the country it was not for pleasure but to supervise their estates, as Madame de Sévigné did. Palladio built his villas in the Veneto as farmhouses, admittedly beautiful ones, for landowners who were intent on being on hand to supervise spring planting and fall harvesting. Part of these villas was set aside for farm use, a fact that explains the hapless sites of many of them. Going away to the country for the summer for Venetians, as was no doubt true for other city dwellers, did not occur until well into the eighteenth century, as we know from the plays of Carlo Goldoni. Even in England and Ireland, where the

*Charles River,
Cambridge, Massachusetts*, 1874.
Collection of Schaffer Library, Union College,
Schenectady, New York. William J. Stillman.

country house is so conspicuous a tradition, the family estate was a source of income and an equally important source of political power. After all, it was the landowner, gentry or titled, who ruled England and Ireland.

All this working countryside is far removed from "living in the country" as we know it today. Most, if not all, of the facilities and rewards of the city are available to today's country dwellers. And when the workplace as well as the shopping are within easy distance, who needs the city? Certainly not the corporation president who, intent on his golf, moves his headquarters from the metropolis to be near his favorite course.

We are equally distant from the eighteenth-century Englishman who, when crossing the Alps, drew the blinds of his carriage. Nowadays we worship nature as we have been doing ever since the romantic era. Our best school of painters, from Thomas Cole to Thomas Moran, glorified nature. (This is the same Thomas Cole who denounced the "Dollar-Godded utilitarians" for building a railroad along his beloved Hudson River.)

The fact is that American painters—and it is also true of our writers and poets—have been much better at evoking the landscape than the cityscape. One would think that New York, which boasts of painters in abundance, would have produced any number who depicted the city with some splendor. I can think of only one, Leon Kroll, whose views of the city give the measure of its grander aspects. No writers have adequately described Wall Street, Park Avenue, or even Fifth Avenue, any more than they have described luxury hotels. A possible exception is Thomas Wolfe, who gloried in the old Pennsylvania Station.

No, the city's visual rewards are not for our writers, so fascinated are they by the urban image reflected in a gutter pool. It might appear, actually, that it is the *image* of the city that many writers flee, at least those who can work in the country, rather than the city itself.

Yet when the people move to the country in crowds, does not the countryside suffer? Somehow we are reminded of New York's Central Park, which in recent years has drawn ever-larger crowds while other city parks are passed by. It is a beautiful spot, made dramatic by the spectacular frame of high buildings. It is also a park amply served with asphalt paths and drives. But this has not kept it from being carved up by man-made trails—on turf, through hedge, and across glade. Much the same casual treatment is found on college campuses, presumably sacred ground compared with public parks. There the expensively maintained lawn is not something to look at—a lawn kept in perfect condition as an object of beauty, worthy of respect—but to sit on or to toss a Frisbee.

In Athens it is easy enough to guess the nationality of the youths reclining on a manicured patch of grass in the center of the Royal Gardens. These innocents abroad cannot see the irrigation channels in the tree-filled parts of the park. It never crosses their minds to consider the cost in manpower and water to have this modest green carpet, purely ornamental, in the dry Mediterranean climate, so accustomed are they to "using" a lawn. We love nature but we like to leave our mark. At the same time those of us who are fortunate to live in the country protest when more people settle in "our" countryside.

It would appear that everything is in place for a continuing invasion. With all of today's facilities, country living is much better than in the days when the poets were declaring its rewards. What is more, a country residence is accepted as almost the highest prize of success.

Other than the disappearance of the working countryside, is there any harm in the change? In a number of instances nature has joined in the invasion. It is said that today there is more woodland in the state of Connecticut than at any time since the first Europeans arrived. Apparently the original dwellers, the Indians, were accustomed to setting fires in the forest to make clearings for game, a practice that was replaced by the far more ruthless conversion of the land to farming.

Besides, what is the alternative to what is accepted as the good life? Ralph Adams Cram, the great architect of the Gothic in this century, found the answer to saving the countryside in confining the population within walled communities. (He, of course, lived much of the time in a countrified suburb of Boston.) *Walled Towns* was the name of the book that announced his scheme to the public. Admittedly, if memory serves, he resurrected the medieval town to the extent of having the good burghers in costume. At least he proposed an answer to the urban swallowing of the landscape.

Far more fashionable fifty and sixty years ago were the denunciations of the city and the proposals to destroy it. Lewis Mumford declared Manhattan's Upper East Side a rich man's slum. Frank Lloyd Wright wanted everyone to live in an endless suburb. Le Corbusier, in a plan financed by an automobile manufacturer, advocated replacing the center of Paris with tall towers set in open spaces. What actually has taken place is probably best depicted in a book published in Switzerland about a decade ago titled *Construction As World-Wide Destruction*. It revealed a spectacle of universal blight, not least in the Swiss countryside, the very country where nature reigns supreme, that same nature that awed the eighteenth-century Englishman.

We tend to accept the new ugliness as part of the price we pay for flourishing populations, convenient transportation, easier shopping, and general ease of living. Yet why the overwhelming failure? What is missing? It is quite simple: we of the Western world have tossed aside our artistic heritage and, in so doing, have encouraged our societies to do the same with theirs. Hence the worldwide destruction.

What is this artistic heritage? It is the classical tradition. And we have substituted for it modern art, the most conspicuous element of which is the cult of ugliness. This is the chief component of the visual nihilism found on all sides, a glorification of the absence of skill. But more detrimental even than these forces is the refusal to accept the concept of adornment.

Of course, such a rejection of an instrument that responds so sharply to a basic human instinct cannot last. Almost a generation ago I wrote a book, *The Golden City*, prophesying as much. Specifically, I saw modern art dying and the classical tradition coming to life. However slow the evolution, there is no question that it has begun. Such evidence can be seen in the new wing of the Frick Collection designed by John Barrington Bayley, in the Benjamin Franklin Dining Room in the United States Department of State, designed by John Blatteau, and in the giant medallion by Pierce Rice and George Kelly on the front of the new Philip Morris Building in New York.

What is strange about the reassertion of the classical is that those who are so concerned with the environment, those who find delight in the countryside, those who have done so much to save our coun-

New York at Night, 1933. The Metropolitan Museum of Art, Photography and the Fine Arts Gift, 1970 (1970.500). Berenice Abbott.

try's natural wonders, have been unable to see what modern art has done to both city and country. Their beloved natural wonders—swampland, beach, forest, and mountain—will be lost to visual nihilism unless they recognize the power of our artistic heritage to create beautiful man-made settings. The city has to be made to rival the country as a magnet. Only in this way will the country be saved.

The visual wealth of art, man-made, must approach that of nature and, by such achievement, end once and for all the drive of construction as worldwide destruction.

Henry Hope Reed is the President of Classical America and author of *The Golden City* and *The New York Public Library: Its Architecture and Decoration*.

Odd and Unusual

To each his own.

Le Palais Idéal, Hauterives (Drôme), France; Joseph Ferdinand Cheval, builder, 1879–1912. Courtesy Bibliothèque Forney, Paris.

La Maison de Piacassiette, Chartres (Eure-et-Loir), France; Raymond-Isidore, builder, 1928–64. Picture Library, Cooper-Hewitt Museum.

76

House, Gondrexange, Lorraine, France. Courtesy of H. Roger-Viollet.

The Glass Castle, Duncan, British Columbia, Canada; George Plumb, builder, begun 1963. Courtesy Mable Plumb.

Residence of G.L. Snow, near Harbour Grace, Newfoundland, Canada, 1980s. Rosalind Pepall.

Residence of Fred Burns, Belfast, Maine, from *All Their Own: People and The Places They Build*, by Jan Wampler (Schenkman Publishing Company, 1977).

House with seashell decoration, Polperro, Cornwall, Great Britain. De Spaarnestad Fotoarchief.

New Towns

They may solve a critical problem.

By Norman Pressman

The "Nelikko" town houses in Tapiola; Aulis Blomstedt, architect, 1962. Courtesy Consulate General of Finland.

Throughout history, towns and cities have been initiated not only by accident but also by deliberate and conscious design. It is an established fact that throughout the millennia of urban evolution there has been a continuous interest in the founding and construction of new towns in virtually every civilization. The significance of city names such as Villeneuve, Newtown, New Harmony, Neustadt, Novgorod, Novigrad, and others has long been forgotten as their newness has given way to a sedate, more aged appearance.

All towns were new at some period in history, when they were conceived by philosophers, architects, engineers, social reformers, and master builders. The army encampments and the administrative and colonial capitals of Greece and the Roman Empire serve as examples. In the fifth century B.C. Hippodamus of Miletus built towns like Piraeus, the twin city of Athens. During the thirteenth century the "bastide" towns of southwestern France constituted one of the largest ventures of new town settlement policy in history. And at the turn of the twentieth century, Ebenezer Howard, Soria y Mata, and Tony Garnier set forth proposals for new towns that were influenced by the technological developments of their times. Le Corbusier and Frank Lloyd Wright proposed revolutionary new cities in 1922 and 1932 respectively; and in our own era, visionary ideas are evolving on a rhythmic basis around the world to resolve a variety of problems created by population growth and by the need to accommodate specialized functions.

The Raison d'être of New Towns

Newly planned settlements have been and continue to be established for a number of reasons. New political capitals are created, such as Brasilia, Dodoma, Canberra, Chandigarh, and Washington. Suburban garden communities are developed to accommodate metropolitan growth in housing and employment markets such as Reston, Virginia; Tapiola, Finland; or Erin Mills, Ontario. New settlements on virgin sites are created *ex nihilo* for resource extraction, such as Fermont, Tumbler Ridge, and Kitimat in Canada and Norilsk in the Soviet Union. New seaports or immigrant absorption centers such as Ashdod and Arad in Israel are established. And the so-called equilibrium towns situated around the Greater Paris Region (of which there are five) are being developed to relieve urban pressures on the older, historic center and to distribute jobs, housing, and recreational facilities throughout a broader metropolitan field in a more carefully planned and rationally organized fashion.

Since new towns are planned on a fairly large scale from the outset, they cannot help but conjure up visions of better spatial arrangements for improved habitats—that is, utopian or ideal city images. They force the societies that build them to address questions that are universal and that exhibit timeless qualities. These questions include the following:

- What should the idealized goals and aims be when creating a new city?

- What type of society does one envisage emerging out of this new framework?

- What means do we possess for transforming society and the physical support-system environment of which it is an integral part?

- Should one attempt to modify social norms through planning or should the urban environment be an exact reflection of an established social order—to remain unchanged wherever possible?

Even if it has been difficult to reach precise answers, these issues have been raised throughout the history of humankind. The answers reflect various cultural values, and they have resulted in a variety of urban configurations. Such issues are even more critical in our own time, when newly emerging technological achievements tend to dictate life-styles and when the vast complexity of social, economic, political, and environmental considerations must be sensitively balanced.

New towns can be viewed as indicators of the quality of life in a range of societies. They indicate the latest social values and often reveal areas of deficiency found in existing settlements. They serve as vehicles for urban experimentation and innovation since the vacant sites on which they are constructed and the speed of their development readily permit controlled application and integration of new technologies, new systems of governmental organization, and alternative patterns of development. New towns can do this more speedily than can already established centers, with their physical and administrative constraints such as zoning ordinances and contiguous uses that may be seen as incompatible with new development. Therefore, new towns can serve as "early warning indicators" of problems that may arise from experimental ideas prior to those ideas being applied on a more massive scale in existing towns.

Some new towns have been built as part of a national strategic plan for recreation and tourism. The French government, to relieve pressure from the Riviera conurbation, has built a system of "holiday villages" or *stations intégrées* along the Languedoc-Roussillon coast, largely between Montpellier and Perpignan. Some of these suffer from a lack of year-round population and diverse employment opportunities. Hence they do not entirely qualify for the nomenclature of a full-fledged new town. Alpine ski stations—planned from scratch—are among such developments, not only in France but also in Switzerland.

Flaine, La Plagne, Tignes, and Avoriaz, some of the well known Alpine resorts on specially designated sites in France, cater to virtually every possible whim of winter-sports enthusiasts. Retirement villages are becoming commonplace in Florida, California, and some sections of the Mediterranean coast, but these cannot truly be viewed as balanced towns where people both live and work. They are, nevertheless, carefully designed for specialized populations and, on the whole, are market oriented in terms of their facilities and organization.

A specialized type of new town that is becoming characteristic of most postindustrial societies is one that is centered around tertiary and quaternary employment with a powerful focus on educational and technology-based research facilities. Akademgorodsk in the Soviet Union is one example. And in Louvain-la-Neuve, Belgium, where the Catholic University of Louvain has played a central role starting in 1971, the core of the town is the university. But academic facilities are intermingled with shops, restaurants, cafés, and public spaces in the center, so that the concept of the town is much broader than an academic site.

Louvain-la-Neuve boasts a scientific park that is attracting national and international research companies and will eventually comprise a population of forty thousand. One of the most attractive features is the town's human scale, which is safeguarded by calm, varied architectural designs and by a very strong pro-pedestrian attitude. Such research-based towns are becoming commonplace in Japan, with innovation as their key feature.

Immediately following World War II, Great Britain, under the New Towns Act of 1946, set up a program to rehouse families affected by the bombing of London. These new communities not only housed families uprooted by the war but also siphoned off London's population growth into attractive planned settlements beyond the existing urban sprawl. These settlements, called Mark I new towns and situated twenty to thirty miles from London, set a precedent throughout the country for urban growth policy.

Towns such as Thamesmead, Cumbernauld, Runcorn, and Milton Keynes have attracted many young married couples with children and tend to exhibit population characteristics representative of typical national income and social groupings. Several dozen towns of this nature have been completed, mainly during the 1960s and 1970s. Moreover, the British have achieved a considerable degree of self-sufficiency in their planned towns.

Sweden's new communities, also largely a post-World War II phenomenon, have been tied to the renewal of Stockholm's central business district and to metropolitan efforts to shape and direct urbanization patterns. Public land acquisition around Stockholm commenced at the turn of the twentieth century—a truly unique accomplishment that enabled land to be used for private and public uses without significant constraints imposed by large, powerful corporations or by private development organizations with vested interests.

From the outset, an efficient rapid transit system tied these communities to one another and to central Stockholm. The early towns of Vallingby and Farsta were exemplary in their landscape qualities and in the separation of pedestrian from vehicular movement. The latest ones of Kista, Akalla, and Husby contain close to thirty thousand people, provide employment for at least half of this population, and offer a wide spectrum of housing types. The open-space arrangements and a carefully orchestrated range of urban designs make the environments more diverse and aesthetically pleasing than those built in the developments of the 1950s and 1960s.

The five new towns proposed in the 1965 regional development plan for the Paris region are now well advanced. Their projected population goal is between 250,000 and 400,000 inhabitants each, in order to provide a critical mass sufficient to support a broad selection of higher-order services and facilities. This goal constitutes a new breakthrough in setting target populations; never before have completely new cities been established on such a large and sophisticated scale.

The scale has required public development corporations to make these undertakings operational—selecting sites, purchasing land, servicing it, and guiding the overall planning and design. In addition, political instruments have been developed to merge existing municipalities and townships on and around the designated sites and to decide among major urban options and on the management of facilities. Coordinating groups have been set up at the national level to see to the administration, research, and financing essential to the creation of these settlements and to assist local municipalities with infrastructure works and budgeting problems.

Cergy-Pontoise, one of these towns with a projected figure of 250,000 people, is located about twenty-five miles north of Paris. One of its aims is the creation of one job for every residential dwelling. Theoretically, people could be able both to live and work there. However, there is a recognition that there will always be some commuting to Paris.

All these towns, like their Swedish counterparts, are tied to the capital city by high-speed rail networks. They espouse a firm desire to offer future inhabitants the greatest possible freedom of choice and a maximum of amenities that would minimize the need to travel to larger urban centers for high-level services.

The French government made it clear in the late 1960s, when it initiated its new-town building program, that innovation and experimentation were to be among the major criteria for gauging success at the national, regional, and local levels. Such innovation was particularly emphasized in the realms of environmental management, transportation, open-space utilization, and housing. The primary methods of generating innovative thought and action were national and international competitions for specific town sites. An essential ingredient of this strategy was follow-up monitoring and evaluation.

In developing nations, where population growth in the larger urban centers expands very rapidly and is frequently difficult to control, new towns serve as reception nodes for rural and unskilled populations who leave the countryside because of overcrowded conditions, lack of arable land, and a paucity of badly needed transportation, education, and health services. Such planned areas keep pressures off the existing cities and help to prevent overspill onto prime agricultural lands surrounding already dense, built-up settlements. They attempt to achieve acceptable housing standards and a subregional distribution of employment opportunities. While resettling both rural and urban poor, their objectives are as much social and economic as they are physical. Very large metropolises such as Alexandria and Cairo have utilized this strategy in areas such as Sadat City and 10th of Ramadan City.

What May Be Expected of the New Towns?

New communities or new towns—whether they be developed on large inner-city parcels of land, on the urban periphery, or in the wilderness—convey a sense of starting from scratch, on a *tabula rasa*. They carry with them a sense of aspiring to build something different from what continually surrounds us, a provision of alternative modes of urban development. Their emphasis is perhaps an improved, expanded vision of life that cannot be mathematically optimized but that represents personal and societal value constructs epitomized in a system of shells, structures, and networks that will enhance life for all urban dwellers. Implicit in such planned developments is a more livable and even a more climate-responsive environment whereby some degree of innovation can be anticipated.

Although these new towns will probably not constitute the ultimate answer to the complex problems confronting our urban civilization, they should furnish the conditions that are vital to high-quality urban life in the twenty-first century. In this regard, they can provide properly diversified services, conveniences, and amenities; healthy living and working environments; abundant green open spaces; effective private and public transportation systems capable of accommodating future demands; sites of exceptional location and visual beauty; and, finally, a wider choice for people selecting their habitats. The new towns can be viewed as a primary force for ensuring that humankind experiences optimum conditions of life, dwelling, work, and intellectual development—to which we are all entitled and which human progress can provide.

Norman Pressman is Associate Professor of Urban and Regional Planning at the University of Waterloo in Ontario, Canada, and author of *International Settlement Strategies: Social Perspectives on Planned Development*.

The Law

What is its influence on housing?

By Timothy Rub

Housing, considered as an economic activity, is among the most regulated of industries, both in the United States and abroad. At first glance, the extent to which housing production is controlled by law might seem surprising. Indeed, many have argued with some justification, that the law as it affects housing—in the form of building codes, various local and national housing acts, and zoning ordinances—is needlessly complex and one of the chief sources of inefficiency in this market. In a broader perspective, however, such complexity is understandable, given the significance of housing in the national economy, its function as an instrument of social policy, and its centrality to the process of city planning. Historically, housing law has been informed by all of these concerns.

The primary mechanism by which legal control is exercised over housing is termed *police power*. This enables the state to limit the uses of private property subject to considerations of public health and safety, the maintenance of property values, and, on occasion, aesthetics. Needless to say, it is difficult, if not impossible, to hold these in balance or, better yet, to weight them properly. To cite one long-standing problem: the stabilization of property values sought by one landowner might be seen as an opportunity cost by another. Thus, the concerns addressed by housing law are often in conflict, resulting in a process that is highly debated and, more often than not, contentious.

In understanding the effect of the law on housing, the critical issue is one of limits. That is to say, the law tends not to prescribe but rather generally to describe what is allowable. For example, a local building code will typically define those materials that are acceptable and set minimum standards for their dimensions, strength, fire resistance, and the like. Similarly, zoning ordinances will set limits with regard to the height, bulk, plot coverage, and use for buildings within a specified district.

It should be noted that such regulations do not usually deal with the issue of aesthetics, for the obvious reason that architectural standards are notoriously difficult to establish—at least more so than sanitary or structural minimums. The exception, and one that has become increasingly well-defined in case law, is the protection from new development or excessive alteration given to historic buildings and districts, based on their educational, cultural, and economic value to the public.

Yet, understood in a broader context, the law has often had a profound influence on the form of housing. In the case of the legislation controlling tenement house construction that was passed by New York City in 1901, the changes brought about were not insignificant. Its requirements regarding maximum allowable plot coverage, the size and placement of interior courts and lightwells, and the minimum dimensions of rooms within an apartment forced the development of new layouts and plan types—most of which represented a considerable improvement over existing conditions (and, as some have pointed out, raised the cost of housing). In this way, the law takes an important place beside technology and social customs as a determinant of architectural form.

Given that housing legislation concerns itself primarily with limiting the rights of individual property holders, it should come as no surprise that its impact is most strongly felt at the urban level. That is to say, the law is designed to encourage a certain uniformity, both of type and within well-defined areas, such as central business districts, industrial parks, or neighborhoods. For example, zoning ordinances will typically delineate several residential districts, specifying for each an appropriate use—for example, single- or multifamily—as well as height limitations, minimum plot size, and allowable coverage.

Early advocates of zoning argued that tools such as these were absolutely necessary to facilitate an orderly planning and development process and, more specifically, to create and maintain homogeneous neighborhoods. As observed in 1921 by Robert Whitten and Frank Walker, authors of a new zoning plan for Cleveland, one of the central functions of the plan was to separate apartment houses and single-family housing so as "to preserve Cleveland as a city of homes." Of the various motives that led to the introduction of zoning ordinances in nearly all of the larger cities in the United States during the 1920s, this was without doubt one of the most widespread and powerful.

The application of construction standards can also serve to encourage uniformity, sometimes in ways that may not have been directly anticipated. New York City's Tenement House Act of 1901, for example, required that all tenements over six stories be fireproof, a condition that made the construction of taller residential buildings prohibitively expensive. Although in many instances the Tenement House Act (and, later, the zoning ordinance of 1916) permitted taller buildings, the differential in returns on fireproof and non-fireproof construction effectively limited the height of tenements in most parts of the city to six stories. For precisely the same reason, the three-story tenement predominated in Chicago.

Insofar as the process of city planning is a dynamic one, there is some question whether housing laws help or hinder that process. Clearly there is no simple answer, because the issues involved in housing are varied and complex. The zoning restrictions by which the character of a residential neighborhood and its property values are maintained may appear perfectly legitimate to some and exclusionary to others. Another often-cited problem is the degree to which zoning guidelines that once served as a blueprint for anticipated growth now tend to inhibit change—specifically, the development of a more fluid and efficient housing market or the revitalization of blighted urban areas.

Finally, a great deal of economic analysis has focused on building codes and the several ways in which they contribute to the increased cost of housing: codes are not uniform but differ from one municipality to the next, and that makes it difficult for builders to achieve scale economies that might be obtained through standardized production. Moreover, codes are updated only infrequently, with the result that there is often a considerable lag between the introduction of more efficient building technologies or less costly substitutes for traditional materials and their incorporation into the revised building code.

In recent years, various mechanisms have been introduced to mitigate some of these problems; the most important is the Planned Unit Development (PUD). The purpose of this is to promote greater flexibility and greater sensitivity in the planning process by permitting departures from local zoning ordinances or from a community's master plan provided that the design strikes a balance between different land uses, open spaces and the density of construction, and the like. The issue is a complicated one; for our purposes it is important only to observe that such an approach has allowed for greater creativity in residential design, particularly the clustering and mix of different dwelling types.

Historically, most housing law is of relatively recent origin; on the one hand, a product of the increasingly prominent role that government has assumed in national economic and social life, and on the other, a function of the dramatic growth of our cities. To be sure, legal controls over building have been with us for a long time—witness the building codes imposed by the City of London in the wake of the Great Fire of 1666; they prohibited projections beyond the plot line and the use of exposed timberwork in facades. But the origin of most housing law, particularly zoning ordinances and acts allowing for slum clearance and the provision of decent housing for the working classes, dates from the latter part of the nineteenth century.

Not surprisingly, Germany (which, of all modern states, had developed the most efficient bureaucracy) led the way in the development of zoning controls, with several major cities adopting comprehensive schemes in the 1890s. American planners, particularly the members of the Heights of Buildings Commission, which drafted the landmark New York City zoning plan of 1916, sought to emulate the German model. They were, however, quick to note that the results would be very different. German zoning ordinances were more rigorous for several reasons, chiefly because municipalities tended to own a large percentage of the unimproved land within their jurisdictions, and therefore could exercise significant control over the development of residential subdivisions. The degree to which this could be accomplished in the United States would be substantially less because of different patterns of land ownership and a tradition of limited public control over property rights.

This brief and idiosyncratic digression into the history of zoning is intended simply to demonstrate the importance of context in determining the influence of the law on housing. To a large extent, government intervention is a function of place and circumstance. At one end of the spectrum we find set rules intended to regulate the behavior of private players in the market; at the other end we find direct government involvement in providing housing and an extraordinary use of police power. Witness, for example, the various acts legislated by the English government in the late nineteenth century to ensure the provision of adequate housing for the working classes. Initially, these acts granted to local authorities broad powers to improve or eliminate slum areas (by means of excess or zone condemnation and replotting); and later, with the creation of the architectural department of the London County Council, the means of providing low-income housing where the market had failed to do so.

Similarly, in the United States both the federal and local governments have played an active role in building and financing housing when it was perceived that intervention was necessary. Perhaps the most celebrated examples are the New Deal programs that gave birth to greenbelt communities in several parts of the country, and in New York City to the development of a progressive and efficient housing authority.

That legacy is, of course, still with us, however much of it has been transformed by changing needs and economic circumstances. It is clear that, over time, the influence of the law on housing has grown rather than diminished. Given that our society has become increasingly urbanized and given the role that the law plays in mediating between individual rights and the rights of the public, it will perhaps continue to do so.

The Reason for the Building Line

Values of neighboring residences have been cut in half by this store

These homes have been blanketed by high walls of apartments.

The high Apartment Houses built out to the sidewalk line cut off light and view from neighboring buildings.
When the entire block is built up with similar Apartments there will be no room for lawn or trees— nothing but pavement and bare brick walls.

The Cleveland Zone Plan: Report to the City Plan Commission, Robert H. Whitten and Frank R. Walker, City Plan Advisors, City of Cleveland, Ohio, 1921. The New York Public Library, Astor, Lenox and Tilden Foundation.

Timothy Rub is an architecture historian, and Assistant Director of the Hood Museum of Art at Dartmouth College in New Hampshire.

Shelter Magazines

They set the expectations.

By Clifford E. Clark, Jr.

Pick up a housing magazine such as *House and Garden* or *Family Circle* today and you will find advice on all sorts of subjects: food and nutrition, health, home decoration, and house design. The same has been true since the early nineteenth century, when *Godey's Lady's Book* and the *Illustrated Annual Register of Rural Affairs* mixed short stories and food recipes with the latest designs for fashionable houses. For the past hundred and fifty years, house and shelter magazines have helped define and shape middle-class ideals of house design and family behavior. Although the advice and suggestions of housing magazines have rarely been completely accepted, they have nevertheless functioned as a benchmark against which middle-class Americans can test their own experiences.

Since magazine writers have always paid close attention to the house designs that their competitors were promoting, they have developed a common vocabulary and set of images to describe their house plans. A brief look at the popular house magazines of any period, therefore, will uncover the important assumptions that were used to justify contemporary designs.

One of the earliest successful publishers was Louis A. Godey of Philadelphia. From 1830 until the end of the century, Godey, in his fashionable *Godey's Lady's Book* magazine, waged a campaign to encourage his readers to build their own homes. In almost every issue, the magazine's hundred and fifty thousand avid subscribers could read about the latest innovations in house layout and decoration. Godey published 450 different house plans, explaining the advantage offered by each style.

One of the designs that Godey promoted, for example, was that for a rural Gothic revival cottage. Houses in the Gothic revival style were easily identified by their steeply pitched roofs, decorated gables, and vertical board-and-batten siding. Known as the "pointed style" because of the emphasis on verticality created by the sharp-peaked gables and tall chimneys, Gothic revival cottages were considered by Godey to be the ideal home for the Christian family.

For Godey as well as for other magazine and plan-book authors, the Gothic cottage could function as a miniature family church, complete with stained-glass windows, cross plan, and parlor pump organ. No wonder that Sereno E. Todd, a nineteenth-century housing promoter, wrote, "Home is not merely four square walls adorned with gilded pictures, but it is where love sheds its light on all the dear ones who gather round the sweet home fireside, where we can worship God with none to molest or make us afraid."

As Todd's comments reveal, popular housing magazines like Godey's helped

THE HOUSE BEAUTIFUL

Vol. SIXTEEN   **JULY, 1904**   No. TWO

The Only Magazine in America Devoted to Simplicity, Economy, and Appropriateness in Home Decoration and Furnishing

SOME BEAUTIFUL BUFFALO HOMES; A MODEL BATH-ROOM; THE LOG CABIN; AN AMERICAN LACE-MAKER; CRESTED PORCELAIN; THE HOME GARDEN; CROSS-STITCH AND BEAD WORK

The Vital Things in the Home
How to Make the Most of $3,500 a Year
NEARLY FIFTY ILLUSTRATIONS

TWENTY CENTS A COPY   TWO DOLLARS A YEAR

TRADE MARK REGISTERED   ALL RIGHTS RESERVED   COPYRIGHT, 1904 BY HERBERT S. STONE

Picture Library, Cooper-Hewitt Museum.

persuade the middle- and upper-class public at mid-century that housing was more than simply shelter. A properly designed house, the reformers insisted, could provide the ideal moral environment for family life. This moralistic approach to housing, with its tendency to label different styles as good or bad, honest or dishonest, permeated the writings of magazine authors, architect essayists, and plan-book promoters.

For those well-off enough to build their own houses, the promotional literature in magazines and plan books provided a new rationale for home design and furnishing. According to one account, readers of *Godey's Lady's Book* in a single decade built over four thousand houses from plans provided by the magazine.

The influence of magazines on popular house design increased dramatically in the 1880s and 1890s as several new journals revolutionized the industry. Some of these new magazines, such as *House Beautiful* (1896) and *House and Garden* (1901), were designed to present the latest designs of professional architects and to create a new canon of taste for household art. Others, like *Ladies' Home Journal* (1883), *Woman's Home Companion* (1897), and *Good Housekeeping* (1885), were directed toward a female audience that increasingly sought to develop a science of house decoration and house management. Among these, *Ladies' Home Journal* was clearly the leader. Under the able direction of Edward W. Bok, the *Journal* expanded its readership from six hundred thousand in 1891 to over one million in 1903.

Appealing to a middle-class audience that was eager to learn the latest about fashions, cooking, and household design and decoration, *Ladies' Home Journal* supported the ideal that the house should be considered a personal statement and that women, through the cultivation of their artistic talents, could make the

home environment into an expression of their artistic tastes. Displaying the latest in female stitchery and interior decoration, the *Journal* suggested that women expand the older cult of domesticity, which stressed their leadership in household affairs and child rearing, into a new expression of artistic achievement. By then, the house was still considered to be the quintessential moral environment, but it was also to be recognized as a work of art.

Encouraged by magazine writers and advice columnists, Victorian Americans followed their suggestions by building elaborate Eastlake and Queen Anne houses. The public saw complex and often idiosyncratic combinations of massive front porches, textured exterior surfaces, towers, turrets, and tall chimneys on these houses as grand artistic statements, fitting the social status and accomplishments of their owners. Surveying the many articles in the *Ladies' Home Journal*, architect Stanford White wrote, "I firmly believe that Edward Bok has more completely influenced American domestic architecture for the better than any one man of his generation."

At the turn of the century, popular housing magazines like *Ladies' Home Journal* and *House and Garden* were joined by more specialized journals in promoting a radically new set of housing ideals. Journals as different as *The Craftsman*, edited by Gustav Stickley, and *Country Life in America*, which catered to the wealthier segment of the population, espoused a new ethic of spartan simplicity and functionalism. They were particularly interested in popularizing a new house, which they labeled the bungalow. Known by its wide, low-pitched roof, which was connected in one unbroken line to a spacious porch that extended across the entire front of the house, the bungalow was extolled in the popular housing magazines as the very antithesis of the earlier

Victorian mansion.

Whereas the Victorian house was known by its two- or three-story size, elaborate exterior, and complex rooflines, the bungalow was an unimposing structure whose simple lines and broad, sheltering roof made it appear to have been hewn out of a single block. Bungalow magazine promoters like Gustav Stickley, who advocated a return to solid, handcrafted construction, stressed the importance of using natural materials—rough cedar shakes and cobblestones. For the interior, they favored heavy oak moldings and beamed ceilings. Where the large Victorian houses had contained elaborate front and back parlors to separate the entertainment of guests from the activities of the family, the bungalow now had a "living room" that served both functions.

Since bungalows had originally been associated with camp and vacation houses, the magazine promoters also stressed the informality and functionalism of bungalows in contrast to the formalism of their Victorian predecessors. Built-in buffets, fireplace inglenooks, and bookshelves minimized the amount of additional furniture that families would need and simplified the business of everyday life. Magazine writ-ers asserted that the veranda or front porch should be the center of home life. "They should be broadly built," commented one writer, "furnished with screens, against the wind or sun, and well-supplied with easy chairs, hammocks, and all the paraphernalia of an outdoor summer parlor, for here will be gained the object of the bungalow, the utmost benefit of life in the open air."

Magazine writers singled out the bungalow as a healthy and sanitary environment in which to raise children. Magazines such as *Good Housekeeping*, *Cosmopolitan*, *House Beautiful*, and *Craftsman* were joined in this crusade for good health by more specialized journals such as *Mother's Friend*, *Today's Housewife*, *Hearth and Home*, *Mother's Home Life*, and *American Kitchen Magazine* in urging that the house be made more healthful. Articles on "The Bacteriology of Household Preserving," "How Any Woman Can Become a Sanitarian," "Science in the Model Kitchen," and "The Bedroom: Health and Economy in an Anti-Microbe Sleeping Room Which May Serve as a Hospital" continually reinforced the need to rethink the design and use of kitchens, bedrooms, and bathrooms.

The growing popularity of house and shelter magazines in the progressive era prior to World War I encouraged publishers to target their articles toward specific audiences. The *Ladies' Home Journal* stressed the inexpensiveness and simplicity of bungalow design and printed articles dividing bungalows into price categories appropriate for "the business woman," "the young bride," and "the bachelor girl." *Sunset* magazine emphasized the easygoing, informal life for those who owned bungalows in southern California. *House Beautiful* and *Country Life in America*, catering to a more expensive market, underscored the ways in which well-designed bungalows might satisfy the artistic concerns of their owners.

Even during the Great Depression of the 1930s, housing magazines managed to keep their audiences by explaining how home owners might remodel their basements into recreation rooms or might en-close a porch to gain an extra bedroom. At a time when new housing construction had fallen dramatically and incomes were limited, housing magazines focused on how the middle class might recycle what they had and make more efficient use of their resources.

When housing starts skyrocketed after World War II, the circulation of housing magazines purchased by those looking for advice climbed precipitously. *Better Homes and Gardens* nearly doubled between 1944 and 1955, selling 4,133,000 copies, while the circulation of *House Beautiful* and *House and Garden* increased 139 percent. By the 1960s, these

magazines, together with those that catered primarily to women, could boast of more than nineteen million readers. Sold on newsstands and in supermarkets, the popular housing magazines promoted the new "ranch house" and "Cape Cod" styles as the ultimate in comfort, convenience, and "livability."

Acutely aware that housing demand was outrunning availability, housing magazines used social science surveys to gain a more systematic understanding of their readers' views. Between 1936 and 1950, more than forty-one surveys were taken. Perhaps typical was that done by Walter Adams for *Better Homes and Gardens* in 1946, based on a questionnaire answered by 11,428 families. Adams discovered that most families wanted a three-bedroom house, all on one floor, with space in the kitchen to eat breakfast and lunch.

Since few people surveyed had an accurate idea of what such a house would cost, *Better Homes and Gardens* and other housing magazines ran articles advising people how to save on construction and make do with smaller houses. Porches were replaced by outdoor patios; garages were scaled down into carports. Increasingly, the popular housing magazines presented themselves as showcases of "ideas" for house plans, home maintenance, interior decoration, and cooking.

Thus, over the past century and a half, the influence of housing and shelter magazines has remained fairly constant. They have continued the emphasis, seen earlier in *Godey's Lady's Book*, on the house as a moral statement and form of personal expression. A recent issue of *Metropolitan Home* put it succinctly when it featured an article on a "Sanctuary and Showcase House." Local carpenters and small developers, moreover, continue to copy model houses from popular magazines and to build them in subdivisions in small towns and suburbs around the nation.

Housing magazines, therefore, continue to serve an important function for the middle class. By introducing their readers to the latest fashions in house design and decoration, and by serving as an "expert resource" to answer everyday questions about construction and planning, housing magazines have helped to establish popular criteria that the middle class can use as a yardstick to judge its own dwellings. If few people use many of the vast quantity of ideas put forth by magazine writers, many families, in search of the house of their dreams, still turn to the articles in housing magazines for suggestions and advice.

Clifford E. Clark, Jr., is Professor of History and M.A. and A.D. Hulings Professor of American Studies at Carleton College in Minnesota and author of *The American Family Home, 1800–1960.*

Architectural Elements

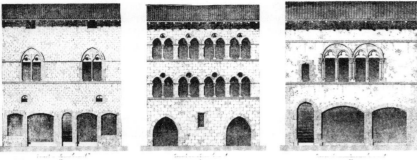

Houses, France, 12th century. Picture Library, Cooper-Hewitt Museum.

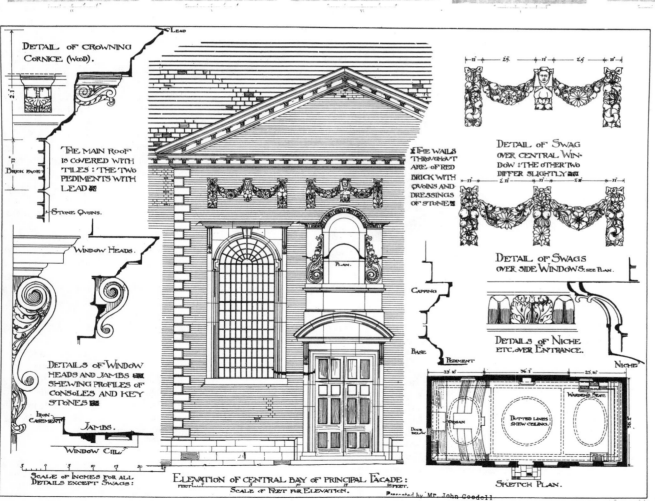

DETAIL OF CROWNING CORNICE (WOOD).

THE MAIN ROOF IS COVERED WITH TILES : THE TWO PEDIMENTS WITH LEAD

STONE QVOINS.

WINDOW HEADS.

DETAILS OF WINDOW HEADS AND JAMBS SHEWING PROFILES OF CONSOLES AND KEY STONES

IRON CASEMENT

JAMBS.

WINDOW CILL.

SCALE OF INCHES FOR ALL DETAILS EXCEPT SWAGS :

ELEVATION OF CENTRAL BAY OF PRINCIPAL FAÇADE : SCALE OF FEET FOR ELEVATION.

THE WALLS THROUGHOUT ARE OF RED BRICK WITH QVOINS AND DRESSINGS OF STONE

PLAN.

DETAIL OF SWAG OVER CENTRAL WINDOW : THE OTHER TWO DIFFER SLIGHTLY

DETAIL OF SWAGS OVER SIDE WINDOWS : SEE PLAN.

DETAILS OF NICHE ETC. OVER ENTRANCE.

CAPPING

BASE   PEDIMENT

NICHE

DOOR BELOW

ORGAN   DOTTED LINES SHEW CEILING.   WARDENS SEAT.

SKETCH PLAN.

Presented by Mr. John Goodell

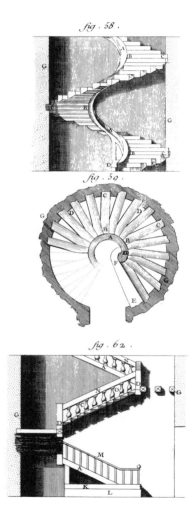

fig. 58.

fig. 59.

fig. 62.

Timber framework: staircases, from Denis Diderot, *Encyclopédie, Vol. I, Receuil de Planches sur les Sciences, les Arts Libéraux et les Arts Méchaniques avec leur explication,* Paris, 1763. Cooper-Hewitt Museum Library.

Parquetry floors and borders. Picture Library, Cooper-Hewitt Museum.

Double doors, from *Journal für Tichter,* 1858. Picture Library, Cooper-Hewitt Museum.

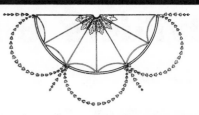

Ceiling design, Joseph Cabot house, Salem, Massachusetts, from *American Architect and Building News,* © 1900. Picture Library, Cooper-Hewitt Museum.

Column bases. Picture Library, Cooper-Hewitt Museum.

Doorway from Project for a town mansion, Italy, 1770–1775. Cooper-Hewitt Museum, Gift of Mrs. Edward D. Brandegee.

Column. Picture Library, Cooper-Hewitt Museum.

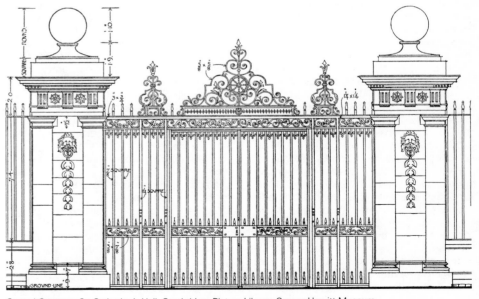

Central Gateway, St. Catherine's Hall, Cambridge. Picture Library, Cooper-Hewitt Museum.

Builders' Guides and Plan Books

The advice was practical.

By Dell Upton

For two hundred years, house builders and their clients have been deluged by published advice. Although writings on domestic architecture were most influential in the nineteenth-century United States, architectural handbooks date back many centuries in both Western and other cultures. Moreover, while periodicals have been the most common means of disseminating architectural ideas since the late nineteenth century, all kinds of books continue to be written and read.

Architectural publications vary in type, purpose, and effect on domestic architecture. Oldest are the technical books. Some of them described standard building practices in a comprehensive manner to aid in specifying and evaluating builders' work. Li Jie's twelfth-century manual *Yingzao fashi* was intended to guide Chinese bureaucrats charged with overseeing building projects. All parts of the traditional Chinese building were related to one another according to a proportional system, as were all the varieties of labor involved in construction. The price books of European and American organizations of carpenters, joiners, and other craftspeople served a similar purpose. They established not so much fixed prices as relative values for various kinds of work. These publications were by nature conservative, for they discouraged undertaking work that was not comprehended in the established system.

Other technical books taught building practices. Joseph Moxon's *Mechanick Exercises: or the Doctrine of Handy-Works*, published in two volumes in 1678 and 1684, revealed to lay people the trade secrets of carpenters, joiners, bricklayers, and turners, along with smiths and printers, as a contribution to practical knowledge. Moxon also wanted to instruct beginners in the craft techniques, recognizing that he could impart information if not the manual skills acquired through experience. His work was among the first of a long tradition of manuals intended for untrained builders. Nineteenth-century writers told farmers about log, *pisé* (rammed earth), and other cheap methods of building that they could attempt themselves, whereas twentieth-century writers instruct middle-class home-improvement buffs in the rudiments of the building trades.

Builders' guides, which combined technical information with architectural details, began to appear in Europe in the seventeenth century and flourished in the eighteenth and nineteenth centuries. They were imported to the American colonies throughout the eighteenth century, and in 1797 the first of a long series written by Americans, *The Country Builder's Assistant*, was published by Asher Benjamin of Greenfield, Massachusetts. Benjamin's book follows a formula universal among Anglo-American writers.

Like his colleagues, Benjamin compiled exercises in drawing and geometry; sections on the theory and drafting of the classical orders; architectural details of all sorts, from moldings to door and window frames to mantelpieces and designs for plaster ceilings; and explanations of technically difficult aspects of carpentry that involved complex problems in solid geometry, typically calculation of the lengths and angles of rafters in irregularly shaped roofs, and the laying out of curved stairs. At the end of a builders' guide like Benjamin's, the reader might find one or two illustrations of complete buildings. These were not offered to be copied, but as examples of ways the ideas in the book might be put together.

Builders' guides were aimed at experienced craftspeople, and were intended to supplement knowledge acquired through apprenticeship. Builders used them to give an up-to-date veneer to otherwise traditional structures. They made similar use of more intellectual architectural works. Since Roman times, Western architects had written elaborate treatises on architecture and planning that were intended to demonstrate their design prowess and to propagate their aesthetic theories. Andrea Palladio's *Four Books of Architecture* (1570) is the best known, but the eighteenth century experienced the first great outpouring of treatises.

Architects like James Gibbs, who presented his work in *A Book of Architecture* (1728), or Robert Morris, who wrote a series of Palladian tracts, addressed their works to a genteel public. Many of their gentlemen readers valued treatises for their intellectual content, but the books were used most extensively by builders, who treated them as visual sources like the builders' guides. The eighteenth-century Virginia mansion Mount Airy is famous for being derived from plates in Gibbs's book, the favorite treatise of colonial Americans. Virginia gentleman Thomas Jefferson and Rhode Island gentleman Peter Harrison also lifted designs for whole buildings from Gibbs. It was far more common for builders, like the Chesapeake joiner William Buckland, to adapt and combine decorative details from several books freely than to copy entire plates from single sources.

While the price books were conservative in their effect, the builders' guides and treatises of the eighteenth and nineteenth centuries introduced builders to change by ridiculing traditional standards in favor of an architectural *taste* or good judgment that required cultivation. Increasingly, they equated taste with constantly changing fashion. The successful builder was one who consulted architectural handbooks to remain current, and the wise client relied on his builder's, and later his architect's, expertise. Through such arguments, architectural books acted as primary agents in adapting Euro-American housing to the new market economy of the Western world.

The appeals to fashion and expertise were even more explicit in a third kind of architectural publication, which was created in England in the eighteenth century and introduced into the United States in the 1830s. The English called them "villa books," whereas American historians prefer the terms "style books" or "pattern books." The works of landscape gardener and publicist Andrew Jackson Downing were among the first and most influential American examples, but they were only the most conspicuous of many. Style books offered model designs for houses, farmsteads, and outbuildings. The accent was on external style and imagery, and few structural or decorative details were included. They were addressed directly to the consumer. Where the builders' guides used scaled technical drawings, the style books typically rendered their buildings in perspective. Houses were depicted in attractively landscaped surroundings and peopled with middle-class occupants (often women and children without men). The accompanying text argued for the design's tastefulness and appropriateness to modern life.

In their theorizing, style books were related to architectural treatises. In other respects, they belonged to the long tradition of advice-and-conduct books that stretched back to the Renaissance. Architectural good taste was presented as a form of good manners and even of morality. Architectural writers intruded on the domain of conduct and self-improvement books when they presented good domestic design as a means of promoting domestic happiness. Conduct-book writers like Catherine E. Beecher agreed that architecture could be the means to promote "Christian homes," and included model designs for houses in their works. Beecher and her colleagues were more interested in spatial arrangements than in appearance. Both architects and conduct-book authors claimed furnishings, hygiene, heating and ventilating, and household technology as their domains.

Style books were designed to promote architecture as consumer goods. They were advertisements for architecture. As a corollary, change was not only assumed, it was celebrated in these books. Yet they were subject to two limitations. First, books were poorly adapted to promote rapid change. Even after prices dropped in mid-century, they could not reach enough people often enough or quickly enough. Within a few years of their appearance in the United States, popular magazines like *Godey's Lady's Book* began to issue architectural designs more cheaply and quickly than book publishers could. At the turn of the century, the *Ladies' Home Journal* was prominent in promoting new architectural fashions. Through it Frank Lloyd Wright's "Fireproof House for $5000" became a staple of suburban architects across the country. The second limitation of style books was that the architect-author was rarely the direct beneficiary of his advertising. Style books promoted architecture in general.

After the Civil War, a new kind of book appeared in the United States that exploited the marketing possibilities of the press more directly. Introduced by George Palliser of Bridgeport, Connecticut, the plan book offered sets of working drawings for direct-mail purchase from the author. Plan books flourished at the turn of the century, when firms like the Newsom Brothers of California and the Radford Company of Chicago offered cheap plans for nearly every kind of small building as well as for apartment houses and commercial structures.

From the sale of plans, it was only a short step to the sale of entire prefabricated buildings. Prefabrication itself was not new, nor were books advertising mass-produced parts of buildings. The large-scale marketing of manufactured houses through books *was* new. Giant mail-order corporations like Sears, Roebuck added houses to their wares, while firms like the Gordon-Van Tine Company of Davenport, Iowa, and the Aladdin Company of Bay City, Michigan, focused on domestic buildings.

With the shift from the marketing of general images in style books to the sale

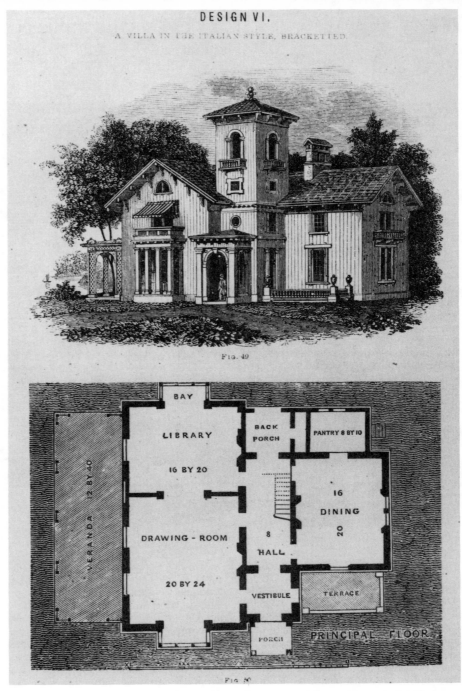

"A villa in the Italian style," from *Cottage Residences*, Andrew Jackson Downing, 1842. Cooper-Hewitt Museum Library.

of specific buildings in plan books and prefab catalogs, the appeal to the reader changed as well. Aesthetic argument was replaced by advertising copy, and the relation of occupant to house was reconceived. Early nineteenth-century clients were urged to consult architects and to build individualistic houses that suited the (male) owner's social standing and personality. By the end of the century, the emphasis had shifted to conformity and salability. The variety of predetermined designs should be sufficient for anyone. Readers were urged to avoid individualism and "extremity" and, with an eye to resale value, to select houses that would appeal to everyone.

Architectural publications are normative. That is, they tell people what they should do, rather than describing what they actually do. Their popularity is evident: vast numbers have been published since the seventeenth century, and all the major types are still being written and sold. But their influence on domestic architecture has been less direct than is traditionally supposed. Proportionately few houses were taken directly from books: even the closest copies show significant departures from the models. Plan-book and prefab-catalog houses, which are literal versions of their printed sources, form a small fraction of the buildings in any locality; only corporate builders of company towns used them in large numbers. Throughout their history, pattern books have served as sources of details that were attached to buildings of traditional or widely used popular form. They have presented *images* of fashion: readers get the idea rather than copying the specific forms. Most important, they have helped to accustom readers to the *idea* of change. But change in domestic architecture has rarely taken the precise direction advocated in the books: new ideas must be assimilated into the vernacular tradition.

Dell Upton is Associate Professor of Architecture at the University of California at Berkeley and author of *Holy Things and Profane*. He is editor of *Common Places: Readings in American Vernacular Architecture* and *America's Architectural Roots: Ethnic Groups that Built America*.

Transportation

The traffic crisis conditions our planning.

By C. Kenneth Orski

The recent migration of office jobs to the suburbs has profoundly modified metropolitan travel patterns. Today, most people work and live in the suburbs and only a small proportion of commuters travel to work in the central city. In a typical metropolitan area, suburb-to-suburb commuters outnumber suburb-to-downtown commuters by four to one. Even in Washington, D.C., with its heavy concentration of federal employment in the central business district, only 18 percent of all commuter trips in the region have a downtown destination. And recent data show that the proportion of commuters who live and work in the Washington suburbs is still growing—at something like 8 to 10 percent a year.

The suburbanization of office employment promises to have far-reaching implications for urban mobility. For one thing, it has enormously complicated the job of public transit. As long as the bulk of office jobs was located in the central cities, public transit systems functioned relatively effectively. Buses and trains collected commuters at suburban staging areas—rail stations and park-and-ride lots—and took them directly to their places of employment in the central business district. However, today, with a vast proportion of commuter trips ending as well as beginning in dispersed suburban locations, there simply is not enough "mass" to make mass transit work effectively. One consequence is a growing dependence of commuters on the automobile.

To be sure, buses and trains continue to play a role, but their market niche is diminishing as more and more jobs move to the suburbs. Already today, surveys indicate that fewer than 5 percent of suburban office workers take transit to work. As trip patterns become ever more diffuse, the proportion of commuters that can conveniently use mass transit is likely to grow even smaller.

Traffic congestion, New York. Adams & Adams Photographers.

The increasing dependence of suburban workers on the automobile has placed a tremendous strain on existing metropolitan road systems, which were not designed for today's traffic volumes. Traffic jams, once associated primarily with the central business district and the downtown commute, have migrated to the suburbs—the very places that people sought not so long ago as a refuge from the hustle and bustle of city living. As traffic invades the once tranquil suburbs, it begins to intrude upon the lives of an ever growing number of people. Getting stuck in traffic jams now affects virtually everyone.

Not surprisingly, traffic congestion has become the top-ranking concern of suburban voters, superseding such traditional concerns as crime, housing, and unemployment. In San Francisco, traffic has been singled out by Bay Area residents as the number one problem for three years in a row. In Atlanta, Washington, D.C., and Long Island, public opinion surveys echo these results.

One tangible manifestation of this concern has been increasingly vocal citizen opposition to suburban office development. Antigrowth sentiments are nothing new, but unlike the growth control movement of the 1960s, which was distinctly a "liberal" cause fueled by a desire to pre-

Highway interchange, San Francisco, 1968. © Robert Perron.

But severe political and environmental constraints are attached to this strategy. Most proposals for new roads meet with intense citizen opposition and become mired in protracted legal battles. Moreover, given current budgetary constraints, there is little chance that new highway construction could keep pace with the rapid growth of the suburbs.

Even a sharp infusion of new tax dollars would not necessarily provide a sure remedy for traffic congestion. Experience attests that new roads tend to fill up quickly with traffic, leaving travelers no better off than they were before. The Dulles Toll Road, for example—a commuter highway in the Washington, D.C. area—had reached near saturation levels only two years after its opening.

And so, a growing number of jurisdictions are shifting their attention to the other side of the equation. Instead of seeking to expand highway capacity, they are striving to reduce transportation demand on the existing highway facilities.

Demand can be reduced in two ways. In the short run, local governments can remove some peak-hour vehicle trips from existing roads by persuading commuters to shift to more efficient transportation modes and to travel during less congested hours of the day. In the longer run, however, the solution lies in enabling people to live closer to their jobs. This, of course, will require a major rearrangement of urban spaces, and an end to the present segregation of land uses.

Are we prepared to accommodate these changes? There is growing evidence that we are, as witnessed by the massive increase in suburban employment and the rise of the suburban office centers and research facilities. If present trends continue, the opportunity to live near one's place of work will increase dramatically by the end of this century.

Moving jobs closer to where people live is not only the best way, it is the only way of saving our metropolitan areas from debilitating traffic congestion, and thereby of ensuring their continued economic vitality.

C. Kenneth Orski is President of the Urban Mobility Corporation in Washington, D.C.

serve the bucolic character of suburban communities, the current traffic-induced anti-development fever cuts across ideological lines. As one California politician has put it: "The pervasive issue in every local election in California today is development—the impinging of commercial development and traffic on neighborhoods. Growth control has become a banner held up by everybody, from San Diego conservatives to San Francisco liberals."

The problem of escalating traffic dominates the agendas of neighborhood associations, city councils, and county commissions across the nation. It has become the subject of intense political debate in such widely dispersed locations as Contra Costa County, California; Fairfax County, Virginia; Du Page County, Illinois; Atlanta, Georgia; and Princeton, New Jersey. As congestion becomes a permanent feature of the metropolitan landscape, balancing the competing needs of development and transportation promises to emerge as a central challenge confronting local governments across the nation.

What can be done to improve suburban mobility and alleviate the growing traffic problem?

The customary response to rising congestion has been to build more highways.

International Building Expositions

How wide an impact have they had?

By Norbert J. Messler

The fictitious "All-Purpose Cottage" of Louis Ferdinand Céline's 1936 novel *Death on the Installment Plan* caricatures the enthusiasm for light, do-it-yourself dwellings at the end of the nineteenth century.

> ... "Your own house," absolutely detachable, tippable (that is, transportable), shrinkable, instantly reducible by one or more rooms at will, to fit permanent or passing needs, children, guests, alterable at a moment's notice . . . to meet the requirements, the tastes of every individual . . . An old house is a house that doesn't move! . . . Buy young! Be flexible! Don't build. Assemble! To build is death! Only tombs can be built properly. Buy a living house! Live in a living house! The "All-Purpose Cottage" keeps pace with life! . . .

Céline presents the cottage at the equally fictitious "Future of Architecture" exhibition held in Paris in 1898, at the Gallery of Machines. Designed for "families with insignificant incomes, homeless young couples, and colonial civil servants," and to be quickly set up with a "movable roof, 2,492 nails, 3 doors, 24 sections, 5 windows, 42 hinges, wood or muslin partitions according to the season," it actually ridicules a genuine goal of the turn-of-the-century Arts and Crafts movement—to encourage craftsmanship, to oppose standardization, to escape the evils of high-density housing in the city. In the midst of this movement a vogue for the suburban bungalow emerged, especially in England, where rampant building, according to Nikolaus Pevsner, degenerated into "bungaloid growth." As for the "All-Purpose Cottage," it must have been *too* light a dwelling: "The populace burst in so frantically, between the walls . . . that the little marvel was instantly torn apart, washed away, swallowed up! . . . absorbed like a pimple."

In the main, international building expositions are a twentieth-century phenomenon. From the mid-1920s to the 1930s and beyond, from the legendary Weissenhof-Siedlung of 1927 in Stuttgart to the Berlin Building Exposition of 1931 and the Interbau-Exhibition in the bombed-out Hansa district of Berlin in 1955–57, they have served as catalysts in launching new concepts of housing.

After the Town-Planning Exposition of 1910 in Berlin, European countries, with Germany as the spearhead, effectively responded to the ongoing demands that housing put on societies, communities, and architects. The expositions organized by the Deutsche Werkbund and its counterparts in Austria, Switzerland, and Central Europe prior to World War II were most significant in defining theoretical positions as well as in showing the cultural implications of various new residential concepts.

"The era of monumental expositions that make money is past," Ludwig Mies van der Rohe said, previewing the Exposición International de Barcelona of 1929, "today we judge an exposition by what it accomplishes in the cultural field."

Although the language of modern housing—slabs, row houses, apartment complexes, and the like—was clearly composed at national and international building expositions, not every housing style had an instructive show of this kind behind it. There is, however, an extra reward in reviewing the so-called Great Exhibitions, such as the World's Fairs, for modern housing prototypes: from Chicago's World's Columbian Exposition of 1893 with its voluptuous "White City," to Montreal's Universal and International Exhibition of 1967 with Moshe Safdie's minimalist "Habitat 67" in the "Man in the Community" section. Le Corbusier, for instance, claimed that his controversial "Pavillon de l'Esprit Nouveau" at L'Exposition Internationale des Arts Décoratifs et Industriels Modernes of 1925, in Paris was the prototype for his "Immeuble-Villa" living units, the first of which

(the "Unité d'Habitation" at Marseille, itself a collective housing prototype), was not to be realized until between 1945 and 1952.

Of quite a different *esprit* was the advertising campaign for the ideal American home, run by the *Ladies' Home Journal* in the 1930s. It reached its apogee in fifteen model homes at the New York World's Fair in 1939 that were dubbed the "Town of Tomorrow." Intended for low-cost maintenance, most of these houses carried that unmistakable bungalow-esque stamp of the American single-family house. Only house Number 11 ("House of Vistas"), with its white-cube geometry and horizontal fenestration running around corners, alluded to the aesthetic sensibility of the European modern movement. As one out of fifteen, this house could have been approved by James Ford in his *The Modern House in America* of 1940 as a "considerable departure" from houses built in America prior to 1934. This

Temple of Ho-o-den, World's Columbian Exposition, Chicago, 1893. Chicago Historical Society.

departure was made possible by the hegira of European talent to America in the 1930s.

Most of the pre-World War II building expositions were put together under the auspices of the Deutsche Werkbund and its European affiliates. The highlights were, apart from Weissenhof: Novýdum (new house), Brno, 1928; Home and Work Exhibition, Breslau, 1928–29; Neubühl-Siedlung, Zürich, 1930; Berlin Building Exposition, Berlin, 1931; Vienna Werkbund Exposition, Vienna, 1932; Baba, Prague, 1932.

Whereas the history of these expositions and their influence on housing is yet to be written, there can be no doubt about their universally effective implications. Consider the Weissenhof example: no program or manifesto surpassed this concerted action of international genius—Gropius, Hilbersheimer, Mies van der Rohe, the Taut brothers, Oud, and other modernists—in proselytizing the broad public about what was later called the international style.

Weissenhof provided the pilot scheme for the others. Together, they stressed standardization, flat roofs and cube geometry, a minimum of form and a maximum of unified space, flexible plans—in short, a radically new way of housing middle-class families, families with restricted incomes, and single people. Everything expressed the industrialized home, mass production, low-cost maintenance, and functionality—the last a concept that had already been outlined in the "Experimental House" at the Bauhaus Exhibition of 1923 in Weimar.

The two Czech building expositions at Brno and Prague are frequently neglected in modern housing history, but deserve special notice. The excellent work shown at Brno, for instance, chiefly single-family houses designed by such architects as Fuchs or Visěk, was a genuine contribution to the form language of the international style. Reductionist as they were, the Czech buildings apparently were more at ease with the sites they were occupying than their Western European counterparts.

Briefly, here are the others: the Breslau-Exposition of 1928–29 specialized in variations of the single-family house. At Neubühl in 1930 the sociological impact of modern housing was made the most important factor. Architects here emphasized flats for families and single people, introducing studios and row houses of various sizes. In Berlin in 1931 Mies van der Rohe repeated his legendary Barcelona Pavilion of 1929 in less costly materials, demonstrating the functional implications of its highly aesthetic concept. In Vienna in 1932 different types of single-family houses were tried out, including the work of such prominent architects as Rietveld and Lurçat. Lurçat's project for row houses, Roger Sherwood maintains, was the show's momentous event. It successfully eliminated dark interior spaces, the dilemma of traditional row houses, by utilizing very narrow units that could go on a shallow lot. For this and many other reasons, it seems logical to agree with Sherwood's evaluation in 1979, that "this adaptability to changing needs and family sizes makes the Lurçat project a particularly attractive solution to present problems."

Whereas these expositions were designed to tighten and strengthen the reductionist concept of housing within the modern movement, the more elegant argument of the art deco style in housing was, for instance, developed in the less appraised regions of architectural modernism. Pierre Patout's "Pavillon d'un Collectionneur" at the Paris Exposition of 1925, gloomy and ornate as it was, could at best have served as a model for modernistic *pompes funèbres*. Yet it is not merely a blank in housing history. Countless European and American houses of the late 1920s and early 1930s display related stylistic elements in form and décor. They perfectly characterize art deco's somewhat aristocratic deflection from the ongoing mainstream of simplification in modern housing.

Although most art deco residences reflect the French idiom, others suggest a related Mayan Revival Style. One authority, Marjorie Ingle, identifies the architectural prototypes of some Californian art deco residences of the 1930s in various reconstructed showpieces of pre-Columbian architecture at the Chicago Exposition of 1893. These walls of yesteryear initiated a Mayan revival style in housing the better-to-do. In quite a similar way, Henry-Russell Hitchcock suggested that the Panama-Pacific Exposition, held in San Diego in 1915, with Goodhue's "quite archaeologically handled" Spanish baroque, caused a renaissance of Spanish colonial architecture.

The influence of conceptual building expositions and of the Great Exhibitions on housing can indeed be subtle, operating almost unnoticeably. Few examples combine the subtle and the obvious. Among these, a final example from the Chicago Exposition of 1893 is paramount. The Ho-o-den, the Japanese pavilion at the fair, did not bow to the neo-academism of the White City. It consisted of three small wood buildings, presumably a reconstruction of the Ho-o-den complex (or Phoenix Hall) of 1053. As such it was roundly mocked, ridiculed, and basically misunderstood. As the first introduction of traditional Japanese craftsmanship and architecture to the United States, it shocked the public with its simplicity. Instead of monumentalism, it featured the calm aspects of Japanese design: harmony and irregular interval, horizontalism, open plan, respect for nature, general tranquility. The Ho-o-den (demolished during World War II), as has been proclaimed by many critics, clearly inspired the young architect Frank Lloyd Wright, who in 1893 was still in his formative period. Analyzing Wright's Winslow House, in River Forest, Illinois, of 1893–94, Grant Manson, for instance, asserts "the extension of the great eaves . . . the subdivision of the interior . . . all these and more have been suggested by the lesson of the Ho-o-den, as salutary improvement as yet missing or undeclared."

While the Asian look of the Winslow House intimately reflects the spirit of the Ho-o-den, the building itself clearly lacks the hoary otherness of the ancient Japanese temple and shows a young American face. And while this particular story is by no means the end of the legends wrought around the Ho-o-den (it is also believed to have launched the California Bungalow mode of the period), it indicates that there is similarly no end to the creative impulses on housing that are to be gained from international expositions.

Norbert J. Messler is a member of the American Studies faculty at the Ruhr-University in Bochum, West Germany, and author of *The Art Deco Skyscraper in New York*.

Winslow House, River Forest, Illinois; Frank Lloyd Wright, architect, 1893–94. Courtesy of The Frank Lloyd Wright Memorial Foundation.

Modern Masterpieces

What are some of our century's best?

Clockwise, left to right:
Habitat '67, Montreal, Quebec; Moshe Safdie and Associates, Inc., architects, 1967. John Ingwerson. Jerry Spearman.

Maison de Verre, Paris; Pierre Chareau, architect, 1928–31. Courtesy Dalsace-Vellay Archives.

Villa Savoie, Poissy-sur-Seine, France; Le Corbusier and Pierre Jeanneret, architects, 1929–30. Picture Library, Cooper-Hewitt Museum.

Palais Stoclet, Brussels; Josef Hoffmann, architect, 1905–1911. Courtesy Belgian Tourist Office.

Fallingwater, Kaufmann Residence, Bear Run, Pennsylvania; Frank Lloyd Wright, architect, 1937. © 1986 Hedrich-Blessing/Bill Hedrich.

Images of American Life

Monkey see, monkey do.

By Brendan Gill

Giuseppe Barberi, elevation of a town mansion, second quarter 16th century. Cooper-Hewitt Museum, Friends of the Museum Fund.

The relationship between movies and architecture has always been a close one, even as in earlier stages of history the relationship between the stage and architecture was close. The open-air Greek theater offered its audiences a proscenium backed by a masonry wall that was, in effect, the visible portion of a house (or a temple, or a citadel, or whatever else might be required by the play being enacted). That Renaissance masterpiece, Palladio's great Teatro Olimpico, in Vicenza, depicted a proscenium so grand that many a local go-getting dignitary, eager to be seen to have made good, encouraged his house architect to emulate

it. When the Bibienas began to design stage sets, it was again the case that their dreams of urban opulence—avenues of high-roofed baroque palaces receding into an infinite distance—influenced the design of entire cities, newly rich and newly ambitious.

In England in the sixteenth and seventeenth centuries, Inigo Jones designed settings and costumes for over thirty masques and again established styles that parvenus at the courts of James I and Charles I were eager to introduce into their houses. The realistic stage settings of the nineteenth century were so quickly copied that it was often hard to be sure

which had come first—the drawing rooms onstage or the drawing rooms in Park Lane and on Fifth Avenue. So-called society architects in our own century borrowed heavily from stage designers—indeed, it became a usual adverse criticism of certain architects in Palm Beach, Los Angeles, and the Gold Coast of Long Island that they provided their clients with stage sets instead of authentic houses worthy of being lived in.

No sooner had movies gained a measurable place in our culture than their influence upon hairstyles, clothing, and architectural design became evident throughout the country on many levels, whether social, financial, or aesthetic. Movie stars were not only heroes and villains in more or less plausible on-screen fictions: they were also role models *within* their roles. How they walked and how they lit their cigarettes was how we learned to walk and light our cigarettes. (Heaven forgive Bogie for the number of macho young men to whom he introduced a death-dealing addiction to tobacco.) Pretty young women from coast to coast batted their eyes in the way that Bette Davis batted hers; university professors heard themselves inadvertently saying "Yup" because Clark Gable said "Yup."

Life imitates art far more often than art imitates life, and in the 1920s American millionaires built themselves Tudor mansions partly because rich men in movies were seen to live in Tudor mansions. (Agreeably enough, some of those American millionaires were movie actors; the cowboy star Tom Mix lived in a Tudor house in Beverly Hills and was given to riding his horse Tony into the paneled great hall.)

Sometimes art imitates life imitating art, as when William Randolph Hearst's architect, Julia Morgan, gave him in San Simeon a realization in stone and mortar of a Spanish castle plucked from one or

another of Maxfield Parrish's immaculately painted fantasies. A further step was taken by *Citizen Kane*, in which a movie set imitates San Simeon, which imitates, etc., etc. No doubt somewhere in the dark heart of South America a cocaine-rich potentate is even now ordering his bespoke tailor-architect to run him up a duplicate of Kane's baronial drawing room.

Proof of the influence of movies on architecture and interior design may be found in scores if not hundreds of movies that tens of millions of Americans have sat through in the past half century. Often consciously but more often unconsciously, we have had the manner in which we live radically altered by these movies. Let a few examples stand now for many.

When the style called art deco became fashionable in the early 1930s, it was taken up by such skillful movie-set designers as Cedric Gibbons of MGM, and for a while we were all at the mercy of their infatuation with a chic that had far more to do with Paris, France, than with Paris, Kentucky. Our living rooms, bedrooms, and bathrooms, our bars and lavatories, our china and silverware were suddenly slim and shiny and streamlined; everything we looked at or touched appeared intended to travel at high speed, even if it were only a cocktail shaker or perhaps a pencil sharpener.

Gibbons was a brilliant designer in the art deco mode, and when it befell him to marry the movie star Dolores Del Rio, he built for her a ravishing house of steel, concrete, and glass, with green bronze trim and a dressing room and bathroom so entirely mirrored that one could see oneself multiplied to an extent that only the most narcissistic of beautiful women would have found bearable, much less pleasurable. By what may only have been a coincidence, when the vogue died, so did the marriage. Luckily, the house re-

Movie set from *The Single Standard*, MGM, 1929. The Museum of Modern Art, Film Stills Archive.

existence the masterpieces that a world of soft-hearted second-raters is unready for. In the movie, Roark is played by Gary Cooper, who says "Yup" every bit as convincingly as Gable ever did and who argues in court that he has done well to commit a crime—the destruction of an unfinished housing project of his design—because lesser men had been tampering with its perfection. Roark's eloquence is such that he is immediately acquitted. Hard as it may be to believe, this immoral and wretchedly written novel is a perennial best-seller; moreover, it has induced innumerable young men and women to become architects and to design—or attempt to design—buildings according to Roark's consummately selfish standard.

A third and final example leads us onto sunnier, higher ground. One of the most popular movies of all time—*Gone With the Wind*—has many memorable characters; it also has a house called Tara, and for uncounted numbers of Americans the house appears to have made every bit as deep an impression as Scarlett O'Hara herself. This high old many-columned southern mansion has been reproduced in one fashion or another all over America, on no matter how inappropriate a scale or in however inappropriate a climate. There are tiny Taras and tremendous ones; there are Taras in the hilly suburbs of Kansas City and in the flat wastelands of Houston. Hollywood itself has a Tara or two and it is only to be expected that Georgia should be overrun with them.

Plainly, we are right to be awed by the capacity of movies to induce in us a desire for change even on the most fundamental level of our culture, which is to say on the level of shelter and creature comfort. To watch a movie is no simple thing; it turns us willy-nilly into amateur architects and interior designers and places members of those professions (or, rather, their pocketbooks) in desperate peril. In a thinly disguised form, we moviegoers are all "monkey see, monkey do." Though not a lofty fate, it is nearly always a happy one.

Brendan Gill writes "The Skyline" column on architecture in *The New Yorker* and is author of *Frank Lloyd Wright*.

mains, as coolly elegant as it was on that long-ago day when the bridal couple took possession of it.

A second example of the influence of movies on architecture amounts, in a sense, to an incestuous one, being *The Fountainhead*, a movie about architects and architecture, taken from a novel by Ayn Rand. The hero of the novel and movie is an architect named Howard Roark, who embodies Rand's ideal human being: one who fulfills himself as an individual without any tiresome nonsense about being his brother's keeper. Roark is a genius, constantly battling to bring into

Residential Construction

It mirrors the economy.

By George Sternlieb

Housing construction is the roller coaster of the American economy. In peak construction years more than two million units are built. Yet not uncommonly they are followed by annual levels of half that. It is, or at least has been, the classic counter-cyclical tool. When the economy heats up, interest rates typically rise—and housing consumption falls. Conversely, at least historically, slack in the economy has generally been accompanied by low interest costs, and by a greater absorptive capacity on the part of consumers. In the very best of years, however, we add fewer than 2 percent to the housing stock. Alterations and improvements are increasing in dollar terms far more rapidly than new construction. Currently the former is running roughly 40 percent of the latter.

The primary product of this country's housing industry is single-family homes. Except when augmented by specific governmental incentive programs the level of housing starts on singles runs approximately three to one against multifamily units, that is, those with five or more units to a structure.

The potency of housing is only hinted at by direct employment, with some half million workers involved in residential construction in 1980 versus seven hundred thousand in 1986. This understates the enormous multiplier (and a singularly domestic multiplier) of ancillary services and goods that are purchased. For example, approximately three-quarters of all furniture purchases are made within eighteen months of moving into a new dwelling unit.

New residential construction tends to follow population. Thus, while the 1970s saw an upswelling of construction outside of standard metropolitan areas, this has now been reversed. It is the suburbs that are securing by far the vast bulk of housing starts in parallel with a reconcentration of population. But there is relatively little spillover to the central city. Rather the suburban ring dominates the scene, increasingly providing not only bedroom space but job and entertainment linkages as well.

This is one of the factors that has substantially increased housing costs: the growing potency of land as a percentage of total construction costs. Whereas in the immediate post-World War II years, the first wave of suburbanization occurred within a land cost context of little more than 10 percent of the total sales price, the figure is now double that.

A great regional population redistribution is followed as well as facilitated by new construction both in volume and, perhaps equally important, in price. In 1985, for example, the north and Midwest shared equally about a half million housing starts. The West by itself equaled this figure. But all three regions were dwarfed by southern housing construction, which was in excess of three-quarters of a million units. The South tends to have not only the highest level of housing starts and lowest housing costs, but generally the highest level of vacancy rate. The median house in this last region would have cost $75,000, whereas the northern equivalent cost slightly in excess of $100,000. In general, most federal housing subsidy programs have generated much more than a proportionate share of their start activity in the South. In very large part this is because of income/cost limitations, which are very much more easily met there than in the other regions.

Picture Library, Cooper-Hewitt Museum.

Low-Cost Housing

The United States is unique among major industrial countries with regard to the relatively small direct role that the federal government plays in housing. In the mid-1980s, when private construction was running in excess of $100 billion a year, the state and federal level was less than $2 billion. But this understates the potency of government policy. Mortgage guarantee programs such as the Federal Housing Authority, or tax incentive programs for lower-cost housing have provided major incentives and a broadening of the market to low- and moderate-income individuals.

However, there is little in direct input toward social housing by the federal government. In its place are the beginnings of efforts at the local and state levels to lower the price of selected portions of new facilities through such means as inclusionary zoning, which requires some

Housing construction site. U.S. Department of Housing and Urban Development, photo #5393C = 14.

low-income housing to be included as part of major projects. There has been a virtual wipeout of tax incentive programs, which provided a major impetus for relatively inexpensive multi-housing family starts. With the demise of nearly fifty years of federal subsidy mechanisms launched by the New Deal, low-cost social housing has largely been left to the same mechanisms as low-cost private transportation, such as used cars, and traded-down housing.

Efforts at innovative housing construction have yielded relatively little product. Building materials in the United States are far cheaper than in Western Europe and even more so than in Japan. In turn this has limited the efforts at innovative construction methods. Even mobile or manufactured housing's share of the market has remained relatively stable, typically approximating a fifth or a sixth of conventional housing starts, with little in the way of upward trend to suggest a major shift from this country's favoring of conventional units. The very largest of our residential developers accounts for no more than 2 percent of starts. Small-scale builders of less than ten units a year account for at least half the dollar volume of production.

In very large part this reflects a basic dynamic of this country's new housing construction. Ours is essentially a post-shelter society rather than one seeking shelter per se. In the latter case the consumer is looking for shelter from the elements, places that don't leak when it rains, that can be heated when it is cold, that have basic life-support systems. In very large part, housing here is bought to be sold. Purchasers of new houses may rattle off a series of likes or dislikes about the houses but the one that is most binding is "If I buy it, can I resell it?"

Within an inflationary pattern this insistent dominance looms ever larger. In studies of American wealth, if the top 3 percent of households by income is excluded, the bulk of the stored wealth of the vast middle is in the equity in their housing. Thus, Le Corbusier's doctrine of "housing as a machine for living" and the efforts at innovation of architects tend to be stymied by the American priority given

to resalability—and increasingly at a profit. As such, style and configuration are enormously conservative. Only the rich can afford experimentation. Only the poor are subjected to it. The middle must hoard their key-wealth depository.

The old political coalitions that provided a broad spectrum of clout for housing subsidy mechanisms for the middle class, and that yielded results for lower-income individuals, have broken apart because of this gap in priorities. Despite the shrinking size of American households, the median size of new units being constructed has expanded relatively steadily. The classic Levitt house of the post-World War II years was barely eight hundred square feet. The median size of new housing at the time of the Korean War had expanded to some eleven hundred square feet. Currently it is half again as large. Typically it is not built for first-time housing occupants but rather for trade-up households. In a typical year, between half and three-quarters of all the new single-family houses that are built are sold to people who are moving from previously owned facilities.

The Future

The changing configuration of household incomes in the United States, with a growing number of those who cannot afford the American dream, may alter the pattern of housing construction. This is emphasized by the increasing importance of minority households. Approximately a quarter of the growth of households in the 1990s will be in this sector. But this is taking place in the face of declining population growth and lower household formation rates. This suggests a decline of private housing construction, but also an increasing demand potential for adding to it through direct government input. This comes, however, at a time of low ebb in terms of public dollars, if not political verbiage, accorded to housing.

In the immediate future we need substantial growth in less expensive formats of housing, particularly common-wall row housing and housing for rental as against purchase. Unless there is a significant shift in household income distribution,

Ben Shahn, *Carpenters*, study for Social Security Building mural, Washington, D.C., 1942, tempera on paper. Southwestern Bell Corporation Collection, St. Louis, Missouri.

housing construction will increasingly mirror a bifurcated market: on the one hand, luxury housing for the new elite of our society, notably two full-time professional wage earners and, on the other, basic housing for the less affluent. Whether the political stresses that presently have divided the shelter and post-shelter societies can accommodate this

is a major issue that will determine the pattern of new housing construction in the years to come.

George Sternlieb is Director of the Center for Urban Policy Research at Rutgers University in New Jersey and one of the authors of *America's Housing: Prospects and Problems.*

Framing Up

Let's build us a house.

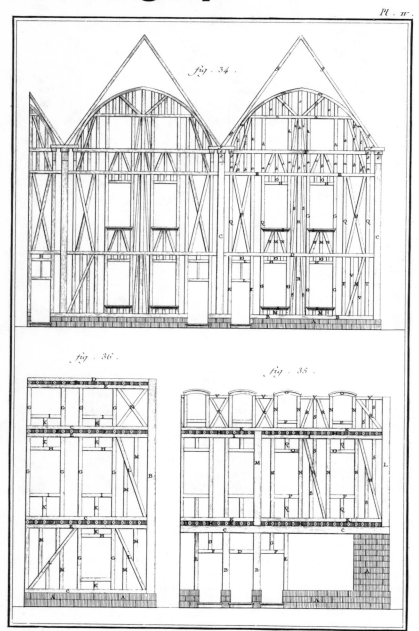

"Looks like housing starts are up in this area."

"Noah's Ark" from the *Nuremburg Chronicle*, Nuremberg, 1493. Cooper-Hewitt Museum Library.

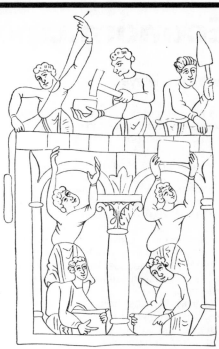

Reproduced from an illuminated manuscript, France, 15th century. Picture Library, Cooper-Hewitt Museum.

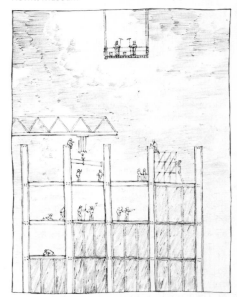

"Plan Ahead," from *Great Moments in Architecture*, by David Macaulay. Copyright © 1978 by David Macaulay. Reprinted by permission of Houghton Mifflin Company.

Economics of Housing

Many forces affect it.

By Martin Mayer

The provision of housing is to other economic activities as the staging of opera is to solo recitals. Both cost of production and perceived value—the blades of the great scissors of pricing—are sharpened and guided by an almost endless variety of societal and sometimes natural forces.

The best American construction lumber comes from southern forests, and lumber is cheapest where it is milled. But people who live in the South build their homes of concrete block, made from limestone that must be trucked great distances, because termites don't eat concrete block.

Virtually identical houses, upper middle-class homes on manicured lawns beneath spreading trees, vary in price as much as 35 percent on opposite sides of State Line Avenue in Kansas City, because on the Missouri side of the line residents have to pay for private school or have their children bused to urban slum schools, while on the Kansas side children breathe the sweeter air of ambitious suburban education.

In Denver a few years back, there was a street that divided densely packed houses from an empty expanse of dusty sagebrush: one side was in a fire district where homes could be insured (and thus banks would write mortgages); the other side was without fire department services.

There are historical patterns with origins that nobody knows. In Boston, the typical lower-income pattern was the three-flat building where the owner lived on one floor and rented out the other two as separate apartments; this turned out to have considerable strength as a source of residential stability and maintenance expenditures, and has been more or less imitated in Newark, New Jersey, especially in a Portuguese enclave (an interesting fact because Boston's three-flat community is also fairly heavily Portuguese).

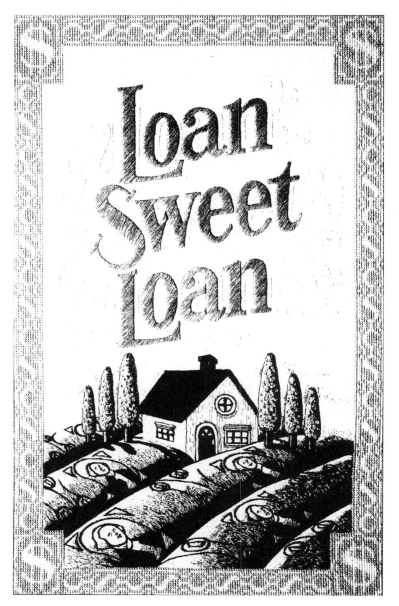

Margaret Cusack, embroidered sampler, Brooklyn, New York, 1987. Courtesy Federal Home Loan Mortgage Corporation.

Philadelphia and Baltimore are communities of tiny row houses, only twelve-feet wide, with alleys down the center of the blocks for deliveries and garbage disposal. In New York, Chicago, and Paris, rich people are happy to live in splendiferous downtown apartment houses; in London, San Francisco, and St. Louis, anybody who can afford a house of his own wants a house of his own. California home owners will put up with crowded conditions—four or five homes to an acre of land is not uncommon in areas where three hundred thousand dollars is a routine price for a house—while better-off families east of the Mississippi want as much opportunity as possible to look at their own grass, not to know who their neighbors are or what they do.

People may be "house-proud" or "house-poor" or "underhoused"; there are even people who economize on housing expenses because they would rather have a fancy car or a lavish vacation.

The dominant variables in the cost of housing are the price of land and the interest rates for long-term loans. On a three-year, $10,000 auto installment loan, the monthly level payment at a 10 percent annual interest rate is $322.67, and an increase to 11 percent raises that payment only $4.72. On a thirty-year, $100,000 level-payment home mortgage, the monthly payment at 10 percent is $877.57, and a one percent increase in the rate lifts that by $74.75. These giant disparities occur even though the average monthly amortization of the two loans is identical over their entire life. The level-payment self-amortizing mortgage is one of the great social inventions, enabling almost two-thirds of American households to own their homes. But it sets compound interest working against the home owner.

In theory, one would expect that a rise in interest rates would force the seller of the house to reduce his price and absorb some fraction of the added cost of money. Looked at another way, the $877.57 payment that services a thirty-year $100,000 mortgage at 10 percent will pay out a mortgage of only $92,150 at 11 percent. But in reality, a rising interest rate usually reflects a stronger expectation of inflation. Inflation lifts the price of real assets, like houses—indeed, it was the common cant of the 1970s and early 1980s that the home was the best repository for a family's savings. This led many families to buy (and probably enjoy) more home than they could really afford, because they regarded part of their payments on the house as their savings; it also meant that the savings rate as conventionally measured fell dramatically in the United States, forcing what was for most of the period the richest country in the world to import capital to finance industrial investment and then government deficits.

If the increase from 10 percent to 11 percent in the mortgage rate reflects expectations of an increase from 5 percent to 6 percent in the inflation rate, and if the rate of depreciation on a residential structure can be taken as 2 percent a year, the anticipated value of today's $120,000 home at the end of a thirty-year mortgage goes up from $291,000 under the assumption of 5 percent inflation to $389,000 at a 6 percent annual inflation rate. Thus we often get the oddity of home prices rising most rapidly when interest rates are also rising; the seller might in fact be able to *increase* the asking price for the house in the face of a rising mortgage rate.

Historically, home mortgage interest rates have been somewhat higher than rates on corporate bonds of similar duration, partly because the work of collecting many individual payments imposes costs on lenders, partly because mortgages tend to be paid off before their full term: people sell the house and move, or refinance when rates go down. But computers and associated equipment have greatly reduced the cost of processing mortgages: General Motors Acceptance Corporation, once exclusively a lender on automotive-related paper, entered the mortgage business in the mid-1980s and claims to be able to handle all the "paper-

work" associated with a seasoned mortgage—collecting from the borrower and paying to the lender and the local tax collector—at a cost of only fifty dollars a year per home.

Since the mid-1970s, with considerable help from government and quasi-governmental agencies, many bankers and investment bankers have been packaging groups of mortgages into bond-like instruments for sale in the market, enlarging the universe of potential lenders. Duration questions remain tricky—"pass-through certificates" leave the lender uncertain how much of his investment will be repaid each month, and "bonds" that promise a scheduled return and repayment must be "overcollateralized" with mortgages that can be substituted for those initially in the package that are paid off. Still, the "securitization" of the mortgage market has probably knocked as much as a percentage point off the interest rates home owners pay, and as noted above, that's not peanuts.

Land prices are determined, an old saw says, by three factors: location, location, and location. Like most old saws, this one remains more or less true, provided you define the word "location" broadly enough. Tax burdens on land and improvements tend to hold down or elevate the price of real estate. Already built-upon land beside the Pacific Ocean is much more valuable than it would otherwise have been because the Coastal Commission has virtually stopped the use of still-virgin plots along the shore. In towns where the local council has required developers to pay all the costs of providing sewer systems, schools, recreational fa-

cilities, and fire departments, similar land may sell for less than it does in nearby communities where the town asks current residents to help new neighbors get started.

Zoning plays a role, but sometimes a less potent role than the alternative uses to which the land can be put. Chateau Haut Brion has been surrounded by the expansion of the Bordeaux suburbs, but no building or set of buildings put on that property would equal the cash flow from making a first-growth claret. Stretches of Route 128 around Boston are zoned for both industrial and residential use, but electronics manufacturers always outbid apartment builders.

The cost of labor and building materials has on the average risen much more slowly than the cost of land and money (from 1970 to 1980, labor costs rose 130 percent and materials costs rose 154 percent—but land costs rose 248 percent, and financing costs rose 381 percent). By 1980, the monthly mortgage payment on an average new home was absorbing almost 40 percent of the median family income—and the mortgage payment, of course, is only part of the cost of a house. At that point, the fraction of Americans able to afford the median new home was down to about 20 percent. But reductions in interest rates and, to a degree, in land prices have reversed the trend in the 1980s, and in 1986 the Realtors announced, perhaps a bit optimistically, that by the rules of thumb historically applied by lenders, the median American family could once again afford to buy the median American home.

Home ownership has been subsidized by the United States government through tax laws that permit the deduction of mortgage interest payments and real property taxes from taxable income. Moreover, the federal government has never asked home owners to include in their incomes the "imputed rent" that they do not have to pay thanks to their equity interest in the property in which they live (as economists but no one else would consider correct tax policy.)

Rental housing, subject to similar cost increases, has been granted benefits relating to depreciation schedules at a time of increasing values; this has permitted investors to shift money from taxable income to capital gains. The new tax law reduces, though it does not eliminate, the tax savings of home ownership, and puts a stop to most "tax shelters" relating to rental housing. Its effects are entirely uncertain. Several municipalities have greatly reduced landlords' incentives to maintain rental properties by legislating rent control.

It is unclear whether the spreading blight of homelessness should be considered an economic phenomenon or not. The number of persons per housing unit in the United States has fallen steadily for half a century, and the number of square feet per person has risen. Quite apart from the contribution to the problem made by governments happily abiding by court orders that compelled the release of the incompetent, it is at least arguable that greater public provision of accommodations for the homeless, plus the great growth of public interest and sympathy, has hardened the hearts of heads of households, already burdened, who would in the past have accepted additional sacrifices to shelter unlucky relatives or even long-standing friends. Under any scenario, however, the abandonment of hundreds of thousands of livable apartments in the cities was a significant contributor to the current tragedy. The partial rehabilitation of some of these shells will be required to end the tragedy, and only governments can pay for that.

Martin Mayer is author of *The Builders.*

Industrial Villages

By Gillian Darley

The planned settlement, industrial model village, or community experiment, as the case might be, was the only testing ground of any significance for working-class housing in Britain during the eighteenth and nineteenth centuries. Some of the British model villages, for example, the Moravian settlements, had direct links with American equivalents, while less direct but no less important links were established between European paternalistic industrialists and their nearest American counterparts.

The only example of religious/utopian settlements in Britain to have more than theoretical importance was the Moravian communities, which were successful examples of economic self-sufficiency within purpose-built settlements. At New Lanark, Robert Owen followed the lead of the Moravians (probably inspired by their example, since he was still living in Manchester when the largest of their communities was founded nearby). Nevertheless, Owen was grafting his social experiment onto an existing mill village, which he then expanded. His ideas for Villages of Cooperation were enormously important, but they remained on paper.

The Moravian experiment was notable because it reflected and established the priorities of the community itself, made up of artisans and laborers in the Moravian congregation. The brethren, as they were called, operated within a carefully structured system of decision-making committees, and were building settlements worldwide for their own needs and abilities. This was community architecture two centuries before the term was coined.

The sites chosen were close to major conurbations in order to allow the brethren to market their produce and goods, but they still remained rural, gaining the benefits of open landscape with farming as part of their ventures. The two major Moravian settlements in Britain

Tenements, New Lanark, Scotland, 1790s. Gillian Darley.

were Fulneck, in West Yorkshire, begun in 1746 and Fairfield, in Droylesden (outside Manchester), founded in 1785. Housing was for families and for single brethren, with the chapel and school physically separating the premises for men and women. Built in a plain, late eighteenth-century vernacular, with classical detailing to distinguish the principal buildings, the architecture is reassuringly practical without the aesthetic purity of the Shaker villages. However, the planning, especially at Fairfield, is sophisticated—here a square within a square—indicating the privacy of the community without excluding it from the outside world. Although family life was central to the Moravians, there were also large numbers of single men and women, and the plan ensured that their quarters were separated.

While the Moravians founded a handful of villages in England (and one in Ireland), they set up numerous settlements in northern Europe and in North America as well as farther afield. Bethlehem, Pennsylvania, was, for example, a Moravian foundation. One fascinating link between the two congregations was the fact that Benjamin Latrobe cut his architectural teeth at Fairfield, before he left for the United States and greater things. His father had been the head of the Moravian establishments in Britain from 1764.

The nineteenth-century industrial village, both in Britain and the United States was based on a single mill or factory, rather than on the variety of cottage industries that the Moravians gathered into their communities. The innovation was to move industry into the countryside. The overindustrialization of the major man-

ufacturing cities was fast making them uninhabitable, and this was the obvious antidote. The background can be drawn from appalling statistics and vivid contemporary observations; for example it was estimated in 1842 that 22 percent of Liverpool's population of 175,000 lived in dank, desperately overcrowded cellar dwellings. Worse still, these were regarded as preferable to much else available because they, at least, meant privacy with an individual front door. Charles Dickens's *Hard Times* or Mrs. Gaskell's *North and South* set the scene all too literally.

So a village such as Saltaire, built by Titus Salt from 1851 onward in fine countryside in the Aire valley, a few miles from Bradford in Yorkshire, was an exercise in urbanism and paternalism. It was a mixture of expedient and undoubted philanthropic motives; it provided the workers in his alpaca wool mill with terraced cottages, usually with two bedrooms, according to their status on the factory floor. Managers, like foremen in railway villages, got superior residences, usually at the end of the terrace and with an extra story.

Lockwood and Mawson, the local architects who designed Saltaire, followed an urban pattern, providing municipal open spaces for all the world as if they were building in the center of a city, rather than a few hundred feet from magnificent open moorland. The Italianate factory of 1853, complete with campanile, was as much the hub of it all as was the Palazzo Communale in Siena; it was a symbol of the mercantile *raison d'être* of the new village. Accepting a 4 percent return on his housing investment, Salt could not be accused of profiteering in this venture.

By 1871 Saltaire consisted of 775 houses, 45 almshouses, and a population of 4,400, on a site of 25 acres. Amenities included schools that provided elementary education for 700 children; the Literary Institute replaced the village pub; and for spare moments, allotments of land for vegetable gardens were provided—in recognition of the fact that many of the population would have previously been outworkers, who combined home-based work in textiles with small holdings of land for farming in a traditional fashion.

Port Sunlight, begun near Birkenhead twenty years after Saltaire was completed, followed some of the same principles. It was a company village that provided all that was needed for employees without the pernicious attractions (particularly alcohol) that undermined the working man in the large cities. Architecturally, however, it bore no comparison to Saltaire. It was planned on informal lines, in an eclectic manner designed by various architects who agreed to mix historic references, as well as a wide range of building materials and finishes. Far less regimented, Port Sunlight emphasized the rural setting, albeit with the factory in its midst, more than had been the case at Saltaire. Its architectural links are with the informality of the early London County Council cottage estates, several of them designed and built before World War I.

Port Sunlight has to be seen against a changed background; public intervention in housing and social provision was beginning to gather momentum. The 1870 Education Act preempted the private provision of schools, and in 1893 the London County Council, just four years in existence, set up its Housing of the Working Classes Branch within the Architects' Department. By the time Port Sunlight was completed, the state was providing an Old Age Pension. The shoulders of philanthropists were being unburdened by the intervention of the state. Municipal housing was gathering momentum, and the war effectively brought an end to private housing ventures of this sort.

In Europe there were parallel attempts. The "chocolate village" at Noisiel, not far from Paris, was built by Meniers from 1874 onward. It consisted of over three-hundred brick semidetached cottages with generous gardens, each planted with a dozen fruit trees. A square and a park added to the "garden village" air, and the amenities included a store, bakery, laundry, baths, and free schools. Each cottage had four rooms and "a unique system of drainage with periodical flushing." Rents were reduced in accordance with length of employment in the factory, until retired employees were housed, gratis, in the almshouse.

In Germany the Krupps built eight colonies around Essen from the mid-nineteenth century until the turn of this century. The most attractive of them were the garden villages of Altenshof and Alfredshof, which consisted of groups of picturesque cottages subdivided into apartments, two or four in each.

The American industrial settlement took various forms; the cooperative village of Leclaire, across the river from St. Louis, was begun in 1890 and was based on residents buying a plot, with the infrastructure fully installed, and building their own houses. The village, set up by Nelson O. Nelson for the employees of the N. O. Nelson painting and plumbing firm, was provided with numerous facilities, all of which contributed to Nelson's aim "to make favorable conditions for work, intelligence, recreation, and duty." Beyond that, the intention was also to encourage cooperative ownership of all the facilities.

Leclaire contrasts favorably with Pullman, built outside Chicago in the early 1880s and famed for the catastrophic strike and lockout of 1894 as well as for the company's intransigence over its employees' right to acquire land or houses. Yet in architectural terms Pullman remains impressive, with its arcaded Italianate market square as the focus of the settlement of over fifteen hundred houses.

By early in this century the influence of the English Garden City movement had become central to new industrial communities in the United States. Availability of land made this kind of low-density planning more suitable here than in the densely populated parts of southern England, where the early Garden Cities of Letchworth and Welwyn were developed.

In the United States such development tended to form the basis of sizable cities. Gary, Indiana, is one example, although Kohler, Wisconsin, incorporated in 1913, remained on a village scale. The villages built for the employees of the Waltham Watch Works in Waltham, Massachusetts, near Boston, or the Crane Paper Mills, near Pittsfield, Massachusetts, played heavily on the imagery of a rural setting—the latter described as "consisting of the cottages and gardens of employees, with the homes of the directors here and there."

The English industrial planned village served as a blueprint for much of the first generation of public housing; the American examples tended to exert less influence on the form or direction of housing but were often to be the foundation stones of vast modern industrial conurbations. It would be hard to detect the Moravian village buried in Bethlehem, Pennsylvania, yet it was from that small community's acumen that an industry sprang, but deserting, as it expanded, the humane objectives and the spirit of cooperation of the original venture.

Nevertheless, the real difference in the importance of these settlements is more fundamental; it highlights the different ethos of England, still feudally inclined, and of the United States in the late nineteenth and early twentieth centuries. As one writer observed of Pullman, "Although the vice-president of the company disclaimed all idea of paternalism in the plan, it was evident that sufficient freedom of action to suit the American mind was not permitted, and the feeling that even in their houses they were not beyond the master's reach seems to have galled from the first."

Workers' housing, Port Sunlight, England, 1890s. Gillian Darley.

Gillian Darley is author of *Villages of Vision*, and is preparing a biography of Octavia Hill, the Victorian housing reformer.

Workplace and Residence

Industrialization brought many changes.

By James E. Vance, Jr.

Much of what we know about prehistoric peoples we have learned from the decoration of the "housing" that survives, found in the caves of France, Spain, and elsewhere. That legacy of wall drawings tells us of a fundamental tie that has accompanied human residence from the very beginning. It is fairly clear that most persons, or at least families, in earlier millennia had to be self-sustaining; if that subsistence shifted geographically over time, or during the annual cycle of biological productivity, these hunters and gatherers had to move with their prey.

So long as rough self-sufficiency persisted, workplace and residence were geographically highly coincident. But the specialization of labor that has permitted the growth of culture and technology—the rise of civilization—has slowly forced upon workers an increasing separation of workplace and residence. Thus, along with growing specialization of labor has gone an increasing complexity in the pattern of worker housing.

There have always been workers of such particular skill that they do one job better and commonly quicker than another does it. For that reason it would be incorrect to portray work throughout most of history as general and self-sufficient. Still, only in the rise of cities was labor specialized, and thereby housing specialization forced upon whole and often large communities. Summarizing the result, we know from Greek and Roman cities that the workshop pattern of housing became the most common there. Biological families tended to occupy quarters of buildings where they carried on a specific trade.

The next critical element in the evolution of worker housing, the rise of the occupational household, cannot be firmly dated. The origin of the biological family needs no further explanation; the rise of the occupational household does. Once labor specialization became widely prac-

Houses, Garden City, New York, about 1875–80. Brooklyn Public Library, Brooklyn Collection, Brainerd Collection.

ticed, already in classical times, there would have been the desire to pass on that skill to further generations, and in doing so, apprentices from outside the family would have been accepted for training along with sons or daughters. On completion of their training some apprentices would go out on their own; whereas others would remain as what came to be known in the Middle Ages as journeymen—those who were not their own masters but worked for daily wages.

The previous family workshop housing structure became transformed into a larger establishment now combining the housing of a biological family, often extended to several generations, with the sheltering of apprentices indentured to the master and of the journeymen normally in his employ. Thus emerged the extensive occupational household with its considerable demands for space. It re-

mained the dominant form of worker housing until the onset of the Industrial Revolution of the eighteenth and nineteenth centuries. Living space provided as an adjunctive responsibility of offering employment and apprenticeship predominated in cities. The rural solution to shelter came probably in a clustering of cottages and outbuildings, again in an occupational hamlet or village, with work and housing normally in the same building.

Such "domestic" manufacture could produce large quantities of goods, but their quality was variable, the labor cost was high (keeping wages low), and production could not be expanded save by enlarging the workforce—not always an easy thing to do. As merchants sought to gain greater quantities of goods and to lower their prices if at all possible, production was shifted into large buildings

where work could be standardized, quality improved, and, ultimately, simple hand-operated machines might be introduced. The factors, men who had organized the earlier domestic production, created these "factories," which for the first time shaped a physical separation of work and residence. Since most of this activity took place in what had been rural industries, no housing problem arose so long as the cottages and hovels of occupational villages could still be used to shelter the workers.

This transitional stage of factory workshops and cottage housing came in the seventeenth century. Once the factory with simple hand-operated machinery had been introduced, it was fully expected that large and more complex machines would be developed, to the point that other than hand power would be required in their operation. Thus, the Industrial Revolution of the second half of the eighteenth century was initially rural and of necessity water-powered.

Because the rural population in England was heavily committed to agricultural employment on large estates, with villages of employment-tied housing, there was no extensive body of geographically and occupationally mobile workers. Recruitment of employees came quickly to mean that employers—factory owners—had to provide housing in order to secure their hands. What has come to be known as the "Arkwright village," a water-powered mill with its attendant housing for workers, began to dot water-power sites in rural areas and to continue the long-standing practice of employment-tied housing.

The paucity of unused "water powers" in Britain, and elsewhere in Europe, forced the effort to secure additional power to turn to steam engines, bringing about a sizable growth of industry in steam-powered factories even before the nineteenth century. Once this geographically more mobile power—produced from coal that might be transported over considerable distances, particularly by water—came into use, it was possible to move the factory site to the potential labor pool, largely in or near ports.

For the first time since the Industrial Revolution, manufacturing grew as an urban undertaking, greatly transforming the provision of housing for the workers. Because in cities there was commonly a pool of potential laborers, employers quickly gave up the provision of housing (often with a hidden subsidy), throwing workers into a "generalized" housing market that operated as a strictly capitalist undertaking. The investors built tenements that they sought to rent for sums that were often expeditious, frequently extravagant, but always sufficient to repay their investment. Whatever housing the workers occupied was determined totally by their rent-paying abilities, frequently a limited and sometimes declining power. Deterioration was sufficiently rapid that, by the middle of the last century, reports on the social situation of the working class centered on the poor state of their housing, through crowding, unsanitary conditions, and pathologies to be found in their social environment.

Wherever industrial employment was urbanized, the preindustrial housing provision was quickly so overtaxed that by the American Civil War, active "housing reform" was seen as a critical need in industrializing countries.

In the late nineteenth century, that reform came first through the efforts of private individuals—George Peabody and Octavia Hill in Britain and A. T. Stewart in America. Their efforts showed a strongly environmentalist quality, arguing that socially and physically poor surroundings created indolence and, in turn, that fecklessness made slums of otherwise sound properties. This environmentalist thinking was the main generator of the efforts to improve housing in the last century.

A. T. Stewart, the New York City department store owner, sought in 1869 to remove his workers and those like them from the "bad influences" of the city by promoting Garden City, Long Island (the first in what became a movement) as a wholesome suburban solution to the housing problem, using cheap transportation and cheap outlying land to permit reasonable shelter for the working class.

A distinction arose between Britain and America: in America the rapid inclusion of successive tracts of cheap, outlying land into the fabric of the metropolis made great improvements in the urban environment, whereas in Britain advance came through improving the physical quality of inner-city housing, as in the case of the "Peabody Houses" erected in working-class parts of London at the middle of the last century. It was in suburban and rural industrial areas that America gained the edge with the rapid spread of the "American suburb," a form of open, largely single-family housing that was available to the working class in a degree unknown in Europe.

Efforts of the reform movement focused on sanitary conditions, viewed broadly as including adequacy of domestic space along with more traditional aspects of sanitation. Interwoven was the problem of the affordability of housing for families of lower economic classes. After the 1880s outright public ownership of worker housing grew rapidly in Britain, France, Germany, and other industrialized nations. The rise of socialism (which began first in cities) encouraged that solution to the degree that by the interwar years Britain had a majority of worker housing in public hands.

Many social critics have drawn a most favorable contrast for the United States, arguing that there was little or no public housing here, and scant regulation of private provision of urban housing. This narrow view overlooks the contrasting form of American housing policy. Here "cheap land and cheap urban transportation" became an alternative to public construction. The trolley worked a geographical revolution of the city when it burst upon American cities in the late 1880s, using the zoneless "nickel fare" to open vast areas of cheap peripheral land to the housing of all but the lowest economic classes.

Economic and social problems of the interwar years brought the penultimate phase of worker housing. This was largely a shift brought on by passage of time

Shively Sanitary Tenements, New York; Henry Atterbury Smith, architect, 1910–1911. Picture Library, Cooper-Hewitt Museum.

rather than a major structural change: Europe increased the role of public housing to encompass the sheltering of the working class in both countryside and city, and in ever-greater numbers. In the United States the Federal Housing Administration Act of 1934, part of the New Deal, brought the government into the business of guaranteeing mortgage repayment for the private housing of most Americans, even those of modest means, assuring that in the post-1945 years the American suburb became the home of the greatest number of Americans.

The most recent phase of worker housing began around 1970, when more than a generation of experience with the various interwar solutions rapidly turned negative. In Europe the provision of public housing, left almost entirely to planners and architects to implement, had been carried to a "logical," if inhumane, extreme: the construction of "megastructures" and "point blocks" appealed to the innovative obsession of designers freed of the restraint of the market, but seemed to carry environmental determinism beyond the edge of human tolerance.

Public housing has sought more humane structures, and countries have returned to greater reliance on private housing. In America the private provision of housing, aided by Federal Housing Administration mortgage repayment guarantees, declined rapidly when mortgage interest rates rose, fortunately only briefly, to some 20 percent. Even though rates subsequently dropped, they did so slowly, reaching a floor far higher than had characterized the period of the "suburban solution" that had lasted for nearly a century.

For the first time, multiple-unit rental housing entered heavily into the American experience, both in the suburbs and the city. In this most recent phase we have certainly not reached an ultimate form of worker housing. We never shall. We have, instead, witnessed what may be the end of a consciously distinct provision of housing for "workers." Today housing in Western society has truly become generalized for the vast mass of the population—nearly a century and a half after that process first entered our experience.

James E. Vance, Jr., is Professor of Geography at the University of California at Berkeley and author of *Housing the Worker* and *This Scene of Man*.

Workers' Housing

It has been a major design concern.

By Helen Searing

With the Industrial Revolution, workers' housing came into new prominence as a building type, but simultaneously tended to be consigned to the twilight zone between mere shelter and architecture. While the vernacular tradition of preindustrial society had on occasion yielded handsome and sound accommodations for the working and lower-middle classes —witness the Fuggerei at Augsburg of 1519 and the housing for Flemish weavers erected in Amsterdam in 1670— the altered political and socioeconomic conditions attendant upon modern capitalism, when living spaces were detached from the workplace and the dwelling became a speculative commodity, meant that the chief demands placed on workers' housing were likely to be utilitarian and financial. The prevailing wisdom was succinctly expressed in 1871 when a housing reformer wrote that the essential requirements were "economy, firmness, commodity, fitness for health and finally, in the last place, beauty."

Nevertheless, architects made sporadic attempts in the late eighteenth and the nineteenth centuries, and more sustained and vigorous efforts in the twentieth, to drag this humble building type onto the stage where it could hold its own architecturally with grander institutional structures like city halls and museums, and vie aesthetically with the nobleman's palace and the merchant's town house. Gradually the profession came to recognize that housing could be as much an architectural opportunity as a social problem—after all, many commissions rivaled in scale the most grandiose public projects of the age. From the mid-nineteenth century on, model housing schemes have consistently been displayed at international expositions, and competitions underwritten by public and private bodies have sought to solve the housing crisis that, with urbanization, had steadily grown. From the 1890s, housing moved

to the forefront of architectural consciousness, and often was in the vanguard of artistic and technical innovation.

The history of housing is riddled with controversy and challenge. The architect who wrestles with the problem is faced with the need to reconcile, if not celebrate, the tensions between the claims of the individual occupants—usually anonymous users whose wishes differed from family to family, and from generation to generation—and those of the community, between the private and the public realms. Toward this end two antithetical strategies have evolved: disguise

Project for a Graphic Arts Center, New York; 4,050 dwelling units clustered around service cores, designed for the Amalgamated Lithographers of America; Paul Rudolph, architect, 1968. Ezra Stoller, © ESTO.

and revelation. Some architects have chosen to cast housing into the mold of a more pretentious building type, like the urban palazzo, the bourgeois mansion, or the rural manor. Others have used the specific programmatic constraints to generate a direct expression of the functional and social givens of the commission, through creation and repetition of simple, standardized elements.

A related dichotomy concerns the preferred physical model: self-contained cottage or multifamily block. From the beginning of the nineteenth century, the former paradigm had been the ideal, but the other has remained the more realistic alternative. Tied to this question is the location and arrangement of housing ensembles. Many architects and reformers, seeking a *tabula rasa*, have looked to sites outside the cities, in country and suburb, whereas others have argued for insertion into the existing urban fabric.

The alternative ways of composing housing estates have been the subject of equally tendentious debates. From the 1890s through the 1920s there evolved from the *mietshaus* (rental treatment) of continental notoriety the *Höfe* (courtyard superblock), with dwellings grouped around the perimeter, enclosing interior courts and gardens, often including communal service buildings for laundries, kindergartens, public baths, and dining facilities; these were particularly characteristic of workers' housing in Vienna and in the Netherlands and Scandinavia. But such "fortresses of the people" have been opposed by those who considered them too dense, preferring a new type of settlement that came into fashion in the 1920s, the *Siedlung* (self-contained estate), which was composed of open rows of dwellings set amid generous green spaces. At the *Siedlung*, the cottage, transformed into flat-roofed volumes grouped into multiple series, remained the basic dwelling type, but much taller blocks or towers that came into being with the introduction of the elevator could also be accommodated there.

All these issues touch on the question of appropriate architectural language for workers' housing, a question best considered through specific historical examples.

Karl-Marx-Hof, Vienna, Austria; 1,382 dwelling units; Karl Ehn, City Planner, 1926–30. Picture Library, Cooper-Hewitt Museum.

Before the involvement of the public sector, any attempt to give housing an architectural presence occurred under paternalistic auspices, when the royal patron, bourgeois proprietor, or philanthropic society recognized that deliberate aesthetic effects could have a positive value—to reinforce the image of kingly power, to encourage a more productive workforce, or to maintain social stability.

Probably the first time that the workers' dwelling could rival in formal invention and grandeur the abode of the aristocrat was in 1775, at Arc-et-Senans, near Besançon. There, Claude-Nicolas Ledoux designed a series of gently curved buildings containing small suites, ranged to either side of a communal parlor with hearth, to accommodate the laborers and craftsmen of the French monarch's salt factory. A carved motif showing saltwater congealing into crystals adorns the stone walls of these dwellings, illustrating the source of the precious substance produced by the fledgling industrial com-

munity. The assumption that the tenants' occupations and place in the social hierarchy could provide inspiration for the architectural and decorative treatment of housing has remained operative in subsequent design.

Ledoux's masonry blocks, with their heavy proportions and simplified classical details, are representative of the movement known as romantic classicism that dominated architectural design and theory from the 1770s through the 1820s. Making a virtue of austerity, this severely noble style was appropriate as well for housing erected by middle-class industrialists, as Le Grand Hornu in Belgium, constructed between 1820 and 1835 to the designs of Bruno Renard, testifies.

Across the channel, however, a different vision of workers' housing held sway. The single and double cottages for old-age pensioners at Blaise Hamlet near Bristol, designed in the 1810s by John Nash, with their asymmetrical plans, lively silhouettes, and textured surfaces of

brick, bargeboard, rough-cast stucco and tile, created a picturesque paradigm that was echoed in simpler and more standardized fashion in town and country throughout the British Isles. The two-story cottage, preferably detached or semidetached, emerged among housing reformers as the favored type, which it has remained down to the present, in garden cities and suburbs, satellite towns and city extensions, all over the world.

The more pragmatic solution, however, when the architectural possibilities—and restraints—inherent in the housing program are taken into account, has been the multistory block. A number of utopian schemes for communal dwellings were advanced in the nineteenth century, the most striking of which was Charles Fourier's *Phalanstère*, a people's palace that resembled the château of Versailles in layout. In 1859, J.B.A. Godin realized Fourier's architectural vision in the *Familistère* that he built for his factory workers at Guise. Architecturally, the most notable feature of the design is that the dwellings face inward onto a glass-enclosed court surrounded by galleries that give direct entry to every flat at each floor. Such gallery access became a popular and dramatic feature of twentieth-century housing schemes: it eliminated corridors and, in effect, offered each tenant his own front door. Its first large-scale use on the exterior probably was at the Spangen estate in Rotterdam, where Michiel Brinkman in 1919 employed these "streets in the sky" to bold effect. Subsequently, wide galleries made circulation an exciting social experience in such municipally sponsored housing projects as the Park Hill Estate in Sheffield, England, of the 1960s, and Bijlmermeer, in Amsterdam, of the 1970s.

Until the end of the nineteenth century, even the most ambitious housing designs continued to reflect the prevailing styles. Thus the London County Council's fine estate at Millbank, in Westminster, erected between 1897 and 1902 to house more than four thousand people, demonstrates the architects' determination to introduce to the workers the charming, eclectic Queen Anne vocabulary that was so popular among the wealthier classes. 107

With the dawn of a new century, however, came successful attempts to give workers' dwellings a style of their own. In Paris, Henri Sauvage developed a fresh vocabulary, both technical and architectural. Using a reinforced concrete frame, he manipulated the building envelope to introduce light and air into street frontages by means of bay windows and terraced stepbacks. In the Netherlands, a group known as the Amsterdam school, led by the brilliant Michel de Klerk, regarded housing commissions as the major vehicle for their romantic ideas about the architect as inspired creator who would embody in his work communal cultural goals. Many of the Amsterdam school members were themselves from working-class families; using native brick and tile, they delighted the inhabitants of the publicly supported housing ensembles through witty details, inventive ornament, and playful compositions.

Antithetical means to reach a similar goal were essayed in the 1920s by architects associated with international functionalism. It was precisely the constraints of the minimal workers' dwelling that these modernists took as the starting point for their solutions, which also envisaged calling into play new techniques for mass production not only of standardized parts but of an entire dwelling. Germany played host to many experiments of this nature, which were supported by the Weimar Republic. Particularly famed for their superb formal discipline were the social housing projects erected in Frankfurt from 1925 to 1930 under the direction of Ernst May, and those in Berlin under the leadership of Martin Wagner, working with such architects as Bruno Taut, Hugo Häring, and Walter Gropius.

Ludwig Mies van der Rohe was in charge of the permanent housing exposition erected in Stuttgart under the aegis of the *Deutsche Werkbund*, an organization of architects and industrialists seeking to elevate the aesthetic quality of German design. Their *Weissenhofsiedlung* of 1927 presented a variety of models for emulation, from the prefabricated single-family house designed by Gropius, to the low row housing of J.J.P. Oud and the four-story apartment block of Mies. All exhibited the stylistic stigmata of international functionalism: planar surfaces, geometric volumes, and reliance on proportion and elegant detailing for aesthetic effect rather than ornament or historical references.

Represented at Stuttgart as well was the Swiss-born Le Corbusier, who probably has had more influence on the architecture of twentieth-century housing than any other figure, so concerned was he with the problem of the dwelling and so fecund was his imagination in dealing with it. In his City for Three Million of 1922, he devised a dwelling type that could be infinitely replicated, either as a single-family house (the cottage ideal) or as a unit in a larger block. This was the maisonette, or duplex, consisting of a double-height living room, a terrace, a small kitchen, and cubicle-like bedrooms inspired by the pullman car and the ship's cabin. In the *Pavillon de l'Esprit Nouveau*, constructed at the Paris Exposition of 1925, he demonstrated one of the actual units; in the same year, there was erected at Pessac a workers' village comprised of detached and semidetached versions of this dwelling type.

After World War II, Le Corbusier explored a much more plastic interpretation, wherein heavy concrete masses replaced the flat planes of the earlier model. He coined the term *Unité d'Habitation* for this building in which dwellings and communal services were combined, recalling Godin's *Familistère*, which had included a theater, school, and dining facilities. The first *Unité* was realized in Marseilles between 1946 and 1952.

Although obsessed with the concept of the standardized dwelling type, Le Corbusier was not insensitive to the fact that occupants of a single housing project might have very different desires. In one of the projects for Algiers that preoccupied him during the early 1930s, he sketched a long curving building with a variety of dwellings—from the *Pavillon de l'Esprit Nouveau* to a Moorish mansion—inserted into the larger structure of the block.

The concept of contrasting scales—the vastness of the modern city versus the intimacy of the dwelling—has been explored further by other architects in the post–World War II period. In the Harumi Apartment Block of 1957 by Kunio Maekawa, a gigantic concrete frame supports dwellings proportioned traditionally according to the dimensions of the tatami mat. In 1960, the Japanese Metabolist group, headed by Kenzo Tange proposed a mammoth extension over Tokyo Bay in which enormous megastructures were to provide platforms on which apartments could be built.

The English Archigram group took this concept to its most utopian extreme in "Plug-In-City." Futuristic cages containing circulation facilities would constitute the more permanent urban fabric; into them could be fitted temporary prefabricated dwelling capsules equipped with novel mechanical services. The number of capsules a given family would occupy would be determined by its spatial needs; as family size changed, units could be added or removed. Similarly, as new mechanical devices appeared on the market, the old capsules could be replaced in the megastructure by technologically more sophisticated ones.

Recent designs for workers' housing have continued to be representative of competing trends and ideologies, many recapitulating or expanding on earlier themes. In his section of the Gallaratese housing project of 1967 in Milan, Aldo Rossi has maintained the reductive forms of modernist housing while instilling in them a brooding power. Modernist too in its crisp detailing and generous use of glass is the municipal housing in Basel by Roger Diener and Wolfgang Schett, but the firm has not entirely eschewed traditional references in the entrance level of their recently completed perimeter block.

More deliberate historical allusions, not only to Fourier and Ledoux but also to ancient and baroque Rome, animate the series of workers' housing projects for the Parisian suburbs of Marne-la-Vallée and Saint Quentin-en-Yvelines, which have been constructed in the 1980s to designs by Ricardo Bofill and the Taller de Arquitectura. The materials—precast, integrally colored concrete elements and mirror glass—are resolutely contemporary, as is the huge scale of the buildings and their details, but the classical vocabulary is not.

A completely different historical model is evoked by Charles Moore in Whitman Village, Huntington, New York, of 1971–75. Moore's inspiration has been the picturesque cottage, as the pitched roofs and shingled surfaces reveal, but unlike his predecessors, he involved the eventual tenants in a dialogue so that an unprecedented level of user participation has shaped this public housing project. Ralph Erskine, the architect of the Bkyer Wall housing in Newcastle, England, of 1972–74, also consulted the future occupants of the community for guidance. Incorporating some existing older structures into the complex, a recent trend in housing design throughout Europe, he selected vernacular clues from the nineteenth-century buildings for the new dwellings of polychrome brick.

During the last decade architects involved with workers' housing have seemed more interested in revitalizing earlier typologies than in exploiting new technological processes. An exception has been Paul Rudolph, who made a series of investigations into what he has termed the "twentieth-century brick"—prefabricated housing modules made by the trailer industry, designed not to stand alone but to be fitted together into more communally conceived housing complexes. Moshe Safdie is another architect who has sought to increase the size and completeness of the module, but the expense of his concrete boxes in such realized projects as Habitat, erected in 1967 for Montreal's Expo, has put them beyond the reach of lower-income families.

Despite the affluence of many Western democracies, housing for the working class will remain a priority, while growing urbanization in the Third World requires that architects continue to address in all their varied dimensions the exciting possibilities and challenging problems of workers' housing.

Helen Searing is Alice Pratt Brown Professor of Art at Smith College in Massachusetts and co-editor of *American Architecture: Innovation & Tradition*.

Homemakers

Bon Ami cleans thoroughly.... *leaves no scratches*
...*has no odor*...*does not redden hands*

New Idea in Vacuum Cleaners

REGINA PNEUMATIC CLEANERS

THE REGINA COMPANY
Union Sq. West
New York
853 McClurg Bldg
Chicago

A woman's work is never done.

Clockwise, from upper left:

Livingston's Stone Tomatoes, Livingston Seed Company, 1930s. Picture Library, Cooper-Hewitt Museum.

Bon Ami, *Good Housekeeping*, September, 1933. Picture Library, Cooper-Hewitt Museum.

Regina Pneumatic Cleaners, *House and Garden*, October 1910. Picture Library, Cooper-Hewitt Museum.

Cream Top, *Good Housekeeping*, March, 1939. Picture Library, Cooper-Hewitt Museum.

Glenwood Gas Ranges, *House and Garden*, April 1930. Picture Library, Cooper-Hewitt Museum.

"Putting Up" Livingston's Stone Tomatoes

A DIRECT-COLOR PHOTOGRAPH TO SELL SEEDS . . . FROM WHICH TO GROW THE
TOMATOES . . . THAT ARE TO BE "PUT UP"

THE GREATEST OF GAS RANGES
Available for any home *in town*
or country

If cooking for your household requires an unusually large and completely appointed range, you will find the Insulated Glenwood De Luxe model made to order for your needs.

... *Insulated.* Its three large ovens are walled with heat-tight mineral wool which makes less gas do more work.

... *Heat-Controlled.* The Glenwood AutomaticCook gives you absolute control, automatically, of every oven heat.

... *Time-Controlled.* The Time Control Clock automatically lights the oven, keeps it at exactly the right heat and turns off the gas when your cooking is done. Nobody has to watch it.

... *"The Shelf that Cooks."* Over the enclosed cooking top is a convenient shelf where things can be kept boiling on heat that is wasted in other ranges.

... *Full Enamel Finish.* The beautiful finish of this range is all clean, shining enamel inside as well as out.

INSULATED GLENWOOD DE LUXE GAS RANGE — MODEL SNJ 24

... *New Vertical 'Broiler.* See how conveniently placed this broiler is. It is lined, vertically, with a special kind of fire-brick which broils by radiant heat on both sides at once and perfectly evenly.

YOU can have this range in your country house although it may be miles beyond the gas main. Let us send you more complete information about this Glenwood Model SNJ 24, and tell you about Pyrofax Gas Service, if you are interested. The coupon is for your convenience.

Insulated Glenwood Gas Ranges *De Luxe*

SEE THEM, IN ALL SIZES, AT YOUR LOCAL GAS COMPANY
Consolidated Gas Company of New York
Westchester Lighting Company
Brooklyn Union Gas Company
And all Offices of
Public Service Electric and Gas Company of New Jersey

GLENWOOD RANGE CO., Taunton, Mass.

FULL-BODIED QUALITY MILK...
...OR CREAM THAT WHIPS STIFF

Housing the Military

By Constance Werner Ramirez and Katherine Grandine

It meets changing standards of living.

Providing housing for soldiers and their families is a major program for the Department of the Army. In 1987 approximately 300,000 soldiers, 12,000 bachelor officers, and 175,000 families were provided with housing by the army in the United States and at installations abroad. This makes the army one of the largest "housing authorities" in the United States, and the largest one in the Department of Defense. The Defense Department (which includes the army, navy, Marine Corps, and air force) provides housing for over 650,000 enlisted personnel and almost 400,000 families worldwide. The congressional appropriation to the Defense Department for this program is currently about $3.2 billion per year for family housing and $1.5 billion for troop housing.

In the present era of a volunteer military service, housing is one of the benefits that accompanies the job. Sometimes housing is tied to specific duty assignments to ensure that military personnel are available when needed. The availability of housing has been a long- and hard-fought amenity for military personnel. The current funding for housing would have shocked the signers of the Constitution. In fact, it was the cost of housing a standing army that was one strong argument proposed against the establishment of a permanent army in the early history of the United States.

The amount of "housing" space and the amenities are determined by the rank of the occupant. The army allocates ninety square feet of space for the lowest ranking unaccompanied personnel. As a person rises in rank, so does the amount of living space he or she may occupy. Few regular army personnel are housed in the traditional sixty-four man wooden barracks of World War II fame, except when on special short training assignments. Most of the dwelling spaces are in barracks that resemble modern college dormitories. Many rooms have private bathrooms and shared or private kitchen facilities. Some barracks provide two-room suites for higher ranking personnel.

Married personnel are provided housing on post or housing leased by the army in the nearest community. In addition the army provides housing allowances to help pay the rent for private off-post housing. For housing on post, the army allows a minimum of 950 square feet per unit with two bedrooms for a noncommissioned officer family to a maximum of 2,100 square feet and four bedrooms for generals and their families. For commanding officers, 10 percent additional space is allowed.

The majority of the 100,000 family housing units on army installations in the United States have been constructed during the last thirty years and resemble middle-income suburban tract housing. About 10 percent of these army family housing units were built prior to 1940. In fact, if you were in the army, you might have had an opportunity to live in the same house in which Robert E. Lee, George A. Custer, George S. Patton, John J. Pershing, Dwight D. Eisenhower, or William C. Westmoreland had lived. These houses are an important part of the army installations in the United States and are an integral part of the image that Americans have of army posts. In addition occupants usually enjoy more space and amenities, such as porches and high ceilings, in the older quarters.

For more than 170 years, the army has been providing family housing at its installations. On most army installations the housing is located adjacent to the parade ground and near the headquarters building as an integral part of the cantonment. Many of the houses have been included in historic districts that are listed on the National Register of Historic Places. Housing, for example, is included in the historic districts of Watervliet Arsenal, United States Military Academy, Fort Myer, Fort Monroe, Rock Island Arsenal, Fort Leavenworth, Fort Riley, Fort Sill, Fort Sam Houston, Fort Douglas, Fort Huachuca, Presidio of San Francisco, Fort Shafter, and about twenty other army installations across the United States. In spite of a change of occupancy every two years, these houses have continued in their original use with few alterations.

Like all federal housing programs, army housing has been influenced by national trends and events. Most important, of course, is the allocation of funds from Congress. In addition, shifting national policies about the size and role of the military and changing responsibilities of the various branches of the army have affected the number and type of units constructed. Some of the earliest housing was constructed by the Army Corps of Engineers, which was authorized after the War of 1812 to build a series of coastal defenses, such as Fort Hamilton and Fort Monroe. Quarters 1 at Fort Monroe, built in 1819, is one of the earliest army houses still in existence and still used for family housing. The Corps was also responsible for construction at the United States Military Academy, which had been established in 1802 to educate engineers. The commandant's quarters there were constructed in 1821.

Besides the missions of defense and education, the army was also responsible for the production and storage of arms and ammunition. This mission was carried out by the Ordnance Department at such installations as Watertown, Watervliet, and Rock Island Arsenals. These installations were managed by a small group of officers who also built housing for themselves. One of these was Thomas J. Rodman, a multitalented officer who developed the Rodman gun. When he was placed in charge of expanding the Watertown Arsenal in Massachusetts in 1864, he built a large (17,840 square feet) brick residence for himself. After complaints about extravagant expenditures, Rodman was transferred to Rock Island in Illinois to construct a new arsenal. He also constructed a commanding officer's quarters in an elaborate Italianate style with a four-story tower. Over 19,000 square feet, the house is, after the White House, the largest quarters owned by the federal government.

As the country expanded westward, the army gained additional missions of protecting the trails and communities of the settlers. This required the Quartermaster Corps to construct many new garrisons. In 1860 the Quartermaster general issued proposed regulations that included plans for quarters for field officers, captains, and subalterns, as well as company quarters, hospitals, laundress's quarters, and ancillary buildings. Since the Quartermaster Corps was responsible for the design and construction of most of the installations established between 1855 and 1940, with such notable exceptions as the Army War College, thousands of houses were constructed in this period to standardized plans. Information about these plans was assembled for the first time in 1986 by Bethanie C. Grashof in A Study of U.S. Army Family Housing Standardized Plans for the Army Housing Office of the Corps of Engineers.

The development of standardized housing plans can be seen in the buildings at Fort Riley in Kansas. Established as a temporary camp in 1853 to protect settlers from Indians, Fort Riley was provided with funds by Congress in 1855 to construct new and more permanent quarters, stables, and storehouses. Several of these new quarters remain, including Building 24. Built of local limestone, and apparently constructed by local civilian stonemasons and carpenters, its two-story design may be attributable to the constructing quartermaster of the post. Five years later, when the Quartermaster

Corps issued a proposed regulation on barracks and quarters, the regulation housing plans greatly resembled the quarters at Fort Riley. This suggests that the nascent standardized housing plans were based on the experience of the constructing quartermasters at various posts, or that the engineers of this period were already aware of headquarter's ideas for house designs.

The subject of standardized housing plans did not emerge again until after the Civil War. Prompted by criticisms of conditions on army posts published in 1870 by the Surgeon General and by disparities in army housing across the country, Quartermaster General Montgomery C. Meigs submitted to Congress a set of plans for temporary barracks and quarters for use on western posts. Dated 1872, these plans consisted of drawings for company quarters, commanding officer's quarters, company officer's quarters, a guardhouse, a commissary storehouse, and a bakehouse. It is not known who was actually responsible for the designs. Although Meigs was qualified to design the quarters (he was later architect of the Pension Buildings in Washington, D.C.), he had also been collecting drawings and plans of army posts since the late 1860s. He may have developed the standardized plans from these. (This collection of drawings is now in the cartographic division of the National Archives and Record Service, Washington, D.C., and is an invaluable record of army buildings standing in the 1870s.) When these plans reached the new posts, many were usually adapted and changed to suit specific locations.

In 1885 Fort Riley entered another building phase when General Philip H. Sheridan was authorized to make it a major cavalry post. Overseeing the new construction was Captain George E. Pond, an 1872 West Point graduate who eventually served in the army for forty years before retiring in 1907. Although he was in charge of all phases of procurement and construction of the new post, he appears to have also been interested in designing buildings, since some of the earliest drawings state, "Designed by Capt. Geo. E. Pond."

The initial officer housing constructed by Quartermaster Pond reflected Meigs's 1872 plans. Pond used the basic house form but added a polygonal bay at the sides and incorporated a full two-story, two-bay projecting front gable that divided the front porch into two sections. While it is known that Pond hired specialists for specific jobs, including an architect, he received public praise for the housing designs used at Fort Riley. Unknown is the role that the architect William A. Goding played in the design of the Fort Riley houses.

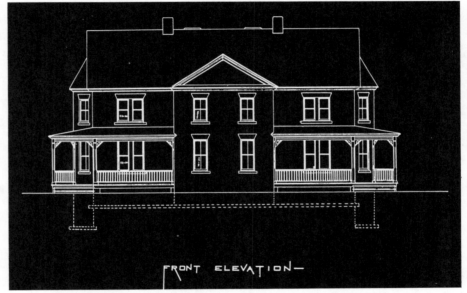

Military quarters, front elevation of duplex, Fort Riley, Kansas; Captain George E. Pond, architect, 1887. Source: National Archives, Cartographic and Architectural Branch, RG-77.

In 1889, a variation of the standard plan for officer housing was introduced by Captain Pond at Fort Riley. It was a duplex with a four-bay gable front. Originally built with Queen Anne decorative elements, this plan was easily adapted to the colonial revival style, which became popular in the army during the first decade of the twentieth century. Whether Goding or Pond should receive credit for this design is not known. All that the records show is that Pond went on to supervise construction at several other installations and that in the 1890s this building was adopted as

the prototype for standardized housing plans issued by the quartermaster general's office in Washington, D.C.

Notable exceptions to the use of standardized plans are the designs for two of the army's most prestigious installations, the Army War College and the United States Military Academy. The Army War College, located at Fort McNair, Washington, D.C., was designed in 1903 by Charles F. McKim, of the architecture firm of McKim, Mead, and White. McKim was a member of the United States Senate Park Commission (The McMillan Commission), which made recommendations for a park system in the District of Columbia. The fifteen officers' quarters that line one side of the Beaux-Arts style campus were designed in Georgian revival style with six two-story columns across each front portico. At the same time, the firm of Cram, Goodhue & Ferguson, the New York City firm renowned for such buildings as the Cathedral Church of St. John the Divine, was at work on housing in the Gothic revival style at West Point.

In 1926 the army began yet another major building program. Responding to a

critical nationwide military housing shortage, the army committed itself to a long-range plan to remedy deplorable housing conditions. By 1933 total appropriations for the program had neared $80 million. The Quartermaster Corps was instructed to develop designs that responded appropriately to the different climatic conditions and to regional architectural styles. House plans were designed in either Georgian revival style with slate roofs or Spanish mission revival style with tile roofs, depending upon the location of the installations. At Fort Riley, the Georgain revival style was constructed of local stone to match earlier construction.

With the conclusion of World War II, the Quartermaster Corps was dissolved and its housing responsibilities turned over to the Corps of Engineers. The Corps of Engineers tried several new ways of providing and managing housing. One of the programs in the 1950s allowed private entrepreneurs to build housing on military installations and to manage it for the army. Through another program, the army designed housing but borrowed funds through a mortgage authority for construction by private contractors. Today, the army contracts locally for both the design and the construction of its housing.

The Department of the Army, then, which currently manages over 1,300 installations in the United States, has a long tradition of providing housing for military families that meets changing standards of living. At the same time, it has pioneered in the use of standardized plans, the integration of housing with a planned community (the military installation), and the adaptation of contemporary architectural styles to military construction. The army is proud that today's officer can still look forward to residing in houses that were occupied by famous predecessors.

Constance Werner Ramirez is the Historic Preservation Officer for the Department of the Army. **Katherine Grandine** is a historical consultant with Traceries, an architectural history and preservation consulting firm in Washington, D.C., currently completing a study of historic army family housing with Mariani & Associates, Architects.

Egalitarian Experiments

Communitarians and feminists designed for diverse households.

By Dolores Hayden

Between 1800 and 1930 hundreds of communitarian socialist experiments and dozens of feminist cooperative housekeeping societies in the United States devised a variety of plans for housing arrangements and domestic reform. Most communitarian socialists hoped to create model towns based on agricultural, industrial, and domestic work. By combining the labor of many workers, male and female, the founders proposed to end the isolation of the individual farmer, industrial worker, and housewife. Improved housing and equal wages were often advertised to make such communities attractive to both men and women. Cooperative housekeeping societies had more limited goals, but hoped to provide women with a chance to limit the hours of domestic work and receive economic compensation for their tasks.

In contrast to the private houses that all these reformers saw as insular, inefficient, and onerous, they hoped to build communal or cooperative housing facilities—physical exemplars of an equal society. The architectural form that new housing took was determined by the economic and social structure of the new community. At least three types of organizations can be distinguished: the rural communitarian settlement functioning as a large family; the rural communitarian settlement containing nuclear families within it; and the urban or suburban cooperative housekeeping society whose members included both nuclear families and individuals.

Communitarians organized as large families of a few hundred or a few thousand members often wished to abolish the nuclear family in order to promote greater attachment to a shared communal ideology. Common ownership of all property and a commitment to free love, which they saw as the sexual counterpart of their economic communism, were sometimes required by such groups.

"The Children's Hour," Oneida Community. Kubler Collection, Cooper-Hewitt Museum.

Others insisted on celibacy. Communal families often preferred large dwellings, where several dozen members or more were housed in rooms or dormitories connected to a shared kitchen, dining room, and nursery.

Shaker communal architecture is celebrated. Among other communal groups less well known in architecture circles, the Oneida Perfectionists, led by John Humphrey Noyes, built a large Mansion House in upstate New York for two hundred members, beginning in 1847. Its eclectic facades were based on the architectural guides of Andrew Jackson Downing. The Perfectionists dedicated themselves to "the enlargement and improvement of home." In 1862, when they moved into their Second Mansion House,

with single bedrooms and sitting rooms planned for "Complex Marriage," they claimed that "Communism in our society has built itself a house." Views of their domestic arrangements were widely published in popular illustrated magazines.

In contrast to those communitarian socialist experiments where specific social, religious, or sexual practices were enforced among members of the communal family living under one roof, communitarian societies containing nuclear families within them offered more diverse housekeeping and child-care arrangements. Usually nuclear families had some private territory to themselves, as well as access to communal kitchens, dining rooms, and nurseries. Some organiza-

tions wanted their housing to take the form of a "unitary dwelling," which contained all of these disparate communal and private facilities; others developed networks of related buildings, including private family houses or small apartment houses and various communal housekeeping facilities. Frederick Law Olmsted visited the North American Phalanx—a farming community of 125 members established in New Jersey in 1843—and admired the communal kitchen, laundry, and bakery that were housed in the same building as family apartments (which had no kitchens) and dormitories for singles. Members who wished, were permitted to build private houses (with kitchens). Members of the Phalanx were followers of Charles Fourier and believed in choice as part of communitarian living.

Other groups designed villages composed of both private apartments and communal housekeeping facilities. The Amana Inspirationists established seven communal villages in Iowa around 1855. Residents dwelt in dormitories and in family apartments that usually had four apartments to a house. Schools, kindergartens, and other workshops were located near the residences and kitchens.

The organizers of cooperative housekeeping services were not communitarian socialists. They believed in private property and the private home, but they hoped to imitate the communitarian socialist housekeeping arrangements previously described and transplant them to urban or suburban neighborhoods. These organizers expected nuclear families to subscribe to a cooperative housekeeping service as a matter of rational self-interest.

Melusina Fay Peirce and members of the Cambridge Cooperative Housekeeping Society, middle-class women, many of them the wives of Harvard professors, organized the first such cooperative housekeeping service in Cambridge,

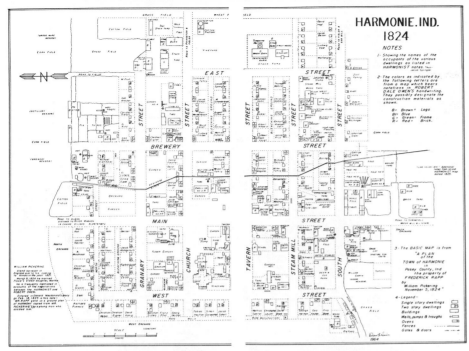

HARMONIE. IND.
1824

NOTES

1- Showing the names of the
occupants of the various
dwellings as listed in
HARMONIST notes (har-
monist Springer)

2- The colors as indicated by
the following letters are
from a map which bears
notations in ROBERT
DALE OWEN'S handwriting.
They possibly designate the
construction materials as
shown.

B= Brown= Logs
Bl= Blue
G= Green= Frame
R= Red= Brick.

3- The BASIC MAP is from
"a PLAN of the
TOWN of HARMONIE
in
Posey County, Ind
the property of
FREDERICK RAPP
by
William Pickering
November 5, 1824"

4- Legend:
Single story dwellings
Two story dwellings
Buildings
Wells, pumps & troughs
Ovens
Fences
Gates & doors

Town Plan, Harmonie (now New Harmonie), Indiana, 1824, from *Harmonist Construction*, by Don Blair (Indianapolis: The Indiana Historical Society, 1964); drawing by Don Blair. Courtesy Indiana Historical Society.

Massachusetts, in 1869. In 1870 they established a cooperative store, laundry, and bakery for forty subscribing households, but they did not provide child care, since the scheme was intended to give women the opportunity to spend more time with their children. In 1871 the Cambridge experiment was discontinued, but Peirce continued to lecture and write for the cause, publishing *Cooperative Housekeeping: How Not To Do It and How To Do It, A Sociological Study* in 1884. She recommended kitchenless houses grouped around a central cooperative workplace as the ideal architectural arrangement.

In *Women and Economics*, published in 1898, the economist Charlotte Perkins Gilman recommended kitchenless houses of a similar sort, suggesting that they could be linked in urban rows or connected by covered walkways in a suburban block. Like Peirce, Gilman also recommended the construction of kitchenless apartment hotels with collective

dining facilities for women with families. Two later books added to this vision: *Concerning Children* (1900) described the benefits of professional day-care arrangements; *The Home, Its Work and Influence* (1903) provided a detailed critique of private, inconvenient domestic architecture.

European enthusiasm for cooperative housekeeping was as keen as American. Melusina Fay Peirce and Charlotte Perkins Gilman had English disciples as well as American ones. Raymond Unwin advocated cooperative housekeeping arrangements in his influential treatise written in 1901, "The Art of Building a House." Gilman interested Ebenezer Howard in cooperative housekeeping as well; Howard organized six experiments in cooperative housekeeping at the garden cities of Letchworth and Welwyn in England. Gilman's disciples in Scandinavia created "service houses," the earliest of which were built in the 1920s and 1930s. These apartment houses, which included

child care and cooked food service, also belong in this housing tradition.

In both communitarian experiments and feminist experiments, housing design was often accompanied by innovative domestic technologies. Economies of scale in domestic life provided an obvious justification for better design and equipment: fifty private families might need fifty kitchens and fifty stoves, but a communal family, with one large kitchen and one large stove, had the resources to invest in additional, more sophisticated laborsaving devices. Both the utopian socialist communities and the cooperative housekeeping societies took pride in providing themselves with the latest in heating, lighting, and sanitation devices, designed to ensure the health of their members and to lighten domestic labor. And what they did not acquire, the men and women of the group might invent.

The Shakers have to their credit an improved washing machine, the common clothespin, a conical stove to heat flatirons, the flat broom, a removable window sash for easy washing, a window-sash balance, a round oven for more even cooking, a butter worker, a cheese press, a pea sheller, and an apple parer that quartered and cored the fruit. Members of the Oneida Community produced a Lazy Susan dining table center, an improved mop wringer, an improved washing machine, and an institution-scale potato peeler. (Their community policy was to rotate jobs every few months, so that a technique learned in one community shop might be the source of inventions to speed another sort of task.) Members of cooperative housekeeping societies designed different types of containers to keep cooked food warm for delivery to subscribers, and sometimes their inventiveness was applied to the design of special wagons and vans for delivery as well.

Inventiveness also extended to developing equipment and spaces for child care. The Amana Inspirationists built large cradles that could hold up to six children for their kindergartens. At the Familistère in Guise, France, great care was spent on designing the perfect individual cradle. The same community devised a special

device for teaching young children to walk, a circular structure of supports surrounding a center filled with toys and games. Other communes had specially designed furniture at child scale, a novelty not to be found in nineteenth-century homes. One commune, the Bruderhof, still supports itself today by manufacturing "Community Playthings." Outdoor spaces might be designed with children in mind as well: the Oneida Community had an extensive landscaped playspace; the Shakers created model farms and gardens for their boys and girls; the Llano del Rio community organized their teenagers to build a clubhouse and dormitory called the "Kid Kolony."

Both communitarian settlements and feminist experiments shared a commitment to space as a social product. Both emphasized the importance of model housing design. They translated their ideas about family life and essential work into physical form in order to provoke discussion about better ways to live. Whether their goal was common ownership or women's liberation, these reformers attacked the mid-nineteenth-century patriarchal family with father as provider, mother as isolated housewife, and children always at home.

In the late twentieth century, a variety of new household types dominate American society, including the two-earner family and the single parent responsible for both earning and nurturing. American architects and planners have not yet designed affordable housing with essential services such as child care for these new household types. Historic communitarian settlements and feminist experiments do offer a legacy of physical innovation in this area. But more important than their kitchen houses, or kitchenless houses, their cradles or "Kid Kolonies," is their recognition that new family forms would require new designs for dwellings and neighborhoods to support their social and economic success.

Dolores Hayden is Professor at the Graduate School of Architecture and Urban Planning, University of California, Los Angeles, and author of several books including *Redesigning the American Dream: The Future of Housing, Work and Family Life.*

113

Communal Living

There is a gap between ideal and real.

By Gilbert Zicklin

The communes of the late 1960s and early 1970s were populated mainly by disaffected young people looking for solutions to problems of contemporary living. They and their older sympathizers started or joined communes to flee from what they perceived as the personal and political failings endemic to our society: an out-of-control competitiveness, a pervasive emotional constriction, and threats to human life from environmental pollution and nuclear war.

From bohemian enclaves in cities mainly on the East and West Coasts, and from campus communities around many of the more liberal colleges and universities, loosely affiliated networks began forming around a core style of art, music, spirituality, drug use, and politics. Such bohemias of predominantly middle-class young people, which were soon written about as "the counterculture," gave rise to a distinctly unmiddle-class set of values. They favored self-expression over self-restraint, the child over the adult, the spontaneous over the planned, the natural over the artificial, cooperation over competition, spiritual awareness and ecstasy over doctrine and petitioning prayer, the experimental and far-out over the ordinary.

As with any set of values that one holds, "ideological work" (in Bennett Berger's felicitous phrase) is often required to square one's actions with one's beliefs, or, for that matter, one belief with another. This danger of walking on the edge of hypocrisy was shared by the counterculture and earlier romantic and rebellious youth movements holding up new sets of ideals, such as the one chronicled by Henri Murger in Paris in the 1830s, or that of the German *Wander-vögel* in the first part of our century. The counterculture was not unique, either, in opposing the settled, quotidian lives of the older generation to its own search for new experience. And while some ele-ments of its praxis paralleled those of other movements (German youth also wore sandals or went barefoot, let their hair grow long, and esteemed the countryside more than cities), some features of mid-twentieth-century counter-cultural life were unique, among them the tendency to form communes.

Now a commune was not simply a place to experience communion with other like-minded individuals (the German youth movement had its version of Woodstock in the form of large groups camping at the foot of "beloved" mountains). It was that, and more. Since a commune was meant to endure for more than the time of a camping trip, it required that certain functions be carried out, with tacit or explicit rules governing the carrying-out of these functions. For example, if the group settled on purchased land and a mortgage was taken out, then some decisions had to be made about how to meet the mortgage payments. Would richer communards be expected to carry the burden of repayment, while poorer ones paid nothing? Would those who had little or no savings be expected to work for their share of the money? Could the group, itself, find a way of collectively earning enough?

One commune chose the latter course and went into the automobile repair and retail parts supply business. In another commune, the income from Aid to Families with Dependent Children (AFDC), veterans' disability checks, and a father's child support was pooled to meet the mortgage payment. In one of the larger communes, members were expected to come up with a proportionate share of the mortgage by working in one of the commune's enterprises, by doing commune-related administrative work and having their wages credited toward their obligation, or by earning income from jobs held "on the outside."

If the need to pay for land forced the

Close Enough Farm, Norwich, Vermont, 1960s. Courtesy DSS.

group into planning for the longer term, it also symbolized the belief in the survivability of the group. Where a group as a whole did not face the mortgage or rent problem, either because the land was owned by one of the members outright or was being paid for by one or more of the wealthier members, their commitment to one another might well be more tentative. For such groups, the major economic constraints were those concerned with daily life: getting food, buying household necessities, paying the electric bill (where there was electricity to buy), keeping a vehicle running.

Here again, the need to provision the group with food raised the same basic questions about how communal the group would be. Would the group try to raise its own food and provide to each unit what it needed? If it did not try for food self-sufficiency, would it pool its money, buying and eating collectively? Or would each individual unit be expected to meet its own food needs from its own efforts to grow or buy it? Such questions were seldom formally decided; they were more likely answered in the practices that the groups rather unself-consciously adopted. Numbers counted. Smaller communal groups (fewer than ten members) tended to have a common refrigerator and take their main meals in common, whereas larger groups tended to have individual domiciles, and if ideology did not suggest otherwise, took

114

their meals in private.

The issue of who could become a member also tended to call for group decision. A few communal settlements were designated as "open land," such as Morningstar Ranch in northern California, where everyone was invited to visit and, at the outset at least, anyone could stay. Others set membership limits and requirements, usually after the founding period. In one communal farm that was oriented to Hindu spiritual practice, some members preferred that anyone with a genuine hippie mentality be allowed to stay, whereas the leadership wanted to confine membership to those who espoused the founder's particular doctrine. Meetings of the membership were held in which both points of view were heard. When the decision was taken to narrow the basis for membership, some communards protested by leaving the group.

Since the counterculture out of which the communal movement sprang tended to be tolerant of deviance and "accepting" of people, it was generally with reluctance that membership issues were acknowledged at all. Most groups did not want to feel they were actively excluding anyone, at least during the initial period after the commune's founding. But as the locations of less obscure communes were publicized in the underground press or passed around by word of mouth, groups sorely pressed by inadequate facilities and "undersocialized" guests felt forced to put up signs limiting visiting to certain days and hours and to discourage any visitor from staying beyond a few days. Visitation rules could be bent for individuals whom the group liked, and, once inside, a visitor might become a member by entering into a couple relationship with someone already in the group. But, for the most part, groups put up barriers to too easy access by outsiders.

The possibility of intragroup sexual relations created another set of problems for commune members. Earlier generations of communitarians tended to solve potential problems of intragroup sexual jealousies and rivalries either by forbidding sex with members (the "incest taboo" solution practiced by the young in many Israeli kibbutzim), or by forbidding sex entirely (the "celibacy" solution of the Shakers), or by institutionalizing intragroup sex and thereby depersonalizing it (the Oneida solution). Contemporary communards tended to allow sex between noncoupled members, with the proviso that at the point where they became "serious" with each other they would accept the norm of relational fidelity (the American solution?).

Some groups valued the personal freedom of having sexual relations outside of one's primary relationship, even with other group members. Those communes took a risk that the tensions created by ensuing sexual jealousies might shake the nascent solidarity of the group. Nevertheless, some groups continued to maintain positive views about intramural sexual freedom, holding to the belief that the problem lay with the jealous individual not with the principle of sexual freedom itself.

Many communes had members with children, and perforce had to make decisions about their rearing and formal education. In smaller communes where people felt particularly linked to one another either emotionally or ideologically, children were more likely seen as belonging to the group. Any adult might assume parental functions of nurturance and discipline and children of different parents might live in a children's room, rather than in the domicile of their parents. Where children were domiciled with parents, they could still take on the identity of being "such-and-such commune's kids," even referring to themselves that way. But, as with the norms of sexual freedom, the opportunity to break down the barriers between adults by sharing responsibilities for the children could also create tensions among adults who were not able to give up the singular identification that parents in our society have with their children.

Children growing up in a commune might come under the authority of nonparental adults whose mode of nurturance or discipline might not coincide with the parents' views. Mothers might become upset at another communard for saying "no" to a child because they did not believe in using the word *no* to teach a child what not to do.

On the other hand, this sort of conflict over nonparental rights to "parent" a child of the commune was not necessarily typical of the way in which biological parents dealt with other adults in relation to their children. Single mothers, especially, were grateful that male communards took an active interest in their children, especially their boy children, but even couples appreciated the attention of other adults to their children. Often this allowed them a respite from parenting responsibilities, but, more so, it was seen to broaden the child's circle of adult intimates in a way that lessened emotional dependence on parents and allowed the child, as an individual, to maintain relationships of his or her own choosing.

Some of these latter parents, who by and large were younger and had spent less time in the counterculture before coming to the commune than people in the more anarchistic communes, did give the counterculture's typical free rein to their children. One example will suffice: an eleven-year-old boy got his mother's permission to leave the commune with a not very well acquainted neighboring sixteen-year-old girl to spend a couple of days at a nearby riverbank where hippie-type young people in the area came to cavort. Explaining her decision to an interviewer, the mother spoke in the language of the counterculture, saying she would rather let him go and take the risk that something might happen to the boy than take away his freedom to explore on his own and encounter new experiences. (On the other hand, this was a boy without a father present, and at a time before this incident, his mother had talked about being worried that the boy was not as self-confidently masculine as were boys with fathers around. Reason, as well, to let him go?)

The communards of the late 1960s and early 1970s were engaged in fashioning little societies of their own. More than most people ever get the chance, they were able to "make history," to affect the events and institutions that in turn were to shape their own lives. By redefining the nature of the ties that bind adults and that bind adults to children—financial, sexual, organizational, and parental ties, to name the ones touched on here—they created new social worlds. They had, still, to operate within the limits of what was legally tolerable to the larger society, though they tested those limits as well. And they had to learn, mainly by trial and error and from the experience of other communes, what parts of their ideologies could profitably be put into practice and what parts had to be shelved lest their implementation generate lethal tensions.

Urban political communes, urban and rural spiritual communes, and rural hippie-anarchist communes all faced similar constraints in trying to create a new moral and social order: the prior socialization of their members in straight society, the gap between ideology and practice, the need to foster commitment to the group while also allowing for personal freedom, the difficulty of achieving consensus in decision-making were only a few.

Most of the communes that were begun did not thrive for very long. A few matured into full-fledged communities (Ananda, for one, a spiritual settlement in northern California) and some remained small, close-knit "families" (the commune that Bennett Berger and Bruce Hackett called "The Ranch," also in northern California, comes to mind). The decline in the commune-building impulse from the mid-1970s on can be attributable to a number of factors: the changing economic picture (from abundance to scarcity); the aging and sorting out of the Woodstock generation into postcollege mainstream institutions; the media surfeit with hippiedom and a subsequent posture of benign neglect; the uncoupling of psychedelic drugs from the spiritual quest.

The communes that survived, like Ananda or The Ranch, were the residues, or, perhaps, are the still-living precipitates of the intense mixture of hope, desire, and belief that something radically new and better in human affairs could be created by the younger generation.

Gilbert Zicklin is Associate Professor of Sociology at Montclair State College in New Jersey and author of *Countercultural Communes: A Sociological Perspective.*

Once Upon a Time . . .

From *Winnie the Pooh*, by A.A. Milne, illustrated by Ernest H. Shepard. Copyright 1926 by E. P. Dutton, renewed 1954 by A. A. Milne. Reproduced by permission of the publisher, E. P. Dutton, a division of NAL Penguin Inc.

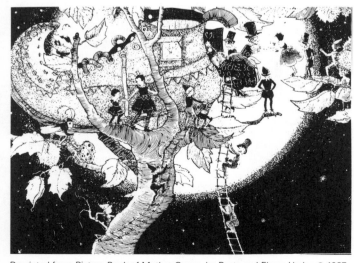

Reprinted from *Picture Book of Mother Goose*, by Berta and Elmer Hader. © 1987 by Berta and Elmer Hader. Used by permission of Crown Publishers Inc.

Illustration by George and Doris Hauman, reprinted by permission of The Putnam and Grosset Group from *Stories That Never Grow Old*, edited by Watty Piper.

Illustration by Lorinda Bryan Cauley, reprinted by permission of The Putnam and Grosset Group from *The Three Little Pigs*, © 1980 by Lorinda Bryan Cauley.

"The Melancholy House of Usher," from *Tales of Mystery and Imagination*, by Edgar Allan Poe, illustrated by Arthur Rackham (London: George C. Harrap & Co. Ltd., 1935). Cooper-Hewitt Museum Library.

From *The Wind in the Willows,* by Kenneth Grahame, illustrated by Arthur Rackham, The Heritage Illustrated Bookshelf (New York: The Heritage Press; The Limited Editions Club, Inc. © 1940).

Paper Houses

By Robert Grudin

Commanded by Zeus to free Odysseus from Calypso's cave, Hermes the messenger flies forth over the sea and finds the goddess at home:

> She was singing inside the cave with a sweet voice
> as she went up and down the loom and wove with a golden shuttle.
> There was a growth of grove around the cavern, flourishing,
> alder was there, and black poplar, and fragrant cypress, . . .
> and right about the hollow cavern extended a flourishing
> growth of vine that ripened with grape clusters. Next to it
> there were four fountains, and each of them ran shining water,
> each next to each, but turned in sundry directions;
> and round about there were meadows growing soft with parsley
> and violets. (*The Odyssey*, trans. Richmond Lattimore)

Hermes, a god himself, is delighted to wonderment by his surroundings. But immediate delight is only part of Homer's literary aim. Scattered throughout his great poem are a variety of dwellings—the sumptuous palaces of Menelaus and Alkinoös, the firelit hut of the swineherd Eumaios, the magical house of Circe, and the fatal halls of Agamemnon and Cyclops—which all serve as foils and echoes of the home Odysseus pines for: the columned hall of Ithaca, where he will defeat the suitors and regain his Penelope. Thus Homer's houses, though different in detail, are all in a sense the same house, serving to develop the profound spiritual event that dominates the epic: the experience of coming home. In celebrating this universal experience, the poet gives us, as a by-product, some of the first detailed descriptions of residence in Western literature.

Homer's literary inheritors have built their houses far and wide, boldly and voluminously, and with small regard for

"House of the Seven Gables," Salem, Massachusetts, c. 1668. Courtesy Historical American Building Survey (HABS); photograph by Richard Cheek.

boundary lines, mortgages, and rights-of-way. Many of these fictional houses are mere contrivances—soulless, two-dimensional backdrops conformable to stylized expectations of geography and social class. But many others are constructed more solidly and expanded to their full mythic dimensions. Great writers, like great architects, do not build mere shelters; instead, just as Homer did, they design structures for classic experience.

What are these structures? The house, first of all, is the physical context of the family, the haven of childhood and adolescence. Specific houses thus become vehicles for the myth and memory we associate with our own origins. Literature takes advantage of this symbolic connection, making fictional houses express the profound experiences of childhood and youth. For young Marcel, narrator of Proust's *A la Recherche du Temps Perdu*

(*Remembrance of Things Past*), an isolated bedroom at Combray is the original focus for a loneliness and longing that will characterize his lifelong experience:

> At Combray, as every afternoon ended, long before the time when I should have to go to bed and lie there, unsleeping, far from my mother and grandmother, my bedroom became the fixed point on which my melancholy and anxious thoughts were centred.

For Yeats, a country house sitting room provides the structure for an evocation of long-past beauty and delight:

> The light of evening, Lissadel,
> Great windows open to the south,
> Two girls in silk kimonos, both
> Beautiful, one a gazelle.

And Augustin Meaulnes, the protagonist of Alain-Fournier's *Le Grand Meaulnes* (*The Wanderer*), finds realized in a strange

chateau the lantern-lit enchantment of adolescent dreams. In all such episodes, the house assumes a distinct temporal spirit. It becomes a shrine of memory, a residence for experience that can be recalled but not repeated.

Fictional architecture may be used as well to convey social criticism and insight into history. When the ten young narrators of Boccaccio's *Decameron* travel from the plague-ridden streets of Florence to the airy gardens of a Tuscan villa, they move figuratively from confusion to clarity and from the confines of medieval ethics to the promise of new values. And when, in *The Merchant Of Venice*, Bassanio takes ship from Venice en route to Portia's country seat at Belmont, he leaves behind the well delineated world of commerce and enters an indefinite sphere of hazard and opportunity. Emily Bronte uses geographical and architectural contrasts between Wuthering Heights and Thrushcross Grange to set up a broader dialectic between the Dionysian and Apollonian poles of her novel; whereas Charles Dickens, whose houses are always physically responsive, establishes with Chesney Wold and Bleak House the contrast between an atrophied social order and the opportunity for renewal and enlightenment.

For Tolstoy, even interior decorations can carry intense moral meaning. His character Ivan Ilyich, newly promoted and intent on furnishing his bourgeois home to perfection, unconsciously type casts himself by including "all things people of a certain class have in order to resemble other people of that class." While hanging curtains, the hero falls and sustains the injury that will bring on his death.

Architectural symbolism is strong medicine that can be toxic in overdose. That the British reading public had suffered such an overdose by the 1930s is suggested by Stella Gibbons's takeoff of the house-mystique in *Cold Comfort Farm*:

Dawn crept over the Downs like a sinister white animal, followed by the snarling cries of a wind eating its way through the black boughs of the thorns. The wind was the furious voice of this sluggish animal that was baring the dormers and mullions and scullions of Cold Comfort Farm.

The farm was crouched on a bleak hillside, whence its fields, fanged with flints, dropped steeply to the village of Howling a mile away. . . . It crouched, like a beast about to spring, under the bulk of Mockuncle Hill. . . . A long corridor ran half-way through the house on the second storey and then stopped. One could not get into the attics at all.

For good measure, Gibbons adds a woodshed, where, many years before, Aunt Ada Doom had been permanently warped by the sight of "something nasty."

To give a house tone or mood is but one step away from giving it an autonomous personality or, alternatively, an indwelling spirit. It may say something about literary psychology to note that such personalities and spirits, when they occur in fiction, are seldom benign. The idea of the haunted house rests on two solid premises. The first premise is that all houses that are not spanking new are vaults of history—that they have been lived in by people other than ourselves and at times beyond our memory. These people shaped the house to suit their own personalities; they endowed it with their otherness; they experienced, within its dark privacy, the passion, resentment, and anguish that they dared not show the world at large.

These intimate emotions, together with the secret actions that tend to follow upon them, are the very stuff of hauntings, both in legend and in literature. The existence, certain or putative, of such past feelings and actions finds echoes in our own loneliness, passion, and fear. Marley's ghost, chained to the symbols of greedy ownership, rattles down the corridors of the house of Scrooge. In the wind and snow, Cathy Earnshaw's longing spirit scratches from outside at a bedroom window of Wuthering Heights.

The second premise for the haunted house resides in an association that is even more profound and pervasive. Not

Grenier, after Tissandier & Gilbert, *Paris qui Travaille*, in *Le Magasin Pittoresque*, 1883. Kubler Collection, Cooper-Hewitt Museum.

only in function but also in form, the house is an icon for the human personality. Cathy's urgent "Let me in!" is not only the cry of a spirit trying to enter a building, but the entreaty of an impulse to break its way into the interior of human awareness. Scrooge's dark house is the macrocosmic image of his dark soul.

Domestic architecture, with its multiple floors, basements, attics, closets, corridors, and rooms, suggests a mental architecture of association, memory, and repression, with consciousness moving, now here now there, like a watchman's candle in a dark palace. Minor writers stick to the parlor, the bedroom, or the kitchen. Great writers take survey of the whole house, from the great halls to the hidden chambers.

At times such surveys end catastrophically. Occupants of hidden chambers can carry messages too terrible to endure. Like Poe's Madeleine Usher, who ascends from her tomb to destroy her brother's mansion, they assert the hegemony of guilt over redemption, of past over present and future. At other times the search, for all its unnerving discoveries, brings reconciliation and self-acceptance. Spencer Brydon, the hero of Henry James's tale "The Jolly Corner," uncovers his own inner self by facing, in the dark and empty halls of a large town house, the ghost of the man he might have been.

But need we enter every room? Other great literature suggests that the riddles of the psychological house, rather than being solved, should be accepted as latent sources of enchantment. Giuseppe di Lampedusa's Don Fabrizio, hero of *Il Gattopardo* (*The Leopard*), owns a huge palace whose rambling courtyards open on many deserted rooms; he remarks that a palace of which one knows every room is not worth living in. Self-knowledge, Lampedusa implies, is less a form of total awareness than a balance of awareness and mystery. Fabrizio's untouched rooms are valuable precisely because they are left untouched.

Robert Grudin is Associate Professor of English at the University of Oregon in Eugene and author of *Time and the Art of Living*.

Domestic Environments

Their design reflects changing functions.

By Jean Gordon

Most writing about American houses concentrates on the history of styles— the saltbox, the Greek revival, the ranch house. But people live in rooms, which over time have changed, not merely in shape, location, and furnishings but also in the way they have been used and experienced by their occupants.

In different periods and regions, different *types* of rooms can be said to exemplify the character of family life existing at that time and place. Type in this sense refers to function; whether the room was used for sleeping, eating, cooking, entertaining, or, as was the case in the earliest houses, all of the above. Type can also be thought of as a stereotype— of the sort found in literature. Fictional stereotypes have the disadvantage of being oversimplified, but they are useful in highlighting differences.

A selection of passages from American writers of the nineteenth and twentieth centuries illustrates the types of rooms that exemplify changes in the American family. These families are by no means inclusive of all Americans. For the sake of simplicity and continuity, the families are white, native-born, middle-class Easterners. A more comprehensive treatment would include blacks, immigrants and Americans from all classes and regions of the country.

In the years before the Civil War, many writers used houses to point up the differences between the plantation South and Calvinist New England. Southern plantation homes were both formal and relaxed. Their focus was outward and diffuse. Doors were left open and there was a constant movement from the relatively few large, squarish rooms of the interior to the many outbuildings that clustered in the back. Being old-fashioned, plantation rooms were relatively unspecialized. One room, however, was customarily the site of the main meal of the day—a major focus of southern rural life. Good food has traditionally been valued by aristocratic societies, and, as southern cookbooks affirmed, a mistress was judged on her ability to provide a daintily spread table at the shortest possible notice. At two in the afternoon the entire family would gather along with visiting relatives and guests for a leisurely dinner lasting two or more hours.

The family of John Pendleton Kennedy's *Swallow Barn* ate in the parlor from a "huge table" surrounded by a legion of "bandy"-legged chairs. The family's "stately china" and "polished silver goblets" were used on a daily basis, and butter, even for a casual evening snack, was formally served in "diverse curiously wrought pyramids . . . tottering on pedestals of ice." The food was prepared and carried in by slaves from a detached kitchen-house, where the family rarely ventured.

In New England, farmhouses were often built in a symmetrical Georgian style quite similar to that of the southern plantation dwelling. But patterns of living were markedly different. Due to cold temperatures and the absence of slavery, the focus of the house was inward. Its heart was the kitchen with its glowing, cavernous hearth. Here, as Harriet Beecher Stowe nostalgically related, the farmer's wife, with the assistance of her daughters and perhaps a paid neighbor girl, carried out the work of the household. The women were so efficient that "every-

Mrs. Rorer's kitchen in *Ladies Home Journal*, January, 1903. Cooper-Hewitt Museum Library.

thing there seemed to be always done and never doing." "A breakfast arose . . . as by magic; and in an incredibly short space after, every knife, fork, spoon, and trencher, clean and shining, was looking as innocent and unconscious in its place as if it never had been used and never expected to be."

The kitchen provided space for sociability and individual projects. "Each member of the family had established unto him- or herself some little pet private snuggery, some chair or stool, some individual nook—forbidden to gentility, but dear to the ungenteel natural heart—that we looked back to regretfully when we were banished to the colder regions of the best room." So central was the kitchen to the New England identity that replicas of it were included in the Sanitary Fairs that were used to raise money for the Civil War, and a New England kitchen was one of the most popular exhibits of the Philadelphia Centennial of 1876.

The New England kitchen, as Harriet Beecher Stowe said, was "ungenteel" and "natural." By the middle of the nineteenth century middle-class families, many recently moved to the city, were more enamored of upwardly mobile stylishness than of old-fashioned naturalness and moral rectitude. They turned with a shudder from the "best rooms" of their parents generation, quailing at the memory of dank shuttered air, slippery horsehair sofas, and somber portraits of deceased relatives. What they wanted was a stylish parlor that would demonstrate to the world that they had "arrived."

Formal parlors of the 1850s might be furnished in suites of French-style furniture, often bought as a package from a professional upholsterer. Later, by the 1880s, when European travel was becoming commonplace, the parlor might display a tasteful, personal assembly of foreign antiques and *objets d'art*. Robert Grant illustrated the two approaches in his novel *Unleavened Bread*. On the one hand there was the parlor of the New York apartment of a young broker and his wife, Flossie. Flossie, wanting to make a showy display, turned to dealers. The result was a room

bright with color. The furniture was covered with light blue plush; there were blue and yellow curtains, gay cushions, and a profusion of gilt ornamentation. A bearskin, a show picture on an easel, and a variety of florid bric-a-brac completed the brilliant aspect of the apartment.

As Flossie explained, "We bought all our things in two days at one fell swoop . . . Gregory gave the dealers carte blanche. That's his way."

By contrast, in the same novel, Mrs. Taylor, the social leader of a smaller, more provincial city, relied on taste and charm rather than on brash new wealth to achieve the personal atmosphere of her drawing room. Externally her house "displayed stern lines of unadorned brick." But the interior exuded "cosy comfort." "Pretty, tasteful things, many of them inexpensive knick-knacks of foreign origin—a small picture, a bit of china, a medieval relic—were cleverly placed as a relief to the conventional furniture." Mrs. Taylor herself completed the effect with her "musical voice, easy speech, and ingratiating friendliness."

By the 1890s spacious Queen Anne suburban homes and showy city apartments were giving way to what the architectural historian Alan Gowans has labeled the "comfortable house." Families who lived in such homes tended to be smaller and more self-contained. Because wives were increasingly forced to assume the duties of cook and nanny, kitchens and nurseries took on a new importance. Few housewives were willing to work in the dank, meanly appointed basement kitchens formerly thought adequate for servants. If a woman was to preserve her self-image as a lady, she required a kitchen that shared the attributes of a well-equipped laboratory and a comfortably furnished sitting room.

The 1905 novel *The Distractions of Martha* centered on the heroine's "art kitchen," where she confronted the mysteries of cookery in a tasteful atmosphere

of gray and blue. Her greatest challenge was a huge, mechanically complex, cast-iron stove, which she satirically dubbed "the shrine." As for the nursery, it was to be practical, healthful, and sufficiently pretty to instill in the children gentle, orderly habits. A 1905 article in the *Ladies' Home Journal* advised mothers that nursery furniture should be painted, not upholstered, carpets replaced by wash rugs, and "nursery picture paper" avoided altogether, "for arsenic is a very bad thing to get into a baby's body through its lungs and pores."

If one aspect of the comfortable house was pleasurable duty, another was pleasurable self-indulgence, a trait that became more important in the 1920s. George Babbitt's Dutch Colonial house in Floral Heights, although not large, had

an altogether royal bathroom of porcelain and glazed tile and metal sleek as silver. The towel-rack was a rod of clear glass set in nickel. The tub was long enough for a Prussian Guard, and above the set bowl was a sensational exhibit of tooth-brush holder, shaving-brush holder, soap-dish, sponge-dish, and medicine-cabinet, so glittering and so ingenious that they resembled an electrical instrument-board.

The ladies of Floral Heights might give themselves up to sensual delight in the dressing room, which, if it followed the advice of Elsie de Wolfe, would have "lots of mirrors, and then more mirrors, and then more!"

After the depression and the sobering pall of World War II, the lighthearted optimism of the 1920s seemed a bit superficial. It was a more self-conscious, serious family that stood behind the United States as a world power. The dream of the 1950s was owning a home in the suburbs. Although husbands commuted to town to work, children dispersed to different schools, and wives spent much of the day in the car, all were expected to reassemble in the evening in the family room.

Betty Friedan dismissed such houses as comfortable concentration camps, but sociologists claim that most suburban dwellers were quite content to exchange the bruising impact of city life for the security of tree-shaded neighborhoods. The rooms of the new ranch houses and split

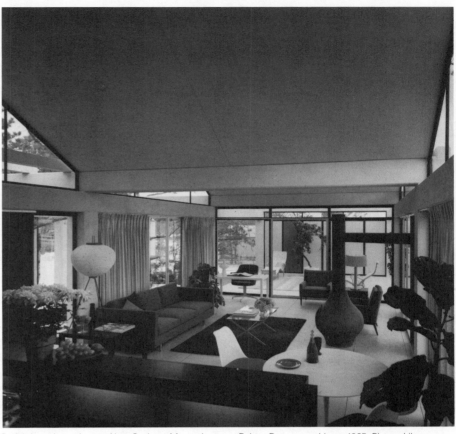

Prefabricated tract house, New Seabury, Massachusetts; Robert Damora, architect, 1965. Picture Library, Cooper-Hewitt Museum. Robert Damora.

levels were no longer self-contained spaces, but flowed expansively into each other, gathering parents and children in a built-in current of "togetherness."

Certainties were less clear in the 1960s and '70s. Inflation and the pill ended the baby boom, Vietnam weakened American self-confidence and the sordid revelations of Watergate cast a shadow over the bicentennial. No wonder many fled into the past through the preservation movement. We can let John Updike speak for such families:

The Guerins lived in an old saltbox on Prudence Street, the timbers and main fireplace dating at least from 1680. The house had been so expensively and minutely restored it had for Foxy the ap-

prehensive rawness of a new home; Foxy empathized with childless couples who conspire to baby the furniture.

For a brief time, uncertainty and nostalgia had brought American interiors full circle. Although the Guerins lived in a saltbox, the New England way of life that had produced it was as remote from the 1970s as the Middle Ages. It was a case of people looking backward to avoid facing the present. Literature will doubtless continue to record the way our houses are used and experienced.

Jean Gordon is Professor of History at the University of North Carolina at Greensboro.

Stately Mansions

The style is grand.

Lyndhurst, Tarrytown, New York; built for William Paulding; Alexander Jackson Davis, architect, 1838, enlarged 1865. A property of the National Trust for Historic Preservation; photo about 1905.

Andrew Carnegie Mansion, now Cooper-Hewitt Museum; Babb, Cook & Willard, architects, 1902. David De Silva.

The Breakers, Newport, Rhode Island; built for Cornelius Vanderbilt; Richard Morris Hunt, architect, 1895. Courtesy of The Preservation Society of Newport County.

Biltmore, Asheville, North Carolina; built for George W. Vanderbilt; Richard Morris Hunt, architect, 1895. Courtesy The Biltmore Company.

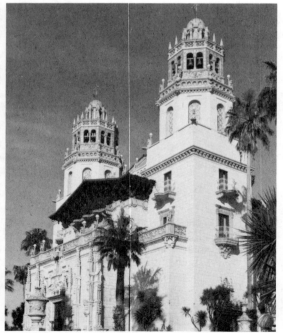

La Casa Grande, San Simeon, California; built for William Randolph Hearst; Julia Morgan, architect, 1919–40. State of California, Department of Parks and Recreation.

Ca' d'Zan the John Ringling residence, Sarasota, Florida; Dwight James Baum, architect, 1924–26. Courtesy of The John & Mable Ringling Museum of Art, The State Art Museum of Florida.

The Client-Decorator Relationship

A client and designer speak.

By C. Ray Smith

Some twenty years ago, when the decorator was pervasive in middle and upper middle-class homes, the distinguished psychiatrist Dr. Milton R. Sapirstein included a chapter on the stresses associated with decorating in his book *Paradoxes of Everyday Life.* It was an inflammatory discussion—pointing out that his clinical practice had revealed that decorating a home was for a woman one of the major traumas of life. Causes of the trauma were indecision, lack of identification with the project, too much belief that the design revealed her innermost subconscious, and so on.

In twenty years, the times and Dr. Sapirstein's views have changed. No longer, he feels, are his patients so psychologically involved with their decorating schemes to care if they are expressions of their own personalities. More and more Dr. Sapirstein finds decorating is just so much stage setting.

What then is today's relationship between decorator and client? To hear truly authoritative opinion, we have asked Gregory B. Smith, an experienced client of decorating, to explain his thoughts concerning the client-decorator relationship. His response is followed by the point of view of Mark Hampton, one of this country's most acclaimed decorators.

Gregory Smith

CRS: Gregory Smith, you have been a client of interior design for a number of years.

GBS: Yes, and really with one decorator—Mrs. Russell Davenport of McMillen Inc. And latterly Benjamin Baldwin designed one apartment for me. Mrs. Davenport and I worked together for almost thirty years, working on about fourteen apartments and houses, I think. So I have had a good deal of experience in this procedure, but only with one decorating firm.

CRS: Do you recall that the procedure of decorating had some consistency from apartment to apartment and house to house?

GBS: Yes, I think it certainly did. One of the interesting things for me over the years has been the learning process. When I look back at the first apartment, I was a babe in the woods, to say nothing of my late wife. And over the thirty years working with Mrs. Davenport I have learned a great deal.

CRS: You knew about history and styles when you began, did you not?

GBS: Yes, I had the advantage—or disadvantage—of having majored in architecture at Yale University. So I had, perhaps, a better background for this than the average American who has bought an apartment in the city or a house in the country and says to his wife, "Let's get in a decorator. We'll do the house up."

CRS: And what is the decorating process from the client's point of view from then on?

GBS: The client has a disadvantage in that the client is ignorant, really, of the process that is involved. In my experience with McMillen, McMillen discusses your problem and intention with you, they look at the apartment, then they disappear for a month or two, and they come back with three schemes—a blue scheme, a green scheme, and a red. And the client is asked to come in for a consultation, where he is presented with the three different schemes.

CRS: Are they essentially the same except for the color?

GBS: I think basically yes. Then the average client has difficulty choosing. I remember Natalie Davenport saying that the problem is that the wife would come to McMillen, review the schemes, and say well I'll take the blue one home and show it to George. Then she comes back for a second time and says George doesn't like blue. The point is that the decorator sometimes has difficulty getting clients to say what they really want or what they prefer, because the average client cannot visualize how the apartment will look given these schemes.

CRS: Do clients give all choice over to the decorator?

GBS: Some clients probably do. I did not. In fact I had some conflict with my wife because she liked blue, and I was not crazy about blue, which I thought was a feminine color. I happen to like autumn colors—red, orange, black. So in my own experience we did have a certain difference of opinion.

CRS: Would you continue explaining how you gradually learned more about decorating?

GBS: Having bought a house in France, I went with Mrs. Davenport to many antique shops in Paris. There is no better way of learning about French furniture than going all over Paris by foot and discussing the virtues of French furniture. As far as materials go, I think once you pick a material and it is installed in your apartment, you learn whether it wears well and, in the case of curtains, whether it blocks the light or not, or whether blue turns out to be the color you thought it would be. You learn a great deal by experience.

CRS: What is the interpersonal relationship between client and decorator?

GBS: In the beginning it is strictly professional, but it can lead to friendship over the course of time. It may not happen when there is only one job, but in my case it was different. If the decorator gets to know the family, how they live, how many children they have, where they go in the summer, then the decorator can visualize more of the client's life. So it becomes more than a business relationship.

CRS: Then when a decorator goes on to an additional project for a client, the first experience gives him or her a headstart in knowing about the life of the client?

GBS: That helps, of course. But my case was unusual. I had a reason—or thought I had a reason—to move every three or four years.

CRS: Were all of your residences equally elaborate?

GBS: I wouldn't say elaborate, particularly. All bore a certain resemblance. One reason was that the furniture from the previous house was used in the succeeding house. I still have some pieces that I had thirty years ago, although my tastes, I think, have changed to something much simpler from my eighteenth-century French days. That is part of the education process that the decorating experience brings about. As you learn more your tastes change.

CRS: What is the greatest advantage of working with a decorator?

GBS: There are practical advantages that you don't think of right away such as measuring everything, getting everything to scale, and in some cases making architectural improvements. And another advantage of working with a decorator is that the average person has no idea about decoration. There is also the advantage in purchasing—decorators know what is on the market and can relieve the client of going to fifty different establishments looking for things.

CRS: Do you feel in the end that it wasn't your own house but their house?

GBS: I didn't, because, for one reason, I always had a lot of books, and they had to plan shelves for my books. And I always had a piano, and they had to put it in one of the rooms—whether they liked it or not. In many cases decorators don't like anything that the client has acquired. They like to get rid of family pieces. In certain cases they look with disfavor on American colonial furniture. I think they would accept good eighteenth-century English furniture.

CRS: That is probably all generational and cyclical.

GBS: I think it is. Then there are economic changes. People don't have the servants they used to have to maintain their establishments.

CRS: How does the decorator help or hinder that?

GBS: I think the decorator can simplify everything so that the key problems are lessened. There is the problem of the working spouse. She doesn't necessarily want a large kitchen. She wants a kitchen where she can do everything herself.

CRS: What are some of the disadvantages of having a decorator?

GBS: Unless you are forceful enough yourself, the decorator may try to force his or her ideas on you. And that definitely is a danger. A client must know what he or she wants. They may have an *idée fixe* of what would look just right for that place in your living room. And you have to fight back, and if you feel very strongly about grandmother's chest of drawers, you should hang on to it. And perhaps don't let them paint it white or some new chic color. I remember one rather interesting Chinese four-poster bed that was cut down because it was too high. I didn't realize it at the time, but having had its legs cut, it lost its value. That is a danger. And an ancestral portrait got cut down because it didn't fit the space and didn't look quite right. That was a mistake.

CRS: Did you ever get to a point in this learning experience where you wanted to do it all yourself?

GBS: No, I have to admit that I never reached that stage. Perhaps selfishly I didn't want to be bothered with the everlasting details involved in measuring or purchasing or working with plumbers, painters, plasterers, and so forth. Also, decorators see so many different establishments that they are in a much better position to compare than the innocent client going off by himself.

CRS: Except for talking about the styles of furniture—eighteenth-century French versus modern—you have not talked about stylistic traditions in interior designing.

GBS: I don't know to what extent the average decorator is influenced by that, or to what extent the policy of the firm dictates individual decorating. For years, McMillen wasn't aesthetically attuned to modern or very modern furniture. I think that has changed. Now they are doing more and more commercial work, too. As I look back on one or two of my former houses or apartments, I now say to myself, I couldn't possibly live with that style anymore. I do not ask how I could have done it, because I think I lived a different life at that time, and that was what I liked. And the decorators produced, presum-

Living Room, Gregory Smith's apartment in the Pulitzer house, 1962; Natalie Davenport, designer; photograph by Henry S. Fullerton III. Courtesy McMillen Inc.

ably, what I asked for. Whereas now, my life has changed and my tastes have changed. Now I have four grandchildren who might possibly want to spend the night, and I want to pull out a sofa where I might put them up from time to time.

CRS: Does the client control the practical aspect of these projects and the decorator the aesthetics?

GBS: We have not discussed the financial aspect. Certain things are limited by financial considerations. The responsibility lies with the decorator to be able to come up with a scheme that fits the financial program of the client. But I suspect that if the decorator comes up with a scheme that requires a certain amount of additional funds, the client has the option of either going along with it or sticking to the original estimate. The original estimate is not always the final estimate.

Interior by Mark Hampton, Greenwich, Connecticut, ca. 1984. New York Times Pictures.

Mark Hampton

CRS: Mark Hampton, what is a typical client?

MH: There is no typical client, in the singular sense of the word. There are typical client types which one encounters. One of the client types, and the best for me is a client who is at least one's age or older, has had a lot of previous experience decorating so that he or she is not constantly and naively alarmed by the difficulties, the expenses, and all the other things that go on in the decorating process that surprise some who have never been through it before. In addition to having experience, my favorite kind of client has three qualities: First, wonderful taste. It's a pleasure to work with people in a kind of give and take situation, but it is boring and defeating to work with people who don't have a personal sense of style, and a rather developed one.

The second quality that I like clients to have is experience. And I love it when they collect something. Sometimes they collect several things—paintings and furniture for instance. Ideally a client should collect some art, because when art is lumped into the list of decorating things to buy, it demeans the art and leads to arid rooms in which the pictures match the decor. And that's not very good. The third quality I like in a client is to have some book life. I don't expect them to collect books as some people do, but I like them to have an active sense of living with books. That is a great indicator in every way.

And the final thing that the ideal client should have is a lot of money. To a professional in the decorating business, whether it is gardens or architecture or decorating, we are talking about beautiful things which are dear. And the ideal client has a sense of luxury and a kind of sporting attitude about pursuing beautiful things, not at any cost, but recognizing that it will be very expensive. That is my ideal client.

CRS: Does the ideal client give you carte blanche?

MH: I have never had anybody who really gave me carte blanche. I have had people who pretended they were giving me carte blanche, but it never really is true. Carte blanche is ridiculous. It means being careless by its very definition. An enlightened, experienced, rich client with a lot of care and input gets the best out of the designer, just as that type of client gets the best out of an architect or a landscape architect.

CRS: Does the client teach the decorator?

MH: Often. Our clients are a great deal older than I am. Many have worked with such decorators as the late Billy Baldwin, the late Rose Cumming, or the late Ruby Ross Wood. Or they have worked with other interesting decorators in Europe. You can learn an enormous amount from a person of great taste who has had all that experience. Many of my clients have three or four houses. In the last thirty

years they might have had ten other houses, apartments, summer places, farmhouses, townhouses, whatever. That kind of experience is full of fascination to me.

CRS: How much, then, of the designer's give and take is his and how much is the client's?

MH: I don't think you can say. If it is a client who has a lot of taste but cannot grapple with things like changing the architectural details of a room, or working with changes in the floor plan of an apartment, you can make an enormous amount of creative input that the client would not be able to do on his or her own. Clients, on the other hand, can say that since this room is going to be like this let's put in an antique floor or let's go shopping for some old paneling, or since we have to do all this why don't we take out these five ugly windows and rebuild this wall. That kind of decision can trigger a whole different thought process and make rooms much more beautiful.

CRS: I had expected you to say that the client is really a critic—"I like it; I don't like it"—rather than a continual door opener to other possibilities.

MH: Oh no. Often clients will come to you with a folder of photographs and articles they have cut out. That's what is in their minds, and when they show it to you it triggers something in your mind. But there is a lot of back and forth and sharing of ideas.

CRS: Besides the princely clients, though, there is a middle-range income group that now goes to designers and decorators. Do you assume that the client relationship is different today or the same?

MH: It can be the same. But I think the best results come if clients are using the decorator for the things they cannot do themselves. There are lots of resources that are not available to people who do not have a decorator. There are a lot of things that people don't have time to do themselves, such as supervising workrooms, shopping for things that are so difficult to find. However, ideally people who are not—to use your term—princely clients, do a lot of it themselves. Natural talent, which, frankly all people whether they use decorators or not, must have if they are to have beautiful houses. We know loads of people who live in lovely houses who have never had a decorator at all. When I was a child forty-five or fifty years ago, the very few people who had a decorator in the Middle West, were thought by my mother and her friends to be people who had given up their individuality.

CRS: Do many clients want to throw everything out and start from scratch?

MH: It is sad when they do that, but sometimes they do. You can't stop them, though you can sometimes discourage them. But the one thing I keep getting back to is that the best client-decorator relationship exists when the client has some creative role that he or she plays.

CRS: One commentator has said that too many houses today are merely stage sets, in which the clients are actors and actresses.

MH: That's right. Traditionally, decorating has fallen into two general categories, the rooms that are one's private realm, and those that are created for other people to admire. I think it is tragic when an entire house has that sort of arid atmosphere of being created for public consumption, a house that would be sullied by reading the newspaper, or taking a nap, or really living in it. I don't mind a house that has a few formal rooms along with rooms that are cluttered and show the happy use that they get every day, but I do think it is sad to see a beautiful room that is never used and a hideous room that is lived in all the time. Why shouldn't the room you live in all the time—with stacks of books and newspapers also be luxurious and stylish?

CRS: What is the relationship between decorating and the functional essence of a residence?

MH: There is a very practical side to decorating that has nothing to do with this ideal client's taste. And that is the practical ability to arrange rooms, to anticipate needs and come up with solutions that will enable the person who lives in those rooms to have them meet his or her needs. A lot of people with wonderful taste and style, for instance, cannot arrange furniture, cannot arrange rooms. They might have a great eye but they do not have an ability to put things together from the mechanical point of view of scale and proportion. They don't know how to make a room comfortable to sit in either for reading or for conversation. And that's where a decorator, in what sounds like a sort of flatfooted way, can be very useful even to a person of great taste. Because the decorator can say if you do this and if you do that, it will make this room, which is a lovely room but it has ceilings that are a little too low, and this will make them look taller; or this is a better way to treat the paint work in this room given the style that you like and are trying to achieve.

A typical example is, if a client says, "I would like to put this mantle in a room," I might say, "It is simply too big. It won't work on the wall." Although the client can't visualize it, he or she will know that what we do is right the minute they see it.

CRS: Is it part of the service to go with a client to find the new residential space?

MH: Oh heavens, yes. I do that all the time. I often work for people with their architects from the day they buy the property. And that is a very real service—how the electrical installation relates to the placement of lamps and furniture for reading, building cabinets for television and music equipment, and all that. It sounds so prosaic, but the functional side of decorating is very important. How high should this be, how long should that be . . .

CRS: How do people find decorators?

MH: The most usual and reliable way is through their friends.

CRS: Do the shelter magazines influence people?

MH: Absolutely. Someone will call up and say, "Oh, I've seen these six rooms you've done and I love them, can we talk." I am pretty faithful in my ability to sense from the first couple of meetings whether or not we are going to get on. One of the main aspects of the client-decorator relationship, and it is twofold, is whether they like one another. Is the decorator going to be reliable? Does he show up on time, does he tell the truth, does he dedicate himself to the job? And is the client reliable, does he or she pay the bills, take the responsibility for the things he or she has approved. You know, this is a real issue with decorating, if you show a client some samples and some model pieces of furniture—perhaps a sketch—and submit an estimate, which the client signs, somewhere in that process some of the responsibility has passed to the client. You do not order a suit, have it fitted, and then take it home and wear it and return it and say, I don't like it. At some point the client has to take the responsibility for having given the go ahead to the project. You have to have a healthy, grown-up attitude about accepting responsibility—both as the decorator and as the client—You don't say I'd love having a room painted that shade of pink, then after standing for two hours while the painter mixes the color, you see it on the wall and then don't like it and want it changed without knowing that you will have to pay for the change.

The other great aspect of hiring a decorator is the whole empirical thing. A decorator who has painted fifty-some beige rooms over the years can come to you with a sample and explain to you what the room is going to look like. And, based on the sharing of ideas, can say this is the color I think we are talking about, and be very right about it.

CRS: That is craft.

MH: It is craft and it is experience. You can talk philosophy forever, but it is when you get down to specifics—this width, that height—that you are into the subject.

"*Our goal is to modernize it but retain the historical flavor.*"

bar

C. Ray Smith is the author of *International Design in Twentieth-Century America: A History.*

Mail-order Residences

Pre-cut houses were sturdy and affordable.

By Katherine Cole Stevenson and H. Ward Jandl

The precut house industry caught hold in America in the last decade of the nineteenth century, capitalizing on the new and growing popularity of general-merchandise mail-order catalogs. Available through specially produced catalogs and later through showrooms, and sent by rail wherever a boxcar or two could pull up, precut houses filled the strong demand for sturdy, inexpensive, yet modern homes in urban and rural areas alike. By 1910 there were over a dozen companies manufacturing and selling precut houses; by 1940 over a quarter million such houses had been sold.

Companies manufacturing precut houses advertised in a variety of sources, including such general circulation magazines as *Ladies' Home Journal* and the general-merchandise catalogs of Sears, Roebuck and Company and Montgomery Ward. Most companies produced annual or semiannual catalogs, displaying a variety of models from which to choose. Typically each model was illustrated with a rendering of the facade and dimensioned plans of each floor. General specifications of the materials supplied and a description of the house's amenities frequently accompanied the illustrations. Some of the manufacturers also included illustrated views of the interiors of the houses, furnished with their own merchandise. Houses ranged in size and style, depending on the company, from two-room bungalows to ten-room colonial mansions; virtually every popular American residential style from the 1890s through the 1930s could be obtained from mail-order catalogs.

Typically the customer selected the model that best suited his needs and budget and sent to the manufacturer either his full payment or, in the case of company-financed houses, the initial deposit. By return mail the company sent detailed blueprints and a construction manual with instructions on assembling the house.

Within a few weeks, materials started arriving by rail, deliveries usually being staggered to provide necessary materials at appropriate times in the construction cycle.

Mail-order house companies sprang up all over the United States, from coast to coast. The success of these early companies is reflected in an article that appeared in 1907 in *World's Work* entitled "How Dealers in Small Cities Compete with Mail-Order Houses." The author describes how mail-order companies were monopolizing the market and offers advice for using local advertising and promoting local examples of good workmanship to combat the growing popularity of precut houses.

The largest and most successful company in the business was Sears, Roebuck and Company. By 1940, when Sears had closed its Modern Homes Department, it is estimated that over one-hundred thousand houses had been sold. Alladin Homes, which stayed in business until recently, also produced approximately one-hundred thousand units. Smaller

Aladdin Homes "Built in a Day" mail-order catalog No. 29, Bay City, Michigan, 1917. Private Collection.

companies, such as the Lewis Manufacturing Company and Pacific Systems, produced fourteen thousand and thirty-eight thousand units respectively.

Some of the companies had their beginnings in supplying precut lumber and trim work, gradually evolving into businesses that supplied entire houses. Some supplied component parts already assembled and some supplied the parts numbered and ready-to-assemble. While most of the precut houses were of frame construction, it was also possible to order forms for cast stone or cast concrete and to supplement the order with millwork and plumbing. Other more specialized services were available by mail, including interior decorating, financing, and landscape design. Sears even provided construction services in some cases. A customer could elect to modify an existing plan to suit his specific needs or, in some cases, to have the company design a house from scratch.

Both Sears Roebuck and Montgomery Ward also sold home furnishings as part

of their mail-order operations. In the 1920s, the Sears staff included an "interior design coordinator" whose sole job it was to help the home owner select curtains, davenports, beds, and dressers. Catalogs of the period frequently showed model interiors that tended to be homey rather than stylish. Typically, cottages were shown spartanly furnished with unadorned plaster walls, metal beds, and plain craftsman-style chairs and tables. More elaborate—and expensive—bungalows contained leaded art-glass windows, built-in bookcases and sideboards, papered walls, and upholstered furniture. The most luxurious mail-order houses featured oak-beamed ceilings, built-in breakfast nooks, brass chandeliers, oriental carpets, and, on occasion, pianos.

Despite the popularity of the mail-order houses in the first two decades of the twentieth century, many companies left the business in the 1930s. Larger companies shut down their housing operations because they had assumed mortgages and were forced to foreclose on thousands of houses. Smaller companies went bankrupt during the depression. Several companies, such as Alladin, remained in business.

The significance of mail-order houses lay in their ability to provide affordable housing to American families at every socioeconomic level. The companies manufacturing precut houses made it possible for families in small towns, without access to architects or mill yards, to obtain quality, modern housing. They simplified the process of selecting, financing, and building houses, offering (in most cases) well-conceived floor plans, premium materials, and solid construction at reasonable prices.

Katherine Cole Stevenson and **H. Ward Jandl** are the co-authors of *Houses by Mail*, published by the National Trust for Historic Preservation.

Cover of *Modern Homes* mail-order catalog, 1908. Picture Library, Cooper-Hewitt Museum.

Industrial Housing

The dream never quite came true.

By Robert Jensen

An architect friend said to me recently, "If we can put a man on the moon and can make all those automobiles, why can't we make houses or housing for everybody?" It is easy to be sympathetic, but I had to tell him I thought his dream was dead.

Somewhere in the mid-1970s the enthusiasm for industrialized housing collapsed, and it has not revived. I am referring to the idea that most or even all of the American single-family house—walls, roof, floors, beams, plumbing, wiring, perhaps even interior finishes—might be efficiently and more profitably put together in a factory and then hauled to a site for construction.

The individualized method of on-site construction and assembly has always worked better here. The same spirit of American home building by contractors, bricklayers, and carpenters has been our construction tradition since the Civil War.

Yet in the 1920s applied technology was imagined to be the means by which every American's wealth, health, and happiness might be secured, and the dream of prefabricating the American house began to grow in that decade. No one tapped this dream better than the mathematician and occasional architect Buckminster Fuller. Fuller invented and promoted a one-family house that was to be made entirely in factories. He called it the Dymaxion House, and, elevated on a single structural mast, it looked like a spaceship. It was a sensation with the public and architects alike.

Besides structural innovations, the house offered such unavailable conveniences as a clothes laundry from which shirts appeared fully ironed in three minutes. Fuller knew it could not be mass-produced then, and said that to develop one fully operating prototype immediately would cost $100 million. But in twenty years, he believed, when Dymaxion Houses—or others like

them—would be produced like Detroit cars, his houses could be made ". . . for about $1500 apiece."

This was an irresistible vision: houses produced the way Detroit makes cars. It was an expansion of America's "can-do" technological spirit. But the vision also sprang from crisis, from the economic depression that began in 1929. An unprecedented financial and intellectual commitment to industrialized housing followed in the next decade.

By 1935 prefabrication was "a movement": thirty-three firms were producing prefabricated housing that year. The very names of these firms ring with the Detroit analogy: American Houses, Inc., of New York; General Houses, Inc., of Chicago; National Homes Corporation of Lafayette, Indiana (this latter firm is still producing houses and housing components today). By the beginning of World War II, few of these companies were really successful (and some had failed), but these were growing pains, it was thought.

Financial, engineering, and sales commitment to industrialized housing increased for five or six years after the war, aided by the need to transform industrial production to peacetime needs. The commitment continued through the 1950s and into the 1960s—though by then it was clear that something was wrong.

The first fact apparent in the prefabrication movement from 1930 through the 1960s is the vast amount of money lost—lost by thousands of entrepreneurs and investors, slowly, grindingly, with agonizing time to watch their money disappear. After they had paid to aggregate the capital, to construct the factories, to hire the sales force, and to create the advertising, the product they made—a soundly constructed, well finished, and market-priced single-family house—was bought by very few Americans.

The market failure signaled intellectual defeat for many bright architects, aca-

"Dymaxion Deployment Unit" grain bin house; R. Buckminster Fuller, architect, about 1940. Picture Library, Cooper-Hewitt Museum.

demics, and foundation presidents who over four decades had applied themselves to prefabrication. One portion of that story has been told by Gilbert Herbert in *The Dream of the Factory-Made House* in 1984, where the thirty-year intellectual commitment of Walter Gropius and Konrad Wachsmann to the concept of industrialized housing is recounted, ending with the complete collapse of their dream through the financial ruin in 1949 of the General Panel Corporation.

In the 1950s, the first doubts were expressed about the potential of the industrialized housing movement, and some of the logistical reasons for its failure up to that time were clarified. Problems were carefully set forth by Burnham Kelly in 1951 in *The Prefabrication of Houses*. But the idea persisted that industrialized housing really should work, and that there would be big money in it for a lot of people when it finally did.

The last public act in the collapse of

industrialized housing in the United States began in 1969–70 with the Nixon administration's Operation Breakthrough, which was directed by George Romney, then Secretary of Housing and Urban Development. Operation Breakthrough was to have learned from all previous mistakes, and was based on what was by then a broad understanding of the economic, technical, and marketing dangers of prefabrication. It was, finally, to be the vehicle for establishing the industrialization of housing on sound foundations. But the financial, political, and intellectual structure of Breakthrough collapsed in 1971 because of undelivered and undeliverable government promises.

What happened to this American dream of industrialized housing? Or, perhaps more to the point, why did it ever exist? The practical problems can be recited quickly:

1. A factory-made house is not a radical improvement over one built conventionally. A factory-made house provides about the same quality and the same amount of space at about the same price as a house built conventionally—but with a lot less choice of how it might look. Large-scale industrialized production has been successful in the United States (and elsewhere) when the product made is vastly superior to what preceded it (just as a car is a radical improvement over a horse and buggy), or when it creates an entirely new human ability (as telephones do). Factory-made houses do neither.

2. Four factors contribute to the cost of building a new house and living in it over time: construction, financing, land, and maintenance. Prefabrication as a "solution" to a housing "problem" addresses only one of these fully—construction. But any of the other three can frequently be more important to the cost of a dwelling, depending on location and scale. If finding solutions to the high cost of housing is the task, the means will be social and ultimately political, more than technical.

But for forty years, much of the energy of individuals in the prefabrication movement was spent looking for the amazing new design, material, joint, or procedure. They investigated wood systems versus concrete systems, panel systems versus box systems, site-assembled component systems versus shipped-ready systems, and so on. Though they usually understood that land, location, and style were crucial to selling houses, their primary solution to housing was construction technology.

Symbol versus Technology

Looking back at the prefabrication movement from the late 1980s, the most intriguing thing seems not its practical problems but its *psychological* problem. The twentieth-century American house has never been about technology: it is about sex and power.

A 1987 issue of *Architectural Digest*, currently a popular magazine depicting homes and their interiors, carried the following headline on its cover: "This Month, Sophia Loren." Inside we visit the actress's new Florida apartment, shared with her movie producer/husband Carlo Ponti. The story begins, "In Florida, where the actress and her family have recently acquired an apartment, there is no sense of one form of beauty rivaling another. Instead, the lush landscape provides a fitting setting for her own sensibility." Her *own* beauty; her *own* sensibility: this is the thrust of the text. It is really Sophia Loren that is being depicted—sensual, unique, and with the enormous power to do whatever she wishes—translated into an American dwelling.

Whether published in 1910 or 1980, such magazines have always been about the same thing: Readers see—through pictures of people in their homes—their *own* possibilities. Because this is the United States, readers believe that something equally expressive of their own uniqueness and their control over their own lives is possible for them. They read about Sophia Loren's new condo within a political/economic context that lets them believe that they too can create whatever they want.

Now, a house is not an individual, and it takes more than things or money to make oneself a sensuous and powerful person. Symbols are not the real thing. Still, context moves our imaginations, or at least our houses. And our context is the United States, with its potential for self-realization.

The real American dream has always been about freedom and its possibilities, in houses as in everything else. So the American dream has little to do with industrialized housing. Actually, industrialized housing is antagonistic to imagining and representing that freedom. It is amazing that so many designers and industrialists have not perceived this antagonism. The public always and inevitably has understood: it does not buy prefabricated houses. They offer no choices. They are boring. (Except for Fuller's house that automatically irons your shirts. That's not boring.)

This condition is in stark contrast to other industrialized places. In England, France, Italy, Germany, Scandinavia, Russia, Poland, Hungary, Czechoslovakia, Israel, and Japan, patented techniques to prefabricate and industrialize housing construction, which similarly began to evolve in the 1950s, are now both profitable and sophisticated. The high-rise apartments surrounding the historic centers of most European cities today are frequently prefabricated buildings. Projects are subsidized by the state; citizens cannot be offered a choice of space or configuration, and apparently do not expect one. This social climate is fundamental to prefabrication. Industrialized housing systems are profitable in the more socialist countries but have never worked here.

Those involved with the housing industry in the United States *do* keep up with technology; but they hide it and treat it like a tool, as they should. From 1945 to the present, the prefabrication of housing components has become standard in this country. For instance, gang-nailed wood trusses are now made in factories, shipped to the site, and set in place quickly, rather than roof beams and roof rafters being custom cut and erected individually, as before. Because of component parts, the once-clear line between standard construction and prefabricated construction is now blurred in the United States.

But there is a critical difference. American component prefabrication is not at all like the European systems just described, or the prefabricated houses attempted here from the 1920s to 1970. Any prefabricated component is available from many suppliers. There is great competition among preassembled window manufacturers, pre-hung door manufacturers, exterior brick panel manufacturers, roof truss companies, and the like. A builder has many choices. So does a buyer. In addition, one prefabricator might make one or two components of a house, while other prefabricators make ten other components. No one tries to prefabricate whole houses, or to make components that fit only other elements manufactured by that company. It would be economic suicide. It *was* economic suicide, for fifty years.

Yet there is another side to this American dream of freedom, also manifest in prefabricated housing. That is the mobile home. Mobile homes began as extensions of the freedom fantasies of Americans and their automobile culture. They were designed to be towed frequently, which was a previously unavailable benefit worth paying for. But today only 3 percent of mobile homes, or "manufactured housing," as producers prefer to call them, are ever relocated. They come from the factory to a dealer and then to one site, and there they stay until they disintegrate.

Mobile homes are perceived as cheap and flimsy by most Americans. They are built to a substantially lower construction standard. Because mobile homes do not meet even the least rigorous city, county, or state building codes (prefabricated housing from the 1920s to 1970 always met or exceeded these codes), a new national code called the "HUD Code" has been created for them. But mobile homes usually have exterior walls only about one and a half-inches thick, as compared with six-inch thick standard construction. They are flimsy.

History reinforces the lesson that prefabrication technology is a tool, merely a tool, and that its value lies in the uses to which it is put.

Robert Jensen is an architect, author, and Associate Professor of Architecture at the New York Institute of Technology.

Mobile Homes

An unrecognized revolution has occurred.

By Margaret J. Drury

Single-section manufactured home, 1980s. Courtesy of Champion Home Builders Co., Dryden, Michigan.

The majority of American households cannot afford to buy new houses because the average price for conventionally built single-family units is now over one-hundred thousand dollars. One of the most important public policy issues facing the nation is how to get more homes for more Americans at prices they can afford. There is tremendous demand for single-family houses that median-income and first-time home buyers can afford—the under fifty-thousand dollar house. Yet, al-

most the only new housing units available below fifty-thousand dollars are factory-built houses that are transported on their own wheels to a site—mobile homes.

Since 1980 mobile homes have consistently accounted for approximately a third of the new single-family home market. When costs for conventionally constructed housing units are rapidly escalating, one wonders why mobile homes have not captured even more of the market, for mobile homes are the affordable

housing of the baby-boom generation, especially those who have chosen to live in nonmetropolitan and urban-fringe areas.

The annual production of mobile homes peaked at around 500,000 units between 1971 and 1973. Since the 1974 recession in the construction industry, annual mobile home production has held rather steady at between 250,000 and 300,000 housing units a year.

The market for manufactured housing declined dramatically in 1986 because

two areas of the country—the South and the Midwest—where mobile home markets have traditionally been strongest, lost many blue-collar jobs. The current depressed conditions in the "rust belt," which has been hard hit by a decline in steel and manufacturing industry, and in the "sun belt," which has suffered along with its oil and gas industry and farming, have weakened the demand for new manufactured homes. The mobile home industry is experiencing a crisis even while the quality and value of its units are at an all-time high.

In 1986 the dramatic lowering of interest rates for conventional mortgages made existing conventional housing more affordable to households that would normally not qualify for mortgages. The median sales price for existing housing in the Midwest was sixty-three thousand dollars and in the South was seventy-seven thousand dollars; this too was a factor in the decline of the mobile home market in 1986.

Since 1980, "mobile homes" have been officially renamed "manufactured homes" by the United States Congress. This change reflects the fact that once placed on a site, only 3 percent of these factory-built homes are ever moved. The wheels and axles of manufactured homes are only a built-in means of transportation from the factory to the permanent homesite. Generally, the size of the units prohibits pulling them behind a family car, and the cost of other transportation and setup discourages repeated moves.

The main difference between manufactured housing and other factory-built housing is the building code that applies to each. Manufactured homes are the only homes governed by a national building code. Since June 15, 1976, a building code administered by the Department of Housing and Urban Development (HUD) has regulated design and construction, strength and durability, fire resistance, and energy efficiency. It also regulates the performance of heating, air-conditioning, plumbing, thermal, and electrical systems. HUD regulates factory inspection of units by federally certified agencies as well. Since the initiation of these standards, the quality of manufactured homes has improved, the average size of units has grown, and fire safety and energy efficiency have dramatically increased. The mobile home units of 1986 are much better products than those of 1972.

The mobile home industry has also made significant progress in solving several of its long-term institutional problems: decreasing zoning restrictions, gaining liberalized financing terms, and overcoming many local building code restrictions.

There have been some dramatic breakthroughs in community acceptance of manufactured homes, but much more work needs to be done to overcome old stigmas associated with "trailer living." There have been great increases in the quality and number of planned community developments involving mobile homes. There have also been major improvements in the quality of parks for manufactured units placed on rented spaces.

The Supreme Court has consistently found it discriminatory to exclude mobile home parks totally from an area through zoning, and there now seems to be more acceptance of multi-section manufactured units for use as compatible infill housing in cities that have numerous small vacant lots. Some small cities have developed local ordinances that allow multi-wide manufactured homes, built to federal code standards, to be interspersed with conventionally built housing when the manufactured units have an appearance, style, and design similar to conventional housing. These ordinances often require the approval of planning commissions and are usually based on unit appearance.

Given the appeal of manufactured units, we may wonder how many have entered the nation's housing stock. In 1985, it was estimated that approximately twelve million people in America occupied more than six million manufactured homes. The Census Bureau found that from 1970 to 1980 mobile homes increased their share of the housing stock by 82 percent, to 3.8 million units, by moving from 3.1 percent to 4.4 percent of the total housing inventory.

Mobile Home Residents

A survey conducted in 1967 by the Bureau of the Census found that the typical head of a mobile home household was under thirty five, had completed three years of high school, and was married. This survey found that mobile homes contributed significantly to the supply of housing in small communities and outside metropolitan areas.

The general characteristics of mobile home residents seem to be about the same twenty years later, as a 1984 nationwide survey of nearly ten thousand mobile home residents sponsored by Foremost Insurance Company showed. In spite of an influx of younger buyers, overall, the age distribution of all manufactured-home owners has shifted toward older age groups. The average age of household heads now is forty-seven years—persons aged sixty and older comprise 33 percent of the occupants. Some 16 percent of household heads were seventy years or over.

The average household surveyed has lived in its manufactured home for almost nine years, 38 percent have lived in their present home for ten years or longer. Some 58 percent of the households owned their units free and clear, although 64 percent financed their homes at time of purchase.

The median education level of manufactured-home household heads was 12.6 years of schooling, and the median household income was sixteen-thousand dollars. Of home owners, 26 percent were retirees on limited or fixed incomes. The average household size was 2.5 members. The majority (66 percent) of households was headed by a husband and wife; 18 percent were households consisting of a woman living alone.

The Foremost survey also looked at the characteristics of new buyers of manufactured homes. About 72 percent of new buyers were under forty with an average age of household head being about thirty-seven years. The median household income of new home purchasers was $19,800. Some 45 percent were blue-collar workers. This reflects a rather dramatic increase in young households—apparently baby boomers have chosen to buy manufactured homes. Fifty-four percent of new manufactured homes were purchased for under twenty-thousand dollars. An unprecedented number (58 percent) of the 1984 new buyers placed their homes on private property. Only 41 percent chose to locate their new homes in a park or subdivision. The study did not indicate whether this was due to the absence of available park spaces or to preference.

The Mobile Home Industry

The mobile home industry has changed dramatically since 1970, when there were 360 manufacturers producing units in six-hundred factories, with ten manufacturers accounting for production of just over half of all units. By 1985 there had been considerable consolidation in the marketplace: only 140 manufacturers producing units in four-hundred factories.

The new safety and performance standards established in 1976 undoubtedly led to the elimination of some of the smaller manufacturers. But the dramatic swings of the economy, due to the energy crisis and inflation, contributed heavily to the reduction of some manufacturers and plants. It is interesting that four of the top five producers of mobile home units in 1970 remained among the top producers in 1985.

In 1985 retail sales of mobile homes amounted to $6 billion. Most sales are conducted by about ten-thousand independent retailers. Some homes are sold through sales centers owned and operated by manufacturers. The multi-section home accounted for one-third of all units produced in 1985. The traditional twelve- to fourteen-foot wide single-section home continues to be a major part (67 percent) of the industry's product. There seems to be increasing acceptance of sixteen- and eighteen-foot-wide single-section homes in some Western states.

Industry leaders emphasize that the industry is basically geared toward production and not marketing. Public perception of manufactured homes could be greatly improved by better marketing. The industry's challenge in the future involves the ability to attract buyers from a broad spectrum of society.

Characteristics of Mobile Home Units

The median model year of occupied manufactured homes is 1974, and fully 59 percent of all occupied units were constructed before 1976. The great majority (78 percent) of owners occupy single units and 51 percent of all occupied units are located in parks or subdivisions specifically designed for mobile homes.

In 1960, 98 percent of mobile homes produced were ten feet wide. This changed dramatically by 1970 with the introduction of twelve-foot-wide units; then about 79 percent of production were twelve feet, 8 percent were fourteen feet and 12 percent were multi-sections or expandable units. By 1985, the multi-wides had become one-third of total production.

The gradual increase in size of units manufactured and the introduction of safety and performance standards tended to accelerate the obsolescence of older mobile homes. The rapid growth of some metropolitan areas, especially on the fringes where so many mobile homes have traditionally been located, has caused displacement for owners of older and especially of narrower mobile homes.

Often mobile-home parks have been located in the growth path of metropolitan areas, resulting in dramatic increases in land values and pressures for landowners to sell for other uses. While park owners may profit from the increased value of their land, owners of mobile home units in these parks sometimes face the difficult, expensive task of relocating their units to another home site or park. A HUD-sponsored study found that from 1973 to 1980 about nine-hundred thousand mobile homes that had been occupied in 1973 were removed from the housing inventory. Much of this loss was undoubtedly due to the age of the units themselves, but some removal was due to urban growth pressure on land occupied by mobile-home parks.

Average sales prices of new mobile homes placed for residential use have increased from $6,100 in 1970 to $21,800 in 1985. During the same period, the average sales prices of conventionally built one-family homes have increased from $18,000 to $100,000, or when land price is subtracted from the total, from about $15,000 to $80,000.

The average cost per square foot for mobile homes increased from about $8 in 1970 to $20 in 1985. Conventionally built single-family houses retailed for about $15 per square foot without land in 1970 and for about $45 in 1985. Overall, mobile home prices have risen about 350 percent during the fifteen-year period, while

Fun N Sun Recreational Vehicle Park, San Benito, Texas. Courtesy Fun N Sun/L.T. Christensen.

conventional one-family housing has experienced a 530-percent increase.

Financing Manufactured Housing Units

An estimated 87 percent of the new mobile homes sold in 1985 were financed. Mobile homes are generally not financed by long-term mortgage loans, but by consumer loans repayable on an installment basis over a period considerably shorter than the typical maturity for conventional loans. The average loan amounted to about $22,000. Down payments averaged 15 percent for new single-section homes and 15.5 percent for new multi-section homes. In 1985 the average loan maturity of new single-section homes was 11.5 years and for multi-section homes, 13.4 years. The interest rate on mobile home credit, due to the risk, has been significantly higher than mortgage credit. Over time, the depreciable nature of mobile homes increases the risk of default.

The volume of credit required to finance manufactured-home purchases has risen steadily. In 1981, high real estate rates in the conventional housing sector and a significant slowdown in the price of manufactured homes made factory-built units relatively more affordable. The effective demand for mobile homes improved in 1983 with lenders reporting $1.16 million in new consumer loans and manufactured home credit outstanding extended to slightly more than $20.9 billion, of which about $4.5 billion was used to purchase new manufactured homes.

The Manufactured Housing Institute conducted a survey in 1983 of 542 financial institutions and found that 185 institutions provided $2.5 billion in wholesale financing for the industry; commercial banks provided 84 percent of this volume.

Future Demand

The demand for manufactured homes will probably increase slightly in the rest of the 1980s even though demand dipped in 1986. This increase is expected because of widening housing-price differences between manufactured homes and conventional new and existing single-family units. The wages of blue-collar workers have not been increasing as rapidly as those of white-collar workers. And, with the 1986 median purchase price of a new conventionally built house exceeding $100,000 and that of an existing house at $80,900, manufactured homes will become even more attractive in non-metropolitan and fringe areas.

In many areas there are shortages of qualified, on-site construction labor, and the high interest rates charged on conventional mortgages in the early 1980s created a long slump for smaller home builders as well as for skilled labor. This has had an adverse impact on the construction industry in some regions. Large builders are expected to play a greater role in housing construction, and they are more likely to use manufactured or other factory-built housing components in the future. Industry economists predict that manufactured homes will continue to hold their 12 to 15 percent market share of United States housing production in the coming decade and will continue to account for about 30 percent of all new single-family site built homes. Should the industry resolve some of its marketing problems and increase the acceptance of multi-wide units in the marketplace, it could capture a larger market share of white-collar and middle-income demand.

Margaret J. Drury is author of *Mobile Homes: The Unrecognized Revolution in American Housing.* Currently she is a principal in the Washington, D.C., firm of Drury and Hendricks.

Scaled Down

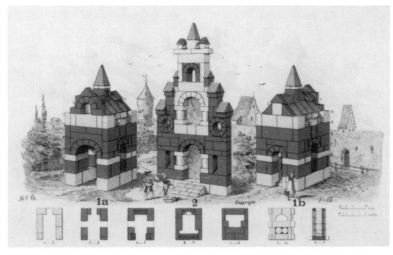

Anchor building blocks, Germany, about 1910. Picture Library, Cooper-Hewitt Museum.

Martin houses, E.F. Hodgson Company, Boston. Picture Library, Cooper-Hewitt Museum.

Dollhouse. Picture Library, Cooper-Hewitt Museum.

Palace, cast iron penny bank, United States, 1885. Courtesy Don R. Duer.

Tree house. Picture Library, Cooper-Hewitt Museum.

133

Underground Living

It is not a new phenomenon.

By Gideon S. Golany

One of the longest-lasting housing concepts has been that of belowground shelter. Natural caves were the first type discovered. Since then mankind has invented extensive and sophisticated forms of shelter involving elaborate site selection and orientation, ingenuity in the usage of building materials, comprehension of environmental constraints and benefits, creative design, economic affordability, selectivity in acclimatization, and energy-saving considerations. For a human being, a house is both a shelter and a home that offers him social entity and identity. These and other themes will continue to be considered for shelter in the future. Present theory holds that house evolution moved from belowground to aboveground and thence to high-rise. In spite of the not always justifiable negative image of belowground spaces, man has continued to use them for shelter.

Although belowground dwellings have been an international phenomenon, certain geographical regions and societies have used such shelters extensively for many centuries. The most commonly known cases are those of China, Tunisia (northern Sahara), Cappadocia (central Turkey), the Mediterranean basin, American Indian cliff dwellings, and North American Eskimos. The most outstanding examples of large-scale uninterrupted developments are the first three. Site selection has evolved primarily because of economic, climatic, or defense considerations.

The Chinese example is the largest in history. The estimated forty million persons living belowground are concentrated within the loess soil zone of northern China. Cave dwellings have been in existence there since 2000 B.C., in the region called the cradle of Chinese civilization, along the lengthy Huang He or Yellow River. Three primary factors operated to make belowground habitats a choice. Loess is a uniform soil, almost free from stone, relatively easy to dig, and structurally sound when moisture-free. The region is arid to semiarid and is defined as climatically stressful, for which cave dwellings are appropriate. The third factor is historical: internal wars created large numbers of refugees and the urgent need to accommodate the soldiers involved in the turmoil.

In some sections of the loess soil zone, such as the rural Qingyang region of Gansu province, more than 83 percent of the total population lives belowground. In the Yan'an City region of Shaanxi province, 90 percent of the urban and more than 65 percent of the suburban population dwells in subterranean housing. Recently, the Chinese government utilized belowground space in the major cities of Beijing and Shanghai for civil defense reasons, construction that is now used for hotels, theaters, shopping centers, hospitals, exhibition halls, and the like.

The Tunisian belowground shelters were introduced by the North African Berber tribes for defense against the Arab invasions of the eighth century. Their location on the Matmata plateau in southern Tunisia is more than five hundred meters above sea level. Presently, there are more than twenty belowground communities, with an average of approximately one thousand persons per settlement. The village of Matmata itself developed around

pit-type cave dwellings and was originally hidden from passersby, though recently aboveground houses have been added. Most other belowground villages feature cliff-type cave dwellings. In spite of the excellent thermal performance of these dwellings, there is a strong tendency for younger people to move outside the village and build above ground.

At Bulla Regia, in northern Tunisia, a city dominated by the Mediterranean climate—dry and warm in summer, cool and rainy in winter—the Romans developed pit-type belowground villas with colonnaded peristyles. They introduced an articulated architecture through consideration of sunshine, light, and ventilation. Our research findings indicate that the Romans used these homes primarily to escape the heat of summer.

The Cappadocian belowground shelters, which are located on the central plateau of Turkey, a semiarid region with cold winters, have continued to be occupied with little interruption since the fourth millennium B.C. The soil is a lava deposit (tufa), subjected to eolian deflation, establishing conically shaped rocks fifty meters high. The rock is relatively easy to cut and excavate, and the cliff dwellings, some more than eight stories high, are interconnected to form highly complicated traffic networks. Some sites have large, wide, high-ceilinged halls constructed and painted like Byzantine churches some fifteen hundred years ago, while others serve as national centers for refrigerated citrus storage. This Göreme valley region has approximately forty belowground communities and is a tourist attraction.

Other examples of belowground dwellings are smaller in scale and have shorter histories. The best known are the American Indian cliff dwellings in the southwestern United States, the cave dwellings in the Merge Trulli region of southern Italy, sites in southeastern Australia,

Pit cave dwellings in Matmata village, southern Tunisia. From Gideon S. Golany, *Earth-Sheltered Dwellings in Tunisia: Ancient Lessons for Modern Design*, reprinted by permission of Associated Presses for University of Delaware Press, Newark, Delaware, 1988.

southern Israel, central France, south-central Spain, and modern sites in the Kansas City region of the United States.

The basic types of subterranean dwellings are the pit and the cliff, each of which includes many variations. In addition, there is the earth-sheltered habitat.

Pit cave dwellings are primarily found on flat or rolling plains; therefore their design is significantly influenced by topographical factors. The overall plan is of a huge pit, eight to twelve meters in length and width, and seven to ten meters in depth, with room units excavated on the four sides. The pit patio, while open to the sky, is not well ventilated and admits less sunshine and light into its rooms than cliff dwellings do. The entrance is usually through a tunnel dug on the south side, with a curving stairway or ramp descending to the patio. In both China and Tunisia, the rooms are dug in relatively soft soil that can support itself when dry. The structural quality of the soil determines the width and height of the rooms: for example, in China the width does not usually exceed 3.5 meters and in Tunisia, 4 meters. The common practice is for height to be correlated to width; thus height ranges between 2.5 and 3.5 meters. The length of the rooms varies between 6 and 9 meters, although some rooms in China total more than 20. Generally, the deeper parts of the rooms are used for storage.

The traditional Chinese architectural concepts of enclosure and intimacy are realized by the pit dwelling's enclosed, belowground courtyard. Because of the high summer humidity in China, rooms facing south are given first preference as living space and are usually reserved for senior family members, the sides facing east and west are given second preference, and the side facing north is used for storage and housing animals. In general, the pit-type dwelling consumes more land than the cliff type does. Recently, some regional governments in China have prohibited the digging of additional pit-type dwellings to conserve valuable acreage.

Cliff cave dwellings are dug into the vertical cliff faces of plateaus, gullies, or mountains. The units can be extended

Cliff dwellings in the tufa rock of Cappadocia, Turkey. Courtesy of the Turkish Embassy, Washington, D.C.

almost to unlimited length, usually with a terrace constructed of soil dug from the cliff to establish a courtyard. The preferred location faces south to realize optimal exposure to natural light and sunshine. In most cases they are constructed on soil that is not suitable for agriculture. In special cases, cliff cave dwellings utilize the geological structure of alternating soft and hard layers, 2.5 to 3 meters thick. The dwellings are created by extracting part of the soft layer and using the remaining hard layers as ceilings and floors.

Cliff dwellers enjoy direct visual contact with their surroundings. They adjust to topographical configurations. Cliff dwellers enjoy substantial natural light and ventilation and are usually in a defensible position. Overall, cliff-type cave dwellings are more advantageous for human habitation and introduce greater architectural variation than the pit-type cave dwellings do.

Earth-sheltered habitats have been reintroduced recently, especially in the United States, as a response to the energy crisis. The structures are aboveground or semi-aboveground and each is covered by soil one-half to one meter thick. They are thermally efficient heat retainers, yet do not match the thermal retentive qualities of cave dwellings. Many modern earth-sheltered structures in the United States are aesthetically designed and articulated, including more than one hundred schools and thousands of personal dwellings.

The cardinal advantage of belowground living space is excellent thermal performance. It is cool in summer and warm in winter. The thermal principle that needs to be understood is twofold: first, that soil functions as an excellent insulator and second, that soil is an efficient retainer of temperature.

Daily solar radiation affects soil to a depth of five to ten centimeters, thus enabling the earth to function as an efficient insulator between the outdoor and indoor environments. In spite of the limited penetration of temperature radiation into the soil, slowly but steadily a wave of temperature is created and moves inward, reaching the indoor environment a season later in a time-lag process. In this way, summer heat will penetrate, be retained and introduced in the winter, and conversely winter cold will penetrate and be retained for the summer. The length of thermal travel is determined by soil thickness, structural composition, and the degree of humidity of the soil. These two basic thermal capacities are not fully comprehended by some modern designers, and consequently they do not fully utilize the optimal thermal efficiency of soil.

The optimal functioning of belowground habitats occurs in such stressful climates as cold and dry (Siberia, north-central Canada) or hot and dry (Sahara, northern China). In regions of high humidity combined with warm temperatures, habitats may encounter problems of dampness that will require intense ventilation. Regions of moderate climate, such as rainy and warm in the summer and cold and snowy in the winter, require careful design considerations since

belowground habitats will function less efficiently. Obviously, historical belowground experiences of human settlement have been primarily in arid and semiarid regions.

Our study in China revealed that modern hospitals using belowground space for patient recuperation after surgery achieved a 25–30 percent reduction in recovery time. This is an economical matter of saving time as well as a matter of health. It results from the basic fact that both relative humidity and ambient temperatures are diurnally stable and therefore are beneficial to healing wounds and achieving steady recovery.

The significance of historical belowground developments in various world sites is that they provide us with elaborate ancient lessons for future design. Modern dispersed cities can achieve diverse land uses and reduce the demand on all utilities, meet the need for new energy resources, and ease the consumption of municipal services with belowground shelters.

The cliff-type habitat is to be preferred over the pit type in modern belowground designs, both because it provides direct visual contact with the outdoors, better light, ventilation, and drainage, and because it permits occupants to ascend rather than descend into the dwelling. Judging by the existing movements in the developed countries, belowground space usage will be on the increase for restaurants, shopping centers, entertainment facilities, schools, offices, industrial plants, hospitals, and many other functions.

The historical bias and negative image associated with belowground habitats should be revised in the light of modern technology and corresponding design innovations. Then we can evolve a new frontier utilizing an ancient concept and can tap its significant economic and environmental potential.

Gideon S. Golany is Research Professor of Urban Design/Planning, Division of Environmental Design and Planning at Pennsylvania State University and author of *Earth-Sheltered Habitat: History, Architecture and Urban Design*.

Tensile Structures

By Nicholas Goldsmith

Tents have always been with us—for nearly every purpose and in every climate. Since the earliest man left the cave, he has been stretching everything over poles—from hides to polyester. Prehistoric campsites for tents found in Russia, date back at least four-thousand years and early pictorial images of tents can be seen in caves that are between ten and twenty thousand years old.

For ages, nomadic cultures developed around tents, refining these forms of shelter into their purest design, in order to support their life-style and provide protection from the most severe environmental conditions. Prevailing winds, unbearable temperatures, and domesticated animals all measured into this equation. Tents developed where two prerequisites prevailed: the need for mobility and a shortage of building materials. Tents used less material mass than other forms of construction and thus were ideal as portable shelter. They could be modified easily according to changing needs. For the nomad, a tent was the ideal house.

The tents of nomadic cultures can be broken down into three general categories: covered cone tents, or tepees; low profile black desert tents; and felt covered cylindrical tents or yurts.

The tepees of the Native Americans were basically tilted cones, the back made steeper than the front in order to brace it against the strong prevailing west winds of the Great Plains. The tilt made for more headroom in the back of the lodge, where most of the activity took place, and allowed the entrance to face east toward the rising sun. The structure of the tepee was basically a frame structure with skins or fabric stretched over it and staked to the ground to stabilize the frame. Similar conical tents existed in Siberia and Lapland; however, the details of how the poles rested on each other were different. Over the centuries there have been a few innovations in the basic design of the tepee. With the introduction of the horse in America in the seventeenth and eighteenth centuries, tepees grew larger because the folded membrane and poles could be carried from place to place

Tent of the keeper of the sacred pipe used at the Northern Arapaho sun dance, 1900. Courtesy Department of Library Services, American Museum of Natural History.

more easily. In the nineteenth century, canvas was introduced as a replacement for buffalo hides because it was lighter and because the white settlers were decimating the buffalo population. As with

any developed culture, the architecture of the Plains Indians developed a language to describe uses of their different tepees. Chiefs, medicine men, and war leaders had their tepees painted to portray their social roles.

Another classic historical example of the use of the tent as housing for vast populations is the black tent of the Sahara and Arabian peninsula. In Arabic, bedouin means desert dweller, and the bedouin people are the nomadic people of Arabia, Syria, Jordan, Iraq, and North Africa. Their tents are made from goat hair spun into thread and woven into long pieces of cloth. These tents served primarily as sunshade protection from temperatures averaging 120 degrees Fahrenheit. They were also required to serve as protective shields against winds (mixed with sand) up to 100 miles per hour. Because of the poor foundation material—sand—the ropes are extremely long and horizontal to minimize the vertical uplift applied to the stakes. It has been said that these horizontal ropes also served as an alarm system at night if someone approached the tent. If touched, they would vibrate and wake the inhabitants.

Structurally, the black tent differed from the tepee in that here, the poles joined reinforced bands of fabric directly instead of creating a frame, thus they invented the model for a column and cable tensile structure.

The third generic type of nomadic tent is the yurt; a cylindrical frame of lattice elements that support conical roof struts. Over the entire frame, a felt cover is secured by ropes, however unlike the black tent, here the membrane acts primarily as cladding and not as a structural membrane. The surface area in yurts is close to a minimum for the space enclosed. Since the entire construction is made of a few repetitive elements (radial roof struts and lattice wall members), the size of yurts was directly dependent on the strength of materials used. Yurts were used primarily in colder climates, since the frame structure worked well in heavy snow conditions.

In a way, the yurt and the tepee can both be seen as the root of a fabric architecture for more northern climates, and the black desert tent with its hovering profile and expanse of shading can be seen as the precursor of a fabric architecture for warmer climates.

These are the earliest tensile structures, that is, structures in which the fabric in a state of tension plays a structural role. The word tent itself comes from the Latin *tentorium* and the verb *tendo* which means to stretch, and that is the essence of tent constructions, both in the past and the present.

Unlike the tribes of Native Americans, bedouins, and herders who were dependent on a nomadic culture where their shelter had to move, Western man's culture grew out of an agrarian condition and portability no longer was a criterion. Tents began to be used only in festivities, carnivals, and wars.

In the field of military campaigns, tents quickly developed as an effective way to shelter armies at war. From Roman leather tents to medieval parasol roof tents to Sibley tents of the Civil War (a westernized version of the American tepee) to our present-day military tents, relatively little change has occurred. They have become larger; decoration has been applied, acting as a text for each culture; and synthetic materials have replaced traditional materials.

Festival tents and canopies of public assembly have developed independently on a larger scale, starting with roofs over Roman coliseums to the great tradition of circus tents. At the beginning of the twentieth century, the technology of cable bridge construction developed to where fabric and cable constructions could permanently span large distances. After World War II tensile architecture was used for public buildings and developed into a new building type. Sports stadiums, concert facilities, and expositions used this technology—from Frei Otto's German pavilion at Expo '67 to the German Olympic stadium in Munich, to the present Olympic stadium complex in Seoul, Korea—the tent as permanent public building has become accepted.

Tenting as housing, however, has lagged far behind, except where nomadic culture has direct ties into the modern world. At the tent cities in the hajj, over two million people live in tents for several days as they make the pilgrimage to Mecca and its surroundings as part of the Moslem religious festival commemorating biblical stories of both Adam and Abraham. Tents have always been a part of this ceremony, which remains today the best living example of a tent city, using 350,000 to 400,000 tents. In Muna, one of the campsites, densities of 5,000 pilgrims per hectare exist. The largest portion of the camp consists of repetitive four-meter (on each side) square tents; however, tents from northern Asia and Africa can also be found.

Frei Otto has recently developed several designs for single-family tent houses. One of them has a dwelling area of about 1,300 square feet and contains two bedrooms, two bathrooms including shower and toilets, and a kitchen.

This tent house is "autarkic," meaning it does not need to be connected to underground services. Each tent house has an electric generator, a freshwater tank, and sewage treatment equipment. The energy source can be fossil fuel or wood.

All larger parts are made of heat-insulated and sound-isolating canvas. Bathrooms and kitchen are lightweight containers that can easily be transported by a car trailer. These tent houses can be erected in about four hours by two to four people; the total weight of the tent, without fuel and water, does not exceed two tons.

Another of Otto's designs for a smaller house is the exterior skeleton frame "umbrella tent." This is a single-room design using a center post that remains above head height and through a series of radial struts applies a prestress to the fabric form.

Other designs for the reinterpretation of the tent as home include Bill Moss's Optimum 200—a small fabric summer home that packs onto a two-foot square box and weighs only fifty-five pounds.

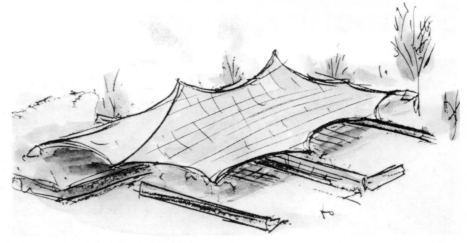

Frei Otto, Sketch of a tent house, 1987.

The firm of FTL Associates in New York has also developed designs for folding summer homes, including one that folds out to form a twelve by twelve foot module only three feet high. Its fabric roof pulls out as the module is deployed to offer a cost effective alternative for a summer home. Another design of FTL was for a resort house for Frank Perdue; it consisted of a 2,000 square foot stone base with a swimming pool, perimeter rooms, and a permanent tensile roof covering the entire complex.

Since World War II camping has mushroomed as a recreational activity, and as a consequence we have several generations of tent development. From the early pole tents, the camping tent industry has moved to self-supporting structures, that is, to rod frameworks with floors and walls that can be prestressed without any staking.

Today fabrics exist with lifespans of over twelve years; they are constructed of glass fiber weaves with teflon or silicone coatings and polyester weaves with vinyl coatings. Multilayer fabric systems can achieve insulation with R values of 6. Computer programs allow architects to design many different shapes for this structural fabric technology. Otto's new fabric construction concepts include sound and thermal insulation using trapped air.

If the technology for permanent tent houses exists, and as previously mentioned, large-scale tent structures have been accepted, why then have tent structures as houses remained primarily concepts on drafting boards? Is it the lingering depression image of the tent as a symbol of poverty? Is it due to our Western cultural tradition of perceiving a home as something permanent and fabric as something temporary? Is it the perceived lack of security of fabric as a building material? Is it due to the fact that fabrics described above are expensive relative to traditional wood building? What will it take to dismiss these associations?

Ultimately the tent as house will become accepted. Its translucency, acoustic properties, portability, and longevity will outweigh the perceived problems that presently hinder its development. But it will do so only after tensile fabric architecture is in use everywhere; after high-rise buildings are clad in fabrics, after concert halls and stadia use tensile constructions, after cities are covered in lightweight fabric enclosures.

Nicholas Goldsmith is a principal architect at FTL Associates in New York City and President of Surface Forms Research Group.

Symbolic Houses

Fishbowl. Courtesy T.F.H. Publications.

Glass House, New Canaan, Connecticut; Philip Johnson, architect, 1949. Richard Payne.

No. 1 Kennel with partition, advertisement, Hodgson Company, 1934. The New York Public Library. The Branch Libraries. Picture Collection.

138

Albert L.U. Hendschel, "The Card House," from Hendschel's *Sketchbook*, 1871. The New York Public Library. The Branch Libraries. Picture Collection.

Almond Street, St. Louis, Missouri, 1867. Culver Pictures.

The White House, Washington, D.C. Courtesy White House.

Roman Catholic Cathedral, Third Street, New York City. Kubler Collection, Cooper-Hewitt Museum.

View of the St. Louis Cemetery, New Orleans, Louisiana, about 1890. Leonard V. Huber Collection, Courtesy Louisiana State Museum, Charles F. Mugnier.

"August Spies, the Chicago Anarchist, as he appeared in his cell," 1887. Kubler Collection, Cooper-Hewitt Museum.

Industrial Servants

Smart houses are a wave of the future.

By Arthur J. Pulos

A century ago most homes were virtually self-sufficient living units. Insofar as utilities go, many had their own water source and waste disposal methods. Communications were either oral or by pen or print. Most people grew their own food or bought and bartered in open markets for what they did not have. The tin can and mason jar were still novelties. Clothing was generally homemade either by hand or with the then-miraculous sewing machine. The arts of living in the home were largely devoted to sustenance and survival.

In 1869, in the dawn of the women's liberation movement, Catherine Beecher and Harriet Beecher Stowe proposed in a small book, *The American Woman's Home*, that smaller homes could be managed by designing conveniences that eliminated the need for servants. "At the present time," they wrote, "America is the only country where there is a class of women who may be described as ladies who do their own work." They anticipated that the true source of emancipation for women lay in the concept of a home as a machine planned along scientific lines.

To give substance to their vision, they designed and illustrated a cooking stove that can still outperform its modern counterpart. With one hod of anthracite coal, they claimed it could keep running for twenty-four hours, keep seventeen gallons of water hot at all hours, bake pies and puddings in the warm closet, heat flatirons under the back cover, boil water in a teakettle and one pot under the front cover, bake bread in the oven, and cook a turkey in the tin roaster in front.

Today's home with its sophisticated appliances may seem to be more independent than the home of the Beecher sisters a century ago. In point of fact it is not. The modern home is only one cell in a complex of thousands that share umbilical utilities of water and waste. It is tied into a nerve system of wire and wireless communications and depends upon power provided by a network of electrical energy. Still, the modern home clings to its dream of independence, and its inhabitants look askance at anyone who tries to survive outside the system.

The current buzz word for the technologically advanced home is the *smart house*. It identifies a long overdue attempt to bring the home into the twentieth century. Except for isolated cases, the architecture of the average home of today is still caught in the Gordian knot of the vested interests of the building trades and the industrial and financial institutions that are supported by them. However, the smart house is exploring changes from the internal systems and functions of the home rather than from its superficial colonial or revamped Queen Anne appearance.

At this point safety and security in the home are dependent on manufactured products and product systems that serve with increasing sophistication as domestic guardians. Smoke and fire detectors that began as clever gadgets to be purchased and installed by the inhabitants are moving up the scale to be retrofitted into existing buildings and installed in new ones as mandated by local laws. In the area of electrical safety, existing systems are now being supplemented by "ground fault interrupters," particularly in high-risk areas such as bathrooms and kitchens. Some manufacturers of appliances and tools have taken electrical safety as their own responsibility by designing products that are double insulated so that, in the event that the integrity of the first level is broken, the second level will protect the user. Electronic equipment is also being produced that offers protection against power surges that may disable computers and other electrically sensitive machines.

The predominance of homes in suburbia has generated a demand for security systems that operate at different levels to make the home as much of a fortress as it is a haven. At one level, hardware is being augmented by electronic systems that are not only keyless but that also signal warnings if they are tampered with. Homes may also be equipped with audible alarms to scare an intruder off or with silent alarms that alert a surveillance center. Domestic lighting may also be tied in with a domestic security system, by which one programs appropriate lights to go on and off as desired. Heat-sensitive switches are available that sense the presence of a person in a room and will turn lights on automatically and then off again when the room is vacated.

Controlling the climate in the home was once the conscious and continuing responsibility of residents using parlor stoves, portable heaters, air-conditioners, and fans that were their property. Today, with rare exceptions (the current fad of turn-of-the-century ceiling fans notwithstanding), original functions have coalesced into a central system that circulates air that is heated or cooled, humidified, and filtered. Moreover, with the increased sophistication of electronic systems, such systems can be programmed to maintain cyclic conditions in different parts of the home.

An important development that has been gaining momentum is the control center in the modern home. Not only does it bring into one location all of the operating systems of the home, it is also becoming a focal point for communication systems both within and outside the home. Moreover, data banks, digital disks, and software for education, entertainment, and personal and professional services may

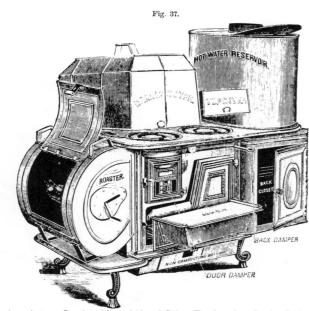

The Beecher sisters' stove. Reprinted from Arthur J. Pulos, *The American Design Ethic*, published by

be accessed in this command and control center.

It is difficult to believe that little more than a decade ago Tandy pioneered the mass marketing of personal computers. Today the success of IBM and Apple computers, among others, has established the personal computer as a basic domestic servant. For adults, it serves professional, social, and domestic needs. For children, it has expanded the horizons for education and entertainment. Original reservations about the invasion of this technological "monster" into the sanctity of the home are disappearing with its transformation into a "user-friendly" genie. The personal computer is becoming indispensable to the home as an office complex—it offers universal access to data banks across the country.

Recently the focus has shifted from electronic education and entertainment in the home to communication. Facsimile (FAX) machines that are capable of sending electronic copies of documents over telephone wires are dropping dramatically in size and cost. Within a year it is expected that they will cost less than five hundred dollars. When one considers that the overnight cost of an air express letter is about twelve dollars, the cost of telephoning a facsimile of a document or photograph in seconds for less than fifty cents makes the FAX machine an inevitable domestic convenience.

The living room, as the focus of family life, is being divided into two different functions. One is the traditional one of personal interchange among family members and with acquaintances; the second is the emerging domestic entertainment complex with its digital audiovisual electronics. One may also expect that today's passive viewers will become interactive participants in future programs. The rapid advance of technology suggests that the next great form for education and entertainment may be a glass box of whatever size in which an electronic stage will present three-dimensional programs through the medium of laser-generated holograms.

First, with the advent of video tapes, then with the development of compact discs, control of video and audio enter-

General Motors' *Kitchen of Tomorrow III*, 1956. Courtesy of General Motors Co., reprinted from Arthur J. Pulos, *The American Design Adventure*, published by The MIT Press, © 1988.

tainment in the home has shifted to consumers. Today, with VCRs and CD players, they plan their own programs independently of public and cable broadcasting systems. Over forty percent of American homes have VCRs and, within five years after the introduction of CD players, annual sales had already jumped to two million a year. On the immediate horizon are digital audio tapes (DAT) that will make sound recordings available to consumers in the same pattern as video tape rentals and libraries make them available today.

With a glance backward to the Romans and other ancient sybarites, the most interesting development is the transformation of the bathroom area of the home into a health center. It is expanding from its essential preoccupation with ablution and elimination to include general hygiene and physical fitness. Access to electronic programs will provide medical and diagnostic information, exercise demonstrations and guidance. One may expect to see a new array of machines,

now in fitness centers, adapted to the domestic environment: jogging and walking platforms (the word treadmill is too negative to use here), exercycles, rowing machines, and other body-conditioning equipment that simulates outdoor sports. Attention will continue to shift from the curative to the far more enjoyable preventative health activities—all of this in response to an increasingly sedentary lifestyle.

The now omnipresent industrial servants in the home—those major appliances developed in the earlier part of the century for food and clothing preparation and care such as stoves, refrigerators, washers, dryers, dishwashers, and the like—have been gradually disappearing into walls and cabinets to become part of the architecture rather than the transportable property of the tenant. Often only their face panels and controls are left to be decorated as desired. Predictions for the Kitchen of Tomorrow and the House of Tomorrow are still being made as they have been since Chicago's

Century of Progress Exposition in 1933–34.

A more recent prediction suggested that the kitchen was disintegrating into a variety of portable appliances such as automatic saucepans, griddles, soup pots, Hotrays, and, most significantly, the increasingly popular microwave ovens. This appears to be in line with the shift from basic food preparation to the purchase of finished foods that have been prepared by specialists and put into forms that can be brought to the table with little additional preparation. One way of assuaging the cook's conscience has been the rise of interest in gourmet cooking and its exotic machines to chop, grind, extrude, blend, and brew. They have Eurostyle names such as Conran's Bistro teapot, Krups Euro-Brew, Ferrari's electric grill, plus such foreign-sounding names as Cuisinart and Dansk. And, most important, the machines themselves become objects of art, to be displayed as evidence of the cook's superior talents.

It appears, however, that most domestic appliances, major or minor, have reached "typeforms" that, while there may be refinements to be made, reveal the products as essentially on a developmental plateau. The best evidence of this fact are the efforts being made by some designers and manufacturers to breathe life into these industries with styling changes—ranging from postmodernist throwbacks to semantics, the latter being a contemporary manifestation of what, a half-century ago, was called streamlining. The difference lies in the fact that in the 1930s aesthetic inspiration came from transportation forms that were shaped to move through the medium of air, whereas the semantic forms of the 1980s take their inspiration from the forms of objects in the vacuum of space, where disassociated Euclidean shapes can be assembled at will to perform a prescribed function. The results are as exciting and as volatile aesthetically as their predecessors were.

Arthur J. Pulos is the former chairman of the Department of Design at Syracuse University, and is the author of *The American Design Adventure*.

Homemakers

By Harvey Green

That the word *homemaker* doesn't appear in the *Oxford English Dictionary* (1970) or the *Century Dictionary* (1889) should surprise no one. The concept is a wholly American one, of recent vintage. It has, however, found its way into newer American dictionaries such as *Webster's Third International* (1971) and the *American Heritage Dictionary of the English Language* (1973). It is even treated—extensively—in the *Americana Encyclopedia* (1986), though it is not to be found in the discreetly British *Encyclopedia Britannica*.

The meanings proffered by those dictionaries tell us much about our own culture, especially about our attitudes toward women, work in the home, and the responsibilities of home life. All the definitions and explorations of the word's meaning combine the twin elements of household management and maintenance with the moral imperative of familial duty. The lexicographers and compilers carefully note that the homemaker is unpaid and is a family member, most often a wife. Unlike those of twenty-five years ago, most current definitions do not presume that women are identified with these roles, suggesting perhaps that some sort of cultural stirring has occurred in very recent years. There is also a careful distinction drawn between paid help and the homemaker.

But as relatively new as the dictionary definition or encyclopedia disquisition are, the ideas and values they contain are at least as old as the settlement of this country. Within the history of homemaking, even though the word itself has not been much in use, is a revelation and elevation of the lives of women, who performed the tasks that Americans have considered central to the survival of this culture.

In the seventeenth century, especially in the modest homes of most people who emigrated to North America from Europe, gender roles were defined by tradition, if not by written code. Most white Americans were farmers, and women performed a mediating central role in the family. Men occupied the positions of provider—in the field as yeoman and in the woods as hunter and fuel gatherer—and of political leader in the "little commonwealth" that was the family.

Women were empowered with the responsibility and authority to transform the raw materials of the field and forest into

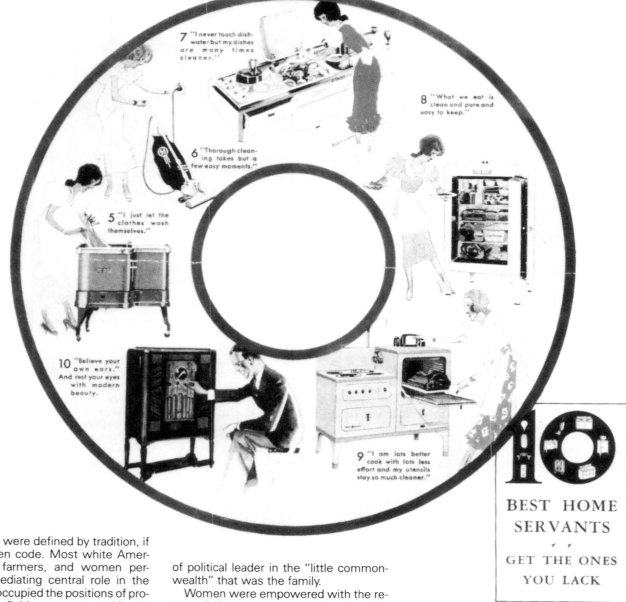

7 "I never touch dishwater but my dishes are many times cleaner."

8 "What we eat is clean and pure and easy to keep."

6 "Thorough cleaning takes but a few easy moments."

5 "I just let the clothes wash themselves."

10 "Believe your own ears." And rest your eyes with modern beauty.

9 "I am lots better cook with lots less effort and my utensils stay so much cleaner."

10 BEST HOME SERVANTS GET THE ONES YOU LACK

"Ten best home servants."
Picture Library, Cooper-Hewitt Museum.

142

usable goods. Thus they preserved and worked foodstuffs—grains, meats, and other produce—into food to be eaten. So, too, they transformed flax and sheep's wool into linen thread and woolen yarn, from which they fashioned clothing and other textiles. Women dressed small game, farmyard animals, and fowls as well as the bodies of their families, and broke both flax and their children's allegedly demonic wills, since most of the responsibility for child rearing also fell to them.

Men performed some of these tasks, too, but most of their tasks were outside the home. They broke land for cultivation, and dressed larger game and domestic animals.

Women operated in the intermediate spaces of the house while performing these functions. The "hall" of the tiny two- or three-room structures in which most lived was a large work area, complete with fireplace for cooking and heat, and often connected to a series of small back workrooms in a lean-to area, where some work was done and goods were stored. Men were lords of the fields and barns, and also of the parlor, in which formal display and religious activity often occurred. The boundaries between authority and responsibility were clearly defined, and understood: women possessed little of the former and much of the latter. Or at best they found themselves in a situation where their responsibility was far greater than their authority. Court records of the colonial era show us that there was little fracture but much friction in this arrangement.

The urbanizing and suburbanizing of American culture that began in the late eighteenth century, and which came to dominate American life in the nineteenth and twentieth centuries, did little to alter this imbalance. By the time the Civil War broke out in 1861, most women no longer had to break flax and spin it or wool into thread, from which they loomed yard goods. Machines had assumed these roles, and women were gladly relieved of the tedium of those tasks. But the new power looms and food-processing mills and factories changed women's and homemakers' lives but a little. Theirs was

Kitchen in 1870. Kubler Collection, Cooper-Hewitt Museum.

still the responsibility to cook, clean, launder, and rear the children. Technology made it possible for women to jettison some activities, usually only to take on others. The same sort of innovation that developed the mill machinery also invented and mass-produced the sewing machine, or "the lady's friend."

The victory over the drudgery of the spinning, weaving, and hand sewing came at a price. The Industrial Revolution brought with it great changes in the economies of both the United States and England, producing consumer-oriented societies in which the newly emerging middle-class household found itself restructured, if not reoriented in its responsibilities. Most popular magazines of the nineteenth century were directed at women readers, and presented ambitious women with elaborate models of fashionable dress, and reams of advice about their work. In the process of disseminating information and offering a multitude of helpful hints, the editors of these "lady's books" and "lady's friends" perhaps unwittingly fed the spirit of social competition and bourgeois insecurity in a

world that was increasingly one of commerce and business, of appearance and status consciousness. The sewing machine made life easier in one sense, but women using it could and did make more and more elaborate clothing, and were roundly criticized for doing so. But the stress of status seeking and the pull of ambition pressed them forward, in spite of reformers' complaints.

Women in the nineteenth and twentieth centuries were driven to do the laundry (which entailed the most physically demanding of jobs—hauling wood, heating water, scrubbing, rinsing, wringing, and hanging clothes), clean the house, cook the meals, and raise the children because they were told that the fate of their families, their nation, and Western civilization depended on them. If their husbands frequented "grog shops" or stayed out for the "late convivial supper" with their male friends, warned M. H. Cornelius in *The Young Housekeeper's Friend* (1868), it was the result of the "total failure of the wife in her sphere of duty." Such dire warnings were not only for the middle class. Working-class

women, whether they worked outside the home or not, had to worry, since "many a day-laborer, on his return at evening from his hard toil, is repelled by the sight of a disorderly house and a comfortless supper."

The home had become—at least in the minds of Americans, if not in fact—the refuge from the commercial and industrial worlds of competition and struggle, a sort of sanctuary or "domestic altar" wherein Christianity might be practiced as it was ignored in the hard world of economics. This division of life's activities into discrete but interconnected parts presented American women of all classes with a nearly impossible situation. Denied economic and political power—women had no vote until the early twentieth century—they were nonetheless responsible for the present and the future. In the twentieth century, the message remains the same, although the presentation is more subtle. *Webster's Third International Dictionary* in 1971 still defined *homemaking* as "the creation and maintenance of a wholesome family environment."

The social, political, and economic movements toward redefining women's roles in the United States have altered some American thinking about homemakers, if only to recognize that the "homemaker" is now also likely to be a wage earner outside the home. Yet even a 1986 encyclopedia entry for *homemaking* still asserts that "today, the homemaker frequently carries dual responsibilities as housewife and wage earner." Men, it seems, are only homemakers if they are single. Marriage (or cohabitation) immediately transfers responsibilities to women, as if their appearance in a dwelling had some sort of magical effect. Perhaps we have not "come a long way, baby," after all.

Harvey Green is the Deputy Director for Interpretation at the Strong Museum in Rochester, New York, and author of *Light of the Home: An Intimate View of the Lives of Women in Victorian America* and *Fit for America: Health, Fitness, Sport, and American Society, 1830–1940*.

The Third World

By Janet Abu-Lughod

Different standards apply.

It is remarkable that over the long expanse of history homelessness has been such a rare and unusual condition—the unhappy albeit temporary fate of groups driven from their usual habitat, by war or natural disaster, or the permanent fate of a few persons who live outside society either because they have chosen it (hermits) or because they have been ostracized for some (unforgivable) crime. Shelter is as basic a need as food, and it has been provided in often ingenious ways by even the most primitive cultures. Throughout history, most people have constructed their shelters themselves, using the raw materials immediately at hand—leafy branches, logs, mud, animal skins, and even, improbably to us, snow.

Yet today we have a housing problem not only in the Third World but in the first as well. The United Nations declared 1987 the Year of the Homeless, focusing on the housing problems of the Third World, but American newspapers now regularly run stories on the plight of the homeless in big cities—not just old-style hobos and bums but also released mental patients and abandoned women and children. Third World cities have their own versions of this housing problem: whole families of street-sleepers in Indian metropolises; residents of makeshift dwellings in the shantytowns or "belts of misery" that encircle most big cities in Asia, Africa, and Latin America; orphaned or abandoned children who sleep in doorways, and conjure up images of Dickensian squalor.

It is obvious that housing problems are the complex result of several factors: changing definitions of what constitutes acceptable or inacceptable housing; new physical and social arrangements that interfere with traditional methods of producing shelter or that mandate a different kind of shelter; and a rapid dislocation of traditionally housed people who cannot bring their dwellings with them to their new environments. These changes in the definition of the adequate house, in the differential access to new types of resources for housing (namely land and cash) that may be unavailable to a large proportion of the urban population, and the temporary (?) misfit between where houses and people are, create shortages of shelter for a population that formerly provided its own, that is, was not homeless.

Rather than beginning with the question of how to solve the housing problem in Third World countries, then, we must begin with a prior question, namely, how much of that housing problem is real and how much of it is created? Only then can we evaluate the means that are at hand to tackle the former and, for that portion due to the latter, a way to redefine both the problems and the types of solutions.

We cannot deny that a large part of the housing problem is real in an important sense of the term. In the rural areas, from which a third to a half of the population now living in the rapidly growing capitals of the Third World may have come, people have a large housing stock that has accumulated over the years as part of their heritage. Some additions have been required by new marriages and some replacements have been needed for deteriorating structures or changing tastes and materials, but these additions were of negligible quantity in comparison with the standing stock. The massive movement of population out of these zones in the period since World War II has left a surplus of housing in the countryside, and inversely, a real shortage of housing stock has been found in the areas to which the population moved.

When new war plants were built in isolated areas of the United States during World War II, massive construction of housing or the moving of prefabricated units nearby was required. Similarly, some of the housing shortage in Third World countries has been generated by migration to the cities. But unlike the United States, whose wealth and motivation allowed it to solve its wartime housing emergency, Third World governments are too poor to make massive and immediate investments in housing for their newly urbanizing populations; besides, they have many pressing demands that compete for their limited resources. Thus, migrants have experienced enormous difficulties: they have neither received aid nor been assisted in providing for their own shelter. Indeed, well-meaning policies have often made matters worse for them.

Whereas migrants are not without skills or the will to make shelters for themselves, their needs in urban areas turn out to be quite different from those in the areas from which they come. The old methods of providing shelter are blocked in the cities by two factors. First, *urban land is not in family or communal ownership nor on the premises of work (the farm), but rather, is a commodity that belongs to others. Newcomers require resources* to obtain rights to build on city land. The lack of free land, then, is a primary cause of housing problems. In cities, land has monetary value determined in part by its accessibility to other urban functions. It should not be surprising that squatters settle on land not yet demanded for other purposes. That land is almost always on the outskirts. Although it is not unowned, owners are holding it for speculative purposes and are therefore willing to tolerate (and even collect fees from) temporary inhabitants, until the value of the land increases sufficiently.

On such sites, however, there are additional problems. First is the availability, or rather the lack of, traditional building materials. Instead of natural materials, housing has to be constructed with the detritus of industrial society—tin cans, packing crates, and the like. Second, development takes place at unprecedented densities; the close quarters make rural methods of sanitation intolerable. Whereas under conditions of low density, simple percolation can clear the ground of human wastes, it cannot do so in dense urban settings. Sewers and complex methods of waste removal are required. The same is true of water supplies. No rural person can raise crops in an area devoid of water, and the same source can be used for irrigation and for personal consumption. Yet many of the marginal urban areas on which squatters are forced to settle lack such resources—or lack enough of them for the large numbers of users who suddenly appear.

So the money needed to bid for land, the lack of normal building materials, and the more complex utilities needed when large numbers of persons share an environment all conspire to cause housing problems of a new sort.

Most important, government regulations, which had often played a negligible role in the countryside, now serve to define the problem of inadequate housing. Low shelter quality may have existed in the rural zones (and indeed still does) but it was, for the most part, invisible. When massed at the edge of the capital—often within view of visiting dignitaries riding into town from the airport—its existence is redefined as a crisis.

Teams of experts flock to this "new" issue, recommending that public resources be channeled into housing, often advocating unrealistic Western standards of adequacy. It mattered little to housing experts that the same resources, invested in rural and small town development through real economic growth, might provide more efficacious aid to the people with the housing problems. (One can think of parallels in American cities, where better care for the mentally disturbed and better supports for families might contribute more to the solution of

Slums of Calcutta, India. United Nations Photo 153,012/Oddbjorn Monsen.

the problem of homelessness than temporary night shelters.)

While in a few Third World countries, governments began first to try to provide public housing for the growing mass of newcomers, demand ran far ahead of any possible supply. Indeed, the shortage of housing was so great that middle-class bureaucrats often arranged to sublet the very units of low-income housing they had assigned to the poor who deserved the subsidized housing but then could not afford to live in it.

Because such approaches proved unviable, policy alternatives have been suggested. The most noteworthy are schemes to provide sites and services to

the poor to encourage them to build their own houses on land provided at low cost by the state. This approach solves one of the basic problems—attaining the right to land in urban areas—but it also generates others. The subsidy of sites and services is often used not to house additional urban dwellers but to relocate traditional urban residents away from their prime downtown locations, whenever those sites are coveted by the modern business sector. Just as in American cities undergoing urban renewal in the 1960s, when renewal all too often turned out to be "poor removal" as expensive central land was recycled for "higher uses," so sites-and-services schemes in many Third

World countries have been used to remove poor people from central areas of high-value land to low-value land a great distance from the city center.

Such removal has had very deleterious effects. It has torn the fragile fabric of proximity that many poor urbanites require to make a living. Few residents of Third World cities work in large-scale industry located on the outskirts of town. Most of the poor, at least, make their livings by offering small-scale services either to one another or to the wealthy who live nearby. Many work at small artisan trades where proximity to suppliers and to potential customers is a *sine qua non* of their viability. Location near the

center of the city is essential to their survival. The increased transportation costs created by their forced removal to the outskirts are often sufficient to reduce marginal workers to unemployed workers, thereby intensifying urban problems.

There is often, then, a perverse mismatch between the goals of government planners and modern real estate interests, on the one hand, and the needs of the poor, on the other. Attempts to solve the housing problem in Third World metropolises have thus often exacerbated the plight of the poor and of new migrants.

What these groups most need is real economic growth and a more equitable distribution of its fruits. To achieve this, Third World countries need massive development in both rural and urban areas. Rural development might not only slow down the explosive growth of large city populations, but it would more fully utilize the existing housing stock and the capacities of the population to continue to provide their own housing. In the cities, decent wages and the control of land speculation might do more to make possible a solution to the housing problem than any direct involvement of government in providing housing.

In all countries, resources are scarce and priorities need to be set for their allocation; in Third World countries the scarcity is even greater, and that means that faulty decisions may be fatal. Minimum expenditures are certainly needed to avert epidemics and health and safety hazards in the cities, but it would be foolhardy to take funds away from development to cover housing for a population that needs employment and income as much as, if not more than, it needs shelter. These, combined with the removal of false problems, such as speculatively induced land shortages and the setting of housing standards more suited to the first than the Third World, would go a long way toward ameliorating, if not solving, the housing problems of the Third World.

Janet Abu-Lughod is Professor of Sociology at Northwestern University, Evanston, Illinois, and at The New School for Social Research, in New York City.

Indigenous Architecture

View of a sixth–seventh century A.D. Buddhist settlement at Bāmīān, Afghanistan. United Nations, 1967.

Papago round grass lodge, Coyote Indian village, Pima County, Arizona. National Anthropological Archives, Smithsonian Institution (2779–M) William Dinwiddie, Bureau of American Ethnology, 1894.

146 View of a section of the city of Dezful, Iran. United Nations, 1972/Witlin.

Pima adobe house, Upper Fresnal, Indian village, Pima County, Arizona, 1894. National Anthropological Archives, Smithsonian Institution (2785–C) William Dinwiddie, Bureau of American Ethnology, 1894.

Hopi dwelling, Walpi, Arizona, 1879. National Anthropological Archives, Smithsonian Institution (1832–D) John K. Hillers, Bureau of American Ethnology, 1879.

A Bemileke village, West Africa. Picture Library. Cooper-Hewitt Museum.

Dwelling in Nigeria, 1960s. Picture Library, Cooper-Hewitt Museum.

Housing in Less Complex Societies

It reveals great ingenuity.

By Gary D. Shaffer

The notion of housing in nonindustrial societies can bring to mind the mud or grass huts of remote peoples in Africa and the South Pacific, the buffalo-hide tepees of the Plains Indians, and even the exotic snow houses of the Eskimo. We might expect such dwellings only barely to provide shelter from the elements and to be dark and smoky, infested with vermin, or of questionable stability.

While in some instances these descriptions may be true, anthropologists and others who have carefully studied the houses of less complex societies have been amazed by the evident architectural sophistication. These researchers have observed craftsmen with great technical and artistic skills, ingenuity, and stamina doing heavy construction work with limited tools. Furthermore, their studies enable us to see how houses reflect a culture's kinship and social organization, religious beliefs, and general world view.

Nonindustrial societies today are found in much of the Third World as well as in remote sections of more technologically advanced countries; additionally, they include most aboriginal groups encountered by explorers and colonists in the past five hundred years.

We also know through archaeology that the industrial societies of today had a rich and extensive nonindustrial *pre*-history. In fact, for over 90 percent of the time that humans have inhabited the earth they have lived in nonindustrial societies.

Caves and rock shelters are the best-known forms of prehistoric housing, but many different kinds were actually used. One of the clearest examples of very early housing was recorded in southeastern France at the Paleolithic site of Terra Amata. There, in the vicinity of Nice, archaeologist Henry de Lumley unearthed traces of more than twenty huts dating back some three hundred thousand years. The structures were oval in

Building an igloo. National Anthropological Archives, National Museum of Natural History, Smithsonian Institution.

shape and up to forty-nine feet long, with walls of wood stakes braced by rings of stone. Much more recent Paleolithic housing is known from several sites on the central Russian plain. At the settlement of Mezhirich, researchers Mikhail Gladkih, Ninelj Kornietz, and Olga Soffer found five fifteen-thousand-year-old dwellings whose foundations were constructed of mammoth bones. Given the age of these buildings, it is interesting to note their architectural variability: Walls were assembled with different types of bones and various arrangements or designs of the skeletal elements.

A very common form in which archaeologists discover traces of prehistoric houses is in outlines of postmolds. Postmolds are discolorations in the soil caused by decayed wood and debris that fill holes once occupied by posts from timber frames. While such evidence might seem very minimal, careful analy-

sis of the diameters, depths, inclinations, and patterns of postmolds can tell us a great deal about construction practices and, indeed, the builders themselves.

To take one example from the Neolithic Age in Europe, archaeologist Sarunas Milisauskas has intensively examined several buildings at the Polish site of Olszanica, dated to the late fifth millennium B.C. These structures, originally with timber frames and walls daubed with mud, were found as postmolds arranged in long rectangular or trapezoidal plans. Milisauskas's study of these buildings demonstrated statistically valid differences in the architecture. One building, which had wider and deeper postmolds, a greater length, and an association with particular stone tools, was also apparently functionally different—perhaps a structure for collective or ritual activities.

Archaeologists who study these and

other prehistoric structures can learn about building technology, the procurement of construction resources, population size, social organization, and settlement patterns. Because excavated evidence can be very limited, however, they often strengthen their interpretations of prehistoric housing through experimentation and the study of dwellings in nonindustrial societies of our contemporary world or the recent ethnographic past.

In this regard, Alistair Marshall's comparative study of contemporary longhouses in Papua, New Guinea, and the Neolithic buildings of central and western Europe is of great interest. The longhouses of Enga Province in the Highlands of New Guinea are made of double rows of wall-stakes, with grass used to pack wall partitions and to thatch roofs. Of importance here are the tapering of these buildings from back to front and their roof beams, which slope down the longitudinal axis to the narrower end. Since the houses are generally aligned toward prevailing winds, these features both minimize the stress of natural elements on the fabric and increase heat retention.

In temperate and subalpine Europe, an environment quite similar to that of Enga Province, archaeologists find Neolithic longhouses in the form of trapezoidal ground plans very reminiscent of the tapering ones in New Guinea. Marshall believes the shape of the Neolithic structures was similar—their roofs also having been pitched down their axes toward the narrower ends. Because these prehistoric European longhouses tend to be oriented in common directions (probably toward prevailing winds), one can argue that they and the Enga examples represent an ingenious parallel adaptation to climate.

Different nonindustrial societies often construct similar dwellings in like climates, but this is not always the case. A survey of architecture around the world reveals that the environment does not determine which building types are made. Instead, builders in given natural areas are offered certain possibilities of construction materials and techniques; and they choose to use and combine them—with the influence of socio-cultural factors—in a host of different ways.

Amos Rapoport's comparison of Native American housing in the southwestern United States illustrates just this point. The Pueblo Indians live in villages (also called pueblos) composed of thick mud- or stone-walled buildings with flat roofs. Dwellings are tightly clustered into groups having several stories. Furthermore, rooms can readily be added on to existing structures, but a plaza is generally kept as an open central area. The compactness of pueblos tends to maximize volume while minimizing surface area. This phenomenon, together with the shading created by adjacent rooms and the heavy mass of construction material, provides excellent, year-round climatic controls in the dwellings.

In contrast to the Pueblos, the Navajo Indians—relatively late immigrants to the Southwest—make a very different form of housing. Their dwellings, or hogans, are of several types, including the forked-stick hogan and the earth-covered variety. The first kind is quite conical in shape, with five logs reaching up from a circular

ground plan to a central point; this timber frame is then covered with sticks, branches, and a plaster of mud. On the other hand, an earth-covered hogan consists of a square frame of four heavy upright posts supporting timber cribbing for a roof. Builders finish these structures by covering the frames with sticks, mud, and dry earth to form a rough dome. Several hogans may occur in groups, but the dwellings are essentially for individual families. Despite these differences between Navajo and Pueblo housing, they both provide more than adequate shelter. Like the pueblos, the hogans are easy to keep cool in summer and warm in winter.

Here we see how different societies may invent different solutions to housing in similar environments. To help explain this situation, Rapoport has detected a number of characteristics of Pueblo and Navajo religion, social organization, and world view reflected in the respective dwelling types. For example, the clustered rooms and additive nature of pueblos well match the family structure of their occupants: the centers of social and economic life are matrilineal clans, composed of extended households of a woman, her husband, their unmarried children, married daughters, and their families. In contrast, the basic social and economic units of the Navajo are the individual biological families; and the separate hogans can readily meet their needs. Social organization and other cultural factors then affect the choices that nonindustrial societies make when deciding upon particular building forms.

As in the study of Pueblo and Navajo housing, social anthropologist Meyer Fortes has noted the close correspondence between homesteads of the African Tallensi people and their family structure. In their homeland of western Africa's Volta River drainage, males and females of the Tallensi utilize separate huts, while other areas in a settlement may have sexually divided or common uses depending on the situation. Perhaps what is most striking about this culture's architecture is the influence of religion on the form of roofs. The Tallensi build circular mud huts decorated with linear and geometric designs. The more common covering of these

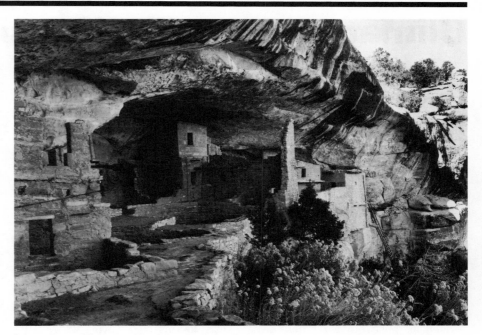

Balcony House cliff dwelling, Mesa Verde National Park, Colorado, built 1200–1276. Courtesy United States Department of the Interior, National Park Service.

buildings is a conical thatched roof. Rarer and more difficult to make are flat roofs of beaten, puddled mud set on strong rafters. Almost all homesteads have at lease one flat-roofed hut whose upper surface is a place for resting, drying plants, and keeping an ancestral shrine. However, some homesteads have flat roofs on all rooms, despite the extra costs of labor and time. In these cases there is a taboo of the Earth: Due to religious proscriptions, almost all men of a certain status have exclusively flat-roofed huts; and those people in recognized zones of principal Earth shrines build only flat-roofed houses.

This brief examination of housing in nonindustrial societies has shown such dwellings to be affected by a number of forces, including religious beliefs, social organization, and the natural environment. Paramount, however, is the fact that different cultures weigh these influences in variable fashions and select building materials and forms from an available range to make particular styles. Those nonindustrialized peoples of the

present and past have demonstrated remarkable inventiveness in providing themselves with shelter, going beyond mere physical needs to invest structures with aesthetic and symbolic value.

In industrialized lands today, one more often encounters mass-produced housing that is sold on an extensive scale. Additionally, with accelerated migration, the more complex societies often blend together architectural styles once characteristic of specific cultural groups and their beliefs. People in industrialized countries frequently have few choices to make with respect to housing construction except building location, size, and decorative details. It is to be hoped that the personal and cultural variability of housing seen in nonindustrial societies will be appreciated and continued in the future.

Gary D. Shaffer, an archaeologist with Christopher Goodwin and Associates of Frederick, Maryland, specializes in the study of prehistoric domestic architecture.

An earth lodge, or hogan, on the Navaho Reservation, Arizona-New Mexico, ca. 1890s. Smithsonian Institution, photo No. 2444.

149

Climate-responsive Housing

By Thomas Fisher

We tend to think of solar housing as a relatively new phenomenon—a direct outcome of the energy crisis of the 1970s. Yet, though the term *solar housing* may be new, the concepts behind it are as old as architecture itself.

The confusion is largely semantic. The word *solar* suggests that a direct connection exists between a house and the sun. In fact, the term is used to describe any house that responds to its climate and respects its physical environment. That includes houses that use the sun for heating. But it also includes houses constructed of indigenous materials, cooled by prevailing winds, or located to do as little damage as possible to their sites.

Seen in those broader terms, solar housing encompasses most housing built prior to the Industrial Revolution. In those previous eras the lack of a centralized building-product industry and of mechanical heating-and-cooling technology left architects and builders little choice but to adapt housing to its immediate environment.

A variety of housing types consequently evolved in various climates. In desert locations housing took two radically different forms: the nomadic tent and the courtyard house. The tent suited its climate not only by providing shade from and a reflective surface to the sun, but also by being able to be closed off from windblown sand, opened up to a passing breeze, or moved if climatic conditions became too difficult.

The courtyard house, with its heavy masonry walls and few exterior windows, was the physical opposite of the tent, but it offered many of the same benefits. Its tightly clustered forms provided shade; its brick or adobe walls, insulation against daytime heat; its light colors, reflection of the sun's radiant energy; and its closed exterior, protection from the wind. The traditional courtyard house also was highly flexible. The use of mobile

furniture allowed inhabitants to move their activities from one space to another depending upon the time of day or the season: living in basement rooms in summer months, for example, or on upper floors and on the rooftops in the winter or at night.

In hot, humid climates a more uniform housing stock evolved. To encourage the maximum amount of cross ventilation, houses typically had open interiors, large numbers of door and window openings, elevated locations, and distant or staggered spacing. Shade from the tropical sun and protection from tropical storms was provided by broad, overhanging roofs. Just as the abundance of raw materials for masonry dovetailed with the need for insulation in the deserts, the abundance of wood proved well-suited to the long spans and large openings required to enhance ventilation in the tropics.

In temperate climates the materials used for housing—typically wood, masonry, or stone—varied from place to place depending upon which was most abundant. The form of housing also varied considerably by location. In warmer regions, broad roofs, open interiors, and ample windows predominated, although rarely to the extent of housing in the tropics. In colder regions, a housing form evolved that had thicker walls for wintertime insulation, lower eaves on the windward sides to reduce air infiltration, large chimney masses to retain heat throughout the night, and relatively few and smaller windows to balance the needs of summer cooling and winter heating.

Such vernacular housing remained essentially unchanged in the United States until the middle of the nineteenth century. Some historians have attributed the decline of such housing to the widespread adoption of central heating and gas lighting near the end of the nineteenth century and of electric lighting and air condi-

tioning in the twentieth century. Those technologies, though, were more the symptoms than the cause, which was a shift in people's perceptions of place and personal comfort.

Among the nineteenth-century forces that most affected people's ties to their localities were the development of a national communications system and the improvement of transportation systems. One greatly expanded people's information about distant places, the other, people's ability to travel there.

Expectations of comfort also changed in the nineteenth century. The growing affluence brought on by the Industrial Revolution certainly had an effect. So, too, did the growth of the service economy in the latter part of the century. Housing conditions became more important— indeed, the subject of legislation—as people themselves became more important to the economy.

Whatever the cause for the decline of environmentally responsive housing, the result was clear. By the middle of the twentieth century, many of the connections between a house and its immediate environment had disappeared. Housing had become a matter of personal preferences rather than a product of local traditions or of local resources. New England Cape Cod cottages went up in Texas as frequently as ranch houses in Massachusetts—many of them built with lumber from the Pacific Northwest and heated or cooled with electricity generated by coal from Appalachia.

That pattern of housing, however widespread, did not go unchallenged. Initially, criticism in the 1950s focused not on the resources and energy required to make such housing possible, but on the loss of regional identity. This regionalist argument recognized an irony in our ability to construct almost any type of housing anywhere. Rather than leading to greater diversity, it made every place look alike. A

regional architectural movement therefore emerged in the 1950s, particularly in areas that once had a distinct local flavor, such as southern Texas and northern California, producing houses that used vernacular forms and indigenous building materials. But the movement remained small and had little influence in more urban and industrialized settings.

The next wave of criticism came in the 1970s with the energy crisis. The object of that criticism shifted from the loss of regional identity to our growing dependence upon finite fossil fuels and upon energy-exporting countries. That shift came at a time when architecture itself was going through an identity crisis as modern and postmodern architects debated questions of style. Energy-conscious design, for some architects, offered an alternative to both camps, based as it was upon functional rather than stylistic grounds.

The first energy-conscious housing in the mid-1970s focused largely on heat collection. Solar collectors mounted on roofs and large expanses of south-facing glass became almost a cliché—an emblem of allegiance to the energy-conservation cause. But collecting heat did little good without some method of storing it, so a variety of thermal-storage techniques was developed. Those techniques included the placement of concrete or masonry surfaces in south-facing rooms and the use of rock beds under the house through which room air was blown. Because of their mass, those materials absorbed heat and radiated it slowly back into the house at night. A variant of those techniques was the Trombe wall, which consisted of a concrete or masonry wall located behind south-facing glass with a space between for the circulation of room air.

Moving air over a sun-warmed mass, though, did little to save energy unless the heated air was circulated throughout

Sea Ranch Condominium, Sea Ranch, California; Charles Moore, architect, 1963–65. Courtesy Charles W. Moore.

ment. Some developments included heat pumps that used ground water for heating or ice ponds for cooling indoor air, photovoltaic chips that used the sun's excitation of silicone electrons to generate electricity, and window glass that changed transparency when exposed to direct sunlight.

Energy conservation began to fade as an important public issue in the 1980s, when oil prices and energy-related federal funding both subsided. Certain energy-conservation strategies, such as the weatherstripping of openings, the addition of insulation, or the installation of more efficient heating systems, have become common practice. But most housing built in 1987 is little more climate-responsive than it was twenty years before.

The decline in interest and support for energy conservation has led to a reevaluation of the whole question of climate response. Traditional housing responded to its climate, not for any one reason such as saving energy or creating a sense of place, but for a host of reasons that might best be described as ecological. The construction and operation of such housing, for example, involved the ecological notion that natural resources were not free to exploit but a precious commodity to be used sparingly and replenished if possible. The same applied to the housing's form and decoration, which was the product not of an individual making an original personal design statement, but that of a society following precedents that evolved in harmony with nature over a long period of time.

Climate-responsive housing, in other words, has become a part of a larger debate over modern consumer culture. By showing us how people once lived, it raises questions about how we now live: wasteful of natural resources, neglectful of regional cultures, and often oblivious to the ecosystems of which we are a part. Solar housing is not just a form of shelter. It embodies a vision of society, and that is what makes such housing important.

the house. That, then, led to the development of more open interiors, which allowed freer movement of air into other spaces. Such interiors also became an important feature of houses in more humid climates, where the judicious placement of windows and walls could induce cross ventilation and reduce the use of energy-intensive air-conditioning.

Throughout this period, engineers also were making improvements in the energy efficiency of products and equip-

Thomas Fisher is Executive Editor at *Progressive Architecture* magazine.

Second Homes

By Steven Holt

There is something strange about second houses. If the second house is what its name implies—a subordinate residence—why do so many of us think of it *first*? It could be many things. It could be desperation. It could be that the grass is always greener on the other side. It could even be that there is something going on there that we should know more about. Whatever it is, second houses are always on our minds, and we are always plotting our next escape to them.

Certainly second houses—or better put, second "homes" to imply the warmth of life within—occupy a special place amid the contemporary American cultural landscape. Important things happen there. Outside the house, we stretch, swim, stargaze, and so forth. And within the walls, countless movies, novels, paintings, designs, business deals and an infinite number of other more or less creative acts have been dreamed of, produced, or done away with.

Over the seasons and years, they are places that we come back to again and again. While we use watches and clocks to tell hourly or daily time, we unconsciously use second homes as a way to demarcate time during the year. "It has been three weeks since I was at the beach house" or "Just think—in two months, I'll be skiing in New Hampshire." We have all heard friends say things like this, and in many instances we have uttered words to these effects ourselves.

But wait. What exactly is a "second home?" Neither the Department of Housing and Urban Development (HUD) nor the Federal Housing Administration (FHA) offers definitions or statistics. The Census Bureau, however, does. In 1970, they queried approximately 61 million households and found that 2,890,000 (or 4.8 percent) of the respondees had "year-round homes held for occasional use, either seasonal or migratory." In 1977, approximately 75 million households were queried, and 3,067,000 respondees (or 4.1 percent) said yes again. The problem is that the Census Bureau considers second homes to be everything from migrant farm worker housing to Napa Valley estates; the wide latitude is confusing rather than clarifying.

Regardless of what second homes are being looked at, it is clear that the answer to questions on second homes depends upon who is doing the surveying and whose interests are being served. Individual counties use differing definitions, for example. Government surveys, if anything, are more concerned with determining basic housing needs than in tracking vacation residences. The second home has as many definitions as design and economics allow, but ownership of a second home usually falls into one of five types: time-sharing; fractional ownership; individual interest; membership in a resort community; and whole ownership.

Our interests force us to focus on whole ownership, because it is in this circumstance that the ideas and issues of home and house are most fully developed. In fact, it is far easier for most of us to describe our mental image—or list the psychological characteristics—of second homes than it is the physical ones. For example, most of us see a house in the country or on the water when we hear the words "second home."

But according to Dr. Steve Miner—research director for Richard L. Ragatz Associates, a Eugene, Oregon, marketing research firm specializing in vacation and resort housing—these are changing times. Miner, who completed his dissertation on the subject of vacation and resort housing believes these houses represent the *undynamic* part of the industry. By this he means that there is little growth (only the changing of owners) in these properties when compared to areas such as time-sharing, camp resort developments and the ownership of a co-op, condo or pied-à-terre in the city.

Whatever their context, second homes are a refuge. They are not always in the country, but they are almost always a sanctuary of sorts. A place where we "get away from it all," "go to unwind," put the world on hold," and "take it easy." Rest and relaxation, however, are only part of their magic. They are also the places we go to do the thing that we have wanted to do for some time. Second homes are hot-beds of mythology and ritual, places where our environmental control is questioned in an interesting way, and where we can focus on our work, hobby or passion without distraction, or at least with a new, fresher set of distractions.

Whether we visit yearly or weekly, second homes imply a physical as well as a mental geography. A second home is a place where a site of scenic beauty reconnoiters with our cerebral landscape. State of nature meets our state of mind. A second home can subsequently take on almost any architectural form as long as it provides the opportunity for us to "distance" ourselves from our normal routinized domicile: a summer place, a vacation cabin, a camp in the woods, or a time-share condo on the beach, or just about any house or house-like structure that is not where we normally live our lives.

No matter the location, having a second home almost always implies privilege. Due to a general rise in wealth across the country, second homes are now a solid middle- and upper-middle-class phenomenon, and have been since the 1960s when the very term "second home" found common usage. Having third, fourth and fifth homes constitutes further privilege and accomplishment, but, like anything else, there is a law of diminishing returns in effect. Who, in the late 1980s, has time to attend to business *and* enjoy a half-dozen or so homes?

Can it even be a "home" if one visits it for only a week a year? Probably not.

Homes need regular residents, although houses do not. The issue of "multiple second homes" versus a single second home is also a point of profound socioeconomic separation. The New Jersey plumber may have a beach house, but is not likely to have beach *houses*; a de Menil or a Getty just might.

This is not to say that second homes are now owned by just anybody. Purchase of such a place still constitutes a kind of societal "arrival." For this reason, second homes are best understood not solely in formal architectural terms but in a myriad of personal, familial, and cultural ways. Partly, this is because second homes are often only occupied during our vacations or on weekends. Partly, this is because a different side of ourselves surfaces during these times. Partly, this is also because there is a material difference between our primary home and our second home—stone and either painted or stained wood dominate. Artificial materials take a back seat.

Comfort is the Key

Whether one's second home is water-bound or landlocked, its fundamental concern is with comfort. These are not expensive, city-slicker comforts, either. You'll find very few satin sheets or bottles of champagne at second homes. Second homes are much more about all-cotton sheets and beer, wine, and rum.

Second houses are about getting back to basics, using all of our senses for example. We smell woods, flowers, and earth; we hear peepers and crickets; we savor familiar foods with awakened taste buds; and we feel the sweet sting of nature against our skins from sunburns, breezes, and bites of all types. Everything seems very alive, even the house itself, which in the best of all possible scenarios will occasionally creak, groan, and make its presence known. With such sensual reward, is it any wonder that so many romances begin at second homes or on vacations?

Sports and games—including the amorous ones—have always been a significant part of the well-functioning second home. Recall, for example, the summer house at Garsington six or so miles from Oxford that Lady Ottoline Morrell oversaw. The house was the site of considerable romantic (not to mention literary) shenanigans among the Bloomsbury set, including Aldous Huxley, D.H. and Frieda Lawrence, Virginia Woolf, Katherine Mansfield, and many of the other bright lights of pre- and post-World War I England. At such a second home as Morrell's, it matters far less if we break a glass, spill the milk on the chair, or burn the bread than that we have fun.

In the end, the most direct route to fun is through being at ease. Being comfortable. Comfort is the rule, the style that unites all second homes. Comfort, to use scientist Gregory Bateson's clever phrase, is part of "the pattern that connects" the second home through past, present, and future. Philosophically, it is the one quality that relates the nineteenth-century Adirondack camp to a late twentieth-century summer house designed by Gwathmey Siegel in East Hampton, New York, and makes these in turn allied to a house by Andres Duaney and Elizabeth Plater-Zyberk in Seaside, Florida.

Comfort is present not only on the level of the environment but on the level of individual objects as well. Furniture, chairs, hammocks, throw rugs, and a hundred other objects differ either by degree (and even logical type) from their first-home brethren. Again, simple, yet rich solutions are emphasized, and the variations on the theme of comfort are infinite. Things no one would dream of doing in the main house one does easily at the second home: patterns go on other patterns, colors collide recklessly, and things we have been taught by critics or designers as being woefully wrong now seem wonderfully right. In this environment, we become literally and figuratively more recreation-oriented. No matter what our age, we play.

This is important, because with even greater frequency, we appear to be turning to our second homes for health reasons. They have become places to live a saner life, places where we can mentally regroup and physically get back in shape.

"Cabin Class." Picture Library, Cooper-Hewitt Museum.

Our current interest in second homes is in many ways tied to our interest in having healthy bodies and minds, which began in the seventies.

Our definition of health, like our definition of comfort, changes regularly, but a concern with both has regularly shown itself in our second homes. We still know surprisingly little about either, and we take them both for granted, except when they are lacking. Because of this, issues of health and comfort are fertile areas for design research, although little has been done so far. The pressing problems of domestic health and comfort simply have not been dealt with. Artists have not built *oeuvres* around these issues, scientists have rarely studied them, and as Witold Rybczynski points out in *Home*, comfort is a subject not even touched upon in architecture schools today, which more than partly explains why it is lacking in so many new buildings.

The Evocative Environment

The design critic Ralph Caplan once said that the chair is "the first thing that we need when we don't need anything at all," and on an environmental level, the same might be said of the second home. We obviously don't require a beach house in Nantucket or Malibu to ensure the propagation of our species. Rather, we have it because we want to do more than merely get by. It has to do with the quality of our lives and that is what makes the second home such a potentially (and peculiarly) compelling symbol of ourselves and of our civilization.

Because we do not, strictly speaking, require it for physical reasons of survival, the second home can offer a rich range of aesthetic, historical, and psychological associations. Such an array of associations has the potential to create especially evocative environments. By design, by accident, or by growth over time, the second home becomes a place where emotion and environment merge together.

In reality, this challenge has been met with mixed success. Far too often second homes have simply repeated the successes and failures of first homes, frustrating host, guest, and architect alike. As a profession, architects have looked knowingly at the form and function of second homes, but have often neglected the *meaning* or the *symbology*. Why adopt the imagery and methodology of the standard suburban tract house for a second home in the mountains or on the coast?

Obviously, because it is more difficult to develop a new language than it is to merely reconfigure an existing one. Significantly, the inverse of this question explains why many second homes are successful: their surroundings are potently reflected or brought into play in the design of the new building. Further, the most successful second homes generally create a new relationship between indoors and outdoors. The two blur together. Planting stimulates architecture; building inspires landscape design. Ultimately, our attitude toward nature is perceptibly altered.

Look at the two great Kaufmann houses, one by Richard Neutra in the Palm Springs desert and the other by Frank Lloyd Wright in the Pennsylvania hills. Our reactions palpably shift in these places. Both houses reconfigure the normal relationship of inside and outside. Both houses manipulate light, space, and volume in the aesthetic service of people. We delight in these transformations, feeling that they are not merely architectonic gamesmanship.

In point of fact, second homes tell us a great deal about our attitudes toward the world. Even the most cursory of glances at today's beach houses will show how desperately we desire contact with nature. Decks, porches, benches, and especially angled windows are all set up to maximize contact with sun, air, and water. Sunrises and sunsets are watched for and discussed, and the weather comes to have daily, even hourly significance.

At second homes, we allow ourselves to be more open to the stuff of life. The material differences of second homes assume significance. Native materials and local craftsmanship are often integral to their structure as well as to their decoration, and bespeak a rich and vital regional aesthetic, one that lends itself to appreciation over time rather than all at once.

This change is particularly dramatic for vertically-oriented city dwellers familiar for most of the year with brick, concrete, and plaster. Wood was the single greatest resource that settlers found when they came here in the sixteenth and seventeenth centuries, and wood has been at the center of the American architecture and design experience ever since. Whether stained, left alone, or painted, wood appears as the dominant element in almost all second homes, inside and out.

Style and typology

No one style typifies the second home, although they tend to fall into one of three categories: the contemporary (the most visible, because they often are about making a statement), the vernacular (the most common, because they are the most affordable), or the colonial (the most sought after, because they signify Old Money). An example of each might be Frank Gehry's houses in Venice Beach, California; the summer camps of the Adirondack Mountains; and the eighteenth- and nineteenth-century farmhouses in the tri-state area that *New York* magazine tells us are the current target of city dwellers in search of a country retreat.

Even these three simple categories have obvious overlaps and omissions, but what is crucial to remember is that the second home must provide sanctuary. Whether working or relaxing, it must be a place where health and pleasure rule. If the primary residence can be construed as a machine (as in Le Corbusier's dictum "machine for living"), the second home may best be viewed as a garden (as in "Garden of Eden").

Paradisical, and occasionally parodoxical in their mixture of disparate stylistic and functional elements, second homes are places, comparatively speaking, of unspoiled beauty and of untrammeled nature. As an adult, one goes to a second house to regroup, to gather one's thoughts and place things back into perspective. Look at recent movies that feature summer places—*The Big Chill*, *Return of the Secaucus 7* or *The Decline and Fall of the American Empire*—and you will see that all are about adults reconnoitering with their sense of self, their sense of others, and their sense of place.

As we reflect on our second homes, we recognize that, if well-conceived and

House in the shape of a ship, North Haven, Maine. From *Summer Places* by Brendan Gill and Dudley Whitney (New York: Methuen, Inc., 1978); photograph by Dudley Witney.

built, they become close friends, epicenters of affection. We give ourselves over to them. Maybe this is because by the time we have the time and money to build a second home, we have a better idea about what we are doing. Like second marriages and second chances, second homes are often more successful.

As owners and as designers, we need to recall the design characteristics that make second homes the wonderful places they are, and we need to see if these qualities can be used in other buildings; our offices, for example, or even our first homes. Second homes favor eclectic spaces and personal inspiration in their design. They favor spontaneity, and they accept the "mistake" with open arms.

Nooks, crannies, hiding places, fireplaces, perches, porches, portals, decks, and all manner of architectural embellishment that stoke a sense of curiosity, wonder, and place are celebrated. Eccentricities that a normal house must disavow a second house can revel in. Whether they be the vernacular cottages of the Virginia coast or the Vanderbilt "cottages" of Newport, Rhode Island, second homes share a similar architectural language yet speak in remarkably diverse dialects.

Second homes imply discovery as well as recovery, qualities that are so worthwhile that many of us should consider (or already have considered) moving into our second homes for the majority of the year. In the end, it may be that the reason we think of second homes first is that they have an effect on our soul not unlike that of a pebble thrown into a still pond—and we live through the year on the strength of those second home ripples.

Steven Holt, formerly the editor of *Industrial Design* magazine, is Design Director of Zebra Inc., a furniture and product design consultancy. He is also Director of the product design program at Parsons School of Design.

Houses in Literature

To be happy at home is the ultimate result of all ambition, the end to which every enterprise and labor tends, and of which every desire prompts the prosecution.
Samuel Johnson (1709–1784)
The Rambler, No. 68, 10 November 1750

The somber comfort, all the peace which springs
From the large aggregate of little things,
On these small cares of daughter, wife, or friend,
The almost sacred joys of home depend.
Hannah More (1745–1833)
Sensibility

'Mid pleasures and palaces though we may roam,
Be it ever so humble, there's no place like home.
J. H. Payne (1791–1852)
Home, Sweet Home

As the homes, so the state.
A. Bronson Alcott (1799–1888)
Tablets

The best security for civilization is the dwelling, and upon proper and becoming dwellings depends more than anything else the improvement of mankind.
Benjamin Disraeli (1804–1881)
Speech in London, 18 July 1874

O fortunate, O happy day,
When a new household finds its place
Among the myriad homes of earth,
Like a new star just sprung to birth.
Henry Wadsworth Longfellow (1807–1882)
The Hanging of the Crane

Peace and rest at length have come,
All the day's long toil is past;
And each heart is whispering, "Home, Home at last!"
Thomas Hood (1799–1845)
Home At Last

He dwells nowhere that dwells everywhere.
Martial (A.D. c. 40–A.D. c. 104)
Epigrams, VII

When I was at home, I was in a better place.
William Shakespeare (1564–1616)
As You Like It

Home is the place where, when you have to go there,
They have to take you in.
Robert Frost (1874–1963)
The Death of the Hired Man

No genuine observer can decide otherwise than that the homes of a nation are the bulwarks of personal and national safety.
J. G. Holland (1819–1881)
Gold-Foil Home

No place is more delightful than one's own fireside.
Cicero (106–43 B.C.)
Epistolae ad Familiares

Home is where the heart is.
Attributed to Pliny (b. A.D. 61)
Claimed by Elbert Hubbard (1859–1915)
Thousand and One Epigrams

But what on earth is half so dear—
So longed for—as the hearth of home?
Emily Bronte (1818–1848)
A Little While

His home, the spot of earth supremely blest,
A dearer, sweeter spot than all the rest.
James Montgomery (1771–1854)
West Indies

Round the hearth-stone of home, in the land of our birth,
The holiest spot on the face of the earth.
George Pope Morris (1802–1864)
Land Ho!

A comfortable house is a great source of happiness. It ranks immediately after health and a good conscience.
Sydney Smith (1771–1845)
Letter to Lord Murray, 29 September 1843

I read within a poet's book
A word that starred the page,
"Stone walls do not a prison make,
Nor iron bars a cage."

Yes, that is true, and something more:
You'll find, where'er you roam,
That marble floors and gilded walls
Can never make a home.

But every house where Love abides
And Friendship is a guest,
Is surely home, and home, sweet home,
For there the heart can rest.
Henry van Dyke (1852–1933)
Home Song

Joy dwells beneath a humble roof,
Heaven is not built of country seats
But little queer suburban streets.
Christopher Morley (1890–1957)
To the Little House

If solid happiness we prize,
Within our breast this jewel lies,
And they are fools who roam.
The world has nothing to bestow;
From our own selves our joys must flow,
And that dear hut, our home.
Nathaniel Cotton (1705–1788)
The Fireside

Be not long away from home.
Homer (c. 800 B.C.)
Odyssey

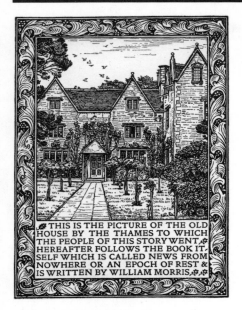

THIS IS THE PICTURE OF THE OLD HOUSE BY THE THAMES TO WHICH THE PEOPLE OF THIS STORY WENT. HEREAFTER FOLLOWS THE BOOK IT.SELF WHICH IS CALLED NEWS FROM NOWHERE OR AN EPOCH OF REST & IS WRITTEN BY WILLIAM MORRIS.

C.M. Gere, "Kelmscott Manor," from William Morris, *News from Nowhere*, 1891. Picture Library, Cooper-Hewitt Museum.

And every one that heareth these words of mine, and doeth them not, shall be likened unto a foolish man, who built his house upon the sand: and the rain descended, and the floods came, and the winds blew, and smote upon that house; and it fell: and great was the fall thereof.

Matthew 7:26,27
The New Testament

A man's dignity may be enhanced by the house he lives in, but not wholly secured by it; the owner should bring honor to the house, not the house to its owner.

Cicero (106–43 B.C)
De Officiis, Bk. i, ch. 39, sec. 139

The house of every one is to him his castle and fortress, as well for his defence against injury and violence, as for his repose.

Sir Edward Coke (1552–1634)
Semayne's Case, 1605. (3 Rep. 186.)

I find by all you have been telling,
That 'tis a house, but not a dwelling.
Alexander Pope (1688–1744)
On the Duke of Marlborough's House

There can be no freedom or beauty about a home life that depends on borrowing and debt.

Henrik Ibsen (1828–1906)
A Doll's House

We said there wasn't no home like a raft, after all. Other places do seem so cramped up and smothering, but a raft don't. You feel mighty free and easy and comfortable on a raft.

Mark Twain (Samuel Clemens) (1835–1910)
Adventures of Huckleberry Finn

Houses are built to live in and not to look on; therefore let use be preferred before uniformity, except where both may be had.

Francis Bacon (1561–1626)
Essays, No. 45, "Of Buildings"

Thou shalt not covet thy neighbor's house. . . .

Exodus 20:17
The Old Testament

By and large, mothers and housewives are the only workers who do not have regular time off. They are the great vacationless class.

Anne Morrow Lindbergh (1906—)
Gift from the Sea, 1955

A house is a machine for living
Le Corbusier (1887–1965)
Vers une architecture, 1923

But all that I could think of, in the darkness and the cold
Was that I was leaving home and my folks were growing old.
Robert Louis Stevenson (1850–1894)
Christmas at Sea

Soldiers are dreamers; when the guns begin
They think of firelit homes, clean beds, and wives.
Siegfried Sassoon (1886–1967)
Dreamers, 1918

What's the good of a home if you are never in it?
George Grossmith (1847–1912)
The Diary of a Nobody, 1894

Walter van Diedenhoven, "Huis en Tuin," reproduced from Wendingen, May 1919. Cooper-Hewitt Museum Library.

May the gods grant you all things which your heart desires, and may they give you a husband and a home and gracious concord, for there is nothing greater and better than this—when a husband and wife keep a household in oneness of mind, a great woe to their enemies and joy to their friends, and win high renown.

Homer (c. 800 B.C.)
The Odyssey, c. 750 B.C.

I do hate to be unquiet at home.
Samuel Pepys (1633–1703)
Diary, 22 January 1669

The great advantage of a hotel is that it's a refuge from home life.
George Bernard Shaw (1856–1950)
You Never Can Tell, 1898

Eden is that old-fashioned House
We dwell in every day
Without suspecting our abode
Until we drive away.
Emily Dickinson (1830–1886)
"No. 1657"

Home is the girl's prison and the woman's workhouse.
George Bernard Shaw (1856–1950)
Woman in the Home

In love of home, the love of country has its rise.
Charles Dickens (1812–1870)
The Old Curiosity Shop

'Tis ever common
That men are merriest when they are from home.
William Shakespeare (1564–1616)
Henry V

Who has not felt how sadly sweet
The dream of home, the dream of home,
Steals o'er the heart, too soon to fleet,
When far o'er sea or land we roam?

Thomas Moore (1779–1852)
The Dream of Home

It takes a hundred men to make an encampment, but one woman can make a home.

R. G. Ingersoll (1833–1899)
Woman

Margaret: She must be lost,
Nicholas: Who isn't? The best
Thing we can do is to make wherever
we're lost in
Look as much like home as we can.

Christopher Fry (1907—)
The Lady's Not for Burning, 1948

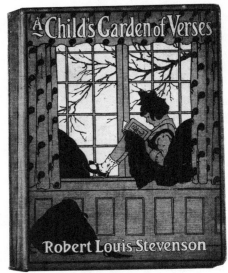

A Child's Garden of Verses, by Robert Louis
Stevenson, illustrated by Florence Edith Storer
(New York: Charles Scribner's Sons, 1909, 1916).

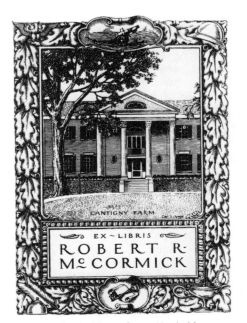

Bookplate. Picture Library, Cooper-Hewitt Museum.

Poverty keeps together more homes than it breaks up.

Saki (H. H. Munro) (1870–1916)
The Chronicles of Clovis, 1911

Old houses mended,
Cost little less than new before they're ended.

Colley Cibber (1671–1757)
The Double Gallant, 1707

Have nothing in your houses that you do not know to be useful, or believe to be beautiful.

William Morris (1834–1896)
The Beauty of Life

. . . A man may build and decorate a beautiful house, but it remains for a woman to make a home of it for him. . . .

Elsie de Wolfe (1865–1950)
The House in Good Taste, 1913

To an open house in the evening
Home shall men come,
To an older place than Eden
And a taller town than Rome.

G. K. Chesterton (1874–1936)
The House of Christmas

A man travels the world over in search of What he needs and returns home to find it.

George Moore (1853–1933)
The Brook Kerith

Where we love is home,
Home that our feet may leave, but not our hearts.

Oliver Wendell Holmes (1809–1894)
Homesick in Heaven

A little house well filled, a little field well tilled, and a little wife well willed, are great riches.

Benjamin Franklin (1706–1790)
Poor Richard's Almanac

Show me a man who cares no more for one place than another, and I will show you in that same person one who loves nothing but himself. Beware of those who are homeless by choice.

Robert Southey (1774–1843)
The Doctor, 1812

An empty house is like a stray dog or a body from which life has departed.

Samuel Butler (1835–1902)
The Way of All Flesh, 1903

Whoever builds a house for future happiness builds a prison for the present.

Octavio Paz (1914—)
Postdata (Postscript), 1870

No house should ever be *on* any hill or on anything. It should be *of* the hill, belonging to it, so hill and house could live together each the happier for the other.

Frank Lloyd Wright (1867–1959)
An Autobiography, 1932

Daughter am I in my mother's house;
But mistress in my own.

Rudyard Kipling (1865–1936)
Our Lady of the Snow

Bookplate. Picture Library, Cooper-Hewitt Museum.

The previous tenant's hardships, how he dwelt; I know it all—

Kobayashi Issa (1763–1828)

In dwelling, be close to the land.

Lao-tzu (6th cent. B.C.)
Tao Te Ching

Gentrification

By Michael H. Lang

Gentrification is one of the most dynamic forces reshaping American center-city neighborhoods in the late twentieth century. The term refers to the economic and cultural ascendency of affluent young individuals and households in formerly low-income areas. It is a widespread phenomenon that is occurring in most large cities and recently in smaller ones as well.

Gentrification results in a significant positive impact. For when newcomers arrive, neighborhoods undergo a rapid socioeconomic change that affects them visually and functionally. The importance of gentrification is that it appears to confound those urbanists who predicted the decline and abandonment of old center-city neighborhoods as they passed through the last stages of their life cycles.

Gentrification reverses this aging process with a series of revitalization stages. An initial pre-gentrification stage occurs when urban pioneers stake out candidate neighborhoods; these pioneers are the artists, students, and others who value the ambience of the city but, due to their low incomes, seek out undiscovered low-cost areas. Such areas are almost always characterized by significant architecture and a convenient location near the city center.

After this initial stage, gentrification manifests itself in terms of historically sensitive housing rehabilitation carried out by more affluent young individuals who are attracted in part by the presence of the urban pioneers. Small real estate developers are quick on the heels of these first gentrifiers. This stage is characterized by an increase in the amount and scale of housing rehabilitation and by concomitant population change. Soon the area takes on the visual and functional characteristics of a gentrifying area, complete with new upscale restaurants, shops, and services that cater to the affluent newcomers and their new life-style. This process represents a reversal of the

prevailing climate of decline and decay that formerly characterized the neighborhood.

Much of the capital that flows into gentrifying areas is due to pro-urban government tax policies and other revitalization programs that encourage private-sector participation. Gentrification is also fueled by individual investors who invest in their own houses or businesses. In either case, the gentrification process signifies the return of market demand and hence private capital to inner city housing markets.

Drawing by Roz Chast; © 1986, The New Yorker Magazine, Inc.

The economic attraction of gentrification today is such that investors can be found to underwrite the historic redevelopment and adaptive reuse of scores of old inner city row houses, warehouses, firehouses, schools, and industrial plants. This creative housing often features unique living areas with exposed brickwork, giant beams, high ceilings, and architectural design and ornamentation of

a bygone and more opulent era. The unique housing and neighborhood environments that are created can make any suburb appear dull by comparison.

Recently, gentrification has led to the creation of some unique and exciting new neighborhood environments. A notable example is the upscale residential development of some of the old finger piers that line the downtown waterfront in Philadelphia and other cities. Here residential units are surrounded by water, urban vistas, new waterside restaurants, shops, and marinas. Again, gentrification has led

to the creation of a new water-oriented life-style as much as it has led to the creation of new neighborhoods and new housing units.

Contrary to what many think, gentrification does not refer to the movement of rich suburban "gentry" back into old downtown neighborhoods. Rather, gentrification is based on newly formed households. Individual members of these

households are introduced to the city for the first time when they arrive to attend college or to work at a first job. Others are original residents of the city but come from outlying neighborhoods. These gentrifiers are typically affluent, well educated professionals, in their twenties or thirties, and it is their upscale tastes to which the market responds. Their impact on a neighborhood can be rapid and profound. Areas that were considered unsafe slums due to high rates of housing and commercial underutilization or abandonment become transformed into chic residential enclaves supported by a strong local economy.

Such rapid renewal exacts a price, however, in the form of rapidly escalating housing costs and commensurate tax rates. The effect of this is to push the urban pioneers, many of whom were renters, further out from the central areas in their search for yet undiscovered neighborhoods as candidates for eventual gentrification. In this way, the process will repeat itself.

Most gentrified areas are near the centers of cities. Proximity to cultural and historic attractions is a crucial part of the gentrification equation. Also important is the presence of expanding institutions such as museums, hospitals, or universities, which serve as economic anchors and provide a pool of professionals as prospective home owners and tenants. But more is needed. Such neighborhoods usually possess physical attributes that set them apart from the more mundane precincts found in our city centers.

While attractive sites with natural vistas are a factor, notable architecture is the most frequent characteristic of gentrified areas. Indeed, it is the restoration of historic buildings and their architectural detail that is the personal or vicarious labor of love for most gentrifiers. Many early gentrifiers went to work armed with only a copy of McKenna's *A House in the City:*

A Guide to Buying and Renovating Old Row Houses (1971). However, not just the individual building but the total neighborhood ambience is important. There must be interesting architecture and it must be in sufficient supply.

People often invest in inner-city housing in emulation of friends who have previously done so successfully. After becoming acquainted with the risks and benefits they are often encouraged to purchase and renovate their own urban dwellings. Whereas gentrification can proceed in a number of ways, the classic and frequently encountered sequence involves the purchase of a low cost, abandoned house or "shell."

The purchase, usually for cash, may be handled privately, through a realtor, or local sheriff's auction of tax-delinquent property. The Department of Housing and Urban Development also auctions off foreclosed properties. Some cities have programs that facilitate the sale of city-owned properties, often for as little as one dollar. Many properties are purchased privately by astute investors who locate owners willing to rid themselves of a burdensome old house. It is not uncommon to be able to purchase such buildings for around ten to twenty thousand dollars depending on their proximity to already gentrified areas. Buildings in this price range can even be found in historic neighborhoods such as the Germantown section of Philadelphia and the Cooper Plaza section of nearby Camden, New Jersey.

The next stage involves financing the renovations. Middle-income households can sometimes qualify for low-cost construction loans, mortgages, and even for grants provided by city and state housing and community development agencies. For the more affluent, a bank may provide a construction loan, which is converted to a standard mortgage after the renovations are complete. In some inner-city areas, bank loans have been hard to get due to poor housing conditions. In such situations creative financing must be utilized. This can entail utilization of savings, a loan from a family member, or a second mortgage on another property. If the property is sufficiently old or historic, a system of significant federal tax credits is avail-able to further defray renovation expenses. Another positive tax feature is the rapid depreciation allowance for renovation expenses.

Today, housing renovation costs for cities in the Middle Atlantic states run from about forty to fifty dollars a square foot. An average three-story urban row house could be completely renovated for approximately eighty thousand dollars, which is considerably below the cost of an equivalent new house. However, it is difficult to describe a typical case study of the renovation experience and the expenses involved. There is a wide range of costs, depending on the neighborhood housing market, the original condition of the building, and the requirements of its new owners. Some may be satisfied with a low-cost fix-up/paint-up, others with varying amounts of reconstruction. A major variable is whether the owner can personally carry out all or part of the renovations. Most gentrifiers hire professionals to do the major masonry and carpentry work and to put in new heating and plumbing systems. Many save on capital costs by moving in when the house is "roughed out" and subsequently complete the trim work and decorations themselves.

The final stage may involve the need to sell the house in order to capture the equity buildup. A buildup results from the rapid improvement in real estate values in neighborhoods undergoing gentrification. This increase in house value gives gentrifiers sizable profits over and above their capital and renovation costs. The profit or equity can then be utilized should they wish to trade up to a larger or more lavish home. Often this profit margin allows a gentrifier to take a second mortgage on a house in order to purchase and rehabilitate other houses for investment purposes.

The risk factor enters when deciding whether investment in a particular neighborhood bodes well for realizing a profit or at least recouping expenses should one need to sell in the future. A miscalculation can lead to the inability to recover costs on an expensive rehabilitation in a fringe area that has stagnant property values. Those who wish to "buy low and sell high" in short order need to be adept at interpreting both neighborhood and citywide economic trends. These trends are somewhat less important for those gentrifiers whose primary goal is the purchase and renovation of a home they intend to occupy for the foreseeable future.

While gentrification is a potent force in the overall urban revitalization process, it is simply not relevant in significant portions of many large cities, since many neighborhoods are inconveniently located or possess poor quality or obsolete housing stock. Philadelphia, for example, has 109 neighborhoods but only 15 are experiencing gentrification.

Among smaller cities, gentrification has become an important component of revitalization plans since it can help restabilize urban economies that have become dominated by low-income households. For such cities the attraction of gentrification is its ability to help reassert an economic balance. Yet in each city there must be those upscale neighborhoods to which residents who have achieved economic success can aspire to move. If such areas exist only in the suburbs, the city will slowly die.

Many positive socioeconomic aspects are associated with gentrification, but there are negative aspects as well. Displacement is one of the negative side effects of gentrification. It refers to the involuntary relocation of those inhabitants who predated the arrival of gentrification. In tight housing markets, the gentrification-induced displacement process has led to outright homelessness. Low-income communities that have a high proportion of renters are clearly at risk due to rapidly rising rents or outright eviction.

Often renters are forced to make multiple moves, forced out repeatedly as gentrification proceeds apace. Numerically the impact of displacement on a neighborhood is a gradual rather than a cataclysmic event. This lessens its immediate political implications, but in no way lessens its cataclysmic consequences for those displaced. Often numerous renters in small apartment units are displaced from a row house that is to be renovated for a single household. This tendency to lower densities might be considered an improvement to some city planners, to displaced residents it is not.

Even when it does not lead to displacement, gentrification has the power to affect the long-standing social fabric of low-income neighborhoods, for the mores and habits of affluent newcomers clash with those of the preexisting community. Indeed, gentrification has engendered considerable local tension and even scattered instances of violence. Viewed in this context, gentrification is an apt name for this process of neighborhood upgrading, since it implies a degree of cultural and socioeconomic distance between the community that used to exist in the area and what it is becoming.

Most urban policymakers agree that the negative effects of gentrification should be controlled. One way to do this is for all cities to enact anti-displacement ordinances that would protect the rights of long-standing residents from the worst effects of gentrification. Additionally, such ordinances can ensure that some of the economic benefits of gentrification will accrue to low- and moderate-income residents of the city and that certain areas will be targeted for gentrification while others will be protected from it.

For instance, a major component of such a program would be to protect long-time home owners from future property tax increases. Additionally, some of the new taxes gained from gentrified areas might be assigned to local low- and moderate-income rental housing programs. Construction jobs in the gentrified areas might be set aside for city and neighborhood youth. Other possible ways of protecting the interests of original residents exist. The problem is to strike a balance between the need to encourage continued gentrification and the need to erect protectionist policies for original residents. If successful, this balanced approach to neighborhood revitalization can measurably improve the future of our older cities.

Michael H. Lang is Associate Professor of Urban Studies and Public Policy at the Rutgers University campus in Camden, New Jersey, and author of *Gentrification Amid Urban Decline: Strategies for Older Cities*.

Homes away from Home

Hotels aim to be good substitutes.

By Nancy H. Ferguson

Almost as soon as permanent settlements were established in America, places of lodging were available, both for new arrivals and for those just passing through. Taverns played several roles in the development of colonial communities: as places of fellowship and refreshment for local residents, as overnight accommodations for travelers, and as centers of communication for both groups.

Taverns were a requisite part of early settlement plans, and laws soon appeared to regulate their operation. A Massachusetts law of 1692 proclaimed "the ancient, true and principal use of Inns . . . is for the Receipt, Relief and Lodging of Travellers and Strangers, and the refreshment of persons upon lawful Business." By 1694 tavern keepers in Maryland were required to keep twelve beds.

Colonial inns provided wayfarers with both sustenance and a warm place to sleep. The latter need was only too easily satisfied, as taverns were usually inadequately supplied with sleeping rooms and beds—both were commonly shared with strangers. Often travelers slept in the taproom after local patrons had gone home. Strangers were welcome guests in colonial taverns for they brought news and fresh stories to the sparsely populated colonies, where letters and publications from afar were few and slow in coming. Often, when correspondence did arrive, it was distributed out of the tavern.

Frequently used as meeting places, taverns occasionally became the settings for momentous events. Angry colonists organized a boycott of British goods at the Raleigh Tavern in Williamsburg, Virginia, and George Washington delivered his farewell address to his generals at Fraunces Tavern in New York City.

An enduring characteristic of both city and country hostelries has been their relationship to transportation. City taverns often appeared along the waterfront to serve trade and businesspeople. In the country, rough roads made travel slow, and frequent resting places were essential. Inns were found along stagecoach routes, or at the termini of ferry crossings. In Manhattan the Hurlgate Ferry House stood where 86th Street now meets the East River.

Throughout the eighteenth century, hanging signboards were required to distinguish tavern buildings from adjacent dwelling houses. It was not until the nineteenth century that the hotel developed as a building type.

By the 1740s the boarding house emerged as a second type of home away from home. Some travelers found the noise and the boisterous atmosphere of tavern lodgings deterrents to sound rest. Families with spare space and the need for extra income opened their homes to travelers. This was viewed as an appropriate business for widows who had been inadequately provided for by their husbands. The boardinghouse remained a staple form of inexpensive lodging, both temporary and extended, through the early twentieth century, until the spread of motels. Indeed, today the boardinghouse is seeing a revival in the bed-and-breakfast establishments that are flourishing in areas particularly rich in architectural charm and historical interest.

The word "hotel" first entered the American vocabulary in 1794 with the opening of the City Hotel on lower Broadway in New York. The term is derived from the French hôtel, meaning town house or palace. The American usage of the word may have been the expression of a desire to evoke a sophisticated or elegant image. In fact the word shares a common root with "hospital" as a place of shelter, and the City Hotel was not much more than a large boardinghouse.

The Tremont House, which opened in Boston in 1829, was the first American structure to be designed specifically as a hotel, and it was graced with many innovative amenities. The architect Isaiah Rogers applied a classical portico to the otherwise austere facade. No traditional tavern sign hung in front; rather, the imposing character of the facade itself was to attract attention. The Tremont was the first lodging in America where one entered into a reception space rather than a taproom, and where the room clerk was not also the bartender. With 173 rooms, each intended to sleep only one or two people, and each with a lock on the door, the hotel was palatial, and a huge advance in American hotel development. Of technological interest were the gaslighting in the public rooms and the indoor plumbing, albeit on the ground floor only. The Tremont House was the site of advances in American cuisine as well. Formerly, lodgers ate from a limited menu and often in the company of the proprietor's family. At the Tremont House à la carte service was introduced, permitting guests to choose their own fare.

Clearly, a new level of comfort and elegance had been attained, and hotels in other cities were swift to follow the Boston example. In 1836 the Astor House opened in New York with water closets and cold running water on the upper floors. As early as 1833 a primitive pulley-operated luggage lift appeared and in 1859, a passenger elevator was in operation at the Fifth Avenue Hotel in New York City. Electric light was introduced to hotel patrons soon after 1881. Americans often enjoyed the benefit of new technology in hotels before it was widely available in private residences. Hotel owners made a point of their modernity in promotional literature.

From 1830 until the Civil War, hotels were the preferred sites for many social functions. Rooms adequate to accommodate a large party were simply unavailable elsewhere. City hotels were also places of business, for in the days before showrooms they provided a place for the display and sale of goods.

As Americans prospered, resort hotels developed to serve those with the means and the desire to travel. The first American resorts were centered around mineral springs to which settlers were introduced by native Indians. The practice of taking the waters for their medicinal benefits was a European tradition as well. The spring at Saratoga, New York, was discovered by Sir William Johnson, the representative of the British crown to the Iroquois. By 1812 there were two hotels there. At first the resort was religious in orientation. When not partaking of the waters, guests could enjoy the innocent entertainments of hymn singing, prayer, and chaperoned buggy rides. The nation's first temperance society was founded there in 1808.

From 1803, more worldly amusements like dancing could be found at nearby Ballston Springs. Saratoga then began a liberalization process that led eventually from cotillions and billiards to gambling and horse racing. Those who missed the religious content moved on to found such communities as Chautauqua, New York, and Ocean Grove, New Jersey. White Sulphur Springs in Virginia, and other Southern spas were more lighthearted in atmosphere from the beginning.

The mountains and the seashore quickly began to attract resort patrons as well, with their promise of clear air and beautiful scenery. Resorts also provided the perennial attractions of new social acquaintances, relief from urban heat and pollution, rest, and, quite simply, a change of scene.

The first resort hotels were modest structures resembling oversized country taverns but with private rooms. By 1830 the typical hotel was a wood building with a porch extending across most of its facade. Although vast public rooms were often provided, guest bedrooms were

Grand Hotel, Mackinac Island, Michigan. Courtesy Grand Hotel.

small and simply furnished, with a bed, dresser, table, and chair. Resort hotels developed alongside their urban counterparts in terms of comfort and amenity. Because of their singular role as places for recreation, resort hotels have generated an intriguing variety of architectural expressions often intended to enhance a particular image or landscape setting.

After the centennial of the United States, the country experienced a dramatic expansion in technology and mobility. The railroad had spanned the continent in 1869, opening the West to souls less hardy than pioneers and prospectors. By 1880 private rail cars permitted the very wealthy to take their homes with them when they traveled. In their walnut-paneled, plush-upholstered cars they could view rugged, forbidding landscapes in luxury. Less affluent tourists could travel in the comfort of equally well-appointed rail cars under the guidance of such expert tour directors as Raymond and Whitcomb, who started taking groups to the Pacific Coast in 1881. Luxurious train cars gave travelers a foretaste of the hotels that awaited them at their destinations. Western innkeepers made every attempt to match or even surpass the level of amenity found at the hotels of Eastern cities.

The railroad age brought about a closer relationship between transportation and hotels, often through common ownership. Henry Morrison Flagler purchased the rail line to Saint Augustine, naming it the Florida East Coast Railway, and built the Ponce de Leon and Alcazar hotels. These grand hotels were clad in ornate, historicizing architectural styles intended to evoke and romanticize Florida's Spanish past. Flagler's Palm Beach hotel, The Royal Poinciana, opened in February 1894, and in April of the same year his Florida railroad began to service the resort. Flagler provided sidings for private rail cars at the hotel, and these served as accommodations for servants.

The Hotel Del Coronado, which opened in 1888 near San Diego, California, serves as a fine example of the relationship of resort hotels to both transportation and real estate development. The opening of the hotel followed rapidly on the completion of the southern California link to the transcontinental system. Housing lots, divided by tree-lined streets, were organized almost immediately. Elisha Babcock, a retired railroad executive from Indiana, owned both the hotel and the real estate. The Del Coronado itself sits on a spit of sand between the Pacific Ocean and San Diego Bay. This slightly offshore position, along with the hotel's bold and fanciful architectural form, must have en-

hanced the early visitor's perception of the place as removed from his or her everyday life.

By the fourth quarter of the nineteenth century, western cities could support sophisticated accommodations. In 1875, The Palace Hotel in San Francisco initiated a new and enduring type of hotel design. The focus of the structure was a seven-story glass-covered courtyard ringed with balconies. The ground floor of the open space was divided between a carriage entrance and a restaurant. The Palace Hotel was destroyed by fire following the earthquake of 1906, but it had several descendants. The Brown Palace in Denver of 1888 is the most prominent example, and it survives today as a fine hotel. Although glass-roofed interiors had several precedents in American commercial architecture, they were a new form in hotel design, unknown in the East. Perhaps such extravagant use of space seemed appropriate only in the seemingly limitless expanses of the American West.

The notion of a place from which to observe the movements of fashionable crowds was hardly new. As centers of social life, American hotels have often included places for patrons to stroll, to see, and to be seen. In resort hotels this place often took the form of a long porch, which also served as a viewing point for the landscape, the original attraction of the resort. The Catskill Mountain House (1828) near Palenville, New York, the Grand Union at White Sulphur Springs, Virginia (1858), and Union Hall at Saratoga, New York (1864), are but a few examples. The Grand Hotel, begun in 1887 on Mackinac Island, Michigan, is graced with the longest front porch in the world—some 880 feet.

In city hotels, lobbies and ballrooms are the usual spots for display and people watching. At the original Waldorf Hotel in New York (1898), a long marble hall linked two restaurants. A society writer of the day gave it the sobriquet "Peacock Alley" because of the elaborate display of finery that was sported there. The name lives on at the current Waldorf-Astoria Hotel, although it now refers to a restaurant.

Hotels have served as permanent homes for different groups of people. They provided the advantages of housekeeping and food service without the responsibilities of home ownership. In 1878 A. T. Stewart opened the Women's Hotel in New York, which was intended as a home for "women who support themselves by daily labor." It proved to be too luxurious, and therefore too expensive, for most working women; besides, there was a myriad of unappealing social restrictions. The building was reopened as the Park Avenue Hotel.

When New York's Plaza Hotel opened in 1907 it was the monumental conclusion to the row of millionaire's homes that lined Fifth Avenue from 50th Street to 60th Street. Such prominent New Yorkers as Alfred Vanderbilt, Oliver Harriman, and George J. Gould all occupied suites overlooking Central Park. The majority of the hotel rooms were booked by permanent residents. The instant and continuing success of the hotel is due in part to the clientele it attracted, as well as to its unusually luxurious appointments.

The widespread use of the automobile following World War I dramatically changed the travel patterns of most Americans. With independent mobility, people began to travel more and to spend less time at each destination. A larger middle class demanded inexpensive accommodations. Motels were introduced in the 1920s, but did not become earnest competitors of hotels until the 1950s, when they began to offer numerous amenities in locations convenient to the roadside.

Since World War II, airplane travel has dramatically altered the way Americans spend their time away from home. Today, American notions of home away from home encompass both the grand hotels of the past and a sleeping bag under the stars. Business travel has insured the survival of many old city hotels, and conventions are often the mainstay of resorts. Thus home away from home is becoming more like home itself, with all its inherent problems and responsibilities.

Nancy H. Ferguson is an architect and co-author of *America's Grand Resort Hotels.*

Natural Habitats

Animal housing tends to be economical.

By Roger B. Swain

Man is not the only animal to need shelter from the elements, a sanctuary from enemies, a nursery to rear young, or a storehouse for food. But, unlike humans with their toolboxes and textbooks, other animals build by leg, beak, claw, and tooth, guided by what are still-mysterious forces. All the more marvelous then is the simplest seashell washed up on the beach or the pigeon nest of sticks on a window ledge. Some animal architecture is famous, some is obscure. The beaver dam across a stream is better known than its builders, but few people recognize the little mud chimneys built by burrowing crayfish.

Animal housing tends to be economical, serving its intended function and little more. A chimpanzee bedding down for the night chooses a firm foundation in the crown of some tree, and then bending nearby branches, weaves them together to form a cushion on which she can lie. The whole procedure takes no more than three to five minutes, and is repeated anew every night. This is not to say that all structures are short lived. Ospreys use the same eyries again and again, adding to the nest until, after decades of use, the built-up accumulation of sticks, seaweed, bones, driftwood, and other detritus can weigh half a ton. Some homes, such as the frost-free caves that bats in the north need for hibernation, are ready-made but in such short supply that their occupants will fly hundreds of miles to return to them every fall.

The simplicity characteristic of many homes of our fellow vertebrates must not be mistaken for a lack of ingenuity. Certain tropical orioles hang their nests in trees that already have wasp nests in them because the wasps chase away parasitic flies that might otherwise attack oriole nestlings. The nest of the American alligator, a yard high mound of dead vegetation, is periodically splashed by the female. The decomposition of this moist heap of compost generates heat needed for the development of her eggs.

Being "higher animals" ourselves, it is easy to focus on the activities of our fellow mammals and on the birds, reptiles, and amphibians. But the truth is that if all the various animal architects alive today were to be baked in a pie, the vertebrates would account for a very thin slice. Invertebrates are the world's most important builders. And on land, top honors go to the social insects, those colony-dwelling bees, wasps, ants, and termites. We have all encountered yellow jackets at picnics, and almost everyone has at some time been stung by a honeybee. But consider the fact that roughly a third of the total animal biomass in an Amazon rain forest has been demonstrated to be ants and termites. Over most of the earth, ants are the principal terrestrial predator of other invertebrates. Termites, in turn, decompose much of the world's dead vegetable matter. We think of worms as the greatest earth movers, when in fact the credit should go to termites, with ants taking second place in most habitats, and earthworms only a distant third. But social insects are more than simply abundant and ecologically dominant organisms, they are house-builders of great originality and perfection.

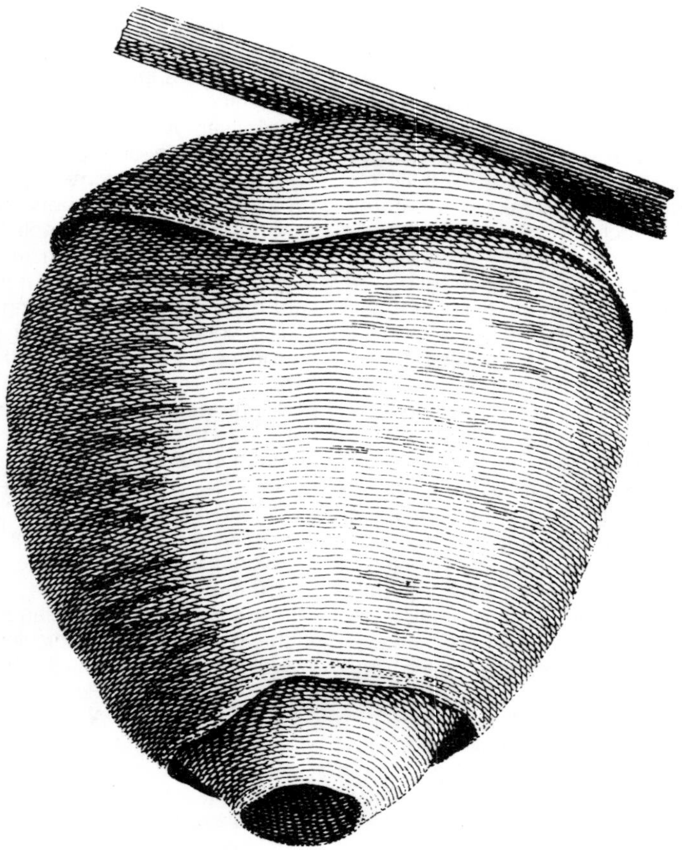

Our own knowledge of making paper from wood pulp is said to have come from watching wasps building their nests. Many species use macerated plant fibers mixed with saliva to construct strong, lightweight combs that will hold developing larvae and to construct papery envelopes that enclose the nest. By aligning the plant fibers longitudinally in the slender stalks by which a nest hangs from its support, the wasps have even invented a paper with load-bearing strength. Yellow jackets suspend a paper nest in an underground cavity that the wasps excavate, undermining and dropping to the bottom of the cavity any stone that is too heavy to carry.

Honeybees nest in preformed cavities, often in hollow trees, and fill the space with vertically hung combs made of wax. These combs do double duty as brood chambers and as storehouses for honey and pollen, since the bees must lay away sufficient provisions to tide them over the season in which plants are not flowering. The wax is produced by glands on the underside of the worker bees' abdomens, and is shaped to form hexagonal cells arranged back to back in parallel series. Each cell is angled up thirteen degrees to prevent stored, but uncapped, honey from running out. Honeybees distinguish themselves not only in their economy of space and material, but in the speed with which they can build. Over 90 percent of a wild honeybee colony's comb is completed within forty-five days of a swarm occupying a new nest site.

Picture Library, Cooper-Hewitt Museum.

162

By far the largest single homes of social insects are those of some species of African termites, whose earthen mounds may reach thirty feet or more in height and ninety feet in diameter at the base. Such a mound may house a couple of million colony members. The queen and her consort are enclosed in a so-called royal chamber—a rock-hard fortress deep within the nest—surrounded by tunnels and chambers that house the rest of the colony. Ventilation is a critical issue in an inhabited structure of this size. How do you regulate air quality and temperature? Solutions vary between, and even within, species. In some nests the heat rises up out of tall chimneys pulling fresh air into the nest at the base. In others, the warm air collects in a large upper chamber and from there moves into a series of ducts just beneath the outer surface of the mound, where it cools, freshens, sinks, and is channeled back to the interior of the nest.

All this architectural diversity pales, however, by comparison with the work of ants. There are more species of ants than all the other social insects combined. Some six thousand species are spread across five continents—from the arctic to the tropics, from the wettest forests to the driest deserts. Some ant colonies, in colder climates, simply excavate a nest beneath a flat rock, using the stone to shield them, to conserve moisture, and to retain the sun's heat. Other temperate-zone ants are mound builders that construct cones of sand and thatch a yard or

more high. The angle of the sides of some of these cones varies with latitude, the better to intercept the sun's rays and warm the ants that occupy the galleries just beneath the surface. Carpenter ants excavate their nests in partly decayed wood (though the fact that they do not eat the wood makes them less of a threat to our houses than termites).

In the tropics, South and Central American leaf-cutter ants tend fungus gardens in subterranean nests, living solely on the fungus that they culture on fresh leaves, which they have cut and carried underground. African and Asian weaver ants nest arboreally, building their homes out of clusters of living leaves pulled together and connected by a silken fiber. The silk is produced by the larvae, and while some workers are pulling the edges of adjacent leaves together, other ants hold the larvae-like shuttles and pass them back and forth across the gap while the silk plays out. Still other ants have dispensed with homes altogether, their legions carrying their young with them, stopping only periodically in bivouacs made of nothing but interlinked ant bodies.

Finally there are those ants that reside in specialized plant structures, from hollow thorns to chambered stems. In the most famous cases, the plants not only provide lodging, but stock the larder as well, producing food specifically for their guests. The benefit is not all one-sided. The aggressive ants chase away insect pests, discourage climbing vines or other competing vegetation, and may in some

Picture Library, Cooper-Hewitt Museum.

cases fertilize the host plant with their waste.

Despite the sophistication of social insects as builders, they work with no blueprints, no foremen, and very limited brains. Their building projects often extend over many life spans, leaving no colony member to witness the entire process. We may like to describe the activity of human construction crews, especially when seen from a distance, as looking like so many ants, but the analogy is not an apt one. The construction of a human domicile is a highly ordered process compared to what one sees inside a beehive, an ant hill, or a termite mound. The latter —perhaps because of a preponderance of chemical communication—borders on chaos.

How any order emerges from the pandemonium of individual building activity in a social insect colony is one of life's great mysteries. In part, the order may come from individuals responding to work already accomplished as opposed to direct communication among nestmates. Thus a termite who encounters the beginning of a wall will instinctively add to it. The term coined to describe this response is *stigmergy* from the Greek meaning "incite to work." This does not of course

explain what causes work to begin in the first place or what causes it to shut down when it is finished. The nests of many social insects are in a state of dynamic equilibrium, being constantly built up and torn down. What we see may simply be the result of a statistical preponderance of certain actions over others.

Clearly the rules of work for insect builders will never be applicable to human ones, even when we fully understand them. Nor should we expect them to be. The protostome line that led to social insects diverged from our own deuterostome line as much as a billion years ago. Insects achieved full sociality a hundred million years before the genus *Homo* even appeared. And yet it is hard for us not to be drawn to the activities of these other social beings, especially the ants. Why have they in particular been so successful? The answer is that they have been able to develop modes of life, and styles of housing, suitable for the most diverse environmental conditions. And that may be a lesson that we can take home

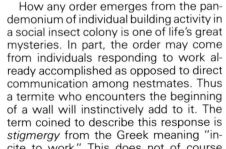

Roger B. Swain is Science Editor of *Horticulture* magazine and author of *Field Days: Journal of an Itinerant Biologist.*

Picture Library, Cooper-Hewitt Museum.

Housing in the Future

By Isaac Asimov

The inexorable pressure on future housing rests on this overwhelming fact: that the human population continues to increase rapidly. The population of Earth at the beginning of the twentieth century was perhaps 1.7 billion. It is now 5 billion. By the end of the century, it may be 6 billion.

Added to this is the fact that the process of urbanization is proceeding even more rapidly as people of the impoverished countryside flock into the cities in search of jobs and services. Some cities in Latin America are housing (or failing to house) twenty million people, and a growth to thirty million is forecast.

Even if population can be controlled without disaster by lowering the birth rate (as China, notably, is desperately trying to do), we will have to face a high plateau of population for a century or two at any rate. What will happen to housing in such a case?

The simplest way of visualizing the future of housing is to suppose a tendency toward decentralization. Present-day technology is pointing to a future in which this will become easy in a way. Computers and the communications revolution have eliminated much of the need for people to be in close contact in order to run their businesses, supervise machinery, take advantage of cultural opportunities, and so on.

Machinery will be increasingly automated, and robots will become more and more important. Consequently, the human role will steadily grow to become that of supervision, administration, decision-making.

Such human activities can be carried through from a distance. Information can be gathered and transmitted, decisions can be made and implemented from the home. There will become progressively less need to commute between home and business. Home and office, or home and workplace, can become one.

Jean-Michel Folon, *Le Regard*, © 1975. Courtesy of John Locke Studios, Inc.

The same technology that would make it possible to do one's work at a distance would also make it possible to gather one's cultural needs at a distance. A computerized library would be at one's fingertips; lectures and concerts could be received in three-dimensional holography. Museums and art galleries could be visited long distance, and so on and so on.

The tendency might then be for cities to melt away and be replaced by a sprawl of suburbs.

However, there are forces that would act against that. Land on Earth is finite in area, and to have human habitations spread outward and outward would consume the wilderness, take up good farmland, crowd out mining areas. In addition, to house a million families in a million separated homes would be incredibly wasteful, since each would have to be supplied with water, heat, electricity, and so on, while provision would have to be made for the delivery of goods and the removal of trash.

There might, therefore, be the tendency to house human beings in moderate conglomerations and to separate those conglomerations.

Thus, the island of Manhattan has achieved an extraordinarily high population density, and yet maintained a comparatively high standard of living by building apartments one on top of another, rather than one beside another.

Would it be possible to continue this tendency over the world generally so that it will become common to have sky-scrapers a mile high—four hundred stories or so—that may comfortably house up to twenty-five hundred families?

Each tower would require an enormously complex system of water supply, waste removal, electricity, gas, elevators, laundries, food supplies, and shops—but surely the total in resources and effort would not be that required by twenty-five hundred separate houses.

If each tower contained a shopping mall, it might rarely be necessary for the families living in such a tower to have to leave it for the sake of everyday needs. Add the facilities of high-tech communications and the need to leave would further decrease.

The mile-high towers would not be viewed as crowding each other. The population of Manhattan could be fitted into about 170 such towers and if these could be evenly spread out over the island, each would be about five or six city blocks away from its closest neighbors. If the base of each tower were to take up a square city block, then only about 2 percent of the land area of Manhattan would be built up. The rest would be open, and could be devoted to parkland, to gardens, even to small farms. Moreover, each tower would receive plenty of sunlight.

Nor need the towers be isolated. In the case of denser areas of population, the towers would be sufficiently close together to be connected by enclosed bridges. That would make it possible for individual buildings to specialize in one thing or another. One building might have a restaurant of particular renown, another a cut-rate appliance store of established reputation. People would travel easily from tower to tower (by small electrical vehicles, perhaps), and individual towers would not be too ingrown. For longer trips, each tower might have a public helicopter-port on the roof.

Of course, the towers possess the capacity for enormous loss. In decentralized

164

buildings a fire in any one of them might ruin only one family. A fire in a tower may ruin a hundred, or a thousand, and may represent an enormous property loss. The towers might be vulnerable to accident also—to collision with aircraft, to windstorms, and to other violent manifestations of weather.

Then, too, a single tower might have a variety of environments. The upper stories would have much more sunshine, since they would rise above the rain clouds at times. They would also rise above much of the dust and pollution at the lower stories. On the other hand, the upper stories would be more vulnerable to the wind, would be colder in the winter, and would have thinner air, which might be an important consideration for those with cardiac or respiratory problems.

•

Is there any alternative that might maintain decentralization, be less sensitive to weather, and yet not take up too much of the surface of the earth?

There is. The future may see humanity take up the fashion of underground living.

It may seem that this is so bizarre as to be instantly judged out of the question. How can people live in buildings cut off from the outside? And yet in the business sections of cities it is quite common for offices to have no windows. And increasingly, especially in subarctic cities, shopping centers large enough to be towns are enclosed or are actually built underground.

In addition to being merely endurable, underground living would have certain strongly favorable features. To begin with, we would move into an environment that is free of weather. There are neither winds nor precipitation. Rain, snow, sleet, and fog will not annoy us. Furthermore, there are no temperature extremes; in fact, the temperature, nearly constant, would be about that of San Francisco. There would be some problems, of course. Droughts would affect the water supply. Rains and floods might waterlog the soil and produce leaks, and there is, of course, the possibility of earthquakes here and there. All these are exceptional circumstances, however.

The underground temperature would be a bit on the cool side—sweaterweather. There would be the need for gentle heating and continuous ventilation, but the energy spent on this would be far outmatched by the energy saved on strong heating and on air-conditioning. What energy is needed may be gained to a large extent by the use of Earth's internal heat, which may perhaps be more easily extracted from a position that is already a substantial distance below the surface.

Then, too, transportation will be simplified. With weather absolutely certain, and never unpleasant, walking would be much more popular. Trains, running through evacuated tunnels on electromagnetic cushions, would move with the speed of airplanes.

Local time would no longer be important. On the surface, the tyranny of day and night cannot be avoided, and when it is one time of day in one place, it is another time of day in other places. Underground, the world might run on a uniform day and night. The whole world could be on eight-hour shifts, with the main "daylight" shift beginning at the same time everywhere. This would ease the problem of world communications, and would eliminate jet lag for those who travel long distances east or west.

The surface of the earth would be saved. With cities and people underground, there would certainly be more room on Earth's surface for wilderness, for farms and pastures, for parks and playgrounds.

And, indeed, living underground would not remove humanity from the enjoyment of nature. Rather the reverse. If you live in the center of a large surface city, and want something more of nature than a crowded park, you may have to drive for an hour or so before reaching a spot, some thirty miles away, that suits you. In a large underground city, you are only a few hundred yards from the countrified surface and can reach it by elevator in a few minutes.

•

On the whole, it is not likely that our descendants will choose a simple strategy. There will be decentralized surface structures, towers, and underground dwellings, all depending on location and tastes. And that perhaps will be best.

CITY OF THE FUTURE

What will the city of tomorrow be like? Here is the giant plastic, metal, and unbreakable glass city of the 21st century. A city of science, of atomic power, of space travel, and of high culture. See page 240 for complete story.

Frank R. Paul, "City of the Future," *Amazing Stories* back cover, April 1942. Joe A. Goulait, Smithsonian Institution.

Isaac Asimov is the author of over 400 books, including the most recent, *Asimov's Chronology of Science and Discovery*.

The Future

Ralph Caplan
Communications Design
Consultant

Housing is of course one of our most sobering public issues. It is also one of our dreariest public concepts. Houses, even ugly houses, have personalities. But housing, however well intended, almost never has. Houses take on the patina of those who have lived in them. The tenants of housing leave only the traces of anonymity. Houses may become homes; and even if they do not, they become old houses, which in themselves demand a certain respect. Housing, however, resists transmogrification (has anyone ever heard of haunted housing?) although, as in the case of Pruitt-Igoe, it is sometimes vulnerable to dynamite. Admittedly there are more urgent aspects of the designed future, including housing, to worry about, but I hope we can incorporate into our planned dwellings the possibility of delight. That would be truly postmodern.

W. Dorwin Teague
Industrial designer

The big future problems will be to achieve enhanced livability, efficiency, and privacy in the face of the inevitable greater crowding, higher energy costs, and more expensive labor. Some of the advances that will help solve these problems:

• Lightweight, inert, vermin-proof, inexpensive building materials with high insulating qualities, such as foam concrete.

• Prefabricated modular construction systems with leakproof joints, built-in wiring, ducting, and plumbing, easily transportable and quickly assembled.

• A central services module combining efficiency, heating, cooling, and hot

Drawing by Sempé; © 1984, The New Yorker Magazine, Inc.

water with minimal on-site plumbing and space requirements.

- Automatic or manually selectable opacity/reflectance glass for windows to eliminate the need for draperies or blinds (this technology will be available in three years or less).
- Regenerative filtered ventilation for all rooms.
- High-security design features.
- Increased factory-built low-cost housing.

Ivan Chermayeff
Graphic designer

What a sight it is to drive through the South Bronx—"On the Beach," so close to home. It makes one wonder where to begin to avoid the end.

The past mistakes of housing seem to have occurred for reasons far beyond architecture—certainly beyond architects and planners, whose pretensions do not stretch into the realms of politics and poverty. People need to make something for themselves of the place where they live, to feel a part of it. Alienation, to be overcome, requires the eradication of gross inequities. The housing of the future has to have more to do with participation than with shelter. Short of that, housing will be forever built only to be destroyed. A truly expensive proposition.

M. Paul Friedberg
Landscape architect

As shelter explores protection from the environment, so housing provides the human counterpart, the social "art of living." Our world of affluence and technology provides us with a preeminent opportunity for choice in how we live. For us, housing codifies and defines lifestyles and allows us to choose: to live in intimate or ceremonial surroundings; to live alone or in concert with others; to live within varied definitions and delineations of space; to live in or be protected from nature.

In the future we will wear our housing as we now wear our wardrobes, and we will act our new roles and fantasies. Having mastered the art of shelter, housing will reflect this new "social art."

Cesar Pelli
Architect

I will write not about what I believe and fear will happen, but instead about what should happen to housing in the future. Perhaps the first step would be to stop thinking of housing as architectural (and political) projects, and to think instead of housing as dwellings that are an integral part of the tissue of a living city, a city not divided artificially by function or income. I see it not as an architectural problem, but fundamentally as a social one. Its solution will require a public commitment to a better life for our cities and for all their citizens.

Niels Diffrient
Industrial designer

It was Edgar A. Guest who said, "It takes a heap of living to make a house a home." The point is that a house should not get in the way of making it into a home. An architect I once knew boasted that he could bring about a divorce in any family just by the way he designed its house. Whether an architect designs a house or a builder proceeds with a non-design; whether the house is mass-produced or handcrafted; those who plan and build houses should bear in mind that the most important thing is what happens after the houses are built and the occupants move in.

Ulrich Franzen
Architect

The design of large-scale housing projects will become one of the most urgent issues of the late 1980s. The failures of design and the failures of social policy have caused the virtual abandonment of

housing in the recent past in this country. The new challenge will be to fill the desperate need for low- and moderate-income housing and, most importantly, to develop design theories and methodologies that will reflect the humanistic and contextual design notions of today.

James Stewart Polshek
Architect

In the future, the public policies that have, for the past decades, been fueled by private (read selfish) needs and political expediencies must change. American housing, like the American automobile, is currently built to be obsolete. However, we are encouraged by what amounts to little more than "loansharking" and excessive advertising to trade in the car every few years. Obviously this cannot be done with a house or an apartment. What the Japanese are doing to us in the auto industry we are doing to ourselves in the housing industry. The lack of technological research as well as disastrous planning strategies have created suburbs that already look like automobile graveyards, their "tin lizzies" pasted together by do-it-your-selfers. This country must put the systematic creation of affordable quality shelter on a wartime footing, because if we do not have the national resolve to do so we will all soon be homeless.

John Hejduk
Architect

It is always a tentative proposition to speculate on futures. I would prefer to refer to one of the most important and celebratory achievements in social housing during the past ten years, namely the solid commitment and productivity of the City of Berlin through its *Internationale Bauausstellung* headed by architects Josef Paul Kleihues and Hardt-Waltherr Haemer. I believe this is a proven example of excellence in housing and planning. If its quality could be matched in the future in other cities, particularly New York, this would certainly be a worthy goal.

Richard Meier
Architect

Housing in the future will occur in even stranger locations than we have witnessed in the past twenty years. Since 1969, when we were involved in the design and construction of what was then called the adaptive reuse of Westbeth Artists' Housing, we have thought that creative loft-type space would be appropriate not only for creative artists but for individuals in all fields of endeavor. This has come to pass to some extent in places like Soho, Noho, and Hobo (Hoboken). However, public financial support of housing has diminished to the point of being almost extinct. In the future, private enterprise will need to develop more flexible and less conventional housing types in the cities as well as in the suburbs.

Amanda M. Burden
Urban planner

In response to the critical shortage of affordable housing, it now appears that new cost-saving technologies will play a key role in New York's residential development. In the future, manufactured preassembled housing may well be indistinguishable from conventional construction and, therefore, accepted by many housing markets. Units may thus become more standardized, but the need for family-sized apartments will require a built-in flexibility for each unit. To respond better to family needs within cost constraints, residential building design should incorporate common or shared facilities. Finally, the quality of the streetscape will become an increasingly important amenity for marketing in all economic sectors.

Edward L. Barnes
Architect

There must be subsidized housing for the growing numbers of people below the poverty level. I believe that the political pendulum will swing back to the left and that housing for the poor will again be 167 addressed. When this happens, I hope we will have learned not to build high-rise file cabinets, but moderately scaled dwellings that are truly humane.

Albert Hadley
Interior Designer

With the advancement of science and technology come new ways and means by which we employ more elements—both old and new—that are suitable reflections of our time and place. As architecture, interior design, and decoration (along with all other art forms) have always keenly reflected the influences of the social, religious, and political structures of any given historical period, so, too, our time and place are recorded with clarity and meaning. Ours is a knowledgeable, inquisitive, imaginative, creative, and sensitive society. Housing, both public and private, shows great evidence of these positive qualities.

Though the glass of fashion mirrors countless changing ideas of attractiveness and often fleeting passions, even sometimes for bizarre and crude forms and concepts, the great stabilizing factor represented by an enlightened design community—and its educated audience—ensures a future that is rich in both the aesthetics and the humanities.

Where there is exuberance, it is hoped that there will be discipline. Where there is aggressiveness of form and idea, it is hoped that there will be gentleness. For the future of our housed—and our homes—it is hoped that there will be a strong measure of the Great American Spirit. What more can we ask?

David Rowland
Industrial designer

The future of home is improvement. But what is improvement? Is it to be primarily a merry-go-round of change, change, change as influenced by consumer magazines? I think not. I think people will mature beyond that. They will learn to differentiate between mere change and real improvement. They will expect better ways of building, better materials, auton-

omous energy, better performance, so that their homes do more for them than ever before. Walls and roofs will move, as weather permits, to allow man to interrelate more with nature. Windows will be automatically light-modulating. But while there will be many marvelous hardware features, the mental satisfaction of feeling emotionally and intellectually nourished will become major goals and accomplishments in tomorrow's home.

John M. Johansen
Architect

All housing, whether public or private, multi or individual, low-cost or luxury, will, I believe, move in two different directions. First, building technology and mass production of building elements will be more in evidence; city services and mechanical plants more effectively distributed; structures more flexible and adaptable; and all this depersonalized. On the other hand, cybernetic controls in the manufacturing process will result not in the marketing of identical products for house assembly, but move toward (back to?) individualized products, from "off-the-rack" products to "custom-made" products.

Secondly, within the standardized and impersonalized utilitarian aspects of house construction, a realm of greater personal choice, diversity of architectural expression, and response to regional conditions will be fostered. Upon or within the high tech, highly processed aspects of structure and mechanical plant, and now electronic equipment, will be found opportunities whereby each owner will "do it him/herself." Owners participation, handcraft, and hobby work will be more in evidence about the house, and a new phase of physiological balance and well-being may develop.

To this, add the effects of the electronic or communication age, which will bring about the "work-live house" or apartment, from which owners will conduct their businesses yet still enjoy the comforts and closeness of family life. Communication will bring to the house education, medical diagnostics, marketing, and democratic networking processes. For

psychic balance, meditation chambers may become popular. Programming the needs for the house will be totally rewritten. And indeed the architectural expression of all this is difficult to visualize. But one can predict an element of greater convertibility, flexibility, transformation. One can predict the interplay of lightness and "scene changing" in contrast to the stability and permanence of heavy masonry; an interplay of the "here and now" with the profound basic special symbols of "all time and all place," which have preserved our psychosocial balance for some six thousand years, and will for equal time to come.

Robert Venturi
Architect

I think in the future we will have to be less dogmatic and simplistic about the form, symbolism, and location of housing—acknowledging that housing for low-income families and the elderly should be less concentrated and more scattered throughout communities so as to diminish ghetto effects and to promote richness and variety socially and formally within the city. This will acknowledge the heterogeneity of these groups and the different ways they can relate to and contribute to the rest of the community.

Ward Bennett
Designer

What I hope will not continue is the pollution of the landscape by the sheetrock-Swiss cheese-postmodern-Bridgehampton style of architecture. Houses of the future will, I hope, depart from the clever, amusing, and fashionable design epitomized by the Memphis look. Instant anything by popular decorators and public relations architects should be shunned. A personal involvement with the environment requires more than purchasing model rooms from a department store and/or pseudo-New England condominiums in a complex outside Phoenix, Arizona.

I hope that designers in the future will begin to respect and use the materials of

the area, and pay attention to the architecture of the house next door. There are guides to beauty, culture, refinement. The ABCs of good regional architecture and furniture are readily available. Lessons can be learned by studying Georgia O'Keeffe's house in New Mexico, Dominique de Menil's residence in Houston, Mies van der Rohe's apartment in Chicago, Sir John Soane's house in London, and Luis Barragan's house in Mexico City. All these houses express very different and very personal ways of life, but all have the level of quality that Thomas Jefferson's masterpiece Monticello has.

We can learn from the past, but we must reject ready-made history. The owners of houses should seriously study the best examples of furniture, decorative objects, architecture, and landscape design in museums and libraries—such as the Cooper-Hewitt. It is equally important for people to understand how they live—before hiring a designer to interpret those particular needs.

William Ellis
Architect

Housing, especially public housing, has an image problem: it looks too much like *housing*. The architectural challenge for the future lies in finding models for housing that transcend its own short, brutish tradition. There must be models that can help accomplish this—English terrace housing, the French *hôtel particulier*, American picturesque cluster housing, waterside hotels, to name a few; there are surely many others.

The need may be obvious and the task incredibly difficult, but since the deadly economics of housing will no doubt persist outside the control of architects, what else of any importance is left for us to do but to concentrate on amenity at the level of fundamental architectural arrangement.

Robert A. M. Stern
Architect

The future of housing depends on whether we can succeed in creating

"Coming Soon," from *Great Moments in Architecture*, by David Macaulay. © 1978 by David Macaulay. Reprinted by permission of Houghton Mifflin Company

Jack Lenor Larsen
Designer

I so firmly believe that the prototype of tomorrow's housing is today's industrial loft. For too long a time now, most of us have not been able to afford architects for residential work—and the architects have not been able to afford to do houses either. The idea of building loft-like boxes that could be dropped by helicopter into wooded hills, or stacked up in cities, makes sense. An architect could be involved in such unspecific, undetailed containers—*and* they would be affordable to the occupants who would build them out as their needs and incomes permitted. In this way, they would be individual and personal spaces. Let us hope it will be soon.

Hugh Hardy
Architect

A negative future for housing in the private sector would result from the same forces of aesthetic miniaturization that have blighted past generations: little thin-walled suburban villas designed to recall the houses of the rich. The public sector would continue to be traumatized by past failures, using high-rise towers to lodge the poor.

A positive future for housing would require new partnerships between the public and private sectors to use architectural images both more personable and more intimate than those of the past three decades. This future must also offer new forms of financing, which can lead to new concepts of equity, thus ensuring that house and home are one.

Rubén De Saavedra
Interior Designer

Fewer outside windows, more fortress-like, more skylights. Fewer windows because of security and desire for privacy, also energy saving. . . . The advent of families living crowded together in dense cities like those in the Orient. . . . Fewer antiques, which will be used more as objects of art. . . . Smaller private rooms and large common room(s).

places—environments that allow a fabric of related experiences based on the specific features of site and history—and not merely developments. There are three principal locales for housing today: the center city, the "middle city" between the urban core and the distant suburbs, and the suburb; each calls for a different strategy of place-making. In the center city, we are relearning the vital importance of the public street and the private facade, and the necessity of thoughtful contextual-ism. In the middle city we have failed miserably by attempting the non-place architecture of high-rise apartment slabs. Now we are reexamining pre-World War II models in which the greater city is conceived as a collection of urban villages, still tied to the city grid and public transportation system, yet with the advantages of a "village" green—the ideal subway suburb. In the far suburbs, the failings of the impersonal subdivision are well-documented, but we are beginning to employ historic and contemporary models that integrate the predominant realm of the single-family house with a variety of housing types and public places. I am optimistic about our renewed understanding of housing as an environmental and cultural act, and believe that we are in the midst of a new era of making art out of circumstance, of preserving the special places and making new ones as powerfully resonant as those we made in the past.

169

Colonies in Space

A new renaissance is anticipated.

By Gerard K. O'Neill and Gregg E. Maryniak

When people think about housing in space, a common picture is of a dome on the surface of the moon or some other planet. It now appears, however, that the most likely type of space-housing will be in cities that have been constructed in free space from material mined initially from the moon and later from the asteroids.

Contrary to predictions that telecommunications advances will do away with cities and the urban life-style, physical and social realities will encourage the creation of cities in space.

Life in these new space-cities will be an integral part of a new renaissance. This renaissance will be triggered by an actual increase in energy and material available to humanity as we learn to harvest the ocean of resources that surrounds our planet. It will also be initiated by an awareness of the potential for growth and freedom made possible by the use of these new resources.

How can we talk about constructing entire cities in space, given that the present cost of launching material from the earth's surface into orbit is several thousand dollars per pound? The answer is as old as the history of mankind, new only when applied to space.

Throughout human exploration of the earth, pioneers learned to use locally available materials as they settled new areas. When settlers built houses in the early colonies they did not import building materials from the Old World. They brought only their tools, and used materials available here. Their first houses were simple shelters constructed from logs, earth, and other materials that required little processing. Later, as the colonial infrastructure included quarries, sawmills, and forges, more sophisticated forms of housing were constructed.

Today, for all aspects of space activity, we still rely completely on imported ma-
170 terials. Soon, however, we will reach a

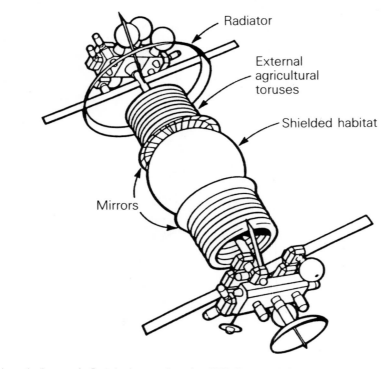

Schematic diagram of a Bernal sphere configuration, 1975. Courtesy NASA.

point where the demand for building materials and other bulk goods will make it far less expensive to "live off the land" using resources already in space.

The first source of nonterrestrial materials is likely to be a sort of space debris: the Shuttle External Tanks, which are larger than the Shuttle orbiter and weigh more than the Shuttle's payload. In the past, these tanks were discarded and forced to burn up in the earth's atmosphere. Studies undertaken by the nonprofit Space Studies Institute and others indicate that these tanks can be saved and used for many types of space construction and activity.

The main source of space materials is likely to be our nearest celestial neighbor, the moon. The moon is about one thousand times closer to the earth than the next closest planet. It is so close to the earth that machinery on its surface can be operated in real time by people working from the earth. Thanks to the Apollo expeditions we know that the moon's surface materials contain a vast storehouse of oxygen, silicon, and metals. Best of all, the moon's low gravity and lack of atmosphere make it possible to launch materials into free space at very low cost.

Instead of using costly and complicated chemical rockets, a cheap, reliable form

of electric motor called a mass-driver can catapult a steady stream of packets of lunar soil into space. Mass-drivers have been built and tested. At present levels of performance, a machine about one-and-a-half times the length of a football field could accelerate packets of lunar soil to escape velocity.

Once these materials have been delivered to free space they can be used for radiation shielding and protection against meteorite or space-debris impact or they can be processed into feedstocks for space construction and industry. Incidentally, it makes economic sense to do most of this processing in space instead of on the surface of the moon, since energy in the form of sunlight is freely available on a twenty-four-hour basis. By comparison the surfaces of the moon and other planets, while material rich, are energy poor.

We have a good idea of what these cities in space will look like. During the 1970s the National Aeronautics and Space Administration (NASA) sponsored two studies on the design and construction of cities in space. Earthly cities provide various elements of life support, such as water, gas, electricity, sewerage, garbage disposal, and transportation. Modern architects and city planners think in terms of cities as machines for living. This will be even more apparent in space-cities. In addition to the above functions, space-cities will also have to provide atmosphere, food production, shielding against radiation, and artificial gravity. Rotation will provide a substitute for gravity. Many possible designs for space-cities permit rotation. Cylinders, rings, and dumbbell-shaped habitats are all plausible. When all factors were considered in the NASA studies, the preferred shape proved to be a sphere.

A permanent space-habitat for ten thousand people would consist of a sphere about five hundred yards in diame-

In the diagram: Radiator, External agricultural toruses, Shielded habitat, Mirrors

ter. The sphere would be an inside-out world with acceleration equivalent to Earth-normal gravity at the "equator." As a person walked toward the internal "poles," he would feel less and less weight. These areas near the spin axis might be used for hospitals, where patients could recuperate in low gravity. Low-gravity ballet might become a popular pastime along with sports such as human-powered flight.

Windows made from lunar glass would allow sunlight to be admitted. Plants and animals would be raised in agricultural areas outside the habitat sphere, where optimal growth conditions can be maintained without discomfort to human residents.

In addition to the habitat sphere and agricultural areas, the space colony would consist of a long rotation axis with non-rotating docking ports and radiator panels to dissipate waste heat.

Although economics would dictate careful use of the internal living space, there would be sufficient room throughout the sphere for parks and garden pathways. Walking and bicycling would provide transport; larger habitats would have electric vehicle-and-transit systems.

Space-cities will result from a number of forces. The first of these is economics. Once space becomes an arena of human activity, it quite rapidly becomes less expensive to provide comfortable and safe housing for workers and their families on a permanent basis than to rotate crews back and forth from the earth.

The use of material resources already in space will seed new industries, and they will create the need for space habitats. One of the most promising of these industries will be the construction of large power-collecting satellites. They will collect the abundant solar energy that presently streams past the earth and will transmit it to the surface of the earth. Each satellite will provide enough power to fulfill the energy needs of a large city on the earth. Such satellite designs have been studied in the past but were only marginally economical because of the enormous cost of launching construction materials from the surface of the earth. Nonetheless, the Soviets and Japanese are engaged in projects that will lead to solar-power satellite construction in space. Recent studies now indicate that over 99 percent of such space-energy collectors could be made from lunar materials. By using lunar materials instead of brute-force launching from the earth, power satellites could become an important part of our world's energy production system.

Power from space would be especially important for the Third World. Whereas a typical solar-power satellite would add about 2 percent to the United States' power capacity, the same satellite would add about 40 percent to India's capacity. The technology required to build receivers for space power is relatively simple. Most of the world's people live in energy-poor conditions. Women in many countries spend a majority of their working time scavenging for cooking fuel (often creating dust-bowl conditions and extending deserts in the process). Lack of available energy is cited as the principal impediment to extending the benefits of the "green revolution" to the Third World.

Providing a means of meeting the rapidly increasing energy demands of the less-developed portions of the earth with alternatives to fossil-fuels is of vital importance to our entire planet. Even if the developed nations dramatically alter their energy-consumption patterns, the rest of the world has the potential to alter or even destroy the earth's biosphere unless non-polluting energy systems are implemented.

Just as Earth's cities are built near rivers, oceans, and other forms of transportation, space-cities will be constructed in free space, rather than on the surface of a planet. In addition to having the advantage of twenty-four-hour solar energy, cities in space will enjoy low transportation cost for their products.

Ultimately, the construction of space-cities will be an industry in itself. Unlike their terrestrial counterparts, space habitats can be mobile. Groups seeking religious freedom or a homeland of their own will have an alternative that is unprecedented in human history. Scientists foresee a gradual migration of the human species throughout our solar system.

Mary Petty, *Interplanetary "Modern,"* about 1954. Courtesy of the Syracuse University Art Collection.

Self-contained space habitats may even make possible expeditions to nearby stars.

In addition to the physical benefits of using space resources to improve the quality of life on the earth, the social and psychological aspects are likely to be dramatic. Just as the knowledge of an expanded "world" beyond Europe helped trigger the Renaissance, the hope generated by our exploration of the High Frontier will be a profoundly positive aspect of life in the twenty-first century.

Gerard K. O'Neill is President of the Space Studies Institute in Princeton, New Jersey, and author of *The High Frontier* and *Interstellar Migration and the Human Experience.* **Gregg E. Maryniak** is Vice-President of the Space Studies Institute.

Selected Reading

Abrams, Charles. *The City Is the Frontier*. New York: Harper and Row, 1965.

Abrams, Philip, and Andrew McCulloch. *Communes, Sociology, and Society*. London: Cambridge University Press, 1976.

Aladdin Company. *Aladdin Homes, 1918-19: Catalog No. 31*. Bay City, Michigan, 1919. Reprint. Watkins Glen, New York: American Life Foundation and Study Institute, 1985.

Albrecht, Donald. *Designing Dreams: Modern Architecture in the Movies*. New York: Harper and Row, 1985.

Allwood, John. *The Great Exhibitions*. London: Cassell and Collier Macmillan, 1977.

The American Institute of Architects Task Force on Aging. *Design for Aging: An Architect's Guide*. Washington, D.C.: The AIA Press.

The American National Standard for Buildings and Facilities—Providing Accessibility and Usability for Physically Handicapped People. New York: American National Standards Institute, Inc., 1986.

Anderson, Martin. *The Federal Bulldozer*. Cambridge, Mass.: MIT Press, 1964.

Andre, Rae. *Homemakers—Forgotten Workers*. Chicago: University of Chicago Press, 1981.

Apgar, William C., Jr., H. James Brown, George Masnick, and John Pitkin. *The Housing Outlook, 1980-1990*. New York: Praeger Publishers, 1985.

Appelbaum, Stanley. *The Chicago World's Fair of 1893*. New York: Dover Publications, 1980.

Archer, John, ed. *The Literature of British Domestic Architecture, 1715-1842*. Cambridge, Mass.: MIT Press, 1986.

The Architectural League of New York and The New York City Department of Housing Preservation and Development. *Vacant Lots: A Study Project on In-Fill Housing in New York*. Spring, 1988.

Ardrey, Robert. *The Territorial Imperative*. New York: Atheneum, 1967.

Aries, Philippe. *Centuries of Childhood: A Social History of the Family*. Translated by Robert Baldick. New York: Alfred A. Knopf, 1962.

Barnett, Jonathan. *Urban Design as Public Policy*. [New York]: Architectural Record Books, 1974.

Bauer, Catherine. *Modern Housing*. Boston: Houghton Mifflin, 1934.

———. *Social Questions in Housing and Town Planning*. London: University of London Press, 1952.

Beattie, Susan. *A Revolution in London Housing: LCC Housing Architects and Their Work, 1893-1914*. London: Architectural Press, 1980.

Becker, Franklin D. *Housing Messages*. Stroudsburg, Pennsylvania: Dowden, Hutchinson and Ross, 1977.

Beecher, Catherine. *A Treatise on Domestic Economy for the Use of Young Ladies at Home and at School*. New York, 1841. Reprint. New York: Schocken Books, 1977.

Beecher, Catherine, and Harriet Beecher Stowe. *The American Woman's Home*. New York: J.B. Ford, 1869.

Bemis, Albert Farwell, and John Burchard II. *The Evolving House*. Vol. 1. *A History of the Home*. Cambridge, Mass.: The Technology Press, 1933.

Benevolo, Leonardo. *History of Modern Architecture*. Cambridge, Mass.: MIT Press, 1971.

Benjamin, Asher. *The American Builder's Companion*. Boston, 1827. Reprint. New York: Dover Publications, [1969].

Berger, Bennett M. *The Survival of the Counterculture: Ideological Work and Everyday Life Among Rural Communards*. Berkeley: University of California Press, 1981.

Bernhardt, Arthur. *The Mobile Manufactured Housing Industry*. Cambridge, Mass.: MIT Press, 1978.

Bestor, Arthur. *Backwoods Utopias: The Sectarian Origins and the Owenite Phase of Communitarian Socialism in America, 1663-1829*. Philadelphia: University of Pennsylvania Press, 1970.

Bettelheim, Bruno. *Children of the Dream*. New York: Macmillan Co., 1969.

Bodfish, H. Morton. *History of Building and Loan in the United States*. Chicago: United States Building and Loan League, 1931.

Boxandall, Rosalyn, Linda Gordon, and Susan Reverby. *America's Working Women*.

Bratt, Rachel G., Chester Hartman, and Ann Meyerson, eds. *Critical Perspectives on Housing*. Philadelphia: Temple University Press, 1986.

Bullock, Nicholas, and James Read. *The Movement for Housing Reform in Germany and France*. Cambridge: Cambridge University Press, 1985.

Burchard, John, and Albert Bush-Brown. *The Architecture of America*. Boston: Atlantic Monthly Press, 1961

Burnett, John. *A Social History of Housing, 1815-1970*. London: Methuen, 1978.

Bush-Brown, Albert *The Architecture of America*. Boston: Little Brown, 1969.

Chapman, Stanley D., ed. *The History of Working-Class Housing; a Symposium*. Newton Abbot: David and Charles, 1971.

Cichy, Bodo. *The Great Age of Architecture from Ancient Greece to the Present*. New York: G.P. Putnam, 1964.

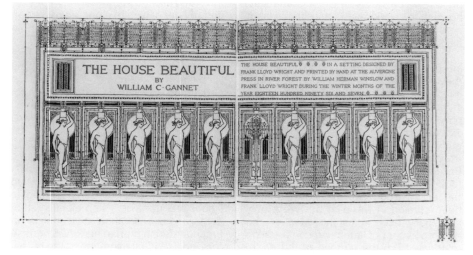

Title page, *The House Beautiful,* by William C. Gannet, 1896. Courtesy Chicago Historical Society.

Clark, Clifford Edward, Jr. *The American Family Home, 1800-1960*. Chapel Hill: University of North Carolina Press, 1986.

———. *Domestic Architecture as an Index of Social History*.

Clay, Phillip L., and Robert M. Hollister. *Neighborhood Policy and Planning*. Lexington, Mass.: D.C. Heath, 1983.

Cook, Jeffrey. *Award-Winning Passive Solar Designs*. New York: McGraw-Hill Book Co., 1984.

Cowan, Ruth Schwartz. *More Work for Mother: The Ironies of Household Technology from the Open Hearth to the Microwave*. New York: Basic Books, 1983.

Curtis, William J.R. *Modern Architecture Since 1900*. Englewood Cliffs, New Jersey: Prentice Hall, 1983.

Darley, Gillian. "The Moravians, Building for a Higher Purpose," *Architectural Review*, April 1985.

———. *Villages of Vision*. London: Architectural Press, 1975.

Davey, Norman. *History of Building Materials*. London: Phoenix House, 1961.

Davidson, Harold A. *Housing Demand: Mobile, Modular, or Conventional?* New York: Van Nostrand Reinhold, 1973.

Davidson, Marshall B., author and ed. *The American Heritage History of Notable American Homes*. New York: American Heritage Publishing Co., Inc., 1971.

Davis, Allen F. *Spearheads for Reform: The Social Settlements and the Progressive Movement, 1890-1914*. New York: Oxford University Press, 1967, 2d ed. New Brunswick, New Jersey: Rutgers University Press, 1984.

Davis, Sam, ed. *The Form of Housing*. New York: Van Nostrand Reinhold, 1981.

Degler, Carl N. *At Odds: Women and the Family from the Revolution to the Present*. New York: Oxford University Press, 1980.

de Wolfe, Elsie. *The House in Good Taste*. New York: The Century Co., 1913.

Diamond, Stephen. *What the Trees Said: Life on a New-Age Farm*. New York: Delacorte Press, 1971.

Diamonstein, Barbaralee. *Remaking America: New Uses, Old Places*. New York: Crown Publishers, 1986.

Dickinson, Peter A. *Retirement Edens: Outside the Sunbelt*. New York: Dutton, 1981; Washington, D.C.: American Association of Retired Persons, 1987.

———. *Sunbelt Retirement*. New York: Scott Foresman and Co. for the Association of Retired Persons.

"Die tschechische Avantgarde." *Stadt*, May 1982. Hamburg, Germany.

Dorsey, Leslie, and Janice Devine. *Fare Thee Well*. New York: Crown Publishers, 1964.

Downing, Andrew Jackson. *The Architecture of Country Houses*. New York: 1850. Reprint. New York: Dover Publications, 1969.

Drury, Margaret Josephine. *Mobile Homes: The Unrecognized Revolution in American Housing*. New York: Praeger Publishers, 1972.

Dubos, Rene. *Man Adapting*. New Haven: Yale University Press, 1965.

Duncan, James S., ed. *Housing and Identity: Cross-Cultural Perspectives*. New York: Holmes and Meier Publishers, 1982.

Edel, Matthew, and Elliott Sclar. *Shaky Palaces*. New York: Columbia University Press, 1986.

Edwards, Carlton M. *Homes for Travel and Living: The History and Development of the Recreation and Mobile Home Industries*. East Lansing, Michigan: C. Edwards, 1977.

Engel, Heinrich. *The Japanese House: A Tradition for Contemporary Architecture*. Rutland, Vermont: C.E. Tuttle Co., 1964.

Evenson, Norma. *Paris: A Century of Change, 1878–1978*. New Haven: Yale University Press, 1979.

Fathy, Hassan. *Natural Energy and Vernacular Architecture, Principles and Examples with Reference to Hot Arid Climates*. Chicago: University of Chicago Press, 1986.

Fitch, James Marston. *Walter Gropius*. New York: George Braziller, 1960.

Foley, Mary Mix. *The American House*. New York: Harper and Row, 1980.

Ford, C. Daryll. *Habitat, Economy and Society: A Geographical Introduction to Ethnology*. New York: E.P. Dutton and Co., 1963.

Ford, James, and Katherine Morrow Ford. *The Modern House in America*. New York: Architectural Book Publishing Company, 1940.

Fortes, Meyer. *The Web of Kinship Among the Tallensi*. London: Oxford University Press, 1949.

Frampton, Kenneth. *Modern Architecture*. New York: Oxford University Press, 1980.

Frank, Ellen E. *Literary Architecture: Essays Toward a Tradition*. Essays by Walter Pater, Gerard Manley Hopkins, Marcel Proust, Henry James. Berkeley: University of California Press, 1982.

Friedman, Arnold, John F. Pile, and Forrest Wilson. *Interior Design*. New York: Elsevier, 1976.

Friedman, Lawrence. *Government and Slum Housing*. Chicago: Rand McNally, 1968.

Fuerst, J.S., ed. *Public Housing in Europe and America*. London: Croom-Helm, 1974.

Gale, Dennis. *Neighborhood Revitalization and the Postindustrial City*. Lexington, Mass.: D.C. Heath, 1984.

Gans, Herbert J. *The Levittowners: Ways of Life and Politics in a New Suburban Community*. New York: Morningside Books, 1982.

———. *The Urban Villagers*. Lindemann, New York: The Free Press of Glencoe, 1962.

Garrett, Elisabeth Donaghy. "At Home" series in *The Magazine Antiques* (January, February, March 1983; October 1984; August, December 1985).

Garvin, James L. "Mail-Order House Plans and American Victorian Architecture," *Winterthur Portfolio 16*, no. 4 (Winter 1981): 309–34.

Gelfand, Mark I. *A Nation of Cities: The Federal Government and Urban America, 1933–1965*. New York: Oxford University Press, 1975.

Giedion, S. *The Beginnings of Architecture*. New York: Pantheon Books, 1964.

———. *Mechanization Takes Command*. New York: Oxford University Press, 1949.

Gillis, A.R. "High Rise Housing and Psychological Strain," *Journal of Health and Social Behavior*, no. 18, (1977): 419.

Gilman, Charlotte Stetson. *The Home: Its Work and Influences*. New York: McClure, Phillips and Co., 1903. Reprint. New York: Source Book Press, 1970.

Girouard, Mark. *Life in the English Country House*. New Haven: Yale University Press, 1978.

Goering, John, ed. *Housing Desegregation and Federal Policy*. Chapel Hill: University of North Carolina Press, 1986.

Golany, Gideon S. *Earth-Sheltered Habitat: History, Architecture and Urban Design*. New York: Van Nostrand Reinhold, 1983.

———. *Earth-Sheltered Dwellings in Tunisia: Ancient Lessons for Modern Design*. Newark, Delaware: University of Delaware Press: forthcoming.

Goldberger, Paul. *The Houses of the Hamptons*. New York: Alfred A. Knopf, 1986.

Gowans, Alan. *The Comfortable House: North American Suburban Architecture, 1890–1930*. Cambridge, Mass.: MIT Press, 1986.

———. *Images of American Living: Four Centuries of Architecture and Furniture as Cultural Expression*. Philadelphia: J.B. Lippincott Co., 1976.

Green, Harvey. *Light of the Home: An Intimate View of the Lives of Women in Victorian America*. New York: Pantheon Books, 1983.

Greenfield, Ellen J. *House Dangerous*. New York: Vintage Books, 1987.

Greer, Nora Richter. *The Creation of Shelter*. Washington, D.C.: The AIA Press, 1988.

———. *The Search For Shelter*. Washington, D.C.: The AIA Press, 1986.

Greer, Scott. *Urban Renewal and American Cities: The Dilemma of Democratic Intervention*. Indianapolis: The Bobbs-Merrill Company, 1965.

Grinberg, Donald T. *Housing in the Netherlands, 1900–1940*. Rotterdam: Nijgh-Wolters-Noordhoff, 1977.

Grudin, Robert. *Time and the Art of Living*. New York: Ticknor & Fields, 1982.

Guidoni, Enrico. *Primitive Architecture*. New York: Harry N. Abrams, 1978.

Gutman, Herbert C. *The Black Family in Slavery and Freedom*. New York: Pantheon Books, 1976.

Hall, John R. *The Ways Out: Utopian Communal Groups in an Age of Babylon*. London and Boston: Routledge & Kegan Paul, 1978.

Hamlin, Talbot. *Greek Revival Architecture in America*. London: Oxford University Press, 1944; New York: Dover Publications, 1964.

Hancock, Judith Ann, ed. *Housing the Elderly*. New Brunswick, New Jersey: Center for Urban Policy Research, Rutgers University, 1987.

Handlin, David P. *The American Home: Architecture and Society, 1815–1915*. Boston: Little Brown, 1979.

Hare, Patrick H. *Alternative Housing Arrangements*. U.S. Department of Housing and Urban Development, Office of Policy Development and Research.

Hartman, Chester, Dennis Keating, Richard LeGates, and Steve Turner. *Displacement: How to Fight It*. Berkeley: National Housing Law Project, 1982.

Hatton, E. M. *The Tent Book*. Boston: Houghton Mifflin, 1979.

Hayden, Dolores. *The Grand Domestic Revolution: A History of Feminist Designs for American Homes, Neighborhoods and Cities*. Cambridge, Mass.: MIT Press, 1981.

———. *Redesigning the American Dream: The Future of Housing, Work, and Family Life*. New York: W.W. Norton, 1984.

———. *Seven American Utopias: The Architecture of Communitarian Socialism*. Cambridge, Mass.: MIT Press, 1976.

Heinz, Thomas A. *Frank Lloyd Wright*. New York: St. Martin's Press, 1982.

Herbers, John. *The New American Heartland*. New York: New York Times, 1986.

Heskin, Allan. *Tenants and the American Dream*. New York: Praeger Publishers, 1983.

Hitchcock, Henry-Russell. *American Architectural Books: A List of Books, Portfolios, and Pamphlets on Architecture-Related Subjects Published in America before 1895*. New expanded ed. New York: Da Capo Press, 1976.

———. *Architecture: Nineteenth and Twentieth Centuries*. Harmondsworth, England: Penguin Books, 1977.

Hochland, Michael Aaron. *Homes on Wheels*. New Brunswick, New Jersey: Rutgers University Press, 1980.

Holcomb, Briavel H., and Robert A. Beauregard. *Revitalizing Cities*. Washington, D.C.: Association of American Geographers, 1981.

Holloway, Mark. *Heavens on Earth: Utopian Communities in America, 1660–1880*. 2d ed., rev. New York: Dover Publications, 1966.

Home Sweet Home: Housing Designed by the London County Council, 1888–1975. London: Academy Editions, 1976. Foreword by Kenneth Campbell.

Hudson Home Guides, *Two Hundred Affordable Home Plans*, New York: Bantam/Hudson Plan Books, 1979.

Hughes, James W., and George Sternlieb. *The Dynamics of Housing*. New Brunswick, New Jersey: Center for Urban Policy Research, Rutgers, The State University of New Jersey, 1987.

Ingle, Marjorie. *Mayan Revival Style*. Salt Lake City: G.M. Smith: Peregrine Books, 1984.

Jackson, Anthony. *A Place Called Home: A History of Low-Cost Housing in Manhattan*. Cambridge, Mass.: MIT Press, 1976.

Jackson, Kenneth T. *Crabgrass Frontier: The Suburbanization of the United States*. New York: Oxford University Press, 1985.

Jencks, Charles. *Architecture 2,000: Predictions and Methods*. New York: Praeger Publishers, 1971.

Joedicke, Jurgen, and Christian Plath. *Die Weissenhofsiedlung*. Stuttgart: Karl Kramer Verlag, 1977.

Kanter, Rosabeth Moss. *Commitment and Community*. Cambridge, Mass.: Harvard University Press, 1972.

174 Katzman, David M. *Seven Days a Week*. New York: Oxford University Press, 1978.

Keiser, Marjorie Branin. *Housing, An Environment for Living*. New York: Macmillan Publishing Co., 1978.

Kelly, Burnham. *The Prefabrication of Houses: A Study by the Albert Farwell Bemis Foundation of the Prefabrication of Industry in the United States*. New York: John Wiley and Sons, 1951.

Kennedy, Susan Estabrook. *If All We Did Was to Weep at Home—White Working Women*. Bloomington, Indiana: Indiana University Press, 1979.

Kepes, Gyorgy, ed. *Sign, Image, Symbol*. New York: George Braziller, 1966.

King, Anthony D. *The Bungalow: The Production of a Global Culture*. London: Routledge & Kegan Paul, 1984.

Kramer, J.J. *The Last of the Grand Hotels*. New York: Van Nostrand Reinhold, 1978.

Kristof, Frank S. "Housing in the United States: The Trends Have Shifted," in *Cities: The Forces that Shape Them*. Edited by Lisa Taylor. New York: Cooper-Hewitt Museum, 1982.

Kron, Joan. *Home Psych: The Psychology of Home and Decoration*. New York: Clarkson N. Potter, Inc., 1983.

Lamberg-Karlovsky, C.C., comp. *Old World Archaeology: Foundations of Civilization*. San Francisco: W.H. Freeman and Co., 1972.

Lambton, Lucinda. *Beastly Buildings*. New York: Atlantic Monthly Press, 1985.

———. *Temples of Convenience*. London: Gordon Fraser, 1978.

Lancaster, Clay. *Architectural Follies in America, or Hammer, Sawtooth and Nail*. Rutland, Vermont: Charles E. Tuttle Company, 1960.

———. *The American Bungalow, 1880–1930*. New York: Abbeville Press, 1985.

Lang, Michael H. *Gentrification Amid Urban Decline: Strategies for Older Cities*. Cambridge, Mass.: Ballinger Publishing Co., 1982.

Leavitt, Jacqueline, and Susan Saegert. *Women Manage Housing*. Forthcoming.

Limerick, Jeffrey, Nancy Ferguson, and Richard Oliver. *America's Grand Resort Hotels*. New York: Pantheon Books, 1979.

Lockwood, Charles. *Bricks and Brownstones, The New York Row House, 1783–1929: A Guide to the Architectural Styles and Interior Decoration for Period Restoration*. New York: Abbeville Press, 1972.

Low, S., and E. Chambers, eds. *Housing, Culture and Design: A Comparative Perspective*. Philadelphia: University of Pennsylvania Press, forthcoming.

Lubove, Roy. *The Progressives and the Slums: Tenement House Reform in New York City*. Pittsburgh: University of Pittsburgh Press, 1962.

———. "Homes and A Few Well-Placed Fruit Trees: An Object Lesson in Federal Housing," *Social Research* (Winter, 1960): 469–486.

Lynes, Russell. *The Domesticated Americans*. New York: Harper and Row, 1957, 1963.

Maass, John. *The Gingerbread House: A View of Victorian America*. New York: Rinehart and Company, 1957.

———. *The Victorian Home in America*. New York: Hawthorne, 1972.

Mandelker, Daniel R., and Robert Montgomery. *Housing in America: Problems and Perspectives*. Indianapolis: Bobbs-Merrill Educational Publishing, 1973.

Marcus, Clare Cooper. *Easter Hill Village: Some Social Implications of Design*. New York: Free Press, 1975.

———. *The House as Symbol of Self*. Berkeley: University of California Press, 1971.

———. *Housing as if People Mattered*. Berkeley: University of California Press, 1986.

Mason, Joseph B. *History of Housing in the United States, 1930–1980*. Houston: Gulf Publishing Co., 1982.

Matthews, Glenna. *Just a Housewife: The Rise and Fall of Domesticity in the United States*. New York: Oxford University Press, 1987.

Mayhew, Edgar de N., and Minor Myers, Jr. *A Documentary History of American Interiors from the Colonial Era to 1915*. New York: Charles Scribner's Sons, 1980.

McClung, William. *The Country House in English Renaissance Poetry*. Berkeley: University of California Press, 1977.

———. *The Architecture of Paradise: Survivals of Eden and Jerusalem*. Berkeley: University of California Press, 1983.

McGinty, Brian. *The Palace Inns: A Connoisseur's Guide to Historic American Hotels*. New York: Two Continents Publishing Group, 1978.

McKelvey, Blake. *The Urbanization of America*. New Brunswick, New Jersey: Rutgers University Press, 1963.

McKenna, H. Dickson. *A House in the City: A Guide to Buying and Renovating Old Row Houses*. New York: Van Nostrand Reinhold, 1971.

Meakin, Budgett. *Model Factories and Villages: Ideal Conditions of Labour and Housing*. London: Jacobs T. Fisher Unwin, 1905.

Merilees, Doug, and Evelyn Loveday. *Pole-Building Construction*. Charlotte, Vermont: Garden Way Publishing, 1973.

Mitchell, S. Paul, ed. *Federal Housing Policy and Programs, Past and Present*. New Brunswick, New Jersey: Center for Urban Policy Research, Rutgers University, 1987.

Mollenkopf, John H. *The Contested City*. Princeton: Princeton University Press, 1983.

Moore, Charles, Donlyn Lyndon, and Gerald Allen. *The Place of Houses*. New York: Holt, Rinehart & Winston, 1974.

Moore, W. *The Vertical Ghetto*. New York: Random House, 1969.

Moxon, Joseph. *Mechanick Exercises*. or *The Doctrine of Handy-Works. Applied to the Arts of Smithing Joinery Carpentry Turning Bricklayery*. 3d ed. London, 1903. Reprint. Scarsdale, New York: Early American Industries Association, 1979.

Mumford, Lewis. *The City in History*. New York: Harcourt, Brace and World, 1961.

———. *Sticks and Stones*. New York: Dover Publications, 1955.

Mungo, Raymond. *Total Loss Farm: A Year in the Life*. New York: E.P. Dutton and Co., 1971.

Nelson, George, and Henry Wright. *Tomorrow's House: A Complete Guide for the Home Builder*. New York: Simon and Schuster, 1946.

Newman, Oscar. *Community of Interest*. Garden City, New York: Anchor Press/Doubleday, 1980.

———. *Defensible Space*. New York: Macmillan Publishing Co., 1972.

O'Dea, W.T. *The Social History of Lighting*. London: Routledge & Kegan Paul, 1958.

Oliver, Paul. *Shelter, Sign and Symbol*. Woodstock, New York: The Overlook Press, 1977.

———. *Shelter and Society*. New York: Praeger, 1969.

Olsen, Donald J. *The City as a Work of Art: London, Paris, Vienna*. New Haven: Yale University Press, 1986.

On Being Homeless: Historical Perspectives. Edited by Rick Beard. New York: Museum of the City of New York, 1987.

O'Neill, Gerard K. *The High Frontier*. New York: William Morrow, 1977.

———. *Interstellar Migration and the Human Experience*. Berkeley: University of California Press, c. 1985.

Orfield, Gary. *Fair Housing in Metropolitan Chicago: Perspectives after Two Decades*. Chicago: Chicago Area Fair Housing Alliance, 1987.

Palen, J. John, and Bruce London. *Gentrification, Displacement and Neighborhood Revitalization*. Albany: State University of New York Press, 1984.

Palliser, George. *George Palliser's Model Homes for the People*. Edited by Michael A. Tomlan. Bridgeport, Connecticut: 1876. Reprint. Watkins Glen, New York: American Life Foundation, 1978.

Pawley, Martin. *Architecture vs. Housing*. New York: Praeger Publishers, 1971.

———. *Home Ownership*. London: Architectural Press, 1978.

Peterson, Charles E., ed. *The Rule Book of the Carpenters' Company of the City and County of Philadelphia 1786*. N.p.: Bell Publishing Co., 1971.

Pevsner, Nikolaus, John Fleming, and Hugh Honour. *A Dictionary of Architecture*. Woodstock, New York: Overlook Press, 1976.

Pommer, Richard, guest ed. Essays by Rosemarie Haag Bletter, Dennis Doordan, Mary McLeod, Christian Otto, Richard Pommer, and Helen Searing. *College Art Journal*, Summer 1983.

Post, Emily. *The Personality of a House; The Blue Book of Home Design and Decoration*. New York and London: Funk and Wagnalls Co., 1933.

Praz, Mario. *An Illustrated History of Interior Decoration*. Translated by William Weaver. New York: Thames & Hudson, 1982.

Pressman, Norman. *International Settlement Strategies: Social Perspectives on Planned Development*. Waterloo, Ontario: Faculty of Environmental Studies, University of Waterloo, 1978.

Proshansky, Harold, William I. Ittelson, and Leanne G. Rivlin. *Environmental Psychology: Man and His Physical Setting*. New York: Holt, Rinehart and Winston, 1980.

Prussin, Labelle. *Architecture in Northern Ghana: A Study of Forms*. Berkeley: University of California Press, 1969.

Pulos, Arthur J. *The American Design Ethic*. Cambridge, Mass.: MIT Press, 1983.

———. *The American Design Adventure*. Cambridge, Mass.: MIT Press, 1988.

Rapoport, Amos. *House Form and Culture*. Englewood Cliffs, New Jersey: Prentice-Hall, 1969.

———. *The Meaning of the Built Environment*. Newbury Park, California: Sage Publications, 1982.

———. "Thinking about Home Environments: A Conceptual Framework" in *Home Environments*. Edited by I. Altman and C. Werner. Vol. 8 of *Human Behavior and Environment*. New York: Plenum, 1985.

Rasmussen, Steen Eiler. *Towns and Buildings*. Cambridge, Harvard University Press, 1951.

Reps, John. *The Making of Urban America*. Princeton: Princeton University Press, 1965.

Reynolds, Jack. *Saltaire: An Introduction to the Village of Sir Titus Salt*. Pamphlet published by Bradford City Art Galleries, England.

Rice, Kym S. *Early American Taverns: For the Entertainment of Friends and Strangers*. New York: Sons of the American Revolution, 1983.

Ridley, Anthony. *At Home*. London: Heinemann, 1976. New York: Crane Russak, 1976.

Rifkind, Carole. *A Field Guide to American Architecture*. New York: New American Library, 1980.

Riis, Jacob. *How the Other Half Lives*. New York: Hill and Wang, 1957. New York: Dover, [1971].

Rudofsky, Bernard. *The Prodigious Builders*. New York: Harcourt, Brace, Jovanovich, 1977.

Rybczynski, Witold. *Home: A Short History of an Idea*. New York: Viking Press, 1985.

St. George, Robert Blair. "'Set Thine house in Order': The Domestication of the Yeomanry in Seventeenth-Century New England," *New England Begins: The Seventeenth Century*, vol. 2. Boston: Museum of Fine Arts, 1982 (pp. 159–188).

Schoenauer, Norbert. *Six Thousand Years of Housing*. New York: Garland STPM Press, 1981.

Schuyt, Michael, Joost Elffers, and George R. Collins. *Fantastic Architecture: Personal and Eccentric Visions*. New York: Harry N. Abrams, 1980.

Scully, Vincent. *American Architecture and Urbanism*. New York: Praeger, 1969. New York: Holt, 1988 (rev. & enlarged ed.)

———. *The Shingle Style and the Brick Style*. New Haven: Yale University Press, 1971.

Searing, Helen, David De Long, and Robert A.M. Stern, eds. *American Architecture: Innovation and Tradition*. New York: Rizzoli, 1986.

Shapiro, H.L. *Homes Around the World*. New York: American Museum of Natural History Science Guide 124, 1947.

Shelter. Bolinas, Calif.: Shelter Publications, 1973.

Sherwood, Roger. *Modern Housing Prototypes*. Cambridge, Mass.: Harvard University Press, 1978.

Smith, C. Ray. *Interior Design in Twentieth-Century America: A History*. New York:

Harper and Row, 1987.

Smith, Norris Kelly. *Frank Lloyd Wright: A Study in Architectural Content*. Englewood Cliffs, New Jersey: Prentice-Hall, 1966.

Smith, Wallace, ed. "Housing America." *The Annals of the American Academy of Political and Social Science*. vol. 465, January 1983. Beverly Hills, California: Sage Publications, 1983

————. *Housing: The Social and Economic Elements*. Berkeley: University of California Press, 1970.

Starr, Roger. *America's Housing Challenge: What It Is and How to Meet It*. New York: Hill and Wang, 1977.

————. *The Rise and Fall of New York City*. New York: Basic Books, Inc., 1985.

Sterling, Raymond, and John Carmody. *Earth-Sheltered Community Design: Energy-Efficient Residential Development*. New York: Van Nostrand Reinhold, 1981.

Sternlieb, George, with James W. Hughes, Robert W. Burchey, Stephen C. Casey, Robert W. Lake, and David Listokin. *America's Housing: Prospects and Problems*. New Brunswick, New Jersey: Rutgers University Press, 1980.

————. *Patterns for Development*. New Brunswick, New Jersey, Center for Urban Policy Research, 1986.

Stevenson, Catherine Cole, and H. Ward Jandl. *Houses by Mail: A Guide to Houses from Sears, Roebuck and Company*. Washington, D.C.: Preservation Press, 1986.

Stokols, D., and I. Altman, eds. *Handbook on Environmental Psychology*. Vols. 1 and 2. New York: John Wiley & Sons, 1987.

Strasser, Susan. *Never Done: A History of American Housework*. New York: J.B. Ford, 1869. Pantheon, 1982.

Tafuri, Manfredo, ed. *Vienne La Rouge*. Translated from the Italian *Vienna Rossa*, Milan Electa, 1980. Brussels: Pierre Mardaga, 1981.

Tarn, J.N. *Working-Class Housing in Nineteenth-Century Britain*. London: Lund Humphries, 1971.

Thompson, Elizabeth K. *Apartments, Townhouses and Condominiums*. New York: George Braziller, 1969.

————. *Recycling Buildings: Renovations, Remodellings, Restorations and Reuses*. New York: McGraw-Hill, 1977.

Tobin, Gary, ed. *Divided Neighborhoods*. Sage Press, 1987.

Toll, Seymour. *Zoned America*. New York: Grossman Publishers, 1969.

The Uniform Federal Accessibility Standards, Washington, D.C.: General Services Administration, 1985.

Upton, Dell. *America's Architectural Roots: Ethnic Groups That Built America*. Washington, D.C.: Preservation Press, 1986.

————, and John Michael Vlach, eds. *Common Places: Readings in American Vernacular Architecture*. Athens, Georgia: University of Georgia Press, 1986.

————. "Pattern Books and Professionalism: Aspects of the Transformation of Domestic Architecture in America, 1800–1860," *Winterthur Portfolio* 19:2/3 (Summer/Autumn 1984): 107–150.

Van der Ryn, Sym, and Peter Calthorpe. *Sustainable Communities, A New Design Synthesis for Cities, Suburbs and Towns*. San Francisco: Sierra Club Books, 1986.

Veiller, Lawrence. *A Model Housing Law*. New York: Survey Associates Inc., 1914.

Venturi, Robert. *Complexity and Contradiction in Architecture*. New York: Museum of Modern Art, 1966. 2d ed., 1977. Reprinted, 1979, 1981, 1985.

VIA IV: Culture and the Social Vision. Publication of the Graduate School of Fine Arts, University of Pennsylvania. Cambridge, Mass.: MIT Press, 1980. Essays on housing by Peter Papademetriou, Helen Searing, Robert A.M. Stern, Tom Wolfe, Ronald Wiedenhoeft

Viollet-le-Duc, *Histoire de l'habitation*. Paris: Bibliothèque d'éducation et de récréation, 1875.

von Eckardt, Wolf. *A Place to Live*. New York: Delacorte Press, 1968.

von Frisch, Karl. *Animal Architecture*. New York: Harcourt Brace Jovanovich, 1974.

Waite, Diana S., ed. *Architectural Elements: The Technological Revolution*. New York: Bonanza Books, n.d.

Warner, Sam Bass, Jr., ed. *Planning for a Nation of Cities*. Cambridge, Mass.: MIT Press, 1966.

————. The Urban Wilderness: A History of the American City. New York: Harper and Row, 1972.

Waterman, Thomas Tileston. *The Dwellings of Colonial America*. Chapel Hill: University of North Carolina Press, 1950.

Watson, Donald, and Kenneth Labs. *Climate Design, Energy-Efficient Building Principles and Practices*. New York: McGraw-Hill, 1983.

Weiss, Michael. *Living Together*. New York: McGraw-Hill, 1974.

Wertheimer, Barbara Mayer. *We Were There: The Story of Working Women in America*. New York: Pantheon, 1977.

Wexler, Harry J., and Richard Peck. *Housing and Local Government*. Lexington, Mass.: Lexington Books, 1975.

Wharton, Edith, and Ogden Codman, Jr. *The Decoration of Houses*, New York: Scribner, 1902. Reprint. New York: Norton, 1978.

Whyte, William H. *The Last Landscape*. Garden City, New York: Doubleday, 1968.

Williams, Frank B. *The Law of City Planning and Zoning*. New York: National Municipal League, 1922.

Williams, Norman, Jr. *The Structure of Urban Zoning*. New York: Battenheim, 1966.

Winter, Robert. *The Californian Bungalow*. Los Angeles: Hennessy and Ingalls, 1980.

Wizansky, Richard, et al. *Home Comfort: Life on Total Loss Farm*. New York: Saturday Review Press, 1973.

Wood, Edith Elmer. *Housing Progress in Western Europe*. New York: E.P. Dutton and Co., 1923.

Wright, David, and Dennis Andrejko. *Passive Solar Architecture, Logic and Beauty*. New York: Van Nostrand Reinhold, 1982.

Wright, Frank Lloyd. *The Natural House*. New York: Horizon Press, Inc., 1954.

Wright, Gwendolyn. *Building the Dream: A Social History of Housing in America*. New York: Pantheon Books, 1981.

————. *Moralism and the Model Home: Domestic Architecture and Cultural Conflict in Chicago, 1873–1913*. Chicago: Chicago University Press, 1980.

Wright, Lawrence. *Home Fires Burning*. London: Routledge & Kegan Paul, 1964.

————. *Clean and Decent*. London and Boston: Routledge & Kegan Paul, revised ed., 1980.

Zablocki, Benjamin. *The Joyful Community*. Baltimore: Penguin Books, 1971.

————. *Alienation and Charisma*. New York: The Free Press, 1980.

Zicklin, Gilbert. *Countercultural Communes: A Sociological Perspective*. Westport, Connecticut: Greenwood Press, 1983.